Legal Research

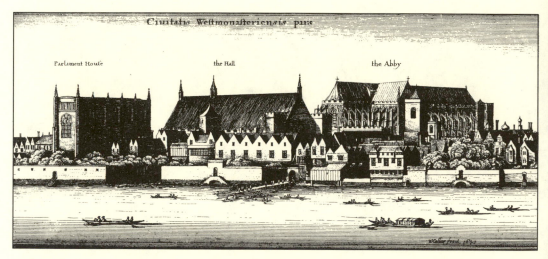

Parliament, Westminster Hall, Westminster Abbey, 1640

Legal Research

Historical Foundations of the Electronic Age

George S. Grossman

New York   *Oxford*

Oxford University Press

1994

Oxford University Press

Oxford   New York   Toronto
Delhi   Bombay   Calcutta   Madras   Karachi
Kuala Lumpur   Singapore   Hong Kong   Tokyo
Nairobi   Dar es Salaam   Cape Town
Melbourne   Auckland   Madrid

and associated companies in
Berlin   Ibadan

Copyright © 1994 by Oxford University Press, Inc.

Published by Oxford University Press, Inc.
200 Madison Avenue, New York, New York 10016

Oxford is a registered trademark of Oxford University Press

Library of Congress Cataloging-in-Publication Data
Legal research: historical foundations of the electronic age
[edited by] George S. Grossman.
p.   cm.
ISBN 0-19-508637-6
ISBN 0-19-508638-4 (pbk.)
1. Legal research—Great Britain.
2. Legal research—United States.
3. Information storage and retrieval systems—Law.
I. Grossman, George S.
K85.L45   1994
340'.072041—dc20   93-23403

246897531

Printed in the United States of America
on acid-free paper

IN MEMORIAM

Jerry R. Andersen	1933–1982
J. Morris Clark	1944–1979
James B. Haddad	1942–1992

Acknowledgments

The groundwork for this book was laid during a term at Cambridge University in 1979, supported in part by a fellowship from the Council on Library Resources. The book was put together ten years later during a research leave from my position as director of the law library at Northwestern University, a position I held until 1993.

Special thanks are due to the staff of Northwestern's law library for being so competent that a leave was possible without detracting from the library's operations. Extra special thanks are due to Marcia Gold Lehr for her invaluable help, to Jessy Johnson, whose word processing skills brought the manuscript into existence, and to Franki Lerman for her encouragement. Barbara Hycnar and Chris Simoni not only acted as codirectors of the law library in my absence but also read portions of the manuscript and made valuable suggestions.

The manuscript was also reviewed by Stephen Presser, whose suggestions are much appreciated, and by Morris Cohen, to whom I am grateful not only for his help on this project but also for his supportive, career-long friendship. J. H. Baker helped plant the seeds in Cambridge fourteen years ago. J. Myron Jacobstein also helped plant the seeds as my legal research teacher and, later, mentor and friend. I also want to acknowledge Roy Mersky's friendship and support.

I have also benefited from reading lists and course outlines provided by colleagues from other law libraries, especially by Al Brecht, Penny Hazelton, Margaret Leary, Terry Martin, and Virginia Wise. Finally, I am grateful to the students who have been exposed to earlier versions of these materials, for their positive, encouraging responses.

Contents

4   Legislation in the United States

III ADMINISTRATION

5 Administrative Publications in England

6 Administrative Publications in the United States

IV SCHOLARSHIP

7 Secondary "Authorities"

8 Legal Periodicals and Sources Beyond the Law

Introduction

Most books on legal research emphasize the development of practical research skills. Consequently, they describe the existing tools of legal research and how to use them. Acquaintance with today's reference sources, however, may not be adequate preparation for the legal information environment of tomorrow. Paradoxically, the best preparation for the high-technology world just dawning may be to return to the medieval world of the plea rolls and the yearbooks to examine the very nature of legal information by tracing its development from those days to now.

The readings in this collection were selected to complement the standard legal research texts. Each chapter consists of selected readings alternating with notes by the editor.* The first six chapters are devoted to primary sources—sources generated by government agencies—and their attendant reference tools. The first two chapters deal with judicial opinions; the next two with legislative publications; and the fifth and sixth chapters with the publications of administrative agencies. The seventh chapter is devoted to secondary sources, largely the work of individual scholars. The Epilogue explores the impact of computer technology.

Although the arrangement of selections and notes in the first six chapters is historical, the aim is not to dwell on historical details—details that may no longer be relevant to contemporary legal research—but to explore basic issues that must be considered in any information system: preserva-

*Sources relied on in the editor's notes are cited in footnotes, but footnotes are omitted in the selected readings.

tion, accuracy, quantity, organization, indexing, timeliness, integration, access, format, and design.

It is instructive to examine causes and consequences in the historical evolution of communication—from the oral tradition to the "artificial memory" of the written record, the reproducibility of the printed book, and the instantaneous, interactive communication of the computer. Just as the transition from irrational to rational decision making, represented in the transition from ordeals to trials by juries, was tied to the development of written records, the use of precedent in judicial decision making could not have developed without the accurate reproduction of court reports made possible by printing. The various historical movements for codification concerned not only the organization of law but also the very core of the legal system. The changes in legal information sources in the 1870s were part of a sea change in legal institutions, legal education, and the legal profession, accompanying revolutions in industry, commerce, and transportation. References in the readings to schools of legal philosophy highlight the links between information sources and intellectual currents.

Such generalizations, however, must be examined in light of the multitude of specific decisions that are made as an information system evolves. To begin with, as each legal institution generates information, decisions are made, consciously or by default, about what is to be preserved. The issue is most explicitly discussed in the debates surrounding the selective publication of judicial opinions but can also be seen in legislative, administrative, and even secondary materials. Complaints about gaps in the legal information system are as frequent as complaints about other shortcomings of legal publications.

The decision to preserve, alone, is not enough if what is preserved is not accurate. Historically, among the most frequent complaints about the legal record has been its inaccuracy. This may be surprising in a profession in which precision is highly emphasized, but perhaps the most revealing aspect of the materials in this collection is their documentation of the "casual and careless" manner in which the records of law have been preserved.

Even more frequent, perhaps most frequent of all, are complaints about the quantity of legal information—a complaint that should not be surprising in a legal system combining the use of judicial precedent with legislation and replicating the legislative and judicial functions in the administrative apparatus of the executive branch. In such a system, no information is ever removed, as even overruled cases and repealed legislation retain both historical interest and value for the interpretation of current law. Complaints related to quantity, however, subsided at various times as organizing devices were found to bring quantity under control.

The organization of legal information is often chronological, sometimes alphabetical, sometimes logical. Whatever the organization, with sufficient quantity, additional aids become necessary to permit the selection of specific information from the mass—outlines, indexes, digests, citation tables, citators, concordances (better known in the computer age as keyword lists). Judicial decisions are published chronologically with digests that have word indexes; legislation is published chronologically, but legislation in force is republished in logical order with word indexes. Such differences reveal much about the nature and authority of courts and legislatures and the way information generated by them is used.

Problems of quantity and organization are compounded by the problem of timeliness. The time gaps between the generation of information and its publication, between publication and distribution, and between distribution and indexing represent major challenges for any information system. For law, the challenges are heightened by the potentially serious consequences of missed information. The challenges involve not only publication, distribution, and indexing but also integration. The characteristically legal updating devices of pocket parts and looseleaf services are designed to meet the need for integration, and that need is perhaps the main reason full-text databases have succeeded in law more than in any other discipline.

Information may also be missed simply owing to lack of access. Key decisions may lie buried in unpublished records or in archives; information may be published but its distribution limited; the cost of information may be a barrier to some.

Access to information is closely related to its format. Paper publications, microforms, and databases are not equally available, and, when available, their use is hedged with differing barriers—physical, mechanical, and instructional. The distribution of information by public proclamation, by mail, or by E-mail results not only in differing levels of access but also in differing challenges for preservation, accuracy, organization, indexing, and currency.

Finally, materials in this collection should raise issues about the overall design of the legal information system. The gaps in some areas of law are ironic in light of the wasteful multiple publication in some other areas. Sometimes the duplication is caused by commercial competition, at other times by overlap between government and commercial publishers, and at still other times by overlap of formats. Such duplication can be wasteful of time as well as paper, space, and money. The waste of time is also evident in design flaws that lead to unnecessary steps in research—as can be seen most clearly in the struggle to bring administrative regulations under control in the United States.

One need not go as far as Marshall McLuhan's assertion that "the medium is the message" to appreciate the significance of the issues explored by the authors in this collection. The methods of generating, packaging, and disseminating information inescapably affect, and are affected by, the substance of the information, the institutions and individuals conveying and receiving the information, and the society in which the communication takes place. It is hoped that the readings in this collection illuminate such cross-influences and, in doing so, will not only increase the reader's skill in the use of legal information but will also help lead to wiser decisions affecting the legal information system of the future.

Additional Readings

For additional readings on research on the law of the United States, the following may be consulted:

M. L. Cohen, *Legal Research in a Nutshell* (4th ed., 1985);

M. L. Cohen, R. C. Berring, and K. C. Olson, HOW TO FIND THE LAW (9th ed., 1989);

J. M. Jacobstein and R. M. Mersky, FUNDAMENTALS OF LEGAL RESEARCH (1987);

C. L. Kunz et al., THE PROCESS OF LEGAL RESEARCH (2d ed., 1992);

A. J. Lewis, USING AMERICAN LAW BOOKS (3d ed., 1990);

C. G. Wren and J. R. Wren, THE LEGAL RESEARCH MANUAL (2d ed., 1986).

For research on specialized areas of United States law—securities regulation, commercial law, federal income taxation, copyrights, labor law, and a growing list of other topics—see:

SPECIALIZED LEGAL RESEARCH (L. F. Chanin, ed., 1987–).

Research guides to the laws of all but a few individual states are also available, although some are quite dated. For a list, see Appendix A to *How to Find the Law* (9th ed., 1989).

Research on the law of the British Isles and other common-law systems is covered in Part II of:

MANUAL OF LAW LIBRARIANSHIP (W. M. Moys, ed., 2d ed., 1987).

Two works on research on the law of the United States, now out of date but still useful for details and historical references, are:

> F. C. HICKS, MATERIALS AND METHODS OF LEGAL RESEARCH (3d ed., 1942);
> M. O. PRICE and H. BITNER, EFFECTIVE LEGAL RESEARCH (1953).

Historical detail on United States law books is also available in:

> E. C. SURRENCY, A HISTORY OF AMERICAN LAW PUBLISHING (1990).

For historical background, useful one-volume, general legal histories are:

> J. H. BAKER, AN INTRODUCTION TO ENGLISH LEGAL HISTORY (3d ed., 1990);
> L. M. FRIEDMAN, A HISTORY OF AMERICAN LAW (2d ed., 1985).

Finally, two general reference sources are available—one a single-volume work from Britain, the other a twelve-volume set with additional supplements from the United States:

> THE OXFORD COMPANION TO LAW (D. M. Walker, ed., 1980);
> THE GUIDE TO AMERICAN LAW (1983–85, supps., 1987, 1990–   ).

I

CASE REPORTING

Reporters in the Court of King's Bench, c. 1675

1

Case Reporting
in England

Note 1(A). The Beginning of Artificial Memory

In the eleventh century, in England and throughout Europe, courts resorted to "ordeals" to decide cases. For example, in one form of trials by ordeal, defendants were required to hold hot iron; later their hands were examined, and the rapid healing of their welts was considered a divine sign in their favor.[1] After the Norman Conquest of England in 1066, trials by battle were also held. According to the British scholar R. C. Van Caenegem:

> We know little about the statistics of these archaic practices because they flourished in periods when writing was absent or rare. What we have are normative texts, prescribing or abrogating the ordeals or indicating how they were to be held; very few texts recording court practice have survived since court rolls tend to begin when ordeals disappear. Fortunately, there are exceptions. The pipe rolls were already being kept when the ordeals were still practised and . . . they contain lists of names of people who were sent to the ordeal and failed. They naturally say nothing about those who succeeded . . . because here there was no royal income to be recorded.[2]

As Van Caenegem indicates, the earliest English government records, the "pipe rolls," were kept for fiscal purposes. The pipe rolls were maintained by the royal treasury—the Exchequer. The courts kept no written record until late in the twelfth century. Prior to the keeping of written court records, knowledge of what was adjudicated could reach back in time

3

only as far as the "living memory"—the memory of the oldest living person.[3]

Trials by ordeal disappeared during the twelfth century. Theologians argued that God should not be "tempted" by being asked to perform miracles in each case.[4]

In place of ordeals, the twelfth century saw the rise of jury trials—not in their modern form, but with jurors serving as both fact finders and witnesses.[5] The same period saw the rise of the royal courts that brought about the "common" law—common to all of England—administered from Westminster Hall in London. The common law rapidly gained ascendancy over most local courts as the king's justices traveled in "eyres" throughout England.

By 1187, the first known English treatise on law was written. Attributed to Ranulph de Glanvill, the treatise describes the writs obtainable to start actions in royal courts.[6] At about the same time, royal courts began to keep records of their adjudications in "plea rolls"—a concept reputedly borrowed from the Exchequer by Hubert Walter, the top legal official of the king (the "chief justiciar"), who was Glanvill's nephew. Somewhat later, courts also produced written dockets of their calendars and written rules of procedures embodied in "paper books."

The public had no access to the plea rolls. They were kept as internal records of the courts. The only early use of the plea rolls, for publication occurred in the middle of the thirteenth century, when the second major treatise on English law was written by a judge, Henry de Bratton, known as Bracton. As a judge, Bracton had access to the plea rolls, and he used them to compile a personal *Note Book* of two thousand cases, citing about five hundred of them in his treatise.

In 1275, a statute was enacted setting the limit of living memory at 1189. Thereafter, the statute needed no updating, and the tradition of relying on memory was superseded by reliance on the written record. This statute has been called "the formal beginning of the era of artificial memory."[7]

Selection 1(A). Plea Rolls and Yearbooks

J. H. Baker, *Records, Reports, and the Origins of Case-Law in England, in* JUDICIAL RECORDS, LAW REPORTS, AND THE GROWTH OF CASE LAW 15–21 (J. H. Baker, ed., 1989).

Although the common law of England began to achieve a distinct identity before the English courts started to keep records, dependence on precedent seems always to have been one of its features. The common law described by Glanvill in the 1180s was conceived of chiefly in terms of remedies, and those remedies (enshrined in the "writs" which commenced actions) were the results of decisions which were rigidly adhered to. . . . Although there was some scope for innovation, . . . the importance of precedent in the writ system was a feature of English law until the nineteenth century. But it is a very rudimentary kind of precedent. The writs were necessary preliminaries to judicial proceedings, and as such provided a framework for legal analysis, but they did not themselves contain propositions of law or indicate in detail what kinds of case fell within their scope.

For the next stage it was necessary to keep records of the decisions of the central courts. The development occurred at an early stage in English legal history, and contributed as much as any other single factor to its distinctive character. If not exactly a by-product of sheep-farming, the common law owed much to sheep. Over a million of them, during six centuries, gave their skins to make the "record"—the continuous parchment memory of the proceedings and judgments in the central courts. To this day it is a remarkably good memory, with few losses and relatively slight deterioration through age.

1. The Plea Rolls

The rolls of the central courts of common law are now generally known to historians as "plea rolls". They commenced in 1194, and the innovation can probably be attributed to Hubert Walter, the chief justiciar. . . . From then until the use of parchment rolls was discontinued in the reign of Queen Victoria, over 10,000 bundles of plea rolls were produced by the clerks of the central courts. These contain the record of all business formally transacted in those courts; and, although undoubtedly not all litigious activities were enrolled, the roll had a status not enjoyed by other forms of memoranda such as dockets and paper books. The roll was the only legally acceptable evidence of what was transacted in court, and for that purpose was conclusive.

. . . The principal purpose of the record was to establish what had been decided, so that the decision might be final: what later lawyers would call estoppel by judgment or *res judicata*. Like minutes of meetings at the present day, they were concerned to record the outcome of proceedings rather than the discussions and reasons which explain how the result was arrived at. The use of Latin—maintained until 1732—helped to preserve the terse formulism of the common-law rolls. At first the entries were very brief indeed, but the classical form of entry as settled in the thirteenth century was: (i) note of the original writ and of the plaintiff's appearance; (ii) (when the defendant appeared), the plaintiff's count (*narratio*) or declaration of his case, the defendant's plea (*placitum*), the plaintiff's replication, and any subsequent pleadings; (iii) the process for summoning the jury (where appropriate) and the result of the trial; (iv) the judgment; and (v) any final process. In practice the majority of cases did not proceed beyond (i), and only a small minority reached (iv). Cases could be discontinued at any stage, with no reason entered; but we may suppose that the usual explanation is a compromise of the suit, or perhaps in some cases a unilateral failure of hope or means on the part of the plaintiff. Since most entries at stage (i) are of pure common form, the bulk of the plea rolls are taken up with matter of minimal legal interest. Even the fuller entries are strictly limited in content. The pleadings, in English practice, were not legal arguments but formulaic statements of fact on which the party relied. As soon as a material fact was asserted by one party and denied by the other, there was a triable "issue" (*exitus*) and the pleadings were closed. The record of the trial, if there was one, gave only the bare essentials: in the case of trial by jury, for example, it noted the process to summon the jurors, the swearing in of the jury, and the verdict, but not the evidence adduced by the parties or the submissions of counsel. The judgment was merely the formal decision as to whether the plaintiff succeeded, and, if so, what relief he should be given. The judges' reasons and the guiding authorities, if any there were, formed no part of the record.

2. The Year Books

If the particular form of the English plea rolls was unique, the idea of keeping a record certainly was not, and it is therefore in the third development—law reporting—that the particular character of English common law seems most obviously to emerge.

The year books, as the early reports are rather misleadingly called, do seem to have been a peculiarly English phenomenon. They reproduce what purports to be a verbatim account, in French, of legal discussions in the royal courts. . . . Doubtless they are not strictly verbatim, in that they are obviously truncated versions of what must in reality have been longer discussions; but they are one of the very few sources from anywhere in Europe in which we can hear the cut and thrust of medieval debate between named people.

The practice of reporting seems to have originated in the 1250s or 1260s in connection with legal education. Maitland considered the immediate predecessors of the year books to have been the books usually now called *Brevia Placitata*, which contained "more or less imaginary reports" designed for the instruction of pleaders; and he thought there was an "almost imperceptible transition" from those to collections of real examples. But Maitland overestimated the distance of time between the two forms of literature, and an alternative possibility is that the examples given in *Brevia Placitata* were already based on real cases, albeit with the details removed, and what we see after the 1260s is simply an elaboration. At any rate, in the parallel series of manuscripts known today by the compendious title *Casus Placitorum*—and which Woodbine considered "the forerunner, and in a way the exemplar, of the Year Books"—use is made of notes or recollections of what identified lawyers said to each other in court, or of what named judges ruled on their circuits. Professor Dunham, who in editing a group of these texts explored their relationship with other early experiments in setting down transactions in court, concluded that the practice of note-taking in court became a professional habit in the 1250s, and that later in the century collections of such notes were made into books, probably for instructional purposes. He also identified two collections of verbatim reports, which may be assigned to the 1270s, and which already show the main characteristics of year-book reporting. It is still a legitimate speculation that the earliest reports of cases may have been designed as supplements to the practical manuals when the newer material became too bulky to be incorporated in the same books. But those manuals may themselves have been the products of an educational routine—in effect lecture-notes—and the exposition of recent cases may have developed into a distinct branch of the course. . . . Unfortunately, the early history of English legal education remains very obscure. Yet, whatever the precise circumstances of its origin, the habit of reporting became permanent, and the copying and studying of reports—stretching back a generation or more even in 1300—helped to establish the tradition that what was said and done in court was evidence of the common law. The law of England was no longer witnessed solely by the plea rolls, but could also be sought in the reports which preserved and explained what had happened in court. Maitland invited us to regard this as "one of the great events in English history":

> Today men are reporting at Edinburgh and Dublin, at Boston and San Francisco, at Quebec and Syndey and Cape Town, at Calcutta and Madras. Their pedigree is unbroken and indisputable. It goes back to some nameless lawyers at Westminster to whom a happy thought had come. What they desired was not a copy of the chilly record, cut and dried, with its concrete particulars concealing the point of law: the record overladen with the uninteresting names of litigants and oblivious of the interesting names of sages, of justices and serjeants. What they desired was the debate with the life-blood in it: the twists and turns of advocacy, the quip courteous and the countercheck quarrelsome.

Although we use the name "year books" for these early reports, for want of another name, the annual arrangement was some time in asserting itself as the norm. Many of the earliest collections are arranged by subject, as befits their supposed origin as supplements to books or lecture courses. Some have little obvious arrangement at all. Others seem to follow particular judges or groups of judges, for instance when they travel on eyre: reports of that kind are found in the 1280s. There are even reports of some discussions in the county courts. The earliest explicitly dated series of Common Bench reports seem to be from the 1290s, and it is only from the end of Edward I's reign [1307] that we have a continuous stream of dated reports. Even for the year books of Edward II, modern editorial work has shown such variety in their order and content that the largest unit which could have existed as a common source seems to be the single case. Hence it has been supposed that these early reports originally circulated as "slips" rather than books, although the point has not been proved. Others believe that they also circulated in pamphlets containing the reports of a single term. This would help to explain the name "books of terms", which they acquired in the course of the fourteenth century, probably before the end of Edward II's reign, and retained until Tudor times. On either view, the books as we have them are in general not "original" year books, but compilations made later, and made from a variety of sources.

Note 1(B). Authorship of the Yearbooks

The yearbooks were the major source for learning about English law for nearly three centuries. In modern times, much scholarly attention has been devoted to them. Yet legal historian J. H. Baker has concluded: "There is still no consensus among twentieth-century historians as to how the earlier year books came to be written."[1] One theory—that the yearbooks were produced by official reporters—is dismissed by Baker. He accepts the view that the main purpose of the yearbooks, at least initially, was legal education, although later, yearbooks outgrew their pedagogic roots:

> [E]vidence from the fifteenth century demonstrates not only that year books were still associated with and used by students, but that they were at the same time owned and much valued by members of the judiciary. The entire profession had come to regard them as "our books", just as to this day law reports are used by bench, bar and students alike.[2]

On the evidence of the fifteenth century, Baker also considers the authorship of the yearbooks:

> One distinctive feature of the year books, at least until the later fifteenth century, is their anonymity. Recording their authorship seems to have been of no interest to contemporary lawyers. This may be because it was common knowledge at the time, or it may be—and this is more likely—because there was no single author. At any rate, the value of the reports does not seem to have been related (as in later times) to the identity of those who wrote them. The question of authorship has, nevertheless, been much discussed by modern scholars, and is obviously material to the interpretation and status of the year books as historical sources.[3]

The best evidence of authorship dates from the latest yearbooks that continued to be produced until the middle of the sixteenth century:

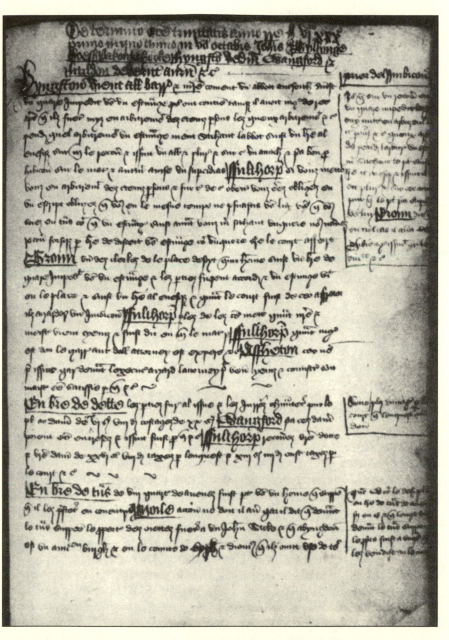

First Page of the Year Book of 31 Henry VI, 1452
(Harvard Law Library, Special Collections)

[I]n the last century of the year books, reporting was carried out by lawyers who made it the habit of a lifetime: by able students destined for the bench, by judges who had begun as students, and by others of intermediate standing. We know, moreover, that they exchanged and circulated material, especially within their own inns, so that any one collection may contain the work of several hands. Is this any different from what had been happening in earlier periods? Perhaps we shall never know for certain.[4]

The chronological regularity of yearbooks also leads to speculation that there may have been an organized method for their production, perhaps through the "law schools"—the inns of court. Another possibility, however, is that chronological regularity is, at least in part, an illusion imposed by the printers who collected manuscripts of yearbooks and republished them in the sixteenth century.[5]

Selection 1(B). Abridgments of the Yearbooks

F. L. BOERSMA, AN INTRODUCTION TO FITZHERBERT'S ABRIDGEMENT 23–26 (1981).

Standardization of the Year Books was inevitable as soon as lawyers, judges and students had learned to depend on them. Two hundred years later, when the bulk of the Year Books had surpassed any compass and rudimentary organization threatened their contents with oblivion, it was argued that in form they were ill conceived. The early fourteenth century did not possess a mass of materials such as accumulated later, and it was doubtless easier at first to issue a series of reports, term by term and year by year, than to revise periodically numerous groups of cases arranged topically. The fact that a chronological arrangement was preferred to a topical one suggests that speed was an important factor in the production of Year Books and that some purpose was served in providing current case-notes. In a period which saw the appearance of the Year Books and encompassed a revolution in litigation and legislation, the value of current case-notes would have been more evident than in a later period when the law was more settled. Topical case-noting presumed a large, fixed body of materials, and if Year Books had employed that organization scheme, they would have burgeoned with each revision and amounted in each instance to a volume scarcely less bulky than the Year Books as a whole. A compromise between the two principles of organization might have obviated some of the difficulties which lay ahead, for if the case-notes of individual terms had been also indexed, the need for abridgements would not have been so great; either future difficulties were not sufficiently perceived at the critical time or contemporary production was not sufficiently organized to achieve an equivalent result, for it was the chronologically-arranged Year Book which prevailed.

Standardization of the Year Books, therefore, left a gap in English law reporting, which the abridgements soon came to fill. Of the diverse elements of which law reporting was composed in the late thirteenth and early fourteenth centuries, expanded case-notes and the chronological method of arrangement became the property of the Year Books, while contracted case-notes and a topical arrangement became that of the abridgements.

The appearance of the Year Books had been connected with the development of pleading in the thirteenth century. It was important for lawyers to know which pleas had been successful in court and to possess ready reference to these pleadings. The Year Books, therefore, noted proceedings in court so as to propagate arguments which were being advanced there with increasingly elaborate invention. Their success can be measured by the centuries that they continued as the chief sources of English law; the draw-back existed, however, that they accumulated in arithmetic progression. They were naturally works of reference rather than record so that their physical bulk made them, in time, decidedly inconvenient for individual lawyers. Unless a researcher knew the year and term of the case-note he was looking for, he had to read through a mass of material to find anything useful, if anything at all. . . .

If the Year Books increasingly required an index, it had to use a method simple enough to make any one of thousands of cases readily accessible to the lawyer. And it had to accommodate the variations in two centuries of Year Books tradition. Separate versions of the same case could vary radically, emphasizing different issues and recording diametrically-opposed decisions. Some duplicated the court record or excerpts from it. The writ could be quoted, the mesne process described, the alleged facts set forth, the pleas recounted, the arguments developed, the issue stated, the verdict and judgment reported: all or any one part of this could be included. In many instances, the note-taker contented himself with a short note, which might or might not reflect the principal issue of the case. In these circumstances, an indexer would have to ignore the degree of formal completeness for any specific note.

For nearly two centuries, Year Books outstripped abridgements in production. Probably, this was because the basic unit—the case-notes of a single year or term—was not large, and numerous copies could easily be made, both at the time of its appearance and afterwards. A collection of several years, moreover, could be made in almost any size by adding together a number of these units. The abridgements by comparison were at a disadvantage. Any of them were likely to be larger than an average Year Book, and with the passage of time, as the reports of years and terms continued to accumulate, their size also tended to increase. In an era in which books were written by hand, it is not surprising that relatively few of them appeared. The contest was apparently equalized by printing, for from the late fifteenth century forward, the abridgements were on the rise and the Year Books in decline. Next to all of the Year Books, printing of even a very large abridgement was a light task. It was not until the late sixteenth century, through the efforts of Richard Tottell, that the goal of printing the Year Books as a whole was even nearly reached, and indeed, the whole has yet to be offered in a single edition. Whereas the abridgements seemingly leapt into print and flourished under the new conditions, the Year Books continued to come out in manuscript form. A baleful conservatism hovered over their last years, for it was only gradually that any of them got into print, and even then, never on a current basis. No year later than 27 Henry VIII (1535) was ever printed, although manuscripts of a later date do exist.

Note 1(C). The Printing of the Abridgments and Yearbooks

Abridgments

The earliest printed abridgment, attributed to Nicholas Statham, was published probably in 1495. It contains about 3,750 notes from the yearbooks arranged in 258 topics. The topics are arranged in roughly alphabetical order, but the arrangement of notes in each topic has been called "a jumble."[1]

Statham's abridgment was soon overshadowed by a much more ambitious work—*La Grande Abridgement* of Anthony Fitzherbert, published in three volumes in 1516. Fitzherbert's abridgment is considered one of the jewels of early English printing.

Although the number of topics in Fitzherbert's abridgment is close to Statham's, the number of case notes is almost four times Statham's. The arrangement of the topics is, again, alphabetical, and the arrangement of notes under each topic is, again, without clear order. Fitzherbert's abridgment, however, is equipped with two additional levels of access. Catchwords or phrases in the margins aid quick browsing (a technique also used in some yearbook manuscripts), and, more important, a "Tabula," listing all 260 topics, with subtopics under each, is keyed by a numbering scheme to the individual notes. The "Tabula" has been viewed as a major advance:

> [T]he "Tabula" was nearly as important as the Abridgment itself; for, without it, the practitioner must have waded through the whole of an alphabetical title in order to track down what he wanted. If the title were a short one, this was a trifling matter, but if it were one like "Briefe," the delay might be irritating, for this occupies 34 folios, has 949 references, and must have been a topic commonly consulted. Here the "Tabula" would greatly reduce labor. Under "Briefe," for example, Fitzherbert composed about 180 short captions spread over 17 folios, and placed the appropriate cases under each of these captions.

With [the] number of the plea and marginal catchword, the searcher had a pretty quick guide to the Abridgment.[2]

The "Tabula" provided a quick reference to the notes in the abridgment, but, in the first edition of Fitzherbert's abridgment, neither the "Tabula" nor the abridgment provided easy reference to the full text of the yearbooks. This may be an indication that Fitzherbert's abridgment was used as a substitute for the yearbooks, rather than as an index to them—although references to the yearbooks are included in editions published after 1565. The fact that the printing press made Fitzherbert's abridgment widely available may well be one reason for the demise of yearbooks in the first half of the sixteenth century. Fitzherbert is frequently accepted as a "primary" authority—certainly for those cases not found in any surviving yearbook manuscript.

Fitzherbert's abridgment was updated and expanded by Robert Brooke. Brooke's abridgment of the yearbooks was published posthumously in 1568 and contains more than twenty thousand case notes divided into over four hundred topics. Although the increase in the number of topics was an improvement over Fitzherbert's arrangement, notes within each topic remained without order.

Subsequent abridgments were based not only on the yearbooks but also on the reports that came to supersede the yearbooks. The leading abridgment of the seventeenth century, written by Henry Rolle and published posthumously in 1668, arranged notes by subtopics under main topics, eliminating the "jumble" that existed from Statham to Brooke.

In the eighteenth century, Charles Viner's abridgment, published in twenty-four volumes from 1742 to 1753, was based on Rolle. Although the set was successful enough to enable Viner to endow the Vinerian Chair in Law at Oxford University (the first holder of which was William Blackstone),[3] it was not a critical success. Nearly a century after its publication, Joseph Story, an influential American scholar, teacher, and later justice of the Supreme Court, reviewed the English abridgments then widely used in the United States; of Viner's abridgment, he wrote:

> [Viner's abridgment] is a cumbrous compilation, by no means accurate or complete in its citations, and difficult to use, from the irregularity with which the matter is distributed, and from the inadequacy, and sometimes the inaptness of the subdivisions. Indeed everything appears to have been thrown into it, without any successful attempt at method or exactness.[4]

Two other abridgments extended Rolle's topical approach. Matthew Bacon (1736) and John Comyns (1762–67) published systematic expositions of the law, using case notes as references. Bacon included abridgments of statutes as well as cases.

Bacon's became the most widely used abridgment for several generations, in part because of its convenient arrangement. According to Joseph Story:

[Bacon's abridgment] consists of a series of tracts, or dissertations upon various topics of the law, generally illustrated by adjudications, and though incomplete, exhibiting a rare union of sagacity and industry. As a text book for students, it has long maintained an unrivalled reputation; and as the expositions of a very able and learned judge upon a large survey of the law, dealing with its history and its reasons, it must forever hold a high rank among the treasures of the profession.[5]

However, the "learned judge" responsible for Bacon's abridgment was not Matthew Bacon but Lord Chief Baron Gilbert from whose manuscripts Bacon was said to have stolen the work.

Joseph Story reserved his highest praise for the abridgment edited by John Comyns:

A work . . . almost perfect in its kind, is the Digest of Lord Chief Baron Comyns. Though a posthumous publication, it has been justly observed, that unlike most publications of that nature, it was left by its learned author, in a state very fit to meet the eye of the public. . . .

Of the plan of his incomparable Digest, it is difficult to speak in terms, which will do it justice, without seeming to be extravagant. . . . [F]or the purpose it proposes to accomplish, no plan could be more judicious, and no execution more singularly successful. . . . [A]s the preface to the first edition states, "the general plan of this Digest is, that the author lays down principles or positions of law, and illustrates them by instances, which he supports by authorities; and these are trenched out and divided into consequential positions or points of doctrine, illustrated and supported in the same manner. By this means, each head or title exhibits a progressive argument upon the subject, and one paragraph &c. follows another in a natural and successful order, till the subject is exhausted."[6]

The popularity of Comyn's work, however, was damaged by editors of subsequent editions:

[I]t has been the hard fate of Comyns to have the symmetry and excellence of his work essentially impaired by the unmerciful interpolations of his later editors. Without any regard to the dependencies of the original text, or the sequence of principles and illustrations, they have thrust in between the different paragraphs, their new matter in a crude state, and often so little sifted, that it is a mere copy of the marginal abstracts of the later Reports. The consequence is, that passages, which are connected in sense in the original text, are often separated by these misshapen adjuncts; and, sometimes, a half page is to be run over by the reader, before he can gather up the *disjecta membra*, the scattered fragments, of the author.

In the art of bookmaking, there is scarcely anything more reprehensible, than this practice, by which an author, singularly clear, exact, and methodical, is presented in the habiliments of a slovenly commonplace man. The only rational course to be pursued, in any new edition of Comyns, would be to leave the text untouched, with all the authority belonging to it from the author's venerable character, and by supplementary volumes, drawn up in the same method, to add the new matter, which has accumulated from the litigation of later times.[7]

In the early nineteenth century, Charles Petersdorff returned to a topical arrangement of case notes without any attempt to string them together into literary statements of general principles. His abridgment, published in 1825, was a model for the digests published in England and the United States in the late nineteenth century and early twentieth, while the Bacon and Comyns works served as the models for the legal encyclopedias dating from the same period.[8]

Yearbooks

Printing of the yearbooks also began in the late fifteenth century. Richard Pynson became the first printer of the yearbooks, gathering existing manuscripts and republishing fifty editions between 1490 and 1530. Beginning in 1553, Richard Tottel succeeded Pynson, publishing 225 yearbooks and imposing a numbering scheme for the citation of the yearbooks he printed. No greater completeness was achieved until 1678–80, when the "black-letter" or "standard" edition of the yearbooks was published under the editorship of Sir S. Maynard.

New yearbook manuscripts continued to turn up. Many were gathered by A. J. Horwood and L. O. Pike in the "Rolls Series," published between 1863 and 1911, and Britain's Selden Society has published more than thirty volumes of previously unpublished yearbooks in scholarly editions, including comparisons with plea rolls, with texts in both original law French and English translations.[9]

As the earliest printed yearbooks and abridgments became available, the regular production of current yearbooks tapered off. The latest yearbook printed in the standard edition covers 1535–36. The following thirty-five years have been called "a period of curious if expectant silence"[10] until the production of court reports resumed in 1571 in a significantly altered form.

Some have speculated that yearbooks continued to be produced in manuscripts, but the manuscripts have not survived because they were on paper rather than parchment. Others have blamed the Reformation for the destruction of yearbook manuscripts; it has been said that "the Catholics destroyed all that was new and the Protestants destroyed all that was old."[11] More likely, the production of manuscripts ceased in response to changes in court procedures, especially a shift from oral to written pleadings. A detailed study of the end of the yearbooks by L. W. Abbott emphasizes that, in the beginning of the sixteenth century, changes in law reporting involved "not so much . . . one system ending and another taking its place; [but] rather, . . . the slow decline of the one and the parallel growth of the other, both unpremeditated and probably unrelated."[12]

Selection 1(C). The Nominative Reports

J. P. Dawson, The Oracles of the Law 65–79 (1968).

The Named Reporters (1550–1790)

The great innovator was Edmund Plowden, author of two volumes of law reports of which the first appeared in 1571. He was the first lawyer in England to publish a set of reports in his own lifetime and under his own name. But his real distinction lay in his high standards of care and accuracy and his concentration on the decisive issues in the cases he reported. Plowden's Reports came closer to meeting the requirements of a modern law report than later reporters were to come for 200 years. It is remarkable and significant that his example was so little followed.

By 1550, when his series of cases began, the subject matter of law reporting had been greatly changed by the shift from oral to written pleadings. The shift had been gradual over the late fifteenth and early sixteenth centuries. It meant that issues were defined outside of court through an exchange of papers, that skills in written draftsmanship increasingly displaced the arts of the oral pleader, and reportable debates in open court were initiated through the specific challenge of a demurrer or, if the case had gone to trial, through the issues raised by a special verdict. The reduced importance of oral pleading may help to explain the altered emphases in the debates reported in the late Year Books—the prominence accorded to propositions in capsule form and long quotations of free-floating doctrine.

The advent of written pleadings had precisely the opposite effect on Plowden and gave him the opportunity to develop a wholly new style in law reporting. By his own account he had begun his notes on current decisions entirely for his own personal use and reluctantly decided to publish them because unauthorized persons had made garbled excerpts that printers might be tempted to publish. Once he had made this decision, he scrapped altogether the notes he had taken in his earlier years, rigorously edited the rest, and preserved only those cases in which an issue of law had been directly presented and decided. The shift to written pleadings enabled him to reproduce in full the record of each reported case, precisely as it was presented to the court for decision. The arguments of the lawyers and the opinions of the judges were also reproduced at length, mostly on the basis of his own notes taken at court sessions he attended. In difficult or doubtful cases he showed his notes to the persons quoted for verification. He thus took every possible precaution to ensure not only that his reports were complete and accurate but that they were sharply focused on the precise legal issues that had been decided.

Plowden's Reports soon acquired an immense reputation. He was already well known as a distinguished lawyer, whose promotion to the rank of serjeant had been prevented by his adherence to the Catholic religion. His reports were a mine of useful information, though he reported only 62 cases in two volumes totaling 567 folios, i.e., 1134 pages. His versions were thus extremely long. But I suggest that it was not their length that discouraged imitators. His careful choice of cases that were worth preserving, his rigorous exclusion of irrelevancies and his painstaking search for accuracy all reflected a theory of judicial decision and conceptions of case law method that were at least two hundred years ahead of his time.

The next set of reports to be published were those of Sir James Dyer, Chief Justice of the Common Pleas for twenty-three years until his death in 1582. They appeared three years after his death and were clearly not written for publication. They were private notes kept for his own personal use. Some must have been copied from manuscripts prepared by others, especially notes on cases that had been decided when he was a child. Dyer's collection was a miscellany, like the late Year Books, and followed them in style and content. Some cases were reported quite fully, with summaries of pleadings and arguments of counsel and statements of outcome with judges' reasons. Other entries were nothing more than detached propositions preceded by such comments as "note for law," or "note by the opinion of all the judges," and with no clue whatever to the context in which they might have been pronounced. Some merely described conversations among judges and lawyers at dinner. There were many reports of questions raised and decided at one of the Serjeants' Inns; in these instances where opinions differed the head counts in voting seemed to rate serjeants on a parity with judges. Altogether Dyer's Reports were most useful. Using a great variety of styles, they described hundreds of cases and gave readers a glimpse into the private world of a leading judge.

Between 1535, when the black-letter editions of the Year Books ended, and 1600, Plowden and Dyer were the only law reports published. The year 1600 is significant because in that year Sir Edward Coke brought forth the first of the eleven volumes of reports that he was to publish in his lifetime. When the series began he held the office of Attorney General, after a rapid rise to prominence in the legal profession. He was appointed Chief Justice of the Common Pleas in 1606 and continued his literary efforts during the stormy ten years of his tenure of judicial office. Many reasons explain the enormous and lasting influence of Coke's Reports—the high offices he held, his great and deserved reputation as a lawyer, the eventual triumph through a revolution of his political views. But to these should be added the extraordinary dearth of published reports. This dearth was to continue. In the 1640's and 1650's lawyers' notes of cases decided under Elizabeth and James were to be published in great volume. During the period intervening, between 1535 and 1640, those outside the inner circle of well-informed lawyers could learn about the work of English courts only from Plowden, Dyer, and Coke. It is no wonder that Coke found an avid audience and that even a not very friendly critic, like Bacon, conceded that he met a great need.

The demerits of Coke as a reporter have been often discussed—the direct falsification of authorities of which he was sometimes guilty, his misunderstanding of the history that he used as his principal weapon, the piled up mass of irrelevancies. There is no occasion here to pass on the more serious charges or on the defenses that have been interposed. Of more interest are the style and format of Coke's Reports, as clues to attitudes. In his first three volumes Coke followed the example of the admired Plowden to the extent, at least, of reproducing in full the pleadings and records in most of the cases reported. In the next volumes of the series this practice was almost wholly abandoned, to be resumed occasionally in the final volumes. In the end he used "every conceivable variety of style and method" in describing not 62, but 467 cases. This mass production by an immensely busy law officer and judge could hardly have been achieved if he had used Plowden's painstaking care in isolating the decisive issues and verifying the statements that were ascribed to others. But it is evident from the most casual reading that Plowden's methods were not for Coke. In substance his reports were disconnected little treatises on topics suggested by the cases, largely written by Coke himself but with only occasional clues to identify his own contributions. The only course that he followed at all consistently was the one that he himself advised, to throw in everything.

An expression that Coke habitually used was that the judges "resolved" a series of propositions or adopted "the following resolutions." The mental operations described by such expressions do not differ greatly from those with which the later Year Books are filled: brief legal propositions quoted by the reporters preceded by "it was agreed as law" or followed by "all the judges and serjeants agreed to (or denied) this." Yet Coke conveys throughout his reports, in almost every case, a distinctly sharper picture of solemn votes taken, at least by a nodding of heads. The culminating feature in his version in almost every case is the set of rules the judges adopted; they are made almost into little legislatures. These oracular pronouncements often reach far beyond the limits of the particular case. In truth many of Coke's "resolutions" were undoubtedly nothing more than casual remarks by judges or lawyers, remarks that no one challenged at the time and that Coke approved and reformulated. At times these judge's "resolutions" flow without a ripple into long disquisitions and masses of undigested citations, peppered with comments like "Note reader" or "Vide" that identify his own insertions. . . .

One abortive effort was made, through the initiative of Francis Bacon, to improve the quality and organize the machinery of English law reporting. Bacon's proposal to King James for the appointment of official law reporters was a part of Bacon's ambitious scheme for the amendment and restatement of English law, including its reduction to a brief and intelligible text. Two reporters were appointed in 1618 and entered on their duties, but only one produced a publishable manuscript. This series, by Thomas Hetley, appeared in 1657, more than twenty years after his death, and fell into well-deserved oblivion. It was a miscellaneous collection of rough notes, mostly very brief summaries of facts and reasons, often giving no facts at all. This experiment with official reporters, publicly appointed and paid, was a complete failure. In England it was never tried again. Perhaps the men chosen were unsuited to the task; certainly Hetley could not have been inspired with any of Plowden's zeal. Perhaps the times were unpropitious, as judges and lawyers became more and more engaged with great divisive issues of public law which were to be resolved eventually by civil war.

. . . .

In the 1640's and 1650's the supply of published reports of English court decisions suddenly changed from conditions of extreme poverty to a somewhat tarnished wealth. The flood of reports that then appeared gave hundreds of cases decided in the sixteenth and early seventeenth centuries. There seemed to be an insatiable curiosity sustaining the market demand, though a high percentage of the cases reported were more than a half century old when they appeared. They were published, of course, long after the deaths of their authors, and few could have been intended for publication. They were private notes and commonplace books of the kind that lawyers kept for their own use and to share with friends. Many similar collections by other lawyers survive in manuscript. They suggest how heavily the working methods of English lawyers had come to depend on self-help measures, supplemented by some mutual aid through borrowing and copying as manuscripts passed from hand to hand among the leading practitioners. Their notes reflected the interests, tastes, and abilities of their authors, so that they varied greatly both in quality and style. Most of them were extremely condensed, stating shortly the issues raised and ending with a proposition or two. Even the notes prepared by judges, on cases in which they had participated, seldom disclosed judicial reasons at any length. As a result of carelessness in editing or translation by unidentified publishers, most of them are suspect. As with the manuscripts of the early Year Books, different or conflicting versions of the same case were given by different reporters. Only rarely could these private jottings have been used, or intended for use, as authorities citable in any court. As the source material for a working system of precedent they left almost everything to be desired. When we apply to them modern methods of case-law analysis we delude ourselves.

There was some, but not much improvement during the century that followed the Restoration of 1660. The whole system of training and promotion in the legal profession had disintegrated as legal education in the Inns of Court fell into total eclipse. The judiciary was degraded by the late Stuart kings who dismissed some judges for nothing worse than political independence. It was not until the Act of Settlement of 1701 that judicial tenure was assured during "good behavior" and no longer depended on royal pleasure. During this dismal interlude there were some able lawyers whose notes on decided cases were published and were deemed worthy of respect. After 1700, when the integrity and reputation of the bench had been restored, there were some reports of improved quality, especially by men who eventually achieved judicial office. But there were others that were so manifestly unreliable that judges complained against them bitterly and even forbade lawyers to cite them in court. Many of them were not published by their authors but by relatives or unknown strangers after the authors' deaths. It was not until 1756, with the first volume of Burrow's Reports, that there appeared a series approximating in fullness and accuracy the standards of a modern law report. Burrow and his followers—Douglas (whose first two volumes were published in 1778) and Cowper (whose single volume was published in 1783)—began a new era in law reporting and made it into a specialized craft.

It is extraordinary and surely significant that the record of English case law was kept for so long by such casual and careless means. The gross inadequacies in the reports were curable, as Plowden had shown long before. If there had been many judges and lawyers who believed that a great deal depended on securing a full and accurate statement of the facts, a clear definition of the issues and precise quotation of the reasons for decision, then surely the considerable effort required could and would have been made. It was not merely that reporting continued to depend on private enterprise, as it had from earliest Year Book times. Private enterprisers here as elsewhere could be expected in the end to yield to the demands of their customers. It was not until nearly 1800 that altered demands brought a regular supply of carefully prepared reports whose fullness and accuracy were sufficiently guaranteed. Before that time, certainly before the advent of Burrow, even the more dependable reports continued to be merely private notes of points or conclusions that seemed interesting to the notetaker and that would be useful in his own professional career or possibly to his friends. What was missing was a sense of responsibility to the profession and the public, and this could only arise gradually as an expectation grew that each judgment with its cluster of decisive reasons would be invested with an authority of its own.

There has been some debate in more recent times as to when conceptions of precedent became sharpened in English law. In contemporary sources articulate discussion of the subject was certainly both late and rare. . . . How could a court be bound by the results and the reasons in some prior case if it could learn of them only through some fallible reporter? A theory of precedent and a highly developed case law method could not emerge because the materials available were insufficient. But it is impossible to identify cause and effect—the materials available were insufficient because theory and method did not yet require them.

If reliability had been a major object, the best assurance would have been for the judges themselves to take on the task of preparing a written record, especially a record of the reasons that had been for them decisive and that they knew best. Occasionally in early eighteenth century reports one finds an opinion whose reasons are written with such fullness and care as to suggest much advance preparation by the judge and precautions taken by someone (perhaps even through consultation between reporter and judge) to ensure that his oral statement had been recorded verbatim. But even model reporters, like Burrow and Douglas wrote only in long-hand and thus were able at most to summarize the reasons stated by the judges orally. As to the notion that the judges should review and approve his work, Burrow's comment was:

> It cannot be expected that the Judges should take the time and trouble to revise it; or that they would do it, upon any application whatsoever.

Note 1(D). Evaluation and Republication of the Nominative Reports

A diverse array of nominative reports continued to be published until 1865. Since the nominative reports varied greatly in quality, the profession needed a guide to assess the reliability of each. Such a guide was provided in 1844 by an American, John William Wallace, in his book *The Reporters Arranged and Characterized with Incidental Remarks* (the fourth and last edition of which was published in 1882). Wallace explained the mission of his book:

> We have, up to this date, nearly fifty scores of different persons who have acted as reporters; nearly all of them self-constituted and without having been subjected to any antecedent test of integrity, education, or general capacity. Besides this, it is known that many volumes bearing the names of eminent lawyers, and purporting to come from their pens, were not designed for the press, were first published generations after their authors' deaths, and from MSS. known not to have been original. It is therefore quite to be expected that these records should possess various grades of merit in almost everything which belongs to reporting; and we find accordingly that the judicial writings frequently contain remarks upon their authenticity, genuineness, and other characteristics. Such remarks, being casual, are scattered through many books; and it is matter of some surprise that in England, at least, no systematic work on the subject has appeared. Nearly a century ago, Sir Michael Foster declared

that these "hasty and indigested Reports" had "become the burden and scandal of the profession;" and the want of accuracy of many of them has been noted both before and since.[1]

Wallace called for scholarly editions of all the yearbooks and reports, providing exact reprints, with translations into English, and "harmonization" of diverse versions of cases, together with "syllabuses" for each case, a table of cases, an index for the whole, and "pervading and accurate reference to all prior and subsequent decisions" concerning the topic of each case.[2]

About a decade after Wallace's last edition, in 1891, a leading legal scholar, Sir Frederick Pollock, began publication of the *Revised Reports*, a consolidated set of the pre-1865 decisions he considered still relevant and important. Sir Pollock's scholarship and editorial aids have been widely praised. The cases included in the *Revised Reports*, however, only reached back to 1785 before publication of the set was discontinued in 1917.

About a decade after Sir Pollock began laboring on the *Revised Reports*, in 1900, a more comprehensive, though less scholarly, project was launched for the publication of all reports prior to 1865. The project, published as the *English Reports: Full Reprint*, was completed in 176 volumes in 1932. The cases in the *English Reports* are grouped by the courts from which they originated, rather than by the reporters who reported them, but a two-volume table of cases and a chart of original citations allow references to the original reports.

Another retrospective collection of cases—called the *All England Law Reports Reprint*—contains cases from the era of the nominative reports, but the editors were highly selective. The cases prior to 1865 take up only eight volumes.

Selection 1(D). The Call for Reform, 1849

Society for Promoting the Amendment of the Law, *Report of a Special Committee on the Law Reporting System, in* W. T. S. DANIEL, THE HISTORY AND ORIGIN OF THE LAW REPORTS 4–12 (1884).

Report.—1849

Your Committee . . . are of opinion that the present system of *law reporting* [is] capable of great improvement.

.   .   .   .

. . . [F]rom the vast increase of new questions of law and practice which at the present day annually arise in our Courts, and the great inducements which then arise for comprehensive reports, a new evil has grown up . . . —that the reports of the decided cases in any year for one term in any of the Superior Courts at the present day exceed, in bulk, those of all the tribunals in the country for the whole year [in the 1770s]. Competition, ordinarily productive of so much good, in this instance adds to the evil. The higher class of reports, which really are or ought to be the records of the existing law, are made as elaborate as the cases will admit of. The whole of the written pleadings, the documentary evidence, the speeches and arguments of counsel, with the various authorities cited on each side, are often given even in cases where the actual decision of the Courts really expounds no new doctrine of law, or is confined to some isolated point. The time which is necessary to effect this, often prevents the decisions of our tribunals being communicated to the public until long after they have been given, and after suitors have taken a course in direct but unconscious opposition to them, and occasionally, even after other judges have unknowingly pronounced directly conflicting decisions. The bulk and expense too of these reports render their contents inaccessible to the great majority of those who are officially or professionally expected to be acquainted with them, and the supply of rival productions simply adds to the cost without diminishing the inconvenience.

It has long been considered a practicable scheme for any barrister and bookseller who unite together with a view to notoriety or profit, to add to the existing list of Law Reports. It may be that such reports may be rarely referred to, that they may be inaccurate, that they may be of little or no authority,—they nevertheless remain. They tend to confuse the science; they muddy the stream. . . . A case of great importance was decided a few years ago upon the authority of a note in Lofft's Reports, which one of the learned Judges observed, with some bitterness, he had never heard three cases quoted from during a professional life of forty years; and some of the inferior law reports of the present day may, perhaps, meet a similar fate. But even if all the reports which are published were correct and given by competent persons, they are now so numerous that they cannot be known to one tithe of the practitioners in the law. They are beyond the reach, not only of the public, but of the great body of the profession. Indeed, it is not too much to say that few of the Judges or the Bar (and hardly any of the solicitors) take in all the current reports. Wherever there is the smallest opening, the profitable trade of law bookselling establishes a fresh series of reports . . . professedly confined to *practice cases, criminal cases, sessions' cases, registration cases, railway cases, parliamentary cases, etc.*, but containing reports of decisions vouched as correct by barristers, whose accuracy must, under the existing system, be assumed.

The competition of the reporting system is thus carried on without regard to the interest of the profession or public. The gentlemen who undertake these reports are often highly competent men; indeed, many of them have been raised to the bench of Westminster Hall. Independent of the profit of reporting, it is a good channel to professional notoriety; but here is one great evil of the system. If the reporter has other professional engagements, he loses his anxiety about his reports, he throws up his office when he pleases (and cannot be blamed for this), and it has been held that the bookseller cannot compel him to perform it. Thus we have chasms in our law reports, which will occur readily to any professional reader, which can never be supplied. It is well known that an eminent counsel (formerly a reporter) practising at the Chancery Bar, has at the present moment notes of the decisions of a deceased Lord Chancellor, taken by the learned counsel in his character of reporter, but to this time unknown as law to all the profession save the parties engaged in these causes. . . .

Thus, under the present system of reporting, the law expounded in Westminster Hall may not only remain for years concealed from the public, but the professed reporter himself, or the counsel in the case, may alone be in possession of the decisions, at the risk of their being used at any moment to contradict the law as universally received amongst the Profession.

This inconvenience is thus alluded to in the preface to Watkins' Principles of Conveyancing:—". . . If conclusions from unquestionable principles are to be overthrown in the last stage of a suit by private *memoranda*, who can hope to become acquainted with the laws of England?—and who that retains any portion of rationality would waste his time and his talents in so fruitless an attempt? Is a paper evidencing the law of England to be buttoned up in the side pocket of a judge, or to serve for a mouse to sit upon in the dusty corner of a private library? If the law of England is to be deduced from adjudged cases, let the reports of those adjudged cases be *certain*, *known*, and *authenticated*."

. . . .

The Reporter, however, under the present system may unavoidably be absent, or purposely omit cases which he deems not to be authorities; and we have heard of an eminent Nisi Prius reporter preserving in MS. a whole pile of decisions of a late Chief Justice which he deemed *bad law*.

The evils, too, arising from the *inaccuracy* of some of the existing reports are often practically felt by the profession. In an article on this subject in the "Law Review" of February, 1848, a long list of instances (taken from the then last numbers of several Reports) is given, where cases solemnly cited and relied on in argument, were denounced as *incorrectly*, *inaccurately*, or *falsely* reported; and it is a common thing to hear of a particular report or set of reports, that they are not *of much authority*. Hence the suitor, even after he has discovered what the law is reported to be, may find to his cost that such report, however authentic in appearance, is inaccurate.

It is but little consolation to say, on the trial of a cause, "That case is not law," after it has misled half the kingdom.

The Committee do not wish to say any thing in this place as to the present style of Law Reporting; still it will hardly be denied that with few exceptions the volumes of reports are commonly too verbose, and too open to the reproach of *book-making*. In a useful article on Law Reports in a recent number of the "Law Magazine", a reform of the existing style of Law Reporting is warmly advocated. "Instead of a collection of judicial decisions," it is observed, "with the facts necessary to support them, and the grounds upon which they are made, carefully and briefly set out, we have volumes upon volumes of reported cases, in which the points important to be known bear but a small proportion to the mass of useless undigested matter with which these volumes are filled. The inconveniences of such a system are evident; instead of having to read through a few pages, and at once obtaining a clear comprehension of a particular point, we have to wade through an enormous quantity of matter, which, so far from throwing additional light upon the subject, confuses by the numerous doubts and difficulties by which each case is surrounded; the consequence is, we do not obtain that certainty in the law which it should be the object of reports to accomplish."

To sum up in a few words the evils and inconveniences of the existing system of Law Reporting, there is no guarantee afforded to the public that the judicial exposition of the law will be reported at all, or reported correctly—or in time to prevent mistakes—or in such a manner, with respect to conciseness, form, and price, as to be accessible to those whom it so vitally affects.

Note 1(E). The *Law Reports*

The 1849 report did not lead to action. The profession's pressures for reform, however, bore fruit when the reform movement gained a leader in former judge W. T. S. Daniel. Under Judge Daniel's leadership, a new committee was appointed in 1863. Although some lawyers were advocating legislative or judicial action to limit court reporting to one official set, the committee recommended the publication of a new set of reports "independently of the Government" under the direction of "an unpaid council."[1]

The Incorporated Council on Law Reporting was named the next year, its members selected jointly by the inns of court and the bar, with the attorney general and solicitor general as ex officio members. The council has been called "thoroughly English," since it "is not founded on any abstract principle; it has no monopoly; it exists because it is useful and supplies a professional want."[2]

The council began producing a new set of law reports, called simply the *Law Reports*, in 1865. In advance of each volume of the *Law Reports*, summaries of current cases were published in *Weekly Notes*. Subscribers to the *Law Reports* also received digest volumes that were consolidated from time to time.

The *Law Reports, Weekly Notes,* and their digests did not succeed in eliminating other reports. Although nominative reports ceased to be published in 1865, a number of publishers continued to publish anonymous sets of reports, and lawyers were allowed to cite any reports in court. If the *Law Reports* was to win predominance over other reports, it could do so only on its merits.

The *Law Reports,* however, failed to outshine its rivals. Twenty years after the *Law Reports* began, Lord Justice N. Lindley published an article critical of the *Law Reports'* "speed of publication, indexes and arrangement." Lord Lindley had found that some cases in the *Law Reports* were published as much as ten months after decision, and he was especially critical of the digests:

> [S]peaking generally, a heading should not begin with an adjective. . . . For example, such headings as "Education" and "Schools" are better than "Elementary Education" and "Endowed Schools." "Lease" is better than "Renewable Lease," which should be a sub-heading of "Lease." "Debt" is better than "Specialty Debt," which should be a sub-heading of "Debt." The editors of the council's Digest have not been happy in their choice of titles. Very few lawyers would think of looking for information under "Lake." They would turn to "Fishing" or "Water."
>
> . . . .
>
> Neither is the matter under each title well arranged. . . . The cases relating to Interrogatories and Production of Documents, instead of being brought together, are to be found partly under the head "Practice, Admiralty," . . . ; partly under "Practice, Chancery," . . . ; partly under "Practice, Common – Law," . . . ; and partly under "Practice, Supreme Court." . . . The decisions on such important subjects as "Interrogatories" and "Production of Documents" ought to have been brought together and made sub-divisions of the title "Discovery," instead of being scattered about the title "Practice." Both for reference and for study it is better to multiply the leading titles than to collect an enormous mass of matter under one title, even if subdivided into sub-heads.
>
> . . . .
>
> Again, the Digest is too much a Digest of Cases, and not enough a Digest of Principles and Rules. There are too many facts introduced, and the law is not sufficiently extracted. Let any one compare the Consolidated Digest with Comyns' Digest, which is almost perfect in this respect, and the difference will be at once apparent. [3]

With respect to arrangement, Lord Lindley suggested the grouping of cases on such subjects as criminal law and bankruptcy so that specialists would not have to buy the entire set of the *Law Reports.* Lord Lindley also advocated selectivity in reporting to keep down the bulk of the *Law Reports.*

The situation was virtually unchanged more than a half-century later, when an article by Professor A. L. Goodhart revived the issue. Professor Goodhart listed eighteen reports being published in 1939 and lamented the expense and space demands the sets placed on the profession. He also pointed out that in much of the reports the same cases were "reported again and again in substantially the same form," and he condemned the lack of coordination among the reports, resulting in text variations, and the lack of an overall digest to all reports:

> It is a striking, although unfortunate, fact that it is less difficult to find the relevant American case among the 40,000 annually reported cases in that country than it is with the 750 in England: this is due to the centralized and efficient indexing system in the American reports.[4]

Professor Goodhart also noted the irony that, despite the multiplicity of reports, it was not uncommon for some important cases to go unreported. According to Professor Goodhart, "the crux of the problem" lay in the selectivity of the *Law Reports*:

> The idea that it is desirable to limit the number of reported cases as far as possible is . . . based on fallacious principle. It is more inconvenient to find that one leading case is not reported than to have twenty unimportant cases in the books. With a proper system of indexing it is possible for a reader to skip those cases which he does not need, but there is no way in which he can conveniently consult an important case which has been omitted. As long as a single case of importance is not reported in the Law Reports but can be found elsewhere it will be necessary for the legal profession to continue purchasing the other reports.[5]

In the same year as Professor Goodhart's article, Britain's lord chancellor appointed a Committee on Law Reporting—the first official body ever appointed to study the topic. The committee's report published in 1940 proposed no reforms beyond encouraging the editors of the *Law Reports* to speed up publication and to "take a more generous view of what is reportable."[6]

A. L. Goodhart, a member of the committee, dissented. He did not, however, propose the comprehensive reporting of judicial opinions as in his 1939 article. Instead, he proposed that judges write their opinions, or that oral opinions be transcribed verbatim by shorthand reporters, and that all opinions be promptly filed and indexed, accessible to the public (after an opportunity for judges to edit transcribed opinions).

The committee rejected the Goodhart proposals, fearing that filed but unpublished opinions would constitute "land mines." It also felt that the various reports were publishing "almost every decision of any possible importance"; according to the committee, "What remains is less likely to be a treasure-house than a rubbish heap in which a jewel will rarely, if ever, be discovered."[7] The committee simply concluded: "we do not think any large measure of reform of law reporting feasible."[8]

Selection 1(E). The Lord Chancellor's Committee on Law Reporting, 1940

P. Clinch, *The Establishment v. Butterworths: New Light on a Little Known Chapter in the History of English Law Reporting*, 19 ANGLO-AM. L. REV. 209, 209–38 (1990).

It is just over 50 years since the largely unremarkable report of the Lord Chancellor's Law Reporting Committee was published. The one controversial and forward looking element in the document was the dissenting report by Professor A. L. Goodhart. . . . There was undoubtedly disagreement in the Committee on how law reporting, that essential yet undervalued element in the system for disseminating English case law, should be organized. Now, for the first time, as a result of access to the unpublished records of the Committee held at the Public Record Office, it is possible not only to identify the real and surprising reasons for the formation of the only official investigation of English law reporting, but also to learn from the hurried and poorly planned course of its deliberations and investigations, to applaud the wide range of proposals for improvement put to it (of which only two appear in the report) and, above all, recognize the considerable influence 'the establishment' had on the work of the Committee.

1. Origins

Market research by Butterworths [Publishers] in 1935 . . . indicated 'there was a definite need' for reports which were quick, contained a full report of the judgment and included a sufficiently wide selection of cases to meet the needs of practising lawyers—wider than any existing series!

This need was fulfilled in the *All England Law Reports* [which Butterworths began publishing in 1936], with the added advantage of cheapness: 2 guineas (£2.10) to the *Law Report*'s 5 guineas (£5.25). That this new and threatening competition to the *Law Reports* was the fundamental reason for the founding of the Committee is easily and clearly demonstrated in the first letters in the PRO file. . . .

. . . Alfred Topham, editor of the *Law Reports*, . . . took the opportunity to present his views on how this unwelcome competition might be ended.

. . . Topham notes the authority of the *Law Reports* and the principles he employs to select cases. He continues:

'I have established a system by which every case which appears in any other series of reports has to be considered by the *Law Reports* reporter responsible, and he has to inform me why he has not thought fit to report it. In doubtful cases I frequently tell the reporter to send in a report, if I think that a full and accurate report may be useful to the profession; but I find that I reject nearly 50% of the cases reported in the *All ER* as not being worthy of a permanent record'.

He grudgingly admits the *All ER* appear to meet a want. 'The legal profession seem to like to get early reports of the recent cases, even in cases where nothing new is decided'. The Council, he suggests, could meet this want by publishing advance reports of verbatim judgments, but his experience is that 'great inconvenience and doubts are bound to be caused' if reports are published before the judges have had the opportunity of approving or revising them.

His remedies are drastic:

> 'one remedy might be to prohibit the publication of verbatim reports of judgments by anyone not authorized to do so, at any rate until they have been revised by the Judges. This might require legislation. Possibly a similar result would be obtained if all the Judges were to agree not to look at reports which are apparently little more than verbatim reports or transcripts of judgments unless they are satisfied that the Judge has had an opportunity for revision. There would, no doubt, have to be an exception in favour of fair summaries published in legal or other newspapers; but these summaries could be treated in much the same way as the reports in *The Times* Newspaper or the *Weekly Notes*'.

Topham proposes either a move towards the schemes of the radical reformers of the 1850's and 1860's where the only judgments which should be available are those that have been authorized, or, the re-introduction, over 100 years after the courts declined to favour it, of the monopoly of exclusive citation. Although he does not explicitly state as much, the impression is that these proposals should be implemented in favour of the *Law Reports* and none else. . . .

. . . .

2. *Proceedings*

The first meeting of the Committee (March 2, 1939) solely considered the question of whether 'a law of non-citation of unauthorized reports' should be implemented. The Chairman may well have had Topham's remedies at the forefront of his mind in adopting this as the Committee's opening discussion point.

On one side of the discussion stood Goodhart and Winfield arguing that exclusive citation would not work (it was employed in India 'and is perfectly useless') and it would not prevent the multiplicity of reports. For the other side Macaskie felt there should be such a rule and Stamp took a middle line, that the rule should not apply until six months after the judgment was delivered. . . .

. . . .

At its second meeting (March 9) the Committee considered the written memorandum of Alfred Topham. . . .

In his written evidence Topham . . . suggests a method of preventing the use of verbatim transcripts for law reports without the Judge having an opportunity to revise them, by vesting the copyright of each judgment in the Judge or the Attorney General on behalf of the Crown. Alternatively shorthand writers could be prohibited by contract from supplying transcripts except to approved persons. He disagrees with Goodhart's . . . article that maintained that every decided case should be reported. The way to reduce the number of 'overlooked' cases would be to employ more people to check other reports and consult Counsel engaged in cases for their opinions on reportability. If exclusive citation were conferred then the decisions as to the selection of cases should rest not with the Editor but with 'some Committee of the Council or other body who could override his decision where necessary'. The next part of his evidence is even more controversial.

> 'If it should be decided that no exclusive privilege should be accorded the *Law Reports*, a good deal might, I think, be done, on the lines of what is sometimes called "rationalization", by the acquisition of rival reports by the Council and reducing the duplication of reports and digest'.

. . . Finally, he turns to the specialist reports including *Workmen's Compensation Cases* noting that

> 'those who specialize in such subjects seem to desire to have every case relating to their special subject available for citation, and it might be advisable to allow certain of these to continue, possibly under license from the Council or some Government Department. If so the question arises whether cases on these special subjects or some of them should not be omitted from the authorized Law Reports.'

. . . .

At the Committee's third meeting on March 23, 1939 it considered the printed memorandum of evidence submitted by Butterworths. . . .

> 'Our opinion is that what the legal public wants in a set of Law Reports is:
>   (1) Reports of all reportable cases.
>   (2) Fullness.
>   (3) Speed of Publication.
>   (4) Accuracy.
>   (5) Full References.
>   (6) Editorial Notes.
>   (7) A good index.'

Coverage, the memo maintains, was not sufficiently comprehensive before the *All England* arrived. . . . An analysis of delay before 1936 indicated that the *Law Reports, Law Journal Reports* and *Law Times Reports* were from five months at best, to eight to nine months in arrears. . . .

As to multiplication of overlapping reports, the memo shows that there were five general series in 1939, the same number as in 1885. . . .

. . . Later in the meeting Goodhart asked questions on overlap between the *All England* and respectively *Lloyds List* and *Workmen's Compensation Cases.* [Representatives of Butterworths] volunteered the view that since the latter are a special series for a specialist public who demand a report of every case that is heard, if the Committee were looking for an instance of over reporting, this would be a good series with which to start. Then Goodhart asked about the opposite—under reporting . . . were there any complaints? Yes, from some solicitors. They sought cases not solely for the legal principle in the judgment but for facts which were analogous to the matter with which they were dealing so they could

> 'use it to see how it was treated, what evidence called . . . to bring their case into line with something already decided on all fours with their own . . . if [a solicitor or barrister] cannot get these [reports] out of a proper legal series then they take them from newspapers and every improper kind of report, and that possibly leads to all kinds of false conclusions.'

This picture of information seeking behaviour and information need may have come as a surprise to some members of the Committee, especially those used normally to taking part in actions in the higher courts of the land. When the Chairman turned questioning to the matter of speed in publication—is there an urgent demand for reports?—some equally unexpected information was provided . . . :

> '. . . before we publish the report of a case we are written to and even telephoned to know if there are reports available . . . [the inquiries are] not the same people every time . . . Solicitors in every case, occasionally a layman asking for an unreportable case . . . a running down case or something of that kind.'

This hunger for early reports was confirmed in the evidence submitted by the editors of the *Times Law Reports* and *Law Journal Reports*.

. . . .

. . . Before the next meeting of the Committee on March 30 Prof. Winfield compiled a note of suggested reforms. He began by placing the schemes in two categories: first, turning law reporting into a government monopoly . . . and secondly, improving the existing system without recourse to the government. . . . 'The *Law Journal Reports*, and *Law Times Reports* and the *Times Law Reports* might with advantage disappear in favour of the *All England Reports*, which are speedier than any of the other series, besides being cheap'. . . . Specialist series should remain largely untouched. . . . The Courts should retain the power to disallow any such citation if they felt the case inadequately reported.

Prof. Winfield's note was an accurate prediction of future events. . . .

. . . .

Market forces caused the cessation of *Law Times Reports* as a separate publication at the end of 1947, when it was incorporated in the *All England Reports*. In 1950 *Law Journal Reports* merged with the *All England*. In 1952 *Times Law Reports* ceased. The following year saw some of Goodhart's proposals set out in the article in *Law Quarterly Review* in 1939 come to pass when *Weekly Law Notes* ceased, to be replaced by the fuller reports of *Weekly Law Reports*. *Weekly Law Reports* were to have a sufficiently wide selection policy to cover cases which ought to appear in any general series of law reports and be published with speed. Each issue would be in two parts, part 2 including only those important cases which would appear later in the *Law Reports* after they had been revised by the Judges. Part 1 would include cases of more passing interest. The Incorporated Council of Law Reporting had promised that 'reports will appear within about three weeks of judgment' and that 'subscribers will have a report of every reportable case, thereby saving the expense of subscribing to any other general series of reports'. Goodhart was concerned that the *Weekly Law Reports* lived up to the expectation of being comprehensive and include 'every reportable case' otherwise 'every unreported case which, in future, is cited in the courts will be regarded as a black mark against the *Weekly Law Reports*'. [Another] reviewer . . . , on the other hand, whilst noting that the competition between the *All England* and *Weekly Law Reports* would 'keep the ICLR up to scratch', observed that unnecessary duplication 'will be a nuisance, and if they report additional cases of minor interest they may be an even greater nuisance'. . . .

Since 1953 many new specialist series have appeared, especially in the late 1970's and 1980's. . . . On top of all these developments, and of much greater significance, has been the introduction of computerized legal information retrieval systems to this country, of which one, LEXIS, survives today.

There are grounds, therefore, for suggesting that there ought to be an official review of the law reporting system to consider the wisdom of such multiplicity of reporting. However, if such an investigation were conducted it would do well to learn from the proceedings of the Lord Chancellor's Law Reporting Committee in 1938 and 1939, to ensure the task is approached in a more open minded, methodical and analytical manner.

Note 1(F). English Law Reporting since 1940

With the demise of the *Law Times Reports* in 1947, the *Law Journal Reports* in 1949, and the *Times Law Reports* in 1952, the *All England Law Reports* is left as the only rival to the *Law Reports*.

The *All England Law Reports* continues to prosper, even though the *Law Reports* has come to enjoy the privilege of primary citation—requiring its citation in court except for cases not reported or incorrectly reported in its pages. The primary authority of the *Law Reports* is based on the fact that opinions reported in the *Law Reports* are read by judges prior to publication. The *Law Reports* also has the advantage of segmentation; it is issued in four series—Appeal Cases, Chancery, Queen's Bench, and Family Division.

The success of the *All England Law Reports* is attributable largely to the shortcomings of the *Law Reports*. Although the *Law Reports* is updated weekly in the *Weekly Law Reports*, the cases reported in the *Weekly Law Reports* are often several weeks old, while the *All England Law Reports* weekly supplements are more timely. The editors of the *All England Law Reports* also do a superior job of headnoting and indexing in many instances, and cross-references in the *All England Law Reports* link the judicial opinions to relevant statutes, regulations, encyclopedia articles, and digest sections. The *All England Law Reports* also includes some cases not selected for the *Law Reports*. In addition to the two general law reports, several specialized reports continue to flourish. Topics include industrial law, company law, criminal law, family law, tax, patents, local government law, shipping, building regulation, and insurance. Each set of specialized reports commonly includes cases not reported in the general reports.

For the most current cases, English lawyers also look to specialized journals. These sources generally do not provide full reports but merely summaries.

Since the 1930s, shorthand transcription of court proceedings has spread throughout the English court system. Since 1968, shorthand transcription has been replaced in most courts by audio recordings. Transcriptions of audio recordings of unreported opinions are available, for a cost, on request.

Thus, there are still overlapping reports and opportunities for "land mines" of unreported cases. However, comprehensive reporting is beginning to be realized by computers. The LEXIS database includes cases reported in all English general reports and most specialized reports since 1945. LEXIS also includes cases not reported elsewhere. Specialized "libraries" in LEXIS bring together case reports, statutes, regulations, and secondary sources on selected topics.

Digests

The main source for subject access to law reports is simply called *The Digest*. (Started in 1919, it was called the *English and Empire Digest* before the imperialist language was dropped in 1981.) Selected cases from Canada, Australia, and other nations, as well as European community cases, are included in *The Digest* following digests of English cases (and in smaller type than digests of English cases). A rival set, *Mew's Digest of English Case Law* started in 1898, ceased publication in 1970.

The Digest is arranged on general principles, much like the widely praised Comyns abridgment of the eighteenth century. In fact, the arrangement of *The Digest* follows closely the arrangement of England's major legal encyclopedia, *Halsbury's Laws of England*. The main topics of *The Digest*, like the topics in *Halsbury's Laws*, are arranged alphabetically, and within each topic subtopics proceed from general principles to specific applications.

Halsbury's Laws of England, published since 1907, includes essays, arranged alphabetically, that are based on cases, legislation, and administrative and other sources, but its treatment of cases is most thorough. *The Digest* can be used to update *Halsbury's Laws*.

In *The Digest*, case digests are followed by "annotations" (also known as "noter-ups" or "citators") listing subsequent cases that cited the digested cases, with brief indications of the import of the citations, such as "overruled," "distinguished," "approved."

Perhaps the major shortcoming of *The Digest* is its annual supplementation. This time gap has left room for a rival digest, *Current Law*, which is published monthly and includes references to legislation and secondary literature, such as articles in law journals, as well as case digests.

Subscribers to the *Law Reports* and the *All England Law Reports* are provided indexes to those sets. The indexes are updated weekly, which makes them more current than any of the digests. The most current updating, however, has become the database of LEXIS, imported to England from the United States.

Selection 1(F). Unreported Cases

R. Munday, *The Limits of Citation Determined*, 80 LAW SOC'Y GAZETTE 1337, 1337–39 (1983).

In his comparative study, *Appellate Courts in the United States and England*, published in 1963, Delmar Karlen examined in some detail the English and American systems of law reporting. Our highly selective method, which sought only to report decisions that enunciated new principles of law, materially modified existing principles, settled some doubtful question or for some other reason were peculiarly instructive, had obvious virtues. Apart from keeping precedent to a manageable size, it could be argued to be less constricting on judges than a system of blanket law reporting in that, theoretically, it permitted the judiciary greater freedom of action (for the very volume of precedent may act as a shackle). Certainly, Karlen felt that the blanket law reporting practised in America brought disadvantages to that legal system. It tended to add to the costs of litigation and to the time required by lawyers to research their cases; the availability of almost unlimited reported case law encouraged the habit of citing dozens of cases where one would do, even to establish a self-evident propo-sition; and, largely thanks to this obsessive citation of precedent, in such a system the danger was that judges and lawyers could easily overlook important cases in the welter of reports. . . .

Such was the position in 1963. English lawyers, if they thought about law reporting, probably were more disturbed at the possible omissions of the law reporters than in the volume of cases being reported. But matters have altered dramatically since then. New specialist series of law reports have burgeoned in remarkable fashion in recent years, the Court of Appeal's unreported cases have become generally available and, more lately, electronic data retrieval systems have become an established part of the lawyer's armoury, retaining every manner of decision, reported or oth-erwise, in the capacious memory stores. The American vices Karlen regret-ted in *Appellate Courts* may now be acquired by the English lawyer. Alarmed at this prospect, and in a bid to prevent their spreading to the English legal system, the Court of Appeal and House of Lords in recent weeks have issued important announcements restricting the use of unre-ported materials which the computer revolution has suddenly made avail-able to the profession. In particular, the House of Lords . . . has effectively outlawed the citation of unreported cases in argument before it. It may be profitable to consider the events which have led up to this uncharacteristic judicial injunction.

The Unreported Case Law

. . . .

One feature of the English legal system has for long been the occa-sional whimsicalities of its law reporting. Because it has deliberately—and rightly—set its face against reporting everything, important cases have on occasion been missed by the major series of reports or even completely passed by. . . . Everyone is aware of this possibility, and courts are not averse to ascribing a lack of authority for a given proposition to the omissions of the reporters. . . .

. . . In part, to overcome these deficiencies, the lawyer has always been permitted to refer to unreported cases, and whether one views unreported authority as the apotheosis of legal learning or as the bane of the lawyer's life, it has an important philosophical bearing on English law: for it acts, in some measure, as a check on what otherwise would be the reporters' law-making monopoly.

Reported cases only represent a fraction of those heard by the courts. Approximately half the decisions of the Civil Division of the Court of Appeal, for instance, remain unreported, and a far higher proportion of first instance civil cases will leave no trace in the reports. The unavailability of transcripts of unreported Court of Appeal judgments at one time proved an intense irritation to some judges and, only following a fierce outburst from Lord Evershed . . . did the Lord Chancellor order that official notes be taken of all Court of Appeal judgments. Transcripts of all unreported decisions of the Court of Appeal (Civil Division) are now retained by the Supreme Court Library and their citation in court has become an everyday matter. The number of first instance cases reported and available to the profession, too, has increased in recent times, owing to the emergence of new series of specialist law reports. However, potentially the most farreaching change in law reporting has been the advent and rapid development of computer retrieval systems. Lexis, for example, now boasts that its 'English General Library' contains more than 5000 unreported cases—the equivalent of 70 volumes of standard law reports—decided by English courts since 1980. Whether or not, as the Lexis publicity claims, these cases are of considerable importance, the fact remains that, confronted with blanket reporting on this scale for any prolonged period, English courts may find themselves unable to cope with the volume of precedent upon which counsel and judge may, and will, make call.

English law reporting has thus far—and probably unintentionally— maintained a fair balance between two competing desiderata: whilst generally ensuring an adequate coverage of the law (and, perhaps, when in doubt erring on the side of over-reporting), the law reports have also succeeded in containing the quantity of reported case law within manageable bounds. The advent of the machine, and the far from remote prospect of a Lexis terminal in every law library and lawyer's office, inevitably impels the legal system towards an extreme with which it will have to come to terms. It may be a comfort to know that significant cases will not be consigned to oblivion if accidentally omitted from the various series of law reports, but as the late Professor Gilmore observed of the American legal system, 'the computerisation of all legal materials, with instant access to everything, has opened up nightmarish possibilities'.

. . . .

The availability of all High Court judgments can only magnify this tendency. As in the USA, it is legitimate to fear that blanket reporting will lead to an excessive citation of authorities which will add little or nothing to the sum total of our legal knowledge. Apart from the futile waste of the courts' time, reporting on this scale will also distract lawyers from the traditional form of legal argument, where the elucidation of principle from authority is paramount, and encourage them to pursue what Slesser LJ once dismissed as 'the unintelligent search for exact precedent'. . . . This latter method characterises to a considerable degree the American legal system. . . . Any such tendencies in this country are to be firmly discouraged, and it is heartening to note that in the last few years the courts have taken an increasingly firm stand on the citation before them of superfluous precedent.

The Defence of Principled Argument

Lord Diplock was amongst the first to comment adversely on the excessive citation of authorities, particularly in commercial cases. By 1977 he feared that it had already become 'an ineradicable practice'. . . . [S]till more recently [he] underlined the dangers of counsel needlessly citing a plethora of authorities which merely illustrate principles whose existence no-one would wish to dispute. Such a practice constitutes an obvious waste of judicial time and the parties' money, and can also mean that the court, blinded by the volume of case law laid before it, finds itself unable to separate the wood of legal principle from the trees of paraphrase.

. . . .

This year, too, the courts have expressed concern at the vast quantity of authority sometimes cited before them. Although this trend was already apparent long before the advent of electronic data-processing appliances, there can be no doubting that such machines have exacerbated the problem. . . .

The Court of Appeal merely expressed the hope that counsel would display suitable restraint in the citation of precedent. The House of Lords, however, . . . went a step further and, in effect, has now forbidden the citation of unreported decisions before it. In *Roberts Petroleum Ltd v Bernard Kenny Ltd* [1983] 1 All ER 564, the House of Lords finally lost patience with counsel who unnecessarily introduce citation into their arguments surplus to requirements. . . .

. . . In a determined effort to prevent court time being squandered, . . . the House declared that in future it would decline to allow transcripts of unreported judgments of the Court of Appeal (Civil Division) to be cited before it without special leave. Such leave would only be granted if counsel was prepared to give an assurance that the transcript contained some new and relevant principle of law binding on the Court of Appeal, and whose substance was not to be found in the reported authorities.

. . . It remains to be seen, of course, whether this stern injunction will serve to cure English counsel of that persistent ailment of the common lawyer, first diagnosed in 1960 by Karl Llewellyn in *The Bramble Bush*, 'cititis', and whether other courts will in turn feel moved to adopt similar practices.

English Law Reporting

Paradoxically, English law, despite its being in the main judge-made, has always been careless of its case law. Historically, law reporting has been left entirely to private enterprise, and attempts in the 1860s and in 1940 to set up a system of official law reporting were strongly resisted. Apart from the 'semi-official' reports published under the aegis of the Incorporated Council of Law Reporting, anyone today is entitled to publish law reports, provided that the judgments reported are attested to by a member of the Bar present at the decision. The disordered manner in which the basic materials of the English lawyer's craft are recorded and printed leads to a number of difficulties. Often the same cases are duplicated in several different series of reports; since no single series will contain all cases needed by the lawyer, libraries and individuals find themselves put to considerable expense subscribing to the necessary series; this, in turn, leads to difficulties in housing reports, in reconciling the textual variants found in different reports of the same case and in actually tracing some authorities. In addition, despite the enormous number of cases reported annually, as we have seen, the law reports still on occasion fail to pick up the odd important decision.

In 1939, the Lord Chancellor set up a committee . . . to report and advise on the problems then posed by the increasing number of reported cases. Apart from Professor Goodhart's sturdy dissenting report, the Committee's findings were bland in the extreme. Published in March 1940, the Law Reporting Committee's report concluded that, although the multiplicity of law reports did pose problems, no large measure of reform was either necessary or possible. Admittedly, in 1940 this country had other and more serious preoccupations. However, with the remarkable proliferation of reported cases witnessed in recent years and the advent of data retrieval systems, it is most unlikely that a similar committee would report today with such equanimity. . . .

The time is past when lawyers could unreflectingly accept the vagaries of their haphazard law reporting arrangements. Occasional eccentricity has been supplanted by a ruthless efficiency and, falling easy prey to the idea that . . . any decided case is a potential authority, the profession has fast been affected by this revolution in law reporting. The upper echelons of the judiciary are clearly anxious about the effects excessive citation can have on the nature and quality of legal argument and, hence, on our law. The promptness and directness of their response to the citation of unreported authorities in . . . *Roberts Petroleum Ltd* is plain evidence that they consider the risks we run are grave. The profession cannot afford to be complacent any longer and, in view of the issues at stake, rather than leaving matters to individual courts to settle, as the House of Lords has done in *Roberts Petroleum Ltd*, the time surely has never been riper for the establishment of a fresh Committee to review the entire system of reporting, citation and storage of English case law. If any degree of control is to be maintained over our present system, the limits of citation soon must needs be deter
mined.

2

Case Reporting in the United States

Note 2(A). The First American Reports, 1789

During the colonial era, courts in British North America relied on English law and English law books. The proceedings of some American trials were published as individual pamphlets,[1] but more for their newsworthiness than for their usefulness to the legal profession.[2] Much like in the yearbook era, lawyers kept private notes of cases; some notes circulated and were hand-copied among groups of lawyers; and unpublished decisions were at times cited by courts.[3]

> Such an arrangement probably worked reasonably well in provincial America. Society was simpler then, and no heavy burdens were placed on the legal system. The bar that practiced before the appellate courts was everywhere a small guild. Attendance at court, keeping a commonplace book, and personal associations with other lawyers apparently met the needs of the legal profession.
>
> The postwar years soon proved different. . . . James Kent when he was elevated to the New York Supreme Court in 1789 . . . declared, "[w]e had no law of our own and nobody knew what it was." Until decisional law was preserved and made readily available through regular publication, there would be no American common law.[4]

Following the Revolutionary War, the publication of reports of American courts was one expression of independence. Almost simultaneously, reports were privately prepared in Connecticut and Pennsylvania. The first to come to press was Ephraim Kirby's Connecticut *Reports*, published in April 1789.

By a statute enacted in 1785, judges in Connecticut were required to produce written opinions. Kirby gathered the "loose papers" of 201 opinions; fleshed them out with notes on the arguments, motions, and process, modeled on the work of English reporters; and provided a detailed index.[5]

Kirby found it difficult to make a financial success of his reports. In part, this was due to the uncertainties of the time; in part, it was also due to the low public esteem of the legal profession. A correspondent wrote to Kirby: "[People] are made to believe that a law book is a very wicked thing and that a man who is the owner is in a fair way to Damnation."[6] Only the purchase of 350 copies for Connecticut's town clerks allowed Kirby to break even. By 1814, however, Connecticut appointed official reporters, and by 1820, seven other states had reporters paid from public funds.

The first to follow Kirby was Alexander Dallas, who published cases from Pennsylvania in 1790. In the second volume of his reports, Dallas began the publication of the opinions of the United States Supreme Court.

Selection 2(A). The Supreme Court Reports

C. Joyce, *The Rise of the Supreme Court Reporter: An Institutional Perspective on Marshall Court Ascendancy*, 83 MICH. L. REV. 1291, 1297–1362 (1985).

. . . With independence, . . . American lawyers embarked upon the daunting task of tailoring English law to American circumstances, when possible, and creating a distinctly American body of law, when necessary. Suddenly, neither English reports nor the notebooks of decisions maintained by many lawyers for use by themselves and their friends would suffice for the practice of law in a new nation. Although a majority of the new American states considered common law decisions announced before the break with England persuasive in their courts, there seemed a pressing need for *American* decisions as precedent. No published reports of such cases appeared in the decade following independence, however, and American courts remained almost entirely dependent on English legal literature for their common law precedents. The law that did develop in American courts was, in the words of Ephraim Kirby, "soon forgot, or misunderstood, or erroneously reported from memory."

Clearly, American soil had become fertile ground for the flowering of "home-grown" law reports. It remained to be determined, however, who would undertake the task and how it would be financed. The contrasting approaches taken in Kirby's Connecticut *Reports* and Dallas' Pennsylvania

Reports are instructive of the problems faced by all of the early reporters, state and federal, and shed particular light on the development of the *United States Reports* under Dallas and his three immediate successors.

From the start, Kirby had significant advantages over Dallas. As early as 1784, the Connecticut General Assembly had recognized the need "to lay the foundation of a more perfect and permanent system of common law in this state," and had accordingly required the judges of the Supreme Court of Errors and the Superior Court "to give in writing the reasons of their decisions upon points of law, and lodge them with their respective clerks, with a view, as the statute expressly declares, that the cases might be *fully reported*." Plainly, Kirby's *Reports*, covering judgments in the named courts from May of 1785 through May of 1788, benefitted directly from the General Assembly's foresight and carried into effect its specified purpose.

Dallas was not as fortunate. Not until 1806, just as he was concluding his *Reports*, did the Pennsylvania General Assembly require judges to reduce their opinions to writing, and then only at the request of the parties or their attorneys. Dallas, therefore, was able to give only the barest description of the earliest decisions in his first volume. For a number of the more recent cases, he had access to the opinions of his patron, Chief Justice Thomas McKean of the Pennsylvania Supreme Court, but generally to no others. Even this limited assistance was unavailable in the instance of the Supreme Court of the United States, whose opinions first appeared in volume 2 of Dallas' *Reports*: while Dallas reported its decisions, the Court apparently failed, even in its most important cases, to reduce its opinions to writing. Certainly, no statute or rule of court required the Justices to do so.

Kirby, like Dallas, undertook his task without benefit of an official appointment as Reporter. The two men's conceptions of their informal responsibilities to the bench and bar, however, seem to have been substantially similar, at least as reflected in their finished products.

. . . .

. . . [I]n many respects, Kirby proved more successful than Dallas at the untried business of law reporting in a new nation. . . . Yet, apparently content to let his fame rest on his first and only volume, Kirby essayed no sequel.

Dallas pressed on, however, perhaps spurred by the prospect of increased sales prompted by the inclusion in his second, third and fourth volumes of the decisions of the federal courts newly located in Philadelphia since the publication of volume 1. But there were numerous grounds for complaint concerning the execution of Dallas' later volumes, particularly by readers interested primarily in the decisions of the Supreme Court of the United States. Those problems (which, in fairness to Dallas, were not to end with his reportship) included delay, expense, omission and inaccuracy.

. . . .

The lion's share of the blame for . . . delays in Dallas' publication of federal court decisions is clearly attributable to the free enterprise character of his venture. Lacking an official appointment and salary from the federal or state governments, and lacking also the comfort of a subsidy, . . . it would be strange if Dallas had not been heavily influenced by commercial considerations. Having commenced publication of his first volume with Pennsylvania attorneys as his primary audience, Dallas may well have thought it prudent to design succeeding volumes in such a way as to maintain that readership as a core for sales. Indeed, the bulk of volume 2 of Dallas' *Reports* was devoted to state rather than federal cases; and its 1798 publication date may well have been dictated by a desire to include as many decisions as possible of the Supreme Court of Pennsylvania. . . .

Whatever the cause, Dallas' tardiness was a major hindrance to those hungry for information concerning the jurisprudence of the highest federal tribunal, particularly its appellate practice. In general, newspaper accounts of decisions were of little assistance in disseminating such information; and, in consequence, counsel who were unable to attend the sessions of the Supreme Court of the United States in Philadelphia found it necessary to inquire of friends at the seat of government whether the Court had decided various issues of interest to them.

Delay, however, was not the only obstacle to the success of Dallas' venture. Expense, too, undoubtedly played a part. Publishing costs in America were generally higher than in England, and American attorneys had grown accustomed to purchasing the less expensive imported volumes. In Connecticut, Kirby's *Reports* had been considered excessively dear at three dollars per copy. Dallas' four volumes, reporting courts as disparate as the Supreme Court of the United States and Mayor's Court of Philadelphia, appear to have encountered resistance at least as stiff from potential purchasers.

Yet delay and excessive expense may not have been the most grave deficiencies of Dallas' *Reports*, at least from a present-day perspective. To these must be added the twin charges that Dallas reported the first decade of the Court's existence both incompletely and inaccurately.

Completeness, or lack thereof, is a matter difficult to decide with certainty. Charles Warren's classic history of the Court claimed that Dallas had omitted at least ten percent of the cases decided during the sixteen active Terms that he reported, including one "of much interest" to a later Court. Chief Justice Hughes, concurring with one of Dallas' successors, thought that Dallas "probably published all the opinions that were filed." Writing more recently, Julius Goebel, Jr., concluded in 1971 that "somewhat less than half of the dispositions made by the Supreme court in the first decade of its existence are reported," although the figure "probably exceeds 70 percent" once the inquiry is limited to cases adjudicated on the merits or on jurisdictional grounds. The dispute, in short, concerns not *whether* but to *what extent* Dallas' three volumes of Supreme Court *Reports* are incomplete.

As to accuracy, the verdict on Dallas' *Reports* is less certain. When, as Goebel notes, an opinion of the Court or of one of the Justices, "as reported by Dallas, is no model of clarity," who is to be blamed: The Justices or the Reporter? If Dallas, and not the Justices themselves, must be held responsible for garbling the opinions that he transmitted to lower court judges and practitioners, the fault would be great indeed in an age when newspaper reports, the primary alternative means of communicating the developing jurisprudence of the Court, "usually [imparted] only the bare outlines of the case and the result."

Any careful attempt to ascertain the accuracy of Dallas' accounts of the Justices' opinions, however, raises an even more arresting question: are the opinions in fact the handiwork of the Justices—or of Dallas himself? Not a single formal manuscript opinion is known to have survived from the Court's first decade; and few, if any, may ever have existed for Dallas to draw upon. Nor may it be confidently assumed that in all instances Dallas was present in court to take down what the Justices said, or that he was able afterwards to consult any notes they may have kept of the opinions they announced. In one instance, Dallas wrote to Justice Cushing for assistance with a series of cases, only to find that Cushing had not retained his notes in certain of the cases, or had not delivered an opinion at all.

Instead, it seems entirely possible that many of Dallas' reports of individual cases were constructed primarily from the notes of other counsel who had attended the proceedings. For example, *Ware v. Hylton* contains an acknowledgment that, having been absent during argument of the case, Dallas had resorted to the notes "of Mr. W. Tilghman, to whose kindness . . . I have been frequently indebted for similar communications, in the course of the compilation of these Reports." A comparison of the arguments as reported by Dallas with the recently rediscovered original of Tilghman's notes, however, reveals that Dallas did more than merely retranscribe his source. Among other liberties taken with Tilghman's notes, Dallas omitted whole paragraphs, while embroidering on, strengthening and shifting emphases in what he retained. The arguments in *Ware v. Hylton*, then, appear to be a combination of counsel's remarks and Dallas' improvements upon those remarks.

Whether the same may be said of the actual opinions in *Ware* is problematical. Having been otherwise occupied during the argument of the case, did Dallas nonetheless find time to attend the rendering of opinions? His report does not say. Justice Chase's rather detailed opinion, as recounted by Dallas, follows Tilghman's notes. Justice Cushing's does not. Dallas attempted to obtain Cushing's notes in *Ware*, but may or may not have succeeded. Does Cushing's opinion as it appears in volume 3 of Dallas' *Reports* depart from Tilghman's notes because of information that Dallas subsequently obtained from the Justice himself, or because Dallas actually heard the opinion delivered in court but recorded it differently from Tilghman, or because Dallas improved upon whatever notes he

obtained, just as he had with Tilghman's notes of the arguments of counsel? On any analysis, the circumstances "cast doubt on the accuracy of the
Cushing opinion as rendered by Dallas."

Delay, expense, omission and inaccuracy: these were among the hallmarks of Dallas' work. His *Reports*, however, had scant precedent in American law, and the task he set for himself in chronicling the rise of the nascent
federal judiciary had absolutely none. The accomplishment, no doubt, fell
short of the aspiration, and perhaps volumes 2, 3 and 4 of Dallas' *Reports*
have found their place in the official *United States Reports* principally "for
want of anything better." In light of the difficulties that confronted him,
however, a more accurate (if still restrained) summation may be that "Mr.
Dallas was a very competent person [who] eventually left things better
than he found them. . . ."

[Dallas's successor was William Cranch. The accuracy of Cranch's
reports remained suspect, and the delays in the publication of his reports
at times rivaled the delays of Dallas. In 1816, following the appointment
of Justice Joseph Story to the Supreme Court, Justice Story's protégé,
Henry Wheaton, replaced Cranch as Reporter.]

In attacking the problem of chronic delay in the appearance of the
Reports, Wheaton moved decisively and victoriously, although not without
a few disheartening moments along the way. The February 1816 Term,
Wheaton's first as Reporter, concluded on March 21, 1816, when the
Court handed down eleven of its forty-three decisions. By early May, he
had completed his work in preparing the opinions, abstracts and arguments
of counsel for the press.

A series of misadventures, only partly the fault of the new Reporter,
then combined to delay the publication of the *Reports* for another seven
months. First, Wheaton himself decided to prepare an extensive set of
scholarly annotations, both in the margins of the cases and in a separate
appendix, to "illustrate the decisions by analogous authorities" and "sub-
join a more ample view" of the Court's developing jurisprudence (particularly in the field of prize law). Second, he allowed himself to become
sidetracked by a number of activities peripheral to the actual publication
of the *Reports*. One was an effort by Story, largely unsuccessful, to coun-
teract negative reaction to *Martin v. Hunter's Lessee*, arising from newspaper reports based on Justice Johnson's concurrence, by encouraging
dissemination of his own majority opinion. Wheaton, agreeing that Johnson's opinion "placed the decision of the Court on a quicksand—yours
on a rock," found himself occupied on and off for the next three months
trying to oversee the placement of Story's opinion in satisfactory forums.
Also, Wheaton further diminished the time available to him for editing the
Reports by an energetic, and for the moment unsuccessful, attempt to
cajole Congress into voting him a formal title and salary as Reporter.

The most serious impediment to early publication of the *Reports*, however, arose from a source utterly beyond Wheaton's control. To his great
dismay, initially not one law book publisher could be found willing to print

the proposed volume on terms he felt he could accept. As Peter S. Du Ponceau, Wheaton's agent in Philadelphia, succinctly advised him: "Bookselling is at present a very bad business, & Booksellers are all out of spirits, & unwilling to undertake any original work." This turn of events ought not to have surprised Wheaton, given his knowledge of the grave difficulties that even Story himself had encountered in trying to arrange the publication of law reports. But the situation did force Wheaton to become painfully practical. He instructed Du Ponceau to offer the right to print the work to Mathew Carcy, a bookseller not generally engaged in the law trade, for a mere $1500 in notes. Carey promptly and emphatically refused the offer. Ultimately, Wheaton had no choice but to let Carey purchase the copyright itself, thereby depriving him of the ownership of volume 1 of his own *Reports*. He received just $1200, payable in notes due up to fifteen months after the date of purchase.

From June 17, when Wheaton reluctantly signed the contract, until December 20, when Carey entered his copyright for the work in the United States District Court Clerk's Office in Philadelphia, six months more elapsed. As summer turned to fall, an embarrassed Wheaton assured Story that the fault lay solely with the printers, who had "sadly procrastinated." As autumn turned to winter, he pleaded with increasing discomfort that "the delay . . . ha[d] been occasioned solely by Mr. Carey's failure to furnish paper from time to time as it was wanted by the printers."

However valid his excuses, Wheaton did not escape the pointed inquiries of those painfully accustomed to the snail-like pace of his predecessors. Attorney General Rush became increasingly impatient, passing from polite entreaty to insistence that the *Reports* issue "before the next [T]erm" to morose musings that Wheaton's first volume would likely be upstaged by the appearance of Cranch's final three. Justice Washington, communicating to the Court's new Reporter through his mentor, Story, noted evenly as the months wore on: "I hear nothing of Wheaton's Reports." Story himself was more direct, pointing out the importance of timely publication of Wheaton's first volume "to justify the Court in their choice of a successor to Mr. Cranch."

Fortunately for Wheaton, the publication of the *Reports* for the 1816 Term prior to the commencement of the 1817 Term answered all doubts regarding the wisdom of the Court in appointing a new Reporter. Dallas, at his worst, had allowed the decisions of the nation's highest tribunal to go unreported for eight years. Cranch, at one point, had permitted a lacuna of six years. Now, for the first time in the history of the *Reports*, the bench and the bar of the Supreme Court had the luxury of preparing for the coming campaign in Washington with copies of the preceding Term's decisions already in hand. Wheaton had accomplished his task, including the preparation of an unprecedented 487 pages of abstracts, arguments and opinions and forty-six pages of notes, in less than nine months. Nor, in retrospect, would this rapidity be seen as an unusual occurrence. Indeed, never again would Wheaton require so *long* to place a volume in print:

typically, later volumes appeared in the summer following the Term reported, and in no instance later than October. Clearly, Wheaton had met and mastered the problem of delay.

Timeliness alone, however, while greatly to be desired, did not itself ensure an increase in the completeness and accuracy of the *Reports*. Indeed, it might have been purchased at their expense. Or perhaps such failings in the volumes of Dallas and Cranch merely demonstrated the limitations inherent in a system dedicated to the preservation of opinions and arguments often extemporaneously delivered from only the most rudimentary notes.

In fact, whether absolute completeness in the *Reports* ought to be sought at all posed, as Wheaton clearly saw, a series of thorny problems. There was, for one thing, the notorious vanity of the Supreme Court's distinguished bar. . . . To what extent, if any, should their orations before the Court be reproduced in the *Reports?* In the preface to his first volume, Wheaton addressed the issue candidly: "Of the arguments of counsel nothing more has been attempted," he wrote, "than to give a faithful outline; to do justice to the learning and eloquence of the bar would not be possible, within any reasonable limits. . . . " Not surprisingly, the bar objected. Responding privately to Webster's public animadversions on this aspect of his reporting, Wheaton observed sardonically to Story: "I bow with submission to [his] criticism as to the inutility of attempting to incorporate into a brief microcosmic sketch of a law argument any of those brilliant displays of eloquence which we frequently hear at the bar." The new Reporter's practice in the matter, however, did not change.

Wheaton's pique was understandable. Reproduction in full would have ballooned his volumes to unmanageable size. What he labored to achieve, and protested that he had achieved, was to assure that the "style and thoughts" of each advocate had been "transfused into the report of his argument," with all "the points and authorities . . . faithfully recorded, where the cases either admitted of, or required, it." Increasingly in subsequent Terms, however, he found it politic and expedient to request assistance from counsel themselves in preparing his summaries of arguments. Most were happy to comply, even to the point of furnishing sketches drafted "as if taken down by you." In due course, the bar became so confident of Wheaton's talent and good will that it dismissed its former anxieties and entrusted matters willingly into his hands.

More troublesome by far was the question of including or omitting certain decisions of the Court. Wheaton's difficulty, as his notebooks show, lay neither in careless preservation of the Court's opinions nor in ignorant underestimation of their utility. He simply recognized that a number of the decisions lacked any precedential value, and thus would take up precious space in his *Reports* without adding measurably to their appeal to potential purchasers. The preface to volume 1 of Wheaton's *Reports* explained matter-of-factly that "discretion" had therefore been exercised "in omitting to report cases turning on mere questions of fact, and from which no important principle, or general rule, could be extracted." Wheaton seems to have continued the practice in his later volumes, with almost no criticism.

Accuracy, on the other hand, would admit of no half measures. In this aspect of his reporting, Wheaton was fanatical to the point of "correcting the proof sheets twice with [his] own hand" to prevent even the most minute error from creeping in. Story, who yielded to none in his devotion to detail, could find but five "errors of the *press*"—*i.e.*, typographical errors—in examining Wheaton's first volume, and none whatsoever in its substance. In fact, the only suggestion of consequential error during Wheaton's entire reportership appears in Justice Johnson's concurrence in *Ramsay v. Allegre*, the last opinion in the last case in Wheaton's very last volume. Johnson's bitter allegation of deliberate misrepresentation in Wheaton's reporting of William Pinkney's argument in *The General Smith* was only one facet of a comprehensive attack ultimately directed at Wheaton's patron, Story, whose expansive views on the federal admiralty jurisdiction the case helped to establish. Wheaton's reply, in a note appended to Johnson's opinion, reveals much about his attitude toward his responsibilities:

> It is a duty which [the Reporter] owes to the Court, to the profession, and to his own reputation, to maintain the fidelity of the Reports, which are received as authentic evidence of the proceedings and adjudications of this high tribunal. If they are not to be relied on in this respect, they are worthless.

In truth, Wheaton's objectives in the preparation of his *Reports* went well beyond unadorned accuracy, embracing as well scholarly excellence and improvement of the law. Cranch, it had been said, "did his work without a spark of enthusiasm, some little of which ingredient is indispensable even to a law reporter." Wheaton's own "enthusiasm for jurisprudence," which he claimed to have caught from Story, quickly became for him not a mere ingredient of reporting but the source of a consuming passion for elaboration. Others might be content to cease their labors upon reproducing correctly the citations of counsel and the Court to leading precedent. Not Wheaton. To these, he added two species of scholarly notes calculated to enhance the utility (even as they greatly enlarged the bulk) of his *Reports*. First, he appended to the cases themselves minor commentaries, which he called "marginal notes," designed "to illustrate the decisions by analogous authorities." The typical marginal note elucidated a point of law referred to, but not explained, in the arguments of counsel or the opinions of the Justices. Second, Wheaton added at the conclusion of his *Reports* a series of scholarly monographs (hereinafter, "appendix notes") intended to provide a comprehensive view of entire areas of law apropos the decisions of the Term. His aim, as he explained in the preface to his first volume, was "to collect the rules and grounds dispersed throughout the body of the same laws, in order to see more profoundly into the reason of such judgments and ruled cases," with the expected result "that the uncertainty of law, which is the principal and most just challenge that is made to the laws of our nation at this time, will, by this new strength laid to the foundation, be somewhat the more settled and corrected." It was an ambitious undertaking: in all, the appendix notes to Wheaton's twelve volumes run to 516 pages.

In the preparation of his notes, Wheaton found in his friend and Washington "chum," Justice Story, an expert and eager collaborator. This was hardly surprising, given their shared interests in prize, maritime and civil law. Story considered these bodies of law to rank among "the most beautiful & scientific efforts of the human mind, & [to be] worthy of the most diligent attention of all the profession." Wheaton now proposed to place his own and Story's best learning on those and other subjects dear to his mentor's heart where they could not possibly escape the profession's notice, namely, in the *Reports* of the Supreme Court of the United States. Within weeks of the conclusion of the February 1816 Term, Story and Wheaton were in constant communication concerning supplementation for the Court's decisions. "Let me know," wrote the Justice to the Reporter, "when you shall want my proposed notes for your Reports. . . .

. . . .

Story's reaction to Wheaton's final product could not have been more laudatory:

> I received yesterday your obliging favour accompanied with a copy of your reports. I have read the whole volume through hastily, but *con amore*. I am extremely pleased with the execution of the work. The arguments are reported with brevity[,] force & accuracy, & the [marginal] notes have all your clear, discriminating, & pointed learning. They are truly a most valuable addition to the text, & at once illustrate & improve it. . . . In my judgment your Reports are the very best in manner of any that have ever been published in our Country, & I shall be surpri[s]ed, if the whole profession do not pay you this voluntary homage.

On the last point, Story was to prove sadly mistaken, at least regarding the short-term reactions most important to Wheaton's pride and prosperity; but time would prove his immediate and sincere praise to have been well founded.

. . . .

One curious aspect of Story's joint venture with Wheaton in the preparation of notes to the *Reports* remains to be mentioned. In the course of five years, Story had contributed to Wheaton's *Reports* 131 closely printed pages of highly sophisticated annotations, or 184 pages overall when marginal notes are included. Yet, in Wheaton and Story's time, this significant and interesting circumstance appears to have been almost completely unknown. The collaborators wished it to be so. Writing confidentially in his memorandum book in 1819, Story noted simply: "It is not my desire ever to be known as the author of any of the notes in Mr. Wheaton's

Reports." Indeed, he said, he had made it "an express condition, that the notes furnished by me should pass as his own, and I know full well, that there is nothing in any of them which he could not have prepared with a very little exertion of his own diligence and learning." Wheaton was properly grateful, but also embarrassed by the praise bestowed on certain of "his" annotations. Neither man, however, revealed the deception. Story's son, William, disclosed a portion of the story after the deaths of both of the principals, and the full record is preserved in their correspondence. But it remains a secret in the official *Reports* of the Court they served.

Whatever the source of the annotations to Wheaton's *Reports*, they were in many respects a considerable success, at least among the leading members of the bar who could afford to possess the volumes. William Pinkney summed up nicely the reaction of this segment of Wheaton's intended audience. Putting his finger on that aspect of the Reporter's accomplishment perhaps most appreciated by his readership, Pinkney wrote: "The promptitude, with which the Reports follow the decisions, greatly enhances their value to us all. We have heretofore suffered a good deal by the tardiness of your predecessor's publications." As to "the Manner in which these reports are given," Pinkney rejoiced that Wheaton had managed to "avoid . . . prolixity in stating the arguments of Counsel," while providing "the substance of them with perfect clearness." The appendices to the *Reports* were "well executed and cannot fail to be useful." In short, said Pinkney, "[t]he Profession [is] infinitely indebted to you. . . ."

One difficulty, however, remained. If omission and inaccuracy had been Dallas' principal weakness and "inexcusable delay" Cranch's, the *Reports* of Henry Wheaton suffered most seriously from inordinate expense. In his zeal for scholarly excellence and improvement of the law, Wheaton had inadvertently pushed the cost of the final product well beyond the reach of the critical market, the mass of ordinary practitioners. The *Reports* of the United States Supreme Court had become a treasure trove of law and learning, but one that required a king's ransom to possess. Wheaton's volumes, more expensive than Cranch's even at the outset, were by the conclusion of his service "exorbitantly dear" at $7.50 each. "[I]t is manifest," as Story so accurately noted in a letter to Wheaton's successor in 1828, "that the profession at large cannot afford to buy" Wheaton's volumes, however valuable.

Not only were Wheaton's *Reports* expensive, but they also lacked reviews in the legal periodicals, at least initially. Without public commendation to mirror the private praise that his efforts had already received, Wheaton soon found himself the victim of slow sales and unexpected financial difficulties. He had arrived in Washington convinced that his appointment as Reporter placed him "in the way to secure an honorable independence." Friends predicted that the profits derived from his new position would "treble those of [his] predecessors." Yet, from the very beginning, Wheaton found himself obliged to "anticipate this income by a loan of $1000 for a year." Three years later, he still could not repay the loan. In regretting his inability to do so, he advised the lender: "I have not yet found the law a thrifty servant. . . . All my calculations as to pecuniary matters have been hitherto so erroneous that I will not now fix the epoch when you may certainly expect payment."

[Wheaton's income improved, but only slightly, as Congress enacted a statute (at Justice Story's urging) to pay him $1,000 per year provided he delivered eighty copies of his reports for distribution to U.S. courts and government offices. Wheaton hoped that his success as reporter would lead to appointment to more lucrative government office—perhaps even to the Supreme Court. However, President Adams offered Wheaton only a minor diplomatic post in 1827. He accepted nevertheless, after twelve years of financial disappointment as reporter. Wheaton's successor as reporter was Richard Peters, Jr.]

. . . .

The end of the [1828] Term brought a flurry of activity, culminating in the publication of Peter's first volume of *Reports* on June 16, 1828. The brief preface to this volume set forth its author's aims in crisp, businesslike fashion. "[I]t has been the [Reporter's] earnest endeavour," he said, "to exhibit the facts of each case . . . briefly and accurately; and to state such of the arguments of counsel, as, in his opinion, were required for a full and correct understanding of the important points of the case, and the decision of the Court." Lest the latter point be lost on "his brethren of the profession," Peters put the matter more plainly still: "It has not been within the scope of [my] purpose, to give, at large, all the reasoning and learning addressed by them to the Court." The decisions, of course, were to be presented faithfully as handed down by the Court. And what of the notes that had so distinguished Wheaton's *Reports?* Of them, Peters said precisely nothing, for the simple reason that his volumes were to contain only the most basic marginal notes, and no appendix notes whatsoever. In short, Peters' plan for his *Reports* resembled the man himself: brisk, practical and determined to avoid unremunerative detours into esoteric scholarship.

The preface did, however, contain two novelties. First, Peters advised his readers that, pursuant to the recently renewed and amended Reporter's Act, he had stipulated with his publisher that the price per volume should be five dollars. What measures had been taken to provide a greater margin of profit at the *Reports'* new, low price, he did not say. Second, Peters drew special attention to his plan for presenting the abstracts (or headnotes) of the Court's decisions: "The syllabus of each case, contains an abstract of all the matters ruled and adjudged by the Court, and, generally, in the language of the decision, with a reference to the page of the Report in which the particular point will be found." Clearly, the provision of page references could only be regarded as an advance over preceding volumes of the *Reports*. Yet, overall, no aspect of Peters' work was to prompt such bitter criticism as the content of his presumably straightforward abstracts.

Predictably, the first assessment of volume 1 of Peters' *Reports* came from Joseph Story. Story's interest in the reporting of the Court's decisions had obviously not diminished with Wheaton's departure. Writing within ten days of publication, Story assured Peters that he had great reason "to be proud of" his initial effort. "[U]pon a general survey of the volume," he could not but commend Peters' "great qualities" as a Reporter. He had performed his task with "fidelity, promptitude, & success." In particular, Story regarded Peters' inclusion of internal page references in the abstracts a useful improvement. On the other hand, there were a number of defects requiring mention. The volume contained a few errors that should be noted in its successor. In future volumes, Peters would do well to allow himself additional time before printing, "not only to accommodate the Printer's Devils, who after all are so mean foes, & much given . . . to misrepresentation, but to have more leisure to examine the proofs and compare the materials." Even more seriously, Story regretted "that the text is so compact & small." He "suppose[d] this was unavoidable in order to bring the work into a moderate compass, so as to afford it at the price established by the Act of Congress. . . ." But, in this respect, he "greatly . . . preferred . . . the 12th of Wheaton."

The first reviews of Peters' initial volume to appear in print displayed an even more profound ambivalence. Boston's *American Jurist and Law Magazine*, for example, thought that Peters had improved on Wheaton "in forbearing to insert at length instruments and documents . . . where short . . . extracts only were necessary." While the *Jurist* pronounced itself "far from being insensible to the extensive research and erudition of Mr. Wheaton," it believed that the profession generally "were hardly satisfied with the high price of his volumes, or with the materials used to swell their dimensions." But Wheaton's prolixity had now been traded for Peters' imprecision, especially in the case abstracts of which the new Reporter had been so proud. An abstract of the case, the review pointed out, should "present briefly and accurately . . . all the important principles which have been decided or discussed" in the course of the decision. Instead, Peters had "heap[ed] into his abstracts incidental observations, reflections, and reasonings of the court. . . . The mass of matter thus thrown together serves to bewilder, rather than to assist the reader," making it almost as difficult "to ascertain the points from the note, as from the whole case." After providing a few particularly garbled excerpts from the volume to illustrate its point, the *Jurist* concluded with pointers for improvement in Peters' upcoming second attempt.

Alas, the *Jurist* found volume 2 of Peters' *Reports* "liable to the same objections," only more so. In fact, "the mode of reporting, adopted in these volumes, not only renders them very inconvenient to readers, but is also likely to diminish very seriously the value and influence of the decisions of the highest tribunal in the country. . . ." Having made due allowance for the arduous labors of reporting and, on that account, forgiven Peters' "little imperfections," the review passed on to those that it found "essen-

tial and glaring." Again, its strongest strictures were reserved for the
Reporter's abstracts of cases, which it charged amounted to little more
than extracting from each decision "a number of sentences or paragraphs,
on what principle of selection it is difficult to say, and plac[ing] them at
the head of the case." In almost every instance, the ratio decidendi of the
case seemed to escape Peters' method: "After studying a page or two of
fine type, [the reader's] mind is in a painful state of uncertainty as to the
points actually decided by the court, and can only be relieved by examining
the body of the decision." Consistently, the Reporter reproduced observations of the Justices out of context, creating the misimpression of general
rather than specific applicability; or he failed to include anything in the
abstract that would alert the reader to the point actually determined by
the Court. In at least one instance, Peters had stated as the holding of a
case a rule "directly the reverse of the opinion" handed down by Marshall.
"Indeed there is scarcely a single abstract in the volume which states the
points in the case definitely and tersely, and which is not open to serious
objections."

Sadly for Peters, the *Jurist* was not alone in its low estimation of his
powers of intellect. To some, his work became a benchmark of mediocrity.
Writing to a friend concerning Wheeler's *Abridgment of American Common Law Cases*, Thomas Day, the Connecticut Reporter, observed in
1833: "As to his digest of cases, he neither gives you the *principle* nor the
case, but generally presents some excerpts, from which one or the other—
or possibly both—may be *conjectured*. He reminds one strongly of Peters'
abstracts in his Reports." And, commenting thirty years later upon the
resignation of one of Peters' successors, a Philadelphia legal newspaper
noted with considerable heat that

> the Reports of the Supreme Court of the United States have been for many
> years past—ever since the time, in fact, that Mr. Wheaton ceased to report
> them—eminently discreditable to our professional character, abroad, and a
> vexatious burden [in] every way to those among us who were obliged to read
> them, at home.

Note 2(B). *Wheaton v. Peters*[1]

What Peters lacked in reporting skills, he made up in business acumen.
Unlike his predecessors, Peters eventually found a way to make the position
of reporter to the Supreme Court pay handsomely. In addition to publishing his own reports, Peters prepared an inexpensive edition of the
reports of Dallas, Cranch, and Wheaton. The four volumes of Dallas, nine
of Cranch, and twelve of Wheaton were condensed by Peters into six volumes and offered for sale beginning in 1829. The *Condensed Reports*
of Peters omitted arguments of counsel, dissenting and concurring
opinions, and reporters' notes and appendices; the type in the *Con-*

densed Reports was also smaller than in the originals, but the price of all six volumes was only thirty-six dollars, less than one-third of the cost of the originals.

Wheaton sued, alleging violation of his copyright, and engaged Daniel Webster to argue his case in the Supreme Court. Webster's skill as an orator, however, was of little avail. Although Wheaton was acknowledged to have a copyrightable interest in the notes, appendices, and other editorial features of his *Reports*—features that Peters largely omitted from his *Condensed Reports*—the Supreme Court unanimously held "that no reporter has or can have any copyright in the written opinions delivered by this court; and that the judges thereof cannot confer on any reporter any such right."[2] In so holding, the Supreme Court endorsed the argument of Peters' counsel:

> Reports are the means by which judicial determinations are disseminated, or rather they constitute the very dissemination itself. . . . The matter which they disseminate is, without a figure, *the law of the land*. . . . Accordingly, in all countries that are subject to the sovereignty of the laws, it is held that their promulgation is as essential as their existence. . . . It is therefore the true policy, influenced by the essential spirit of the government, that laws of every description should be universally diffused. To fetter or restrain their dissemination, must be to counteract this policy. To limit, or even to regulate it, would, in fact, produce the same effect. Nothing can be done, consistently with our free institutions, except to encourage and promote it.[3]

The decision of the Supreme Court in *Wheaton v. Peters* has been considered to have "set the stage . . . for the gradual evolution of the private enterprise system of law reporting into the nationwide phenomenon that is still strong today."[4]

Selection 2(B). Dane's Abridgment, 1823–24

[J. Story, Book Review,] 23 N. Am. Rev. 1, 2–40 (1826).
—*A General Abridgment and Digest of American Law, with occasional Notes and Comments.* By Nathan Dane, LL.D. Counsellor at Law. In eight volumes. 8 vo. Boston. Cummings, Hilliard, & Co. 1823–4.

. . . [W]hatever may be thought of other cases, it is certain, that in the department of law, abridgments are indispensable. Before Reports of adjudged cases were published, no other adequate means existed of acquiring the science of jurisprudence, than what were furnished by a faithful attendance upon the courts, and a diligent collection of the substance of their decisions. The early professors of the common law were compelled to resort to commonplace books, and personal reports of cases, falling under their own observation. Many manuscripts of this description are still extant, exhibiting a patient industry, care, and accuracy, worthy of all praise. The labor indeed of these venerable jurists, almost transcends the belief of students of the present day. They noted every case, in all its points and principles; they abstracted, from records, and general treatises, and private manuscripts, often obscure and crabbed, everything that could be found to aid them in study or in practice. They gathered voluminous collections of special pleadings, and unusual writs and judgments, to suit the exigencies of their possible avocations, and thought no labor too great, which brought any solid addition to their knowledge, or any increased facilities to their clients.

The necessity was the more pressing in those days, from the subtleties, and quibbles, and scholastic logic, which characterized every department of learning. The law then dealt with forms, even more than with substances. . . . There were no public repositories, in which principles or practices could be ascertained by a glance of the eye. . . .

When Reports began to be published, the labor was not materially diminished. The decisions were not uniformly reported at stated times; and many cases were not reported at all. The early reports contain no indexes. The Year Books have not a single line, to direct the student to their contents, and leave their bulky and abbreviated text without title or comment, so mixed up in one common mass, that it requires no small share of historical knowledge to ascertain, who, at any given period, speak as judges or as counsel. When tables of contents came subsequently into fashion, they were so incomplete and incorrect, that they were comparatively of little assistance. . . .

The practice of keeping commonplace books, which was thus begun from absolute necessity by the old lawyers, was afterwards continued from a sense of its convenience. Nor was it generally discontinued by the profession until a late period; and it is not perhaps without some examples, even in the present age. In America, the anterevolutionary lawyers were in the habit of compiling manuscript abridgments for their private use, some of which have reached our times. They also left behind them many notes of adjudications, which are yet to be found in the hands of the curious and the learned. And probably, in most of the states, the practice of preserving short notes of new cases, was common among the leaders at the bar, until the legislature provided for the regular publication of Reports.

It is to sources like those already adverted to, that we owe the early, and perhaps all the abridgments hitherto made of the common law. What was introduced originally from the mere scantiness of public materials, in process of time obtained a continued favor from the unwieldy bulk of adjudications.

. . . Upon the appearance of a new Abridgment of the Law, the question naturally occurs, whether it be necessary, and if necessary, what is the best plan, with a view to comprehensiveness and convenience, on which it can be formed?

In respect to England, there may perhaps be some doubt whether such a work would be of any extensive utility. A continuation of Comyns's Digest seems all that is necessary for lawyers of advanced standing. . . . But we think the subject admits of a very different consideration, in relation to America. The learned author of the 'General Abridgment and Digest of American Law,' has stated the reasoning in favor of it. . . .

'. . . The work is calculated . . . to be purely American, and among other things, to supply the place generally of the English Abridgments and Digests now read, especially by students, very disadvantageously, because, in many respects, inapplicable to our practice. . . .'

. . . .

In regard to the plan most proper for an American Abridgment, various opinions will probably be entertained by the profession. . . .

. . . In regard to one point only, will there probably be much difference of opinion within the profession; and that is, whether local law ought to find a place in the work; and if it ought, how far the selection of the local law of Massachusetts, as a basis, is judicious. On this point let Mr Dane speak for himself. . . .

'. . . [S]tate law [is] so voluminous . . . , and so much of it merely local, in small portions of the nation, that it has been deemed not practicable or useful to include large portions of it in this work, except in regard to a few of the states. . . .

'This being the case in regard to state law, it was found best to select the state law of some one state, to be included much at large in this work. Accordingly, the laws of Massachusetts, in substance including Maine, have been selected for the purpose. . . .

'However, there is embraced in this work much of the local law of the other states in the Union in different ways, especially of New York, Virginia, and Kentucky. . . .

'In fact, on a careful examination, it will be found, that more than four fifths of the decisions made in Massachusetts, New York, and Virginia, stated in this work, have been made on principles and authorities common to twentythree states, and so practised on in all. . . .' . . .

. . . .

We are next to consider the plan of the work. And here again we quote the words of the author.

'It has been a part of the plan, in considering each subject of importance, first to give a general view of it, under the terms, *general principles*, illustrated, usually, by rules and cases; then to enter on particulars on the same subject. . . .

. . . .

'Original authorities have always been preferred, principally relied on and resorted to. Digests and abridgments have been relied only when found correct, or when deemed to be so, by reason of their agreement with known and settled law in other cases; but Cruise, Comyns, Bacon, and other digests and abridgments, have been extensively cited or referred to in the margin, &c. as directing to many good authorities, and as corroborative. . . .'

. . . .

That there are many advantages in this system of arrangement, especially for students, will be denied by few; that it has some disadvantages ought not to be concealed. . . .

The principal disadvantage, in a practical view, to which this method of arranging subjects is liable, is, that it is not of so easy reference in the hurry of consultation. But in Mr Dane's work, this disadvantage is entirely overcome by a general Index to the whole work, occupying, with the names of cases, a volume. This index, we venture to pronounce, absolutely unrivalled in fulness and accuracy, bringing within the reach of the most ordinary diligence, all the leading positions and doctrines of this extensive compilation.

. . . .

Moreover, [the Abridgment] embraces a large collection of decisions, many of which have never before appeared in print, and are valuable from their general applicability as well as the fidelity with which they are reported. Before the publication of regular reports in our country, many questions of the highest moment were litigated and decided in our courts, which form rules of property; and it is no inconsiderable present to the profession to embody these, in an authentic form, as well as to add to some of the cases now in print, reports more full, exact, and satisfactory.

Again, large extracts are introduced from the civil, the French, and other foreign law. The utility of this part of the work cannot escape the observation of the profession. The civil law, modified by French and Spanish ordinances and usages, constitutes the basis of the law of Louisiana and the territory of the Floridas. . . .

. . . .

There has probably never been a time, when the English law, in force here, the French law which we have adopted, and the native American law, could have been better embodied in one 'great national work.' Earlier, perhaps, our native American law, especially Federal, would not have furnished materials; and had it been delayed, our laws might have become too bulky and numerous, to have been abridged in this way.

. . . .

. . . We cannot refrain from expressing our admiration of the patient assiduity, indefatigable industry, and ardent devotion to professional learning, of which this work, more extensive and voluminous, than any that has been published by any individual in our country, on any subject, either in science or literature, is the honorable monument.

Note 2(C). Dane's Progeny

Dane's abridgment was a commercial success, indicating the need of American lawyers for an orderly approach to American law. The profits from Dane's work established the Dane Chair at Harvard Law School, the first holder of which was Joseph Story.

Commercial success, however, was not the same as popularity. Dane's work was "never . . . a great favorite with the profession."[1] Though learned, accurate, and influential, Dane's abridgment was difficult to use.

> Unfortunately, [Dane] did not arrange his material in alphabetical order by topic, but rather, in a progressive development of the legal topics which requires frequent use of the index.[2]

Dane's abridgment was followed by a number of digests, reaching their height with several digests prepared by two brothers, Benjamin and Austin Abbott of New York, in the 1860s and 1870s. These works differed from Dane's abridgment. They did not attempt Dane's scholarly, literary discussion of legal topics, proceeding from general principles to specifics.

Nevertheless, the two Abbott brothers approached the task of digesting in a scholarly manner. They read widely in legal treatises and carefully outlined the organization of each legal topic. Using these outlines, they created a classification scheme for all law that, while alphabetical among its main divisions, was logical within each main topic. The scheme is published in more than one hundred pages in one of their digests;[3] it has come to serve as the basis for the digesting system still in use in the United States today—the "key-number" system of the West Publishing Company.[4]

By the end of the nineteenth century, the mass of law had become too great to be digested by individual editors. Digesting, rather, became the job of editorial staffs at publishing companies. As early as 1847, a national digest was published by Little, Brown and Company; in 1885, the Lawyers Cooperative Publishing Company started a similar set, followed by West Publishing Company.

A scholarly, encyclopedic work like Dane's, however, was not attempted until near the end of the nineteenth century—and then, not as the work of an individual scholar, but as the work of many hands coordinated by the publishers. Encyclopedias following Dane's model claimed to provide comprehensive discussions of the law, but in reality, they relied almost exclusively on cases, to the virtual exclusion of legislation and administrative regulation. Their major value to the legal profession became their case citations rather than the necessarily broad generalizations in their texts.[5]

After an unsuccessful publication in 1883, a twenty-nine-volume set was published by the Edward Thompson Company between 1887 and 1896 as the *American and English Encyclopedia of Law*, covering substantive law; it was followed between 1895 and 1902 by the twenty-three-volume *Encyclopedia of Law and Practice*, for procedural law. Between 1896 and 1904, the Edward Thompson Company also published the *Encyclopedia of Forms and Precedents*, the first collection of forms for national use.

Competition soon followed. The American Law Book Company published the *Encyclopedia of Law and Procedure* between 1901 and 1912, combining substantive and procedural law. To lend prestige to the set, the publisher paid noted lawyers to write some of the articles—a practice not followed in subsequent encyclopedias.

In 1914, the American Law Book Company started a new encyclopedia, *Corpus Juris*, designed to cite "all reported decisions." It took seventy-two volumes and twenty-three years to complete the set. The encyclopedia was eventually bought by West Publishing Company, and its second edition became *Corpus Juris Secundum*, which continues to be published.[6] The second edition, however, did not repeat all the citations in *Corpus Juris*. The two editions are, therefore, often found still shelved together in law libraries.

An alternative to the comprehensive approach of *Corpus Juris/CJS* is a selective rival set published since 1962 as *American Jurisprudence 2d* by the Lawyers' Cooperative Publishing Company. Preceded by a set called *Ruling Case Law*, *Am. Jur. 2d* has a lineage that also goes back to 1914. Selectivity in case citations allows *Am. Jur. 2d* to include increased discussion of statutes and administrative regulations, although case law continues to dominate. Revision of the entire set since the 1960s also gives *Am. Jur. 2d* cleaner cross-referencing and index volumes than *CJS*. A unique feature of *Am. Jur. 2d* is a looseleaf binder and occasional bound supplements for "New Topics."

Encyclopedias and digests have become alternative tools for providing access to case law. At the end of the nineteenth century, however, neither digests nor encyclopedias were well enough developed to satisfy the needs of the legal profession. Moreover, court reports were proliferating, presenting a muddle similar to the welter of nominative reports in pre-1865 England.[7] When the American Bar Association was organized in 1885, one of its first tasks was to form a Committee on Law Reporting and Digesting.[8] Similar committees were organized by state bar associations.

Selection 2(C). Law Reporting in New York, 1873

REPORT OF THE COMMITTEE ON LAW REPORTING OF THE ASSOCIATION OF THE BAR OF THE CITY OF NEW YORK (1873).

To the Association of the Bar of the City of New York:
The undersigned, to whom the subject of Law Reporting was referred

by the Association of the Bar of the City of New York, respectfully report:

. . . .

English Reports

From the year 1307 to 1872—a period of 565 years—there were published in England 1,036 volumes of reports. The great increase of these books claimed the attention of the British bar at various times during the past century.

They felt that they would be overwhelmed if the evil were not checked, and this conviction culminated in the reform inaugurated by the Council of Law Reporting.

American Reports

Our plight, however, is infinitely worse than theirs ever was. From the year 1794 to 1873—a period of 79 years—there were published in the State of New York alone 400 volumes of reports; more than one-third of the reports of Great Britain for 565 years.

If the 190 volumes of the decisions of the United States Courts are added—which should be done to make a fair comparison with the number of English Reports—there are 590 volumes in 79 years; more than one-half of all the reports of England. . . .

Judge Story, in noticing the fact that between the Revolution and the year 1821, more than 150 volumes of law reports had been published in the United States, said: "The danger indeed seems to be, not that we shall want able reports, but that we shall be overwhelmed by their number and variety."

. . . .

Your Committee find that the number of the reports is due to the fact that law reporting has become a distinct business, conducted by private individuals for their own emolument; that book-making is the interest of those engaged in this traffic, and that their profits depend, not upon the excellence, but upon the number of the volumes they edit; the profession having been found ready to buy whatever the publisher would print.

This general charge is fully sustained by an examination of the reports under the following heads:

. . . .

MULTIPLICATION OF REPORTS OF THE SAME CASE

On this point, your committee find that it is common to find four reports of the same case differing very little from each other, three reports of the same case are numerous, and there are two of every important case and of many unimportant cases. . . .

. . . .

INDISCRIMINATE REPORTING

Your Committee find that little or no discrimination is used by any of the present Reporters (except Judge Daly) in the character of the cases they report.

That reports are constantly published which enunciate no new principle and give no useful illustration of the application of an old principle, which are not worthy of preservation, and only furnish false lights to be reversed by the appellate Courts. They have no hesitation in saying, that two-thirds of all the reported cases are of this character, and should not be reported at all.

There will, of course, always be room for a fair difference of opinion as to what should and what should not be reported.

There is no room, however, for any doubt as to the worthlessness of two-thirds of our reports, as herein explained.

APPEALS

. . . An examination of the cases reversed will satisfy any lawyer that a large proportion of them should not have been reported, that they are opposed to well-known principles of law, and were such as must have been reversed on appeal. A similar examination of the affirmed cases discloses the fact that many of the appeals were taken for the purpose of delay; the question involved present nothing new, the judgments were such as must have been affirmed, and the decisions of both the inferior and appellate Courts are, for this reason, unworthy of preservation for citation or reference.

. . . It is a common practice of the Reporters to publish the opinion of the inferior Court at the same time with that of the appellate Court. Where the judgment above affirms that below, the opinion of the inferior Court is generally useless, and merges in that of the appellate Court. Where the judgment is reversed, the opinion below is absolutely valueless. The necessity of book-making, however, disregards all scruples of this kind. It is no uncommon thing to find the opinion of the Courts of first resort reported years after they have been reversed by the appellate Courts.

. . . .

PROLIXITY

Your Committee find that the reports, with few exceptions, are carelessly prepared.

In the more important and intricate cases, involving difficult questions of fact as well as law, and labor on the part of the reporter to condense the facts, it is a common practice to report the opinions alone without any statement of facts or points, sometimes adding "the facts appear sufficiently in the opinion of the Court," while in other, and generally the simpler cases, the pleadings, testimony and arguments are spread, with needless prolixity, upon the record. . . .

Your Committee respectfully call the attention of the Bench to the unnecessary length of some of the opinions. Prolixity is one of the great defects of our system, and so long as it is indulged in by the Judges, the Bar and the Reporters will follow suit. It is unnecessary to point out cases in which opinions of from twenty-five to fifty pages in length have been written, and some of them largely made up of copious quotations from other decisions, when a bare reference would serve every purpose. The labor of condensation is indeed great, but we feel confident that when the extent of the evil is appreciated, the Courts will themselves apply the remedy.

. . . .

RECKLESS REPORTING

The following are a few miscellaneous instances of reckless reporting which have come under our observation:

The Trustees of the Auburn Theological Seminary agst. Calhoun was reported by Barbour in 1872. . . .

It was decided in 1862. The length of time that elapsed between the decision and the report, ten years, is bad enough. But Barbour had reported the same case in almost the same words in 1863. . . .

And to make the matter worse, the decision had been reversed by the Court of Appeals a year before Barbour first reported it.

. . . .

Wait *vs.* Green, . . . Vickery *vs.* Dickson, . . . Crain *vs.* Cavana . . . were decided in 1862. They were reported by Barbour in 1872. He had reported the same cases in [1862], only giving the opinions of other justices as those of the Court.

. . . .

[In] Mayor, etc. *vs.* Erben . . . a dissenting opinion . . . is printed as the decision of the Court.

. . . [Howard's] and Abbott's Digest[s] . . . are misled by the above report, and give as the law established by the Court of Appeals the reverse of what was in reality decided.

. . . .

In Schuchardt *vs.* Mayor, etc, . . . Joslyn *vs.* Fiske . . . there were no judgments, the two judges who heard the cases having disagreed, and yet the cases are reported at length.

Mullford *vs.* Muller . . . has a head-note, containing a single proposition which the Court distinctly said they did not determine.

Alexander *vs.* Hard . . . was carelessly reported. The error is corrected at page 384, at the request of a Justice of the Supreme Court.

. . . .

The opinion reported in Day *vs.* Saunders . . . was not only never adopted by the Court, but was never delivered.

.   .   .   .

DELAY

.   .   .   .

There is no reason why an energetic reporter should not publish opinions in pamphlet form within thirty days after they are delivered. With us, however, years often elapse after the rendition of opinions before they are reported. . . .

.   .   .   .

The reporters of the Court of Appeals Reports, have generally failed to comply with the direction of [legislation], which requires them to issue their reports in pamphlets of 250 pages each as fast as they are compiled.

One of the evils which is experienced by late reporting, is illustrated by the case of—Ferren *vs.* O'Hara . . . decided in 1862 and reported in 1872. The authorities on which the decision rested, were declared, in the interval between the rendition of the opinion and its report, to be of no force.

.   .   .   .

LAWS

Before approaching the remedies for the evils which have been indicated, it will be well to review the legislation now existing upon the subject of reporting.

The Constitution directs that "the Legislature shall provide for the speedy publication of all Statute Laws, and of such judicial decisions as it may deem expedient. And all laws and judicial decisions shall be free for publication by any person." . . . Under this provision the office of State Reporter, and Supreme Court Reporter have been created.

THE STATE REPORTER

The Court of Appeals has an official reporter, appointed for three years, at a salary of $2,000 per annum. It is made his duty to report every cause which the Court shall order reported, and such others as the public interests shall, in his judgment, require. The Judges are directed to deliver their opinions to him. The reporter has no pecuniary interest in the reports, which are reported under his supervision, by contract between him and the Secretary of State and Comptroller, with that publisher who offers to comply with the prescribed conditions, one of which is to sell the reports at not exceeding $3 per volume. . . .

Under the early and the last reporters, these volumes have been generally well edited. Your Committee regret that they cannot say the same of Tiffany's Reports. Besides other criticisms to which they are open, a number of cases were omitted, which should have been reported. This afforded an excuse for the publication of the five volumes of Keyes' Reports, which, considering the existence of an official reporter, and the practice of the Court to designate what cases should be reported, can only be regarded as an audacious attempt to foist another set of generally worthless reports upon the profession, for the sole benefit of the reporter, and without the provision regulating the price of the regular reports prescribed by Statute. Many cases in Keyes' Reports are incorrectly reported; in several instances the dissenting opinion is given as the opinion of the Court, and in others, the report is presented in such a form as to make it impossible to know what was decided.

SUPREME COURT REPORTER

In 1869, the Legislature provided for the appointment of a Supreme Court Reporter. He was to hold office for five years, and it was made his duty to report from among the decisions forwarded to him by any general or special term, such as he should think expedient.

To enable him to perform his duty, the Judges of the Supreme Court were directed to deliver to him their opinions, in all cases in which they should order the opinion to be reported.

Not more than three volumes were to be published annually. The reporter was to receive no salary, and the cost of the reports was limited to $2.50 per volume, of 500 pages. . . .

LANSING'S REPORTS

Mr. Lansing was appointed reporter in June 1869, and since that time has issued six volumes. They are reported intelligently and clearly, and are superior to those of his competitor Mr. Barbour.

BARBOUR'S REPORTS

Since the year 1848, Mr. Barbour has reported the decisions of the Supreme Court, and has now issued his 63d volume. Notwithstanding the Act of 1869, he continued the publication of these reports, as he had a legal right to do, and since then has issued eleven volumes. The existence of two sets of Supreme Court Reports is unnecessary, and an unmixed evil, entailing great labor and expense upon the bar.

While there is no law to prevent Mr. Barbour publishing reports, there is a law requiring Judges to deliver all the opinions which they think should be reported, to the Supreme Court Reporter. If this law had not been very generally disregarded, it would have been impossible for Mr. Barbour to continue his reports.

An examination of his volumes shows many cases decided by one Court or Judge reported *seriatim*, for which it would appear that certain Judges are in the habit of sending him all their decisions.

OPINIONS

It can hardly be necessary for us to combat the idea that Judges have a proprietary right to their opinions, that they may retain them, or give them exclusively to their favorites, that reporters depend upon their courtesy, and not upon their own rights. "Judge made law," is as much the law of the land as the Acts of the Legislature, and is, on principle, entitled to the same publicity.

It cannot be supposed that Judges would permit any feeling of favoritism to induce them to send their opinions to an unauthorized reporter, after a law requiring their transmission to the official reporter had been brought to their notice, and it is hoped that this suggestion will lead to the abandonment of any practice of this kind which may have heretofore existed. The present method, or rather want of method, in the transmission of opinions by the Judges to the various reporters for publication, sometimes leads to unexpected results. And even the care that Judges take to ensure the reporting of their opinions may, in the absence of any system throughout the State for collecting them, increase the difficulty. Thus one reporter may receive the opinion of the Court from the Judge who prepared it, while another reporter receives the dissenting opinion in the same case from its author. Both reporters naturally suppose the opinions sent to them express the decision of the Court, and publish them as such. . . .

. . . .

THE PRACTICE REPORTS

The two reporters of the Practice Reports have no official position. And as long as the bar will buy their reports, no blame can attach to them for publishing them. These volumes constantly contain the same decisions; they often contain cases which are also reported in Barbour, Lansing and the New York Reports. Thus, it happens that we habitually have two reports, often three, and sometimes four of the same case. . . . The Practice Reports, however, have ceased to contain practice cases exclusively. Some of them appear to be made up of whatever comes to hand, without reference to its quality or authenticity. Instances of the latter may be found in . . . [cases] which are reported upon the authority of newspaper articles. . . .

. . . .

CONCLUSION

It may be doubted whether, even if reporters had greater and more varied professional ability, there would be any great improvement while the present system continues. So long as reporting is conducted by private enterprise, for the sole purpose of making as much money out of it as possible—so long as lawyers must buy all the reports, and pay for the chaff in order to get the wheat—the temptation of printing worthless cases and of mere book-making will exist.

Your Committee are of the opinion that all reporting should be official, that the reporters should be responsible to some supervisory body, and should be paid by salaries, and thus made independent of the number of volumes they may be able to publish annually.

Your Committee entertain no doubt that it is the duty of the State to inform its citizens of its laws; and that this duty is not fulfilled so long as it makes only partial provision for reporting judicial decisions.

There are, however, serious objections to committing the practical work of law reporting to any State officer under our form of government. The work is not of a kind to be well done by an elective officer, nor is it likely to be well done by an officer, who, if appointed, goes out of office with changing administrations. A first-class reporter requires particular qualities, and should have a permanent position. If undertaken by the State, and the profits of the office went to the reporter, the place would soon be sought by political aspirants, and . . . the work would be badly done, and soon relapse into the present evils.

Nor should the reporter be in any way dependent upon the Courts, whose favor and friendship it is his privilege to win and enjoy. In a free country, it is well that Courts should feel that they are acting before an intelligent and reading public, to whom their decisions will certainly become known through fearless and independent reporters.

Your Committee are of [the] opinion that the provision of the Constitution permitting any person to publish the laws and judicial decisions, is a wise one, and that counsel should be at liberty to cite any authority from the whole range of literature, leaving the weight of the citations to be judged of by the Court. If these views are sound, any new series of reports that it may be thought wise to edit, must depend for their success upon their merits alone, and must, in the first instance, compete with the reports now in the field. But your Committee are convinced that a new series of the reports, properly edited, and based upon sound principles, would, within a year, compel the withdrawal of all the existing reports; and that while the publication of the reports should be legally free to whoever will undertake it, the State might aid, by necessary legislation, or by reasonable appropriations, any responsible body that would relieve it of the duty imposed upon it by the Constitution of making known its laws to its citizens.

Your Committee, after the thorough examination they have given to this subject, and the knowledge they have acquired of the great success of the English Council of Law Reporting—as shown by the admirable volumes which form the fruit of their labors, and by their financial resources—would have no difficulty in recommending a scheme, which, in their opinion, would ensure the desired reform.

But inasmuch as it is apparent that certain legislation will be needed, and the subject is one which is of deep importance to the Bench and the Bar throughout the State, and it is desirable that the plan to be adopted should comprehend all interests, and have the hearty support and sympathy of all, and is also likely, if successful, to be followed in other States, your Committee have concluded not to recommend at present any definite scheme, but to suggest that this report be published and circulated among the Judges and profession generally throughout the State, with a request that they communicate to this Committee any recommendations or suggestions which may occur to them as valuable, and after considering the suggestions which it is hoped this course will elicit, your Committee will be prepared to report the definite plan of action called for by the resolution under which they were appointed.

Note 2(D). Frank S. Shepard of Chicago, 1875

Six months following its report, in December of 1873, the Committee on Law Reporting of the Association of the Bar of the City of New York submitted a set of recommendations "based upon that of the English Council of Law Reporting."[1] The committee's recommendation differed from the English scheme in one respect—the New York legislature was to be petitioned for twenty thousand dollars per annum to pay the salaries of reporters. The scheme was approved by the association[2] but was never realized.

One of the problems raised by the committee's report was the link between opinions in the trial courts and opinions in the same cases on appeal. Lawyers were unable to readily ascertain when a case had been reversed or overruled or modified. Clearly, some way to link published opinions to subsequent court action in the same case, or in other cases dealing with the same issues, had to be found.

Historically, when the amount of reporting was manageable, lawyers kept track of cases in their "commonplace books" or "marginalia" in the reports.[3] Abridgments and their progeny—digests and encyclopedias—were also relied on to link related cases, but the increasing litigation and increasing legal complexities of the late nineteenth century demanded something more. Relying on the editors of digests and encyclopedias to link cases by topical headings and index terms risked missing a great deal.

In 1821, an American lawyer, Simon Greenleaf (who later became a Harvard law professor and a noted scholar of the law of evidence), attacked the problem with a volume entitled *A Collection of Cases, Overruled, Denied, Doubted, or Limited in Their Application*. The volume consisted of digests of cases with notes on how they were affected by later cases. Not only was this format cumbersome, but the volume also lacked any method for updating except by the publication of new editions. Nevertheless, the book was useful, as evidenced by the publication of three editions between

1821 and 1867. In the long intervals between editions, however, lawyers again were left to their "marginalia."

In the 1870s, a law book salesman in Chicago noticed lawyers writing into the margins of their reports. The salesman's name was Frank S. Shepard, and he went on to make his fortune from that observation.

To save lawyers work, Shepard had little gummed stickers printed up whenever one Illinois case modified a previous case. In 1875, he began selling the stickers to lawyers to paste into their *Illinois Reports.* Upon Frank Shepard's death in 1900, the sticker format was abandoned. Instead, pamphlets and, later, books were published to link the citations of cases to the citations of later cases that affected them.

Rather than exercise editorial judgment on which cases "affected" earlier cases (as lawyers did in their marginalia), the assumption was made that anytime one case is cited by another, the link is worth noting. Thus, *Shepard's Citations* became columns upon columns of citations, comprehensively tracing the web of interconnections between cases, based purely on the incidence of citation.

Editorial judgment, however, was not entirely abandoned. The most important incidents when one case cites another are singled out in *Shepard's*. Such incidents are noted by code letters such as "r" for "reversed," "a" for "affirmed," "e" for "explained," "o" for "overruled," and "q" for "questionned." Moreover, *Shepard's* editors introduced a time-saving device by identifying specific portions of cases cited, including the headnote number of a cited case as part of the citation whenever such limitation can be identified.[4]

It took nearly a century from the time Frank Shepard produced his first gummed stickers to the time *Shepard's* units became available for all state and federal court reports. *Shepard's* also spread to citations of constitutions, statutes, court rules, administrative regulations, and even local ordinances and law review articles. In recent years, *Shepard's* volumes have also been subdivided by topic for specialists. In the meantime, in 1966, *Shepard's* was purchased by a publishing giant, the McGraw-Hill Company.

Shepard's only addressed one of the problems raised by the report of the New York Bar's Committee on Law Reporting in 1873. Other problems called for a total overhaul of court reporting. Especially pressing was the growth in the number of reported cases, which many lawyers saw as a threat to the cohesiveness of law:

> [T]he number of volumes, their great cost, and the rapidly accelerating ratio of their increase . . . has a deeper significance. . . . It can hardly be doubted that the rapid accumulation of so large a mass of precedents, and their constant use in practice, so far from strengthening the foundations upon which our jurisprudence as a system is based, has a well-defined tendency to weaken them by the substitution of precedents for principles in the practical administration of justice. The germinal principles underlying our system of law are of slow

BARBOUR'S SUPREME COURT REPORTS   **Vol. 1**

Vol. 1							
	26AR50n	22NYS¹363	28NW925	1903NYAG	−225−	j48Bar261	20A1468
	102AR576n	100NYS¹470	29P79	[²644	s3San222	j290US305	85A1677
−9−	102AR581n	266NYS¹168	95P317		6Bar²448	j781.E331	109NY‍90
116NY²593	56SW447	j312NYS2d	33SE338	−155−	c24Bar²566	11L.E²35	173‍
23NE²19		[¹410		s1Edm190	c31Bar192	j54SC200	88‍
	−42−	91NE¹270	−85−	3CodR245		84SC²19	‍
−11−	174AR150n	1941NYAG	23FC690	6Bar²462	−227−	18F⁴146	‍W369
2TCSR²433		[296	137F⁴103	7Bar²588	20Hun¹184	4AR1387n	
16Bar⁴593	−48−	77NE78		11AbP²14	36NY²681		−316−
30FC257	1LAn²192	153NW613	−89−	55Bar²613	37NY¹240	−271−	30AN¹416
80P333	4Dal²522	157NW565	16Hun³179	233NY⁴321	19F¹813	a2Bar545	33Hun¹542
391SW725		255P179	25Hun³362	135NE⁴516		4Bar⁶344	86NY¹126
	−53−		25Hun⁴416		−229−	c4Bos⁶582	13NYS¹297
−19−	1CP¹26	−72−	78AS205n	−158−	Case 2	o5Bar⁶133	26NYS¹918
4AbP326	87NY276	2BCh¹396	j130NY³520	a1NY321	6AbPn¹149	25Hun⁵487	50US²29
7AbP¹126	53NW768	2Sween399	18NYAD³304	5Bar²499	7AR78n	26Bar⁶638	13LE²34
16Bar¹393		3RSCR²5	18NYAD³308	5Bar⁴511		99AS158n	135F¹486
24Bar²191	−57−	3RSCR616	46NYS³192	6AbP28	−230−	c6NY⁶352	32AR895n
45HP¹239	s4SanCh434	8AbPn453	46NYS³351	j6Bar¹288	1LAn⁵159	33NY⁶34	15AR265n
q18NY¹163		30HP²341	j29NE³996	6Bar¹300	2Hun108	36NY⁶149	26A1398
74HLR1277	−68−	39HP¹189	93AR17n	16HP¹334	2RSCR¹172	30FC786	20NW875
	s2San568	52Bar²648		26Bar¹459	2RSCR609	36AR665n	3P369
−20−	s3San683	81NYS2d²900	−94−	1P878	3LAn⁵259	74P138	
16NY¹448	s6HP41	20FC1048	2Dem¹139		j3Hun⁴322		−318−
	s3' V525	59NW106⁷	10AS474r	−1°5−	4TC⁻R684	−280−	m3Bar236
	⁻h5'	⁻NW'	⁻⁴ur'	26N' ⁻⁹	‍ ⁻⁷	⁻51'	'Bar'⁷

Shepard's New York Supreme Court Citations, Vol. 1, page 271.
Reproduced by permission of Shepard's/McGraw Hill, Inc.
Further reproduction is strictly prohibited.

In the above example, from *Shepard's New York Supreme Court Citations*, it is indicated that the case reported in volume 1 of *Barbour's Reports* at page 271 is:

—affirmed in volume 2 of *Barbour's Reports* at page 545; and

—cited in volume 4 of *Barbour's Reports* at page 344 specifically in relation to the issue in headnote 6;

—the same issue is explained in volume 4 of New York's *Bosworth's Report** at page 582; and

—the ruling of the court on the issue in headnote 6 is overruled in volume 5 of *Barbour's Reports* at page 133.

The example indicates additional citations of the case by New York courts (Hun, Bar, NY), by a federal court (FC), by a state court in the Pacific region (P),** and in footnotes in two selective reports—volume 99 of the *American State Reports* and volume 36 of the *American Law Reports*.

---

*A list of abbreviations appears at the beginning of each volume of *Shepard's*.
**See Note 2(F), *infra*.

growth, and, as compared with the cases themselves, few in number. The ramifications and refinements, distinctions and modifications, which have been added to these principles under the iniquitous system of reporting are of endless variety and infinite in detail. In the labyrinth of cases through which a lawyer is thus obliged to grope his way in the preparation of a case, there is constant temptation to forget the underlying principle in the search for a precedent exactly in point. The tendency is to try our cases upon precedent rather than upon principle, and it is matter of common remark among the elder school of lawyers and judges that the younger men at the bar rely too much upon books and too little upon the elementary doctrines by which all cases should be decided. That the result, as affecting both lawyers and judges, is pernicious in the extreme cannot be doubted; that this result is in large measure due to the vast accumulation of reported cases seems equally clear.[5]

The first national effort to overhaul court reporting began before the committee issued its report but was perhaps unknown yet to the committee. In 1871, the Bancroft-Whitney Company started publishing the *American Reports*, containing selected current opinions from all state courts. In 1878, the Bancroft-Whitney Company also started publishing *American Decisions*, which aimed at collecting selected decisions from the earliest American cases to 1869. Both sets represented "attempts to sift the American case law for the real gems of the law, to eliminate redundant, regressive cases, and to present a unified system to the practitioner."[6] The preface to the first volume of *American Decisions* described the aim more fully.

Selection 2(D). Selective, Annotated Reports

Object of the "American Decisions," 1 AM. DEC. v–x (1878).

It has been for a long time a constant and perplexing complaint of the legal profession in England, and especially in this country, that the issue of reported decisions proceeded at such an enormous rate as to make it impossible for the profession to become conversant with them, and out of their power pecuniarily to procure the reports as they are issued. Not only on this ground may objection be justly made, but yet more on account of the utter uselessness, to the general practitioner, of a great many cases reported in the volumes; for a vast number of the cases, particularly in the earlier reports, are upon unimportant points now well settled and universally recognized, or are based upon some local statutory law, of no general importance whatever, and of no value outside of the state where the decision is made, or are so nullified by other cases as to be of little or no utility.

. . . From a careful estimate of the reported volumes of decisions, it appears there are nearly 2000 at the present time; and to provide these would require an outlay of at least $15,000. What lawyer is there, even if he could afford the time and the means, would be willing or able to examine such a vast mass of decided cases? And were it practicable, would it be desirable or productive of any adequate advantage? By no means; for to arrive at satisfactory understanding of the value of these adjudicated cases, it will be necessary to find how far they are followed as authority in the state where decided, as well as elsewhere; what construction has been placed on them, either limiting or explaining them; and carefully exclude from them all dicta not bearing on the points decided.

It is therefore apparent, that no one, busied with the requirements of professional life, can afford to follow or examine from the published reports the whole of the adjudicated cases; and a resort is therefore made to text-books to obviate the difficulty, and supply the need. But this can rarely satisfy the conscientious and painstaking lawyer; he must inquire further; he finds, that to understand the value and scope of a decision, he must examine the facts in the case, learn what points were made in argument, and on what particular point or points the decision turned. Hence cases must be studied.

Surely, then, something is needed to obviate these difficulties; there is a strong imperative demand for some publication to meet this need; to remedy in some way this "growing grievance" of the issue of a vast number of hastily considered and trivial cases of no general importance—something that will give the real "kernel of the law," without sacrificing clearness and practical utility. But what is it to be? An abridgment, or digest of decisions, it has been found, will not answer; nor will a series of leading cases on some important topics of the law. Such a series is good enough in its way; but it is too restricted; it does not give a continuity of adjudications to enable us to see the structure and development of a system of legal principles by the tribunals of one jurisdiction as compared with the same structure and development in another.

Nothing will be found to answer the purpose, and relieve the profession from the embarrassment of a tangled and inharmonious mass of decisions, except a revision and compilation of our American reports, from which will be rejected obsolete, overruled and merely local cases, and a selection made of authoritative, well-considered cases of general importance with a careful and accurate statement of the points actually decided, as well as a brief but clear statement of the facts involved. This has been found practicable and successful in the series known as the *American Reports*, begun in 1870, and on the same principle, and to carry out the scheme just indicated, the publication of a series of reports to be known as THE AMERICAN DECISIONS has been undertaken.

Plan of the Work

Scope. It is proposed to include in this series of reports all the cases of any general value and authority from the earliest reported decisions of our several state courts up to the year 1869, after which period the ground is covered by the series known as the *American Reports*. It is not thought desirable to include therein the federal decisions, of which a revision is being published. The decisions of courts of last resort will be mainly considered; but there are decisions of courts of less grade, that have been so long trusted and followed, and cited in our courts and text-books, that they may be deemed of such established authority as to rank with the decisions of the highest courts, and these will therefore demand our attention. . . .

Selection of Cases. In the selection of cases, regard is had primarily to those cases of established general authority, which have been indorsed by subsequent decisions or cited by text-book writers. Cases, therefore, upon local statutory law, not having any general authority out of the particular state where they are decided, are discarded, as well as those on obsolete points of law, having, at the present time no significance or application. When an examination of a report is made in this way, especially one of the earlier reports, it is surprising how small a proportion of the cases are found fit to survive the test here given. . . . For example, in the first volume of Washington's Virginia Reports, out of *one hundred and twenty-five cases* reported, only *ten* cases, regarded with the most indulgent eye, were found to possess sufficient value to entitle them to be reported in our first volume. . . .

But it must not be understood that the pruning knife is ruthlessly applied; it is thought better to err rather on the side of leniency than strictness; and, therefore, to give cases which may be regarded as not possessing a very novel or leading character, but which, nevertheless, are of established general authority, although the points which they determine may no longer be novel. The aim is to give, by a series of continued authoritative decisions, the system of law established in each state as compared with the other states; to show, by a compilation of contemporaneous, collated decisions, the structure and development of our American law; in fact, to give a system of American comparative jurisprudence.

. . . .

Method of Reporting. In reporting the cases selected, the strictest care is taken to see that the syllabus entirely conforms to the decision of the court; that it does not embrace more than is actually decided, and that it covers the points made and determined. Where a case settles a rule or principle of law, that rule or principle will be stated as a general proposition; but where the decision turns principally on some particular facts, such facts will be stated in the syllabus, as the basis of the court's decision. The different points or propositions settled by the decision will be indicated by head-lines prefixed, to give a general idea of the matter decided. This will greatly facilitate the examination of a case, as at a glance any point sought for can be seen.

Notice will be taken of the arguments of counsel, so far as to extract from them the points made, and the authorities cited in support of them. We can but imperfectly understand the cases, if we do not find out just what points were made in argument; for when we see the points which were really made, we can better appreciate the force and pertinency of a decision. It should be remembered that in the preparation of counsel's argument, great research and ability are sometimes shown, and such efforts are often no less instructive than the decision of the court. . . .

When a decision embraces several points, some of which are trivial and of no pertinency at the present day, or turn on mere points of local practice, such will be eliminated, and the point or points which are of any significance or value at present will be noticed, and so much of the court's decision given as goes to support the point noticed.

Annotations. A special feature of these reports, and one which, it is hoped, will be found to much advantage, are the notes affixed to the cases. The compiler will endeavor to bestow great care and research in these notes. All fanciful or digressive discussions will be avoided, the great aim being to make them pointed, compact, and practical; to give, in the first place, by a reference either to text-books of subsequent decisions, some idea of the value of a case as authority, how far it is adopted or modified in the particular state where the decision is made, and how far it agrees with the current of authorities elsewhere. In this way, a system of comparative legal principles will be evolved. In some few instances, a note may be extended into an essay, when an effort will be made to give an exhaustive review of the authorities, both English and American, on the question decided. . . .

Arrangement. The arrangement of the cases is made with a view of showing a connected, regular order of adjudication in each state. Thus the reports of a state for a certain period are taken, and cases are selected in order from them; then the reports of another state are examined for the same period of time, and cases selected in the same manner; and in this way, until a volume is compiled. In the selection of cases for the succeeding volume, the cases are taken up at the point where they were left in the preceding volume. This has been found the most feasible, and it is believed the most advantageous plan; for in this manner, each volume will cover a certain period of time, and the decisions from the reports of each state can be traced in continuous order through the series. Thus in the first volume of the series, the decisions will be given up to about 1801, taken from thirty different state reports.

Volumes of the Series: From an estimate made, it is calculated approximately, that the revision of the reports carried out on the plan here proposed, omitting mere practice reports, will take about seventy-five volumes of this series. There need be little said to show the immense advantage and convenience of these volumes to the active members of the profession, who are not able to purchase the entire volumes of the state reports, or who have no facilities or opportunity for research in law libraries. A lawyer who is provided with his own state reports, and who has besides the volumes of this series, supplemented by the series known as the *American Reports*, may well be considered as completely equipped for the ordinary needs of his practice.

Note 2(E). The Lawyers Cooperative System

American Decisions was completed in one hundred volumes in 1888. That year, *American Reports* changed title to *American State Reports*, while another publishing company, the Lawyers Cooperative Company, started publishing *Lawyers Reports Annotated*, a selective set of reports, similar to the Bancroft-Whitney Company's set. In 1911, the *American State Reports* ceased publication. *Lawyers Reports Annotated* continued, to be succeeded in 1919 by *American Law Reports (ALR)*. Since 1919, *ALR* has been divided at various dates into new series.[1] Since 1969, federal district and circuit court cases have been published separately in *ALR Federal*. All cases from the U.S. Supreme Court, many with annotations, are published by the Lawyers Cooperative Company in *United States Supreme Court Reports, Lawyers Edition (L.Ed.)*.

The survival of the selective-report concept has been due not to its selection and republication of judicial opinions but to the value of the annotations accompanying some of the opinions. The annotations provide a case-finding aid similar to the legal encyclopedias, but are more subject-specific than encyclopedia articles.

An elaborate system of indexing and updating is necessary to keep *ALR* annotations usable and current. The *Index to Annotations* is the main source for locating annotations by subject in all but the first series of *ALR* (1919 to 1948), and, beginning in 1965, pocket parts in each volume of the *ALR* keep annotations up to date. A "digest" approach to locating annotations and cases is also available but is somewhat redundant. For prior years, the indexing and updating of *ALR* is more complex.[2]

ALR annotations can also be located by references from *American Jurisprudence 2d*, the legal encyclopedia published by the Lawyers Cooperative Company. Since 1989, cases reported in *ALR 3d, 4th, 5th, ALR Federal*, and the *Lawyers Edition* of the Supreme Court reports can be searched in a special unit of *Shepard's Citations*. Other units of *Shepard's* also list the citations of cases in *ALR* and *L.Ed.* annotations. However, the citation of *ALR* annotations in cases cannot be traced through *Shepard's*. Tracing such citation is only possible through the on-line databases, LEXIS and WESTLAW.

LEXIS also provides a way to avoid the cumbersome indexing and updating of *ALR*. Annotations from *L.Ed.* and all but the first series of *ALR* are available in fully updated form on LEXIS.

Selection 2(E). John B. West of St. Paul, 1879

A Symposium of Law Publishers, 23 AM. L. REV. 396, 400–407 (1889).

From John B. West, Esq., of St. Paul.

. . . .

. . . I believe it to be the principal business of American law publishers, to enable the legal profession to examine the American case law on any given subject, as easily, exhaustively, and economically as possible. It is a remarkable fact that until within the last few years, there has been no successful attempt to handle, systematically and comprehensively, the current decisions of the courts of last resort, which are constantly developing and modifying the law on every subject; and to so report and digest them, classify and give notice of them, that they shall be promptly available to the exhaustive research of the judge and practitioner.

Until the advent of the *North Western Reporter*, some ten years ago, the prompt publication of opinions was practically unknown to the legal profession in this country. In each State lawyers were compelled to wait in the first instance, on the convenience of their State reporter, whose official duties were more or less subject to the exigencies of his private practice; and in the second place, upon the delays incident to the conflicting business demands of the local publisher. The publication of the decisions, which had, from the time of their delivery, become a part of the law of the commonwealth, and concerning which it was legally assumed every citizen had full knowledge, was made subsidiary in turn to the professional obligations of a legal practitioner, and the private business interests of some local publisher or printer. It is true that there was some publication of current opinions in the law magazines, but this was done in a fugitive and irregular fashion. The opinions were filed away in the offices of the court and were therefore not directly accessible to the editor, while the issues of the magazines and law journals were limited in the number of their pages, and largely taken up with essays and other matter. Such cases as found their way to print reached the editor more or less by accident, and their publication was contingent upon the condition that space be found for their insertion. Some opinions were sent in with the compliments of the attorneys directly interested, or contributed by subscribers who deemed them worthy of publication; the rest were such as had come to the knowledge of the editor accidentally. The element of notice, the bringing of news of the most recent decisions of the courts, was largely wanting under this system, and the prompt and exhaustive publication of all that has been decided, was almost without precedent. The profession was dependent upon such service as could be rendered incidentally by publications designed mainly to serve other purposes,—some of them, primarily mere advertising sheets, only inserting opinions as far as necessary, for the purpose of padding.

When, therefore, a lawyer looking up the case law of a subject, consulted the reports of his own State, he had to ask himself, "Has our Supreme Court rendered any later decision upon this point not yet reported here?" and he had no means of securing a conclusive answer, unless he had access to the files of the court. The "Reporter" plan of publication, first used in 1879 in the Northwestern States, was designed to give lawyers the ready means of keeping themselves informed as to the decisions of their own Supreme Courts, as fast as they should be filed.

But in investigating the case of the whole country, the lawyer was at a still greater disadvantage. Not only did he suffer from the lack of notice, the delays of official reporting and local publication, but in most instances the cost and number of volumes prevented him from taking the official reports when they were published. He was forced to content himself with such information as to these decisions, as he could get indirectly and by accident. He consulted text-books and turned to the title page (or if he was wise, to the copyright page), to see when they were published; then rose the question, "What have the American courts said in the years since this book was written?" If he consulted any series of selected cases, general or topical, he could not hope to find a conclusive answer, and if he searched through the few cases scattered through the law journals, it was with the hope that he might *happen* to find a case in point. At the last he had to go into court uncertain whether he might not be met on the threshold by his opponent, with controlling precedents to which he had not had access, and of the existence of which he had not been aware.

This condition of things perhaps still exists for some lawyers, but is not now necessarily the situation, as it certainly was a few years ago. All opinions are now published promptly and systematically, and are no longer dependent upon professional courtesy or vanity for their appearance in advance of official reports. One can today more readily and far more economically secure the printed copy of any territorial decision, than was possible a few years ago, even in the case of the New York Court of Appeals. The profession have now the immense advantage of being able to turn to a single set of reports and digests, and be sure of finding *everything* which the courts have said on any given subject up to the last decision just rendered. A lawyer can compare the decisions, and advise his client with a nearer approach to certainty. He can see what precedents are available for himself, and also what will probably be cited by his opponents and so thoroughly prepare himself to meet them. This service is rendered by the National Reporter System, which, strange to say, has been wrought out entirely by private enterprise, not through the intervention of any bar association, State or national, or by subsidy from any government.

. . . .

The older and comparatively less important cases are all covered by the *U.S. Digest*, recently incorporated in the System. The latest decisions are kept fully reported and digested up to date, and through the digests and reports of the National Reporter System the lawyer can now, in a short time, examine the case law of a subject with the certainty that no American decisions in point have escaped his attention. These reports are authentic and reliable. The opinions are printed from compared and certified copies of the original, furnished in most cases by the clerk himself, or other custodian; the proofs are read with great care by specially trained law-proof readers; citations are verified by experts from the original volumes; these reports are edited by a corps of men specially trained for that work. These editors are not left to their own individual whim, but act under an elaborate code of instructions, which is the result of experience in reporting some 50,000 cases. Their reports are prepared with the briefs of counsel and "paper books" and other documents before them, showing the cases as submitted. Finally, by the new system recently inaugurated, the judges themselves are enabled to revise the reports of their own decisions in the temporary edition, and have their amendments or corrections incorporated into the permanent or library edition. This practically puts them on a par with the official reports as regards authenticity, while as regards promptness, economy, compactness and convenience of access by prompt current digesting, there is no comparison.

Note 2(F). The West System

In the 1870s and 1880s, a number of publishers began publication of sets combining the judicial opinions of groups of states. In 1879, West Publishing Company of St. Paul, Minnesota, began the *North Western Reporter*, combining judicial opinions from Minnesota and five surrounding states after not finding enough profit in publishing only Minnesota opinions in a publication called *The Syllabus*. The *North Western Reporter* was no different in concept from the sets of other publishers. In 1880, however, West began a unique set combining the opinions of all federal courts, other than the Supreme Court, in the *Federal Reporter*. Soon, other reports of federal courts stopped, giving West a monopoly.

West's *Supreme Court Reporter* began publication in 1882, and in the following five years, West Publishing Company extended the concept of regional reports nationwide, sometimes buying up rival sets. The beginning date of each regional unit of the *National Reporter System* is:

North Western	1879
Pacific	1884
North Eastern	1885
Atlantic	1886
South Eastern	1887
South Western	1887
Southern	1887

West thus made it possible for lawyers to collect the judicial opinions of all states easily.

To achieve national scope, West developed a thoroughly professional operation, establishing and maintaining direct contact with all judges to obtain their opinions. West followed a policy that has been described as "comprehensive reporting of all decisions, no matter how boring or stupid."[1] On the other hand, West broke with centuries of reporting tradition by ignoring the arguments of counsel.

West also hired full-time editors to have all editorial work done in-house. The result was not only high quality but also promptness. To get reports of cases to customers as fast as possible, "advanced sheets" became a permanent part of subscriptions to West reporters. Yet, despite such double publication, West's reporters were competitively priced.

Even the slip opinions of the courts usually did not appear as promptly as the West advanced sheets. In fact, most official reporters were notoriously tardy in publishing the official reports in any form. Nevertheless, some official reporters tried to prevent commercial competition by asserting copyright through the states with which they had exclusive contracts. However, courts consistently followed the doctrine of *Wheaton v. Peters*[2] and ruled against the official reporters. At the same time, West succeeded in gaining copyright protection for its editorial enhancements to the opinions.[3]

Not only were all available opinions reported by West, but all were treated equally—including opinions reversed or overruled and including concurring and dissenting opinions. The only limitations on reporting resulted from the failure of judges to send opinions to West (which became increasingly rare) and from the well-developed tradition that only appellate opinions should be reported (a tradition that has exceptions, most notably for selected opinions of the federal district courts). The result was more comprehensive reporting than ever before. As Grant Gilmore, a noted legal scholar, has written:

> Now, for the first time, all the decisions, not only of the federal appellate courts but of all the state courts of last resort, were made available to lawyers throughout the country. Being available, they had to be used: even a middle-sized law firm in a middle-sized city could not afford to be without a full set of reports. And, as we know to our sorrow, the number of volumes published increased year by year in geometric progression.
>
> The West Publishing Company, whose interest in jurisprudential theory I assume to have been minimal, thus made a contribution to our legal history which, in its importance, may have dwarfed the contributions of Langdell, Holmes, and all the learned professors on all the great law faculties. After ten or fifteen years of life with the National Reporter System, the American legal profession found itself in a situation of unprecedented difficulty. There were simply too many cases, and each year added its frightening harvest to the

appalling glut. A precedent-based, largely non-statutory system could not long continue to operate under such pressures.[4]

The great bulk of the *National Reporter System* had to be balanced by easy access. To this end, the addition of a digest completed the West system. West first bought the *U.S. Digest* from another publisher in 1887 and then replaced it, in 1896, with the *Century Digest*, digesting all American cases that could be located, from the earliest to 1895. To keep the *Century Digest* up to date, *General Digests* have been published since 1896, using West's unique "key-number" system combined with word indexes and tables of case names.[5] The *General Digests* have been cumulated every decade into *Decennial Digests*. Since 1986, cumulations have been published every five years.

Although it does not appear on the title pages, the entire set of West reporters has come to be called the *National Reporter System*, and the West digests have come to be called the *American Digest System*. In addition to the national set of digests, digests are available for nearly all states and for most regional units of the *National Reporter System*. Separate digests are also available for the federal courts, including the U.S. Supreme Court.[6] The West state, regional, and federal digests contain little that is not in the *American Digest System*; the smaller units simply are easier to use and less costly for those who need only local or federal cases.

Reporter volumes are also available for individual states, reprinting from the regional reporters only cases from each state. Libraries that have the regional reporters have no reason to buy these limited reprints, but they are cost-saving for lawyers who only want home-state cases.

The topical arrangement of the digests starts with seven large topics derived from the outline of the Abbott brothers of New York:[7]

1. Persons
2. Property
3. Contracts
4. Torts
5. Crimes
6. Remedies
7. Government

The seven main topics are subdivided and further subdivided into more than four hundred alphabetically arranged subtopics with over forty thousand sub-subtopics. West Publishing Company devised its "key-number" system to avoid the linguistic difficulty of assigning names to all the topics.

Since 1909, West reporters have included the digest paragraphs at the beginnings of cases in the reporters. Such "headnotes" carry key numbers enabling readers to find cases on the same topic in the digests.

The systematization involved in the West key-number system may be largely responsible for rendering the common law manageable enough to survive in the United States.

> [West's] subject arrangement lent its structure to American law. Because it was a universal subject thesaurus, locating every point in every case by subject, then placing the case in a location in the printed Digests, it imposed a continuing structure on the law. Language and concepts were normalized as the West editor prepared the headnotes for each case. . . . Commentators criticized West, but there is no doubt that its family of publications had a profound and continuing impact on the way information about law was organized. West's influence may have saved the myth of the common law from what looked like its inevitable demise.[8]

Continuing survival also requires the adaptability of digests to new topics. Not until 1926 was the need for flexibility recognized, with a new topic for "Automobiles." Since then, workers' compensation, labor law, and other topics have been accommodated, but slowly. When a new digest topic is born, cases prior to the appearance of a new topic can sometimes be traced through tables linking new key numbers to old.

Although the *Century Digest* covers all American cases to 1895, no attempt has been made to republish all American judicial opinions prior to the *National Reporter System*. Only the opinions of federal courts have been collected; they were published (up to 1880) in *Federal Cases*. Thus, for each state that published reports prior to the beginning of the *National Reporter System*, those reports remain necessary for full historical coverage.

Since its inception, the *National Reporter System* has undergone a number of changes:

— In 1932, the *Federal Supplement* was created to remove U.S. District Court decisions from the *Federal Reporter*.

— In 1940, a *Federal Rules Decisions* unit was created to remove U.S. District Court cases dealing with the Federal Rules of Civil Procedure and the Federal Rules of Criminal Procedure from the *Federal Supplement*. It includes relevant articles, speeches, proceedings of judicial conferences and other material as well as cases.

— Since 1888 decisions of New York, and since 1960 those of California, have been separately published in the *New York Supplement* and the *California Reporter*. The decisions of the California Supreme Court are duplicated in the *Pacific Reporter*; the decisions of the New York Court of Appeals are duplicated in the *North Eastern Reporter*, but the intermediate appellate reports of both states are not in the regional sets.

— In 1978, two topical units were started to report the opinions of special federal courts—the Bankruptcy Court, which was new, and the Court of Military Appeals (plus some opinions of the Courts of

Military Review), which existed earlier.[9] Although *West's Military Justice Reporter* contains only the opinions of the military courts, *West's Bankruptcy Reporter* contains not only the opinions of the Bankruptcy Court but selected bankruptcy opinions of the U.S. District Courts (which are not published in *Federal Supplement*) and selected opinions of the U.S. Circuit Courts and the Supreme Court (which are reprinted from the *Federal Reporter* and the *Supreme Court Reporter*).

—In 1982, another specialized reporter started publication—the *United States Claims Court Reporter* (later renamed the *Federal Claims Reporter*)—to report the opinions of the new United States Claims Court,[10] along with the claims opinions of other federal courts reprinted from other West reporters.

—In the 1980s two other topical units were started—*West's Education Law Reporter* and *West's Social Security Reporting Service*. These sets simply reprint cases from the federal and regional reporters, retaining the original page numbers.

The West system has not eliminated duplication of reports. The selective reports (*ALR*) continue to be published,[11] and twenty-eight states continue to publish official state reports. (Other states have recognized the waste and discontinued their own reports, giving official status to the West reporters.)[12] In addition, specialized reports and looseleaf services often report cases duplicating the *National Reporter System* as well as some cases not reported elsewhere.

Cases reported in both the *National Reporter System* and official state reports are required by courts to be cited to both—the state report because it is the official version, the regional reporter because that is the version lawyers are most likely to own for out-of-state cases. Opening page numbers of official citations can be traced in the regional reporters and in a set called the *National Reporter Blue Book* as well as in *Shepard's Citations*.[13] Recent volumes of regional reporters and recent cases on LEXIS and WESTLAW also contain internal page references to the official reports, but for earlier cases, it remains necessary to resort to the official sets.

Shepard's Citations publishes volumes both for state reports and for West's regional reporters. Although the cases reported in both the state reports and regional reporters are the same, the *Shepard's* volumes for each provide different information. The most important difference is that state units of *Shepard's* are confined to intrastate citations, while interstate citations can only be traced in the regional *Shepard's* units.

As West Publishing Company became the only publisher of federal court opinions and the only national source for the opinions of state courts, it attained an unchallenged preeminence in law publishing for nearly a century. In the 1970s, however, a rival appeared in the form of an on-line computer service—LEXIS. LEXIS simply offered on-line access to the full texts of judicial opinions. Without editorial enhancements, the full texts could be searched by key words connected and limited by formal terms developed from Boolean logic. In time, West responded with an on-line service of its own—WESTLAW.

The two rival databases are competing on several levels, including the comprehensiveness of their coverage. Both services continue the tradition of nonselectivity, as voiced by John B. West in 1889.[14]

Perhaps WESTLAW's greatest advantage in its competition with LEXIS is its inclusion of the digests along with full texts of cases, both of which can be searched on-line by key numbers as well as keywords. LEXIS includes only full texts of cases and can only be searched by keywords. Some, however, have speculated that on-line research may do away with the need for digesting cases.[15] At one time, WESTLAW also had the disadvantage of coming at the competition from behind.

Selection 2(F). Enter LEXIS

J. Abramson, J. Kennedy, and E. J. Pollock, *Inside the West Empire,* 5 AM. LAW. 90, 90–95 (Oct. 1983), reprinted as *West Publishing: The Empire's New Clothes,* 12 STUDENT LAW. 17, 17–20, 38–41 (Jan. 1984).

There's a story about West Publishing Company that has become a legend in the publishing industry. Back in 1966, after McGraw-Hill bought *Shepard's Citations,* the company became interested in acquiring a larger chunk of the legal publishing industry. It put its feelers out to St. Paul, Minnesota, where West had quietly dominated the reporting of American case law for almost a century. But instead of jumping at the chance to join up, West's executives responded with a disdainful chuckle. Then they promptly offered to buy McGraw-Hill—for cash.

True or not (and official spokesmen at both companies neither confirm nor deny it), the story sums up West's image. Because the management of the privately held company has always been conservative and intensely secretive, West is an unknown quantity to many outside of the legal community. Within that community, West, with 2,700 employees and annual revenues estimated by industry analysts at more than $220 million, is a power unto itself. . . .

. . . West has made itself indispensable to most lawyers. In fact, this privately held, secretive publisher of court decisions has become, literally, the sum and substance of American jurisprudence.

Jill Abramson and Ellen Joan Pollock were senior reporters and John Kennedy was a summer intern for *The American Lawyer.* This article is republished with permission from the October 1983 issue of *The American Lawyer.* © 1983 *The American Lawyer.*

As publisher of more than 400 titles, including the *Federal Reporter*, *Federal Supplement, Federal Rules Decisions*, West is the only publishing company that attempts to report *all* state and federal case law. The demand for West publications is so great that nine web presses run 24 hours a day at the company's massive plant in the suburbs of St. Paul. There are so many volumes (last year's *Federal Supplement*, for example, included 26 volumes containing 5,500 opinions) that a computer in the plant's storage area must track the location of each publication and issue driving instructions to the storage personnel before a particular volume can be found. The plant employs two full-time postal workers and is itself a postal station.

Even small firms must make a sizable investment in West's books. When he started his own five-lawyer litigation firm two years ago, Sidney Stein of New York's Stein, Zauderer, Ellenhorn, Friedman & Kaplan invested an immediate $30,000 for a basic library consisting mainly of West's federal volumes and state texts. And that was largely for second-hand volumes, at about half the price of new ones. The beauty of "the West system" is that, once having invested in a West library, lawyers have a tremendous incentive to keep updating it with the latest opinions. For instance, New York's Skadden, Arps, Slate, Meagher & Flom, with 275 lawyers, annually spends between $25,000 and $40,000 on new West publications. During the 1982–83 academic year, Harvard Law School spent $61,000 to keep its West library up to date.

These are the kind of figures that make West's major competitors . . . miserable. While West makes no public disclosures about its earnings, industry analysts project that West sales account for 40 to 50 percent of the new law book market.

. . . .

But while West has dominated the law book market for a century, it has been trounced in a field where it should have flourished: computerized legal research. West was extremely slow getting into the computer business, introducing Westlaw in 1975, two years after the first LEXIS terminal was installed at New York's Shearman & Sterling. Ironically, much of the reasons for the lag lies in the very characteristics that have marked West's success in print—the publishing company's conservative, centralized leadership, its lack of serious competition and hence lack of motivation to innovate, even its own faith in the century-old West "headnote" and "synopsis" system.

. . . .

But if West had little incentive to innovate ten years ago, it now has all the incentive it needs. Its initial sluggishness gave Mead Data [the owner of LEXIS] an unexpected opportunity to tighten its grip on the fast-growing computer research market. And in 1975, when West finally introduced Westlaw, its system was fraught with design problems and only increased Mead Data's stranglehold. Now, with more and more lawyers turning to terminals instead of books, . . . LEXIS sales outpace Westlaw sales nine to one, according to industry analysts' estimates. The question is, can West use its century-old hegemony in the print world to reverse its fortunes in computers?

At least part of the answer lies in West's beginnings . . . John West, a single-minded businessman . . . traveled from Massachusetts to found West Publishing with his brother Horatio in 1876. West built up the St. Paul business from a monthly newsletter, *The Syllabi* (which contained excerpts of decisions from the Minnesota Supreme Court and Minnesota federal court) to its National Reporter System. . . .

At the same time, West Publishing developed its American Digest System of indexing court decisions using "headnotes" and "keynumbers," thus enabling lawyers to find particular decisions by subject matter, no matter how voluminous the court reports became.

In a series of buyouts and bankruptcies, West's competitors fell by the wayside in the late 1880s. West was undercutting them in price, and lawyers were finding the uniform, national "West system" more convenient to use than the competitors' regional reporters. By 1888, when West acquired the *U.S. Digest* . . . , it stood alone in the marketplace.

In the same year the U.S. Supreme Court upheld West's copyright on its publications—a major factor in its domination of legal publishing. While there is no property right in judicial opinions per se, the court recognized . . . a right of property in the "intellectual labor" supplied by a private reporter of its decision. West has always claimed copyright over its editorial product—the bound and edited opinions. "We claim copyright on our compilation and editorially added features [headnotes, synopses, keynumbers]," says West editor in chief Arnold Ginnow, "down to the pagination."

. . . .

If the courts have treated West kindly, West has returned the favor in spades. By printing every decision it receives, West offers every judge a ticket to immortality. One of West's top officers, editorial counsel Charles Nelson, 63, is there just to keep judges happy (and to keep them sending their opinions to West).

. . . .

In a letter, West invites all new judges to become "contributing editors" to its publications by sending in their opinions. In return, West offers judges free copies of some of its publications. . . .

. . . .

Mead had difficulty at first getting judges to send their opinions to LEXIS as well as West. According to one former executive at LEXIS, the judges "most certainly were reluctant. Many of them were not used to handing opinions to anyone but West. Some were looking for handouts. One judge even said, "West gives me free law books. What are you going to give?"

. . . .

Ginnow presides over an editorial staff of 200. The heavyweights of the editorial department are the eight classification editors who assign keynumbers to cases. All have had between 10 and 15 years of editing experience at West. It used to be a major event at the company when a new subheading for the various opinions was created. Labor only got its own heading in the 1950s and until recently, according to Ginnow, worker's compensation cases were listed as part of "Master and Servant" law, and products liability was put under "Negligence." Today, however, there are 418 subheadings.

Thirty-four general editors work under the classification editors, writing headnotes and synopses. The manuscript department then adds parallel citations and corrects "routine errors," according to Ginnow. These include wrong statute references, case citations, or misspellings. When an editorial employee finds an error, he must send a letter to the judge indicating the correction. When advance sheets are sent to the judge, he or she sees the correction again.

"We don't edit the language or delete anything," says Ginnow. "We don't alter the punctuation. If a judge likes semicolons, that's fine, too." Opinions are usually printed from 23 to 30 days after arriving at West.

If a judge sends West an opinion, West prints it. "It's strictly a matter of judgment on the judge's part," says Ginnow. "West does not decide what to publish." Inevitably, many decisions go unreported, but Ginnow refuses to estimate the number. "We check advance sheets and other publications," he says, "and if we find something missing, occasionally we do solicit opinions." However, some courts are trying to restrict the number of published opinions. In California, for example, only 15 percent of the decisions of the state's intermediate appellate court are published. The state courts in New Jersey have recently established a Committee on Opinions to determine which opinions should be submitted for publication.

West requires that all editors be graduates of law school and be admitted to the bar. New editors are hired on for a 30-day tryout period, during which Ginnow tests whether they can handle the large volume of work West requires. An editor is expected to plow through at least 12 judicial decisions each day. "We've learned that resumés, grades, and law review don't mean they can understand a simple case," says Ginnow.

. . . .

Whatever its merits, the company's insular management brought West into the 1970s in good shape. The publishing monopoly was untouched and extremely profitable. But in the computer age, West's executives showed signs of being out of their element. . . . Using its copyright as a shield, West has driven all of its competitors away. But in the computer age, West was no longer unassailable. Enter LEXIS.

Until 1973, West was the only comprehensive system that enabled a legal researcher to locate opinions relating to specific points of law. That year, however, LEXIS introduced its full-text, computerized service, ending West's monopoly. Past opinions could now be retrieved through words, phrases, or section numbers specified in the LEXIS user's request.

. . . .

Executives at West were caught off guard by LEXIS's early success. A former employee observes that their surprise "reflects the isolation of some of the more senior people at West. They just don't understand the technology." There were also the more legitimate fears that computerized research would interfere with West's book sales. "It was a matter of priorities," explains Ginnow. . . .

By 1975, Opperman finally realized that West could not afford to let LEXIS monopolize the computer market the way West had always dominated legal publishing. According to a former West employee, "Opperman just came out of his office one day and said, 'There will be Westlaw.' "

But Westlaw's debut was extremely weak. Its early failures have been chalked up to several mistakes by West's top management.

First, instead of taking the time and expense to develop its own software, West purchased a ready-made package, called Quic-Law, from a Canadian company. The system was slow (ironically) and developed a reputation for being "user unfriendly." . . . The result was that Westlaw spent hundreds of thousands of dollars promoting computer-aided law research, and LEXIS gained. "West's entry," recalls one observer, "was the best thing that ever happened to LEXIS. . . . West came in spending zillions on PR, and while that raised everybody's consciousness, everyone also saw that LEXIS was the better system."

Second, instead of bringing in a new management team with computer experience . . . , West turned to its own editorial people to guide Westlaw. But Ginnow and Theodore Herman were so sold on West's age-old system that they designed Westlaw's data base to contain only headnotes and synopses. LEXIS offered full text from the start, and it soon became clear that this was what lawyers preferred. No one was surprised, then, when West, in 1978, announced it was going full text. . . .

Third, West had different salesmen selling books than Westlaw, and there was an obvious conflict between the two. "Westlaw's salespeople were telling customers that they wouldn't have to buy any more books," says a former West books salesman.

These mistakes all compounded one another. The result was badly sagging sales. . . .

Still, West had certain built-in advantages which saved Westlaw from being an utter disaster. West's copyright made LEXIS's attempt to build a data base extremely expensive. West, on the other hand, managed to have all of its reporters, supplements, and digests put on a computer tape free of charge—courtesy of the federal government.

In 1974 the Justice Department wanted to put the entire West system into JURIS, its computer system. Because of West's copyright claim, the department needed West's permission. West agreed to let Justice make the transfer, in return for free and exclusive copies of the tapes. The Justice Department also contracted to pay West $750,000 over five years, to provide JURIS with computer tapes of West's new publications. LEXIS, meanwhile, was spending $5 million to build its data base with the same materials, thanks to having to search through clerk's offices across the country for old opinions.

When LEXIS caught wind of West's contract with the Justice Department . . . Mead Data Central decided to file suit against West. . . .

. . . .

The suit didn't get very far. After two years of procedural maneuvering in which Opperman and Schatz succeeded in getting it moved to Minnesota, Mead Data suddenly withdrew the case voluntarily.

. . . .

Mead's abortive antitrust case created hard feelings between the two companies and made their competition even more intense. One of the ironies of their sore relations is that one of LEXIS's top executives, according to an informed source, had approached Opperman early on to see if the two companies could get together on developing a data base. According to the source, "Opperman screamed and shouted that they were certainly not going to help LEXIS set up a business. . . ."

There are signs that the Mead suit gave Westlaw new impetus to improve its management, software, and sales. In 1978 Thomas McLeod was brought in as the new manager of Westlaw. . . . Earlier West had replaced the Quic-Law software with its own. It then added several improvements, including a unique "Shepardizing function," which permits users to shuttle back and forth between the opinion being researched and the full text of various citing opinions. (On LEXIS, once the user jumps into the Shepard's file, the main case is lost.) . . .

Most important, Westlaw marketing has become more aggressive under McLeod's tenure. All West salesmen now sell both books and Westlaw. . . .

Typically, West's executives refuse to talk about Westlaw's revenues. McLeod talks in general terms about Westlaw's successful marketing attempts at midsize firms. Tostrud adds that Westlaw "is moving very quickly" into law school libraries and claims that Westlaw is about to "make some inroads" into LEXIS's turf, the big firm.

. . . .

Westlaw is clearly playing a game of catch up. "I've never heard anyone say that West has even come close to LEXIS," says Jeffrey Pemberton, who edits *Online and Data Base* magazines. Mead Data's 1982 revenues were a healthy $66 million, and the company projects 1983 revenues of $100 million. The company claims to have terminals in 99 percent of the nation's 150-odd firms with more than a hundred lawyers; in 84 percent of the firms with 40 to 60 lawyers, and in 40 percent of those with 20 to 40 lawyers. In small firms, LEXIS's presence drops sharply, to between 4 and 11 percent. Paul Nezi, Mead's vice-president for marketing, believes that the battle between LEXIS and Westlaw will be waged most intensely in the small-firm market, which is only now being mined.

At the moment, one industry watcher describes the fight between West and Mead as "fierce—about as rough as you can get." The stakes are high. By 1987 computerized legal research is expected to be a nearly $1-billion industry. And for West, the battle is definitely one that will decide whether it retains even a semblance of its century-old predominance. Electronic publishing is expected to grow at twice the rate of hardcovers. That's why West, after a slow start, is fighting back with an energy that recalls the days when John West used to disappear into the Minnesota and Dakota winters and return, weeks later, with his satchels full of subscriptions. In his 17 years as the company's first president, West built a legal publishing empire without rival. One hundred years later the question is, can the empire strike back?

Note 2(G). LEXIS, WESTLAW, and Thamus

Although WESTLAW started from behind LEXIS, it caught up quickly. The texts and headnotes of earlier cases were added to those of current cases until WESTLAW's database of cases has come to approximate the database of LEXIS.

Eventually, both LEXIS and WESTLAW added *Shepard's Citations.* Both also added an abbreviated, rapidly updated citation service—LEXIS named its service Auto-Cite; WESTLAW's service is named Insta-Cite. These quick-cite services list only parallel citations, citations of appeals and other proceedings in the same case and other cases affecting precedential value (e.g., overrulings). Such citations are, of course, also available in *Shepard's,* but the abbreviated services make the information available more promptly than *Shepard's.*[1]

LEXIS also enriched its database by adding the full text of briefs submitted to the United States Supreme Court. Such briefs can be helpful in the interpretation of judicial opinions, as was the reporting of counsels' arguments in early reports, but they are available only at a few depository libraries throughout the nation and on microfiche.[2]

The contest between LEXIS and WESTLAW has extended beyond cases. Both LEXIS and WESTLAW added federal and state legislative materials,[3] administrative materials,[4] and even scholarly writings and non-legal materials.[5] Moreover, specialized topical databases in both LEXIS and WESTLAW bring together judicial, legislative, administrative, and scholarly sources in such federal regulatory fields as securities regulation, tax law, and labor law and even in some state-regulated fields such as insurance and public utilities. Thus, by 1987 it could be written:

> At present, with respect to *legal* data bases, the offerings of the two services are much the same. Both continue to add new materials, and both continue to make the existing files more retrospective. Each occasionally gains some small advantage in one area or another, but overall they are now very close to equality.[6]

As the full-text database of WESTLAW began to catch up with LEXIS, the advantage shifted to WESTLAW. The pure full-text content of LEXIS

NAME	PG	NAME	PG	NAME	PG	NAME	PG	NAME	PG	NAME	PG	NAME	PG
--------------------------------- L E X I S — U S ---------------------------------------								PUBLIC		FINANCIAL		---- NEXIS ----	
GENFED	1	CODES	1	LEGIS	1	STATES	1	CITES	6	RECORDS		COMPNY	17	NEXIS	14
										ASSETS	6	QUOTE	17	BACKGR	14
ADMRTY	2	FEDCOM	3	MILTRY	4	CORP	2	LAWREV	6	DOCKET	6	INVEST	17	BANKS	15
BANKNG	2	FEDSEC	3	PATENT	4	EMPLOY	2	MARHUB	6	INCORP	6	MERGER	17	CMPCOM	14
BKRTCY	2	FEDTAX	3	PENBEN	4	HEALTH	3	LEXREF	6	LIENS	6	NAARS	12	CONSUM	14
COPYRT	2	IMMIG	3	PUBCON	4	INSRLW	3	ABA	6	LEXDOC	9			ENRGY	15
ENERGY	2	INTLAW	3	PUBHW	4	MEDMAL	3	BNA	6	--- MEDIS ---		---- INT'L ----		ENTERT	14
ENVIRN	2	ITRADE	3	REALTY	4	PRLIAB	4	TAXRIA	6	GENMED	16	WORLD	18	INSURE	14
ESTATE	2	LABOR	3	TRADE	5	STENV	4	TAXANA	6	MEDLNE	16	ASIAPC	18	LEGNEW	15
ETHICS	2	LEXPAT	3	TRDMRK	5	STSEC	4	ALR	6			EUROPE	18	MARKET	15
FAMILY	2	M&A	4	TRANS	5	STTAX	4	--ASSISTS--		POLITICAL		MDEAFR	18	PEOPLE	15
FEDSEN	3	MSTORT	5			UCC	5	PRACT	13	CMPGN	15	NSAMER	18	SPORTS	14
						UTILTY	5	GUIDE	13	EXEC	15			TRAN	15

```
_____ WELCOME to the WESTLAW DIRECTORY _____P1_____

    GENERAL MATERIALS         SPECIALIZED MATERIAL    TEXTS, PERIODICALS AND NEWS
Federal              P3      BNA              P516    Law Reviews, Texts,    P462
  Case Law           P4      Other Publishers P550     Journals & CLEs
  Statutes & Regs    P7      Careers          P555    Newspapers & Mags      P268
  Administrative     P11     Dialog Databases P211
State                P17     Gateways (e.g.,  P531           CITATORS
Combined Federal     P16       Dow Jones)             Insta-Cite, Shepard's P512
  & State                    Highlights       P583     Citations, Shepard's
                             Public Records   P585     PreView, & QuickCite
    TOPICAL MATERIAL         Restatements &   P511
Bankruptcy           P284    Uniform Laws                    SERVICES
Environmental        P328                             Dictionaries          P523
Labor & Employment   P391         DIRECTORIES         EZ ACCESS             P593
Securities           P428    West's Legal     P527    Key Number Service    P592
Taxation             P442    Directory                Other Services        P592
....More Topics      P2      Other Directories P524   Customer Information   P594

If you wish to:
    Select the searchable WESTLAW database list, type IDEN and press ENTER
    Select a known database, type its identifier and press ENTER
    Obtain further information, type HELP and press ENTER
```

Directory screens of LEXIS and WESTLAW.

has to compete with the full-text-plus-headnotes content of WESTLAW. While LEXIS advertising made a virtue of the fact that there is no editorial intervention between the full text and the researcher, WESTLAW capitalized on its editorial staff and advertised "full text PLUS," providing the option of pure full-text searching or searching by key numbers or keywords used in headnotes. WESTLAW also developed a "natural language" search technique which frees searchers from the artificial limitations of Boolean searches. LEXIS followed with "plain English" searching.

The added search options on WESTLAW should permit both a higher rate of returns on search queries and a greater degree of precision in search results.[7] However, WESTLAW does not include all headings used in the digests, nor any of the word indexes to the digests.[8] These omissions severely limit the usefulness of the "plus" in WESTLAW and may even be misleading.[9] It has been suggested that the full *American Digest System* should be added to WESTLAW.[10]

LEXIS has responded to West's headnotes and key numbers by adding the annotations of Lawyers Cooperative Company to its database. The annotations—from *American Law Reports* and the *Lawyers Edition* of the *United States Supreme Court Reports*—can serve as alternatives to the West digests for finding and analyzing cases, but they do not provide the comprehensive coverage of the West digests.[11] However, the annotations include citations to cases predating the cases reported in full text, while West headnotes in WESTLAW are only for cases included in the database.

The headnotes and key numbers in WESTLAW and the annotations in LEXIS are, in part, responsive to a number of writers who have raised doubts about the efficacy of pure full-text searching. For example, in one study (conducted on a large database developed by a law firm) keyword searches of full-text records, using Boolean search techniques, retrieved only 20 percent of the relevant documents in the database, and the searches retrieved as much irrelevant material as relevant material.[12] One writer has cautioned that "dependence on words" in full-text systems "grounds search capabilities in the opinion's language rather than its content," which may " 'lose' a very relevant case from a reasonable search," owing to "over-narrowing" that "prevents . . . approaching the issue-at-hand from a general perspective" using "analogies, broad policies, and imagination."[13]

Another writer invoked the legend of Thamus, the Egyptian king who refused to have his subjects taught the art of writing for fear that it would "implant forgetfulness in their souls."[14] And then there is the biblical story of the Tower of Babel . . .

Since the early days of the common law, commentators have warned that a system of law based on the cumulation of precedents must inevitably result in such a large mass of data as to create chaos. As chaos threatened in the nineteenth century, both in England and the United States, information systems were devised—in England by the bar and in the United States by commercial publishers—that for a time channeled the deluge into manageable streams. The initial motivation behind LEXIS was explained by one of its founders in terms that echo the nineteenth century:

> By the early 1960s, there was much talk in the legal profession about the geometric rate of increase in the amount of material a lawyer had to scan to do a comprehensive job of legal research. Simply said, there was more law. Lawyers had begun to see legal research as becoming an almost intolerable burden. What could be done about it? What about those huge, mysterious, and temperamental machines, computers? Could they somehow be programmed to do some of the work of legal research?[15]

Although computerized legal information has been defined as "an entirely new genre of legal literature,"[16] only computer searching is new. The databases of LEXIS and WESTLAW and the preindexed search aids are directly converted from preexisting paper publications.

Headnotes and key numbers in WESTLAW, annotations in LEXIS, and *Shepard's Citations* in both may serve well for a time to balance the excessive freedom of pure full-text searching, but all three are relics of the nineteenth century. The West digests, for example, serve not only to organize but also to confine.

> American legal literature . . . was controlled by a paradigm that was naturally both conservative and orthodox. . . . The West System was conservative in the sense that it resisted change; it was orthodox in the sense that it self-consciously attempted to maintain internal consistency and coherence in American law. The instrument of conservatism was the rigid index. The instrument of orthodoxy was the editorial staff placing new cases into the national index.[17]

The conservatism and orthodoxy may relate not only to structure but also to ideology. For example, it has been alleged that scholars who "have begun to question basic premises" in civil rights law "have found current legal categorization schemes [such as the digests] a hindrance more than a help," since "each system bears a strong imprint of the incremental civil rights approach these writers decry."[18]

As computerized information becomes more and more a familiar and comfortable part of professional life, it is likely to evolve from its nineteenth-century roots. Concepts for the organization and retrieval of data yet unknown should arise from the influence of the technology itself— concepts that take advantage of the computer's capabilities—or from "thinkers able to break free from the constraints of preexisting thought."[19] Experiments now testing the application of videodiscs, of imaging, of artificial intelligence, of new concepts of indexing and thesaurus development may do for the twenty-first century what John West and Frank Shepard did for the twentieth.

In the meantime, as computers were beginning to be applied to legal information in the mid-1970s, the federal courts, and the courts of some states as well, took a more traditional step to stem the growth of legal information. They simply cut down on the numbers of opinions published, creating a controversial new category of unpublished and uncitable opinions.

Selection 2(G). Unpublished Opinions

L. K. Robel, *The Myth of the Disposable Opinion: Unpublished Opinions and Government Litigants in the United States Courts of Appeals*, 87 MICH L. REV. 940, 940–61 (1989).

Since 1976, every federal appellate court has adopted rules that limit the publication of opinions. As a result, only a minority of the federal courts of appeals publish even half of their decisions on the merits. . . .

. . . .

There are differences among the publication plans adopted by the circuits, but the assumptions underlying the plans are fairly uniform. . . . All of the publication plans are based on the central assumption that opinions that serve no lawmaking function should not be published. Clearly, however, appellate opinions serve a host of other purposes: to supervise the lower courts, for instance, or to provide a mechanism . . . to keep track of how an agency is administering a statute. For the most part, however, the policies that inform the publication plans do not consider the plans' impact on these purposes.

Selective publication plans are also premised on the assumption that publication is costly in a number of ways. The judges suffer the costs involved in preparing an opinion for publication. Presumably, the plans will not eliminate the costs of researching the issues to be decided and formulating a rationale for a decision, since these must be done regardless of publication. Rather, the plans are meant to minimize additional special production costs associated with publication: those that arise because judges do not simply decide a case but also—like other published authors—attempt to express that resolution felicitously, to shore it up with citations to authority at every turn, and to anticipate in writing possible criticism of the opinion. . . . Litigants suffer the costs of delays that occur while judges attempt to write. Everyone suffers from added costs associated with increasingly large volumes of the *Federal Reporter*: research becomes more inefficient and time-consuming as the number of published opinions increases, as does maintaining the libraries and citechecking against the possibilities of missed authority.

The argument for nonpublication, then, depends upon the claim that judges (with their staffs) can efficiently identify cases that add significantly to the costs of litigation and decision but add nothing to the law. . . .

The option most responsive to the concerns underlying the publication plans would be to eliminate opinions altogether [by summarily affirming or reversing lower court decisions]. By doing this, the courts would achieve every cost saving that was hypothesized in connection with non-publication, but would avoid entirely the risk of creating a twilight zone of written-but-unpublished work. This option, however, has proven unattractive to litigants and judges alike: summary decision serves none of the legitimating functions of appeal and may leave parties with the feeling that the court never considered their arguments. Instead, the publication plans adopted by the courts are a compromise: they eliminate only *publication of the decision*, rather than the actual writing of the opinion. The resulting "unpublished opinions" are sometimes extremely obtuse, and they are often short, but just as often they resemble in every way the published opinions of the courts: facts are stated, the parties' legal arguments are addressed, and authority is cited and explained. The result of this tension between the need to explain and legitimate results to the parties and the premises of the selective publication plans has been that unpublished opinions are still opinions—providing insights into a court's reasoning and suggesting to advocates the arguments that could win or lose a case.

Disincentives for Use

Lawyers are trained to use opinions: to make arguments based on them, to try to distinguish them, and to consider how they bear on the outcome of their cases. In order to preserve the savings associated with nonpublication, though, lawyers must be persuaded not to use unpublished opinions. . . . [C]ourts employ two mechanisms to discourage the use of unpublished opinions.

First, all but four of the circuits circumscribe, by rule or by practice, the distribution of unpublished opinions. In most circuits, the opinions are routinely distributed to parties to the case and the lower court judge whose decision was reviewed. In six circuits, the opinions are also circulated to all appellate judges on the court. . . . Even though theoretically the opinions are available to anyone who wants to dig through the courts archives to retrieve them, practically speaking they are unavailable because they are neither indexed nor filed in a manner that would facilitate retrieval.[*] . . .

Second, all but the Third and the D.C. Circuits limit citation of the

[*]The Tenth Circuit indexed the opinions for a while but has ceased this practice. . . . [M]ost courts simply file them chronologically in the clerk's office and list the outcomes of the cases on tables in the *Federal Reporter*. However, only three of the circuits that list the results in this manner include *all* unpublished decisions in the list sent to West Publishing Company for inclusion in the *Reporter*. . . . With the growth of legal databases such as *Westlaw* and *Lexis*, unpublished opinions may become more accessible. Both of these services have begun to include many unpublished opinions from federal appellate courts. However, the availability of unpublished dispositions through these databases is not uniform across the circuits.

opinions to the court. Eight of the circuits forbid citation except in related cases or to support a claim of *res judicata*. Four of the circuits allow citation when there is no better precedent available. [However, there is no prohibition on citing an unpublished case to a court in another circuit, and the courts have no way of determining whether the opinions are being used without citation.]

. . . .

The Myth of the Disposable Opinion . . .

. . . .

What kinds of information could litigants get from unpublished opinions that are not foreseen by the publication plans? One important piece of information is the shape of the universe of decisions by a court in a particular area of law. The information might be as simple as knowing the odds. For instance, an attorney in California in 1987 might assess differently an appeal of a decision of the Board of Immigration Appeals (BIA) if he knew that the Ninth Circuit published only 27% of its immigration opinions in that year, and that over half of the reversals of BIA decisions occurred in unpublished decisions. . . .

. . . .

[Moreover,] the published immigration opinions of the Ninth Circuit for the eleven months beginning October 1, 1986, included one concurrence and one dissent. By contrast, there were seven concurrences and seven dissents in the unpublished opinions. . . . Taken together, the large number of reversals and separate expressions in unpublished opinions reveals a good bit of dissatisfaction on the part of the court with a variety of agency practices, as well as a fair amount of disagreement among members of the court about what it ought to require of the agency. It would be difficult to discern this pattern, however, if one were limited to the court's published expressions.

. . . .

. . . The . . . subject-matter areas where unpublished opinions predominate . . . include much litigation in which the government is a party, such as review of agency determinations in immigration and social security cases, Federal Tort Claims Act cases, criminal and habeas appeals, civil rights actions, and employment discrimination complaints against the federal government. On average, these are low-status, low-resources types of appeals, and they are the kinds of cases judges find tedious, with the result that they are often—perhaps usually—relegated to staff handling from start to finish.

In fact, there is some reason to doubt whether judges have much to do with the publication decision in these areas. First, judges themselves do not usually do the initial screening that designates a case as a likely candidate for disposition without argument. That initial decision is made by staff, usually staff attorneys or a circuit executive. A high correlation obtains between cases not argued before the court and cases disposed of without a published opinion. Some of the screening procedures used by the circuits identify entire categories of cases by subject matter as likely candidates for the expedited review that results in nonpublication. This suggests another reason why nonpublication may not be a good indication of the information value of an opinion: Decisions that result in nonpublication have been made in gross rather than individually, at least on the initial level, and judges have few incentives to examine these initial decisions closely. Existing data reveal that judges rarely disagree with the initial decision to decide an appeal on the briefs alone. . . .

In effect, then, the determination not to publish occurs very early in the appellate process, and necessarily so, for to delay the publication decision until after an opinion is written would be to lose the time savings the plans hope to achieve by having judges write with nonpublication in mind. Yet it seems unlikely that it will usually be possible to predict the information value of an opinion before it is written. In fact, many judges have noted how frequently a case's complexities are revealed through the process of writing an opinion. . . .

All of the circuits have mechanisms by which members of the panel of judges that decides the case can force a decision's publication. Available information suggests, though, that panel members rarely do this in cases that have been initially identified for nonpublication by staff, perhaps because in many circuits these opinions are drafted by central staff rather than the judges themselves or their own clerks. . . .

. . . .

The Ineffectiveness of Disincentive Mechanisms

. . . .

Because the plans underestimate the kinds of information attorneys derive from opinions and overestimate judges' abilities to implement the plans' central assumptions, those people who have unusual access to unpublished opinions will gain an advantage over those who do not. Moreover, the limited distribution plans currently operating assure that the people with unusual access to these opinions will be the same litigants who enjoy a variety of other institutional advantages in litigation: the frequent litigants [such as government agencies]. . . . [B]ecause the opinions are most often distributed *only* to parties and judges, the frequent litigants will have unique access to a useful source of information known only to them and the judges before whom they appear. . . .

The no-citation rules also present only a minor disincentive against using these opinions, especially for those litigants who have unusual access to them. This is so in part because the "guts" of the opinion—its reasoning, citations to authority, and such—can still be effectively employed through incorporation in briefs and arguments. . . .

. . . .

Finally, . . . the courts of appeals allow litigants to move to change the status of opinions from unpublished to published. Research . . . has suggested that frequent litigants have more incentive to "play for rules" than do other litigants: That is, they are more likely than other litigants to base litigation decisions on the possibility of creating favorable precedent or avoiding unfavorable precedent, rather than simply obtaining a favorable outcome in the immediate case.

Allowing motions for publication creates a serious flaw in the publication plans because, depending upon the frequency with which they are granted, they allow frequent litigants to stack the precedential deck. . . .

. . . .

The biggest objection most judges have to changing the present system is that any change will increase the demands on judges. Judges generally agree that they cannot be expected to increase their output significantly, nor can they be expected to take on the task of authoring decisions in the large number of unpublished cases. . . .

There is no reason why judges would have to change their behavior to accommodate universal publication. Those opinions that now remain unpublished could instead be published with a legend indicating that they are not to be cited except in those limited instances that unpublished opinions can now be cited. . . . We could then allow attorneys to make whatever use of the opinions is rational, and I suspect that attorneys can be trusted to behave rationally in this regard.

II

LEGISLATION

Parliament in 1523

3

Legislation in England

Note 3(A). The Early Stages of Legislation

Ancient Law

In his classic study *Ancient Law*, Sir Henry Maine describes three epochs in the early development of all legal systems. First is the "heroic age" when law "has scarcely reached the footing of custom" but is pronounced by kings claiming a "divinely given prerogative"; it is an epoch of "patriarchal despotism, . . . controlled . . . by a regimen not of law but of caprice."[1] Next is an epoch of "Customary Law" in which a special class acts as the "depositories and administrators of law":

> Before the invention of writing, and during the infancy of the art, an aristocracy invested with judicial privileges formed the only expedient by which accurate preservation of the customs of the race or tribe could be at all approximated to.[2]

Finally, comes the "era of Codes":

> In Greece, in Italy, on the Hellenised sea-board of Western Asia, these codes all made their appearance at periods much the same everywhere, not, I mean, at periods identical in point of time, but similar in point of the relative progress of each community. Everywhere, in the countries I have named, laws engraven on tablets and published to the people take the place of usages deposited with the recollection of a privileged oligarchy. . . . The ancient codes were doubtless

99

originally suggested by the discovery and diffusion of the art of writing. It is true that the aristocracies seem to have abused their monopoly of legal knowledge; and at all events their exclusive possession of the law was a formidable impediment to the success of those popular movements which began to be universal in the western world. But, though democratic sentiment may have added to their popularity, the codes were certainly in the main a direct result of the invention of writing. Inscribed tablets were seen to be a better depositary of law, and a better security for its accurate preservation, than the memory of a number of persons however strengthened by habitual exercise.[3]

Among the codes developed in the third epoch, Sir Henry Maine cites the "Twelve Tables of Rome," enacted by Rome's assembly in 451–450 B.C., as "the most famous specimen."[4]

Roman Law

The "Twelve Tables" is considered the founding document of Roman law.[5] Thereafter, Roman law developed from a variety of sources. The most important source was legislation enacted by the assemblies of Rome during the Republic (to 44 B.C.) and early Empire, and by imperial proclamations during the later Empire. To interpret legislation, Romans looked not to their judges, or "magistrates," but to *"pontificies,"*[6] who have been described as "priestly officers."[7] Magistrates, however, issued "edicts" that were "proclamations in which they notified the people of their orders and of their intentions."[8] During the later Empire, both pontifical interpretations and magisterial edicts ceased as power was concentrated in the emperor.[9] Another source of law was recognized in "juristic literature" from "books of elementary instruction" to "[s]ystematic general treatises."[10]

As the Western Roman Empire fell to invaders in 476, the heirs to Roman law in the Eastern Empire were faced with a great mass of legislation, interpretations, edicts, and juristic literature. In 527, as Justinian become emperor of the Eastern Empire, he instructed his chief legal adviser, Tribonian, to gather the legal experts of the day and compile the whole body of the Roman Law into one clear, coherent statement:

> Everything obsolete or unnecessary was to be omitted, all contradictions and repetitions were to be removed, additions and even changes might be made, and, where convenient, several enactments might be put together. . . . [All] were to be arranged in titles according to their subject-matter, and chronologically within each title.[11]

First, a "Code" was compiled and enacted. "Thereafter, previous enactments . . . might be cited only as they appeared in the new collection."[12] Next, a "Digest" was compiled of juristic writings, consisting of only what the compilers "thought best wherever they found it." Thereafter, writings not included in the Digest were denied authority, and "commentaries were forbidden, for these, Justinian thought, would only lead to doubt and confusion."[13] Then, the "Institutes" was prepared to serve as an "introductory text-book" for the study of law.[14] Last, the "Novels" were started to collect new legislation following the enactment of the Code, including clarifications of unclear provisions of the Code, which Justinian "ordered to be referred to himself for decision."[15]

Civil Law

The Code, the Digest, the Institutes, and the Novels of the Roman law as enacted by Justinian—together known as the *Corpus Juris Civilis*—form the basis of much of the civil law system of continental Europe. The civil law system continues to be based largely on codes:

> The systematic and comprehensive nature of the code with supporting legislation makes [civil] law statute-oriented to an extent that is otherwise impossible; and the code and supporting legislation provide the skeleton of the whole of private law.[16]

In some nations, even interpretation of the codes is limited to legislators. In most civil law nations, however, the interpretation of codes may be done by administrators and judges who look to custom and to the writings of scholars for guidance, but such "derivative law" is not viewed as a major innovative force. The civil law system remains "basically and primarily statute law."[17]

Anglo-Saxon Law

Soon after the time of Justinian, Anglo-Saxon culture in England was reaching the "Code" epoch, as defined by Sir Henry Maine, with the "dooms" of King AEthelberht of Kent.[18] Laws from other parts of England followed, to be incorporated by King Alfred at the end of the ninth century in "a code of general application for the whole of his dominions."

> Alfred's code is most significant as marking the beginning of a continuous era of legislation which helps make the tenth century the most notable in the history of the Old English polity.[19]

Further legislation of the kings in the tenth and early eleventh centuries was "commonly promulgated at councils held at the principal Church festivals . . . [when] kings held solemn crown-wearings."[20] Then came the Norman Conquest of 1066.

Selection 3(A). From the Conquest to Edward I

F. W. MAITLAND, THE CONSTITUTIONAL HISTORY OF ENGLAND 6–21 (1950).

The Norman Conquest is an event of the utmost importance in the history of English law; still we must not suppose that English law was swept away or superseded by Norman law. We must not suppose that the Normans had any compact body of laws to bring with them. They can have had but very little if any written law of their own; in this respect they were far behind the English. . . .

The proofs of the survival of English law can be briefly summarised. In the first place one of the very few legislative acts of William the Conqueror of which we can be certain, is that he confirmed the English laws. . . . Then again, after the misrule of Rufus, Henry I on his accession (1100) confirmed the English law. . . . Secondly, these confirmations . . . seem to have set several different persons on an attempt to restate what [English] law had been. We have three collections of laws known respectively as the *Leges Edwardi Confessoris, Leges Willelmi Primi, Leges Henrici Primi.* These are apparently the work of private persons; we cannot fix the date of any of them with any great certainty. . . . Thirdly, Domesday book, the record of the great survey made in the years 1085–6—the greatest legal monument of the Conqueror's reign—shows us that the Norman landowners were conceived as stepping into the exact place of the English owners whose forfeited lands had come to their hands; the Norman represents an English antecessor whose rights and duties have fallen upon him. . . .

At the same time it must be admitted that there has been a large infusion of Norman ideas. Occasionally, though but rarely, we can place our finger on a rule or an institution and say 'This is not English.' Such is the case with trial by battle, such is the case with the sworn inquest of neighbours which comes to be trial by jury. . . . The valuable thing that the Norman Conquest gives us is a strong kingship which makes for national unity.

No one of the Norman kings . . . was a great legislator. The genuine laws of William the Conqueror are few. . . . From the lawless Rufus we have no law. Henry the First on his accession (1100) purchases the support of the people by an important charter—important in itself, for it is a landmark in constitutional history, important also as the model for Magna Carta. Stephen also has to issue a charter, but it is of less value, for it is more general in its terms. It is as administrators rather than as legislators that William the First and Henry the First are active. . . .

Henry II (1154–89), Richard (1189–99), John (1199–1216).

The reign of Henry II is of great importance in legal history; he was a great legislator and a great administrator. Some of his laws and ordinances we have, they have been casually preserved by chroniclers; others we have lost. The time had not yet come when all laws would be carefully and officially recorded. At his coronation or soon afterwards he issued a charter, confirming in general terms the liberties granted by his grandfather, Henry I. . . .

. . . [B]y providing new remedies in his own court Henry centralized English justice. From his time onwards the importance of the local tribunals began to wane; the king's own court became ever more and more a court of first instance for all men and all causes. The consequence of this was a rapid development of law common to the whole land; local variations are gradually suppressed; we come to have a common law. . . .

. . . [I]n 1166 . . . Henry began a great reform of criminal procedure. Practically, we may say, he introduced the germs of trial by jury: the old modes of trial, the ordeals and the judicial combat, begin to yield before the oath of a body of witnesses. . . .

. . . .

Henry's reign finished, we look onwards to Magna Carta. Under Richard the tradition of orderly administration, of the concentration of justice in the king's court was maintained. Richard himself was an absentee king; . . . the country was governed by justiciars, by men trained in the school of Henry II. Our materials for legal history now begin to accumulate rapidly. Not that there is much that can be called legislation; but it now becomes the practice to keep an official record of the business done in the king's court. Our earliest judicial records come from the year 1194; thenceforward we have the means of knowing accurately what cases come before the king's justices and how they are decided. During the first half of John's reign the country was decently governed, though the legislative and reforming activity of his father's day has ceased. But then John casts off all restraints, becomes involved in a great quarrel with the church, in another with the baronage, unites the whole nation against him, and at length in 1215 is forced to grant the great charter.

Henry III (1216–72).

The great charter, from whatever point of view we regard it, is of course a document of the utmost importance. The first thing that strikes one on looking at it is that it is a very long document—and a good deal of its importance consists in this, that it is minute and detailed. It is intensely practical; it is no declaration in mere general terms of the rights of Englishmen, still less of the rights of men; it goes through the grievances of the time one by one and promises redress. It is a definite statement of law upon a great number of miscellaneous points. In many cases, so far as we can now judge, the law that it states is not new law; it represents the practice of Henry II's reign. The cry has been not that the law should be altered, but that it should be observed, in particular, that it should be observed by the king. Henceforward matters are not to be left to vague promises; the king's rights and their limits are to be set down in black and white. Apart from the actual contents of the charter, . . . we ought to notice that the issue of so long, so detailed, so practical a document, means that there is to be a reign of law.

. . . .

. . . [W]hen the time for printing came, Magna Carta . . . took its place at the beginning of the statute book. It was constantly confirmed. . . .

. . . From the long reign of Henry III we have not much other legislation; legislation is as yet by no means a common event. The interest of the reign is to be found not so much in the laws that are made but in the struggle for a parliament. Gradually . . . the idea of what the national assembly should be is undergoing a change; it is ceasing to be that of a feudal assembly of barons, it is becoming that of an assembly of the three estates of the realm—clergy, lords and commons. . . .

But it is not only or even chiefly by means of legislation that English law has been growing. The reign of Henry III is the time when a great part of the common law takes definite shape—in particular the land law. The king's court has been steadily at work evolving common law; that law is carried through the length and breadth of the kingdom by the itinerant justices. As yet the judges have a free hand—they can invent new remedies to meet new cases. Towards the end of the reign indeed complaints of this grow loud. It is more and more seen that to invent new remedies is in effect to make new laws; that the judges while professing to declare the law are in reality making law;—and it is more and more felt that for new laws the consent of the estates of the realm, at all event of the baronage, is necessary. . . . We may indeed regard the reign of Henry III as a golden age of judge-made law: the king's court is rapidly becoming the regular court for all causes of any great importance, except those which belong to the ecclesiastical courts, and as yet the judges are not hampered by many statutes or by the jealousy of a parliament which will neither amend the law nor suffer others to amend it. . . .

Edward the First (1272–1307).

Edward I has been called 'the English Justinian.' The suggested comparison is not very happy; it is something like a comparison between childhood and second chilhood. Justinian, we may say, did his best to give final immutable form to a system which had already seen its best days, which had already become too elaborate for those who lived under it. Edward, taking the whole nation into his counsels, legislated for a nation which was only just beginning to have a great legal system of its own. Still it is very natural that we should seek some form of words which will mark the fact that Edward's reign is an unique period in the history of our law. Sir M. Hale, writing late in the seventeenth century, says that more was done in the first thirteen years of that reign to *settle and establish the distributive justice of the kingdom*, than in all the ages since that time put together. . . . Now Hale, I think, hits the mark when he says that more was done to settle and establish the distributive justice of the kingdom in Edward's reign than in subsequent ages. The main characteristic of Edward's statutes is that they interfere at countless points with the ordinary course of law between subject and subject. They do more than this—many clauses of the greatest importance deal with what we should call public law—but the characteristic which makes them unique is that they enter the domain of private law and make vast changes in it. For ages after Edward's day king and parliament left private law and civil procedure, criminal law and criminal procedure, pretty much to themselves. Piles of statutes are heaped up— parliament attempts to regulate all trades and all professions, to settle what dresses men may wear, what food they may eat—ordains that they must be buried in wool—but we may turn page after page of the statute book of any century from the fourteenth to the eighteenth, both inclusive, without finding any change of note made in the law of property, or the law of contract, or the law about thefts and murders, or the law as to how property may be recovered or contracts may be enforced, or the law as to how persons accused of theft or murder may be punished. Consequently . . . , a lawyer whose business lay with the common affairs of daily life had to keep the statutes of Edward I constantly in his mind. . . .

. . . .

The vigorous legislation of the time has an important consequence in checking the growth of unenacted law. Henceforward the common law grows much more slowly than under Henry III. Its growth is hampered at every turn by statute—the judges are checked by the now admitted principle that changes in the law are not to be made without the consent of parliament. Law continues to grow, but it can grow but slowly; the judges are forced to have recourse to fictions and evasions because the highroad of judge-made law has been barred. . . .

Note 3(B). The Five-Hundred-Year Struggle for Parliament

The era of legal development in post-Conquest England had its parallel in continental Europe. At Bologna, academic scholars revived the study of Roman law in the eleventh and twelfth centuries; in the twelfth century, Gratian applied Roman law to compile the principles of canon law. The influence of Roman law thus spread throughout continental Europe.

The influence of Roman law was felt in England as well. Roman influence can be traced in some of the legislation of the Norman kings; it is evident in English ecclesiastical law and the law of admiralty; "civilians" were active in English universities; and Bracton's legal treatise is based in form (though not in substance) on Roman juristic writings. Roman law, however, never came to play a guiding role in English law.

> [F]or a century and a half after the Norman Conquest England was governed by a succession of strong rulers in touch with the main currents of continental thought. They created the centralized institutions in which the English common law originated. Men who knew something of the civil and the canon law so transfigured the old English customary law that they made it a system of law fit to govern a modern state. Hence there was no need, as in those continental states in which the old customary law had not been thus transfigured, to replace it in a later age by a wholesale reception of Roman law.[1]

The distinction between England's common law and the civil law system of the Continent is usually defined by contrasting the influential role of the judiciary in England and the all-powerful role of legislatures on the Continent. In England, as on the Continent, both functions were initially centered in the king. As parliament developed, it also performed both functions.[2] The demarcation of legislative and judicial functions was only vaguely perceived in the thirteenth and fourteenth centuries. As its authority increased, parliament's pronouncements took precedence over the opinions of judges, but parliament never legislated so comprehensively as to displace the judge-made common law.

Nor was a distinction clear between legislative and executive roles. The initial meetings of what might be called parliaments may have been difficult to distinguish from expanded meetings of the king's own council—the *curia regis*. The *curia regis* included the heads of the two main departments—the Exchequer, in control of finances, and the Chancery, which performed a secretarial role including the keeping of records. Also included were members of the nobility and clergy and leading judges.

The *curia regis* occasionally met with groups of nobles, clergy, and merchants to discuss new laws that especially concerned their interests.[3] The meetings became further expanded as lesser landholders and representatives of counties and towns—the "knights and burgesses"—were summoned, since they had to bear much of the burden of new taxes.

The Parliament of Oxford, 1258

According to English legal historian H. G. Richardson, despite "the carelessness of record-makers and . . . the disappearance of many records," a "transition from occasional plenary sessions of the King's court held at no regular intervals to . . . regular and ordered meetings" can be seen "from the middle of the thirteenth century."[4] The development of parliament was accompanied by a change in the character of legislation. The turning point came in the parliament held at Oxford in 1258:

If we were to fix a dividing line between the old conception of legislation and the new, we should, without much hesitation, draw it at 1258, the year of the parliament of Oxford. There had been much miscellaneous law-making earlier in the century; but no one had collected these enactments systematically, and when they were remembered, they were remembered indistinctly and imperfectly. . . . While it is probable that changes in the law of obvious importance were always surrounded with a certain amount of formality, in some cases a new writ apparently passed into use and became part of the accepted law without any public notice. The essential thing was the form of writ or rule of law, not the formal expression of the authority behind it. The law in 'Glanville' is largely the result of deliberate law-making, much of which must have been recorded at the time in writing; but the author of that treatise speaks of the laws of England, even those enforced in the king's court, as unwritten. If he knew of any written records of the legal reforms of Henry II, he was unmindful of them; and this was an attitude that changed but slowly in the course of the thirteenth century. . . . But from the work begun at Oxford in 1258 there issued legislation of a character and quality which, if it had any forerunner, could only be found in the Great Charter. . . . Of all these, many copies were assuredly made . . . and they passed at once into circulation. . . . If the precise machinery by which they became available to the legal profession and to the general public is still to some extent a matter of conjecture, of the fact there can be no doubt.[5]

Sealed Statutes

The distribution of copies of legislation was the task of the Chancery. Clerks in Chancery copied the statutes as drafted by royal officials and approved by parliament, and distributed the copies under the royal seal to ministers, sheriffs, and justices.

[T]he intention was that the contents should be read in open court and other public places and, further, that the document should be preserved for reference by local officials . . . and also, apparently, for the multiplication of copies.[6]

Sealed statutes served as authoritative texts well into the fourteenth century until parliament acquired "a special responsibility for legislation" and more systematic records were developed.[7]

Rolls of Parliament

Systematic records of parliament began at the end of the thirteenth century. From 1290, petitions to parliament, together with "pleadings before the council, interspersed with memoranda of matters relating to legislation and taxation" began to be collected on parchment rolls that have come to be called the Rolls of Parliament.[8] They were drawn on "no uniform plan" and have been called "haphazard," "careless," "repetitive and ill-digested,"[9] but the Rolls of Parliament were a significant advance in parliamentary record keeping.[10]

Statute Rolls

The Rolls of Parliament included statutes relating to individuals (private acts) and specific localities (local acts), but, from 1299, acts of general application were recorded on separate Statute Rolls. Early Statute Rolls suffered from "many instances of errors and deficiencies," but "the status of the roll gradually changed until it would be hard to deny it the right to be regarded as of peculiar authority."[11]

Private Compilations

The Rolls of Parliament and the Statute Rolls, like the plea rolls of the courts, were internal government records, although they were on occasion made available for public inspection. The sealed statutes were the public's main source of information about legislation, but the sealed statutes were indifferently kept. "[N]ot even the most methodical of medieval clerks could have produced at will a sealed copy of every statute it might be desired to consult in court."[12]

Lawyers, therefore, resorted to "private enterprise" to make their own collection of statutes. Such collections were collated when possible against sealed statutes or the rolls, but they were commonly "garbled and mutilated." Still, as often the only statutes widely available, private collections gained the "authority of tradition."[13]

Edward III (1327–77)

Parliament's legislative powers continued to grow as kings needed taxes to support their military adventures or as inept kings weakened royal powers. For example, in 1327, Edward II, the philandering son of Edward I, was overthrown by his wife Isabella and her lover, Mortimer. They placed the fourteen-year-old Edward III on the throne and ruled on his behalf for three years. At seventeen, Edward III took over, had Mortimer executed, and began a reign that was to last fifty years. The turmoil had so weakened royal power that in the first year of Edward III's reign, parliament began to initiate legislation by petitions to the king, instead of following the previous practice of waiting for the king's initiative. This development has been called "a momentous innovation."[14]

By 1340, parliament adopted the slogan "redress before supply"—requiring the king to answer parliament's petitions before parliament would act on the king's revenue requests. In 1341, parliament gained the right to pass on major appointments of royal officers and judges; Edward III had second thoughts and tried to repeal this provision, but parliament reinstated it and established the principle that "only parliament could make and unmake statutes."[15] In this period, the "commons"—or the knights and burgesses, who had been attending parliaments regularly since 1310— became the originators of most parliamentary petitions.[16] This was the beginning of the division of parliament into the House of Commons and the House of Lords. Thus, in the fourteenth century, the "basic foundations of parliamentary government were laid."[17]

During the reign of Edward III, parliament was also assigned its own clerical staff from the Chancery. The Rolls of Parliament, which until then had been irregularly prepared and scattered in several locations, became part of the Chancery's records.[18] The clerks, however, held on to the rolls as long as possible to reserve "the profitable means of providing copies of private . . . acts if any were required in the course of litigation."[19]

The House of Lancaster (1399–1461)

More royal turmoil followed the reign of Edward III as his successor, Richard II, was deposed in 1399 by a nobleman, Henry of Lancaster. The House of Lancaster retained the crown until 1461, but the period was marked by constant strife and, consequently, much-weakened royal power.

The years of Lancaster rule marked a peak in the power of parliament that was not to be reached again until the eighteenth century. Members of parliament gained limited rights of free speech in parliament and immunity from arrest. In 1414, royal attempts to amend statutes were defeated. Thereafter, parliamentary consent was required for amendments as well as for enactments and repeals.

Most important, beginning in 1445, parliament began presenting "bills" drafted in statutory form to the king. Until that time, the parliament drafted only petitions, the king replied to the petitions, and the parliament's petitions and the king's replies were then sent to agents of the king (usually judges) to be drafted into statutes. This gave the king considerable latitude to influence the outcome. With the advent of bill procedure, "the Parliamentary edifice was complete."[20]

Bills

Bill procedure also brought about a new parliamentary record. Bills were drafted on paper and were copied on parchment if they received consideration by the Commons or the Lords. Parchment bills came to be separately enrolled, and some have also been preserved as individual slips.[21] Bills that passed parliament have been preserved from 1497 as "Original Acts," which are the "ultimate source" from which the rolls were copied.

> Unlike the Roll . . . , valuable but not very informative, the Original Acts . . . often contain evidence touching the fortunes of bills during passage, in the form of amendments on the face of the bill, provisos attached to it on parch-

ment schedules, and on occasion paper sheets of amendments proposed by the second House to see the bill which got filed with the act.[22]

The House of York and the Tudors (1461–1603)

The House of Lancaster was deposed in 1461 by another noble family, the House of York, which reigned until 1485 and was then deposed by the Tudors. Both the York and Tudor rulers tended toward royal absolutism and reduced the powers of parliament. "Only abnormal royal weakness permitted such abnormal power to parliament, and parliament quickly lost it under the strong Yorkists and Tudors."[23]

The first Tudor monarch, Henry VII, called only one parliament in the last twelve years of his reign. His successor, Henry VIII, in turn, used parliament to his own ends—especially the so-called Reformation Parliament of 1529, which eliminated the power of the Catholic church and established a national church with the king at its head. Henry VIII was thus able to obtain the divorce he could not obtain from the Catholic church and to fan the growing nationalism of the era. In 1539 he even had parliament authorize, for a time, that royal proclamations were to have the force of statutes (with some limitations, the most important being that proclamations could not impose the death penalty or alter fundamental law).[24]

The last Tudor ruler, Queen Elizabeth, reigned from 1558 to 1603—a golden age of culture and stability but an era in which parliament's powers further declined. Legislative initiative was firmly in royal hands, and the queen severely restricted parliament's rights. "Discussion or action [in parliament] could take place only if [the queen] had given her permission."[25]

Printed Statutes

The records of parliament also underwent considerable changes in the fifteenth and sixteenth centuries. In 1468 the Statute Rolls were discontinued, and all statutes were added to the Rolls of Parliament. Not long after, in 1484, the first statute was printed. From that date on, slips and sessional volumes of public, general statutes have been printed in an unbroken succession.

Journals

In 1503, the House of Lords began to publish a journal recording petitions, proceedings, and other matters, followed in 1547 by the Journal of the House of Commons. Concurrently, beginning with the Reformation Parliament of 1529, the Rolls of Parliament stopped recording such mat-

Statuta apu̅ Westmonasteriu̅ edita Anno primo Re-
gio Ricardi tercij

Richard per la g̃ra & Dieu Roy Dengleterre
& Fraunce e signour Dirland puis la conq̃ste
tierce Al honour de Dieu e & saynt Esglise p
we̅n ꝑfite du Royalme Dengleterre a o̅ ꝓmier pla-
ment tenus a Westm le Biutisme tierce io̅ & Januer lan &
o̅ reigne ꝓmier de ladups e assent de̝ seignours espu̅elz et
temporelz e le̝ we̅ns du dit royalme Dengleterre au dit pa̅
ament sommonez per auctorite & m̅ le parliament a̅d ordey-
ne e establie p quiete & o̅ people et apnez Statutz e Ordina̅
ez en la fourme q̃ sensupe Ca i Primierment p co q̃
per priuez e disconuz feffementz g̃und̅ nonsuerte trouble co
stez e g̃ruez Expacions & iour en io̅ accruont enter le̝ sub-
iectez du roy entant q̃ nult home qui achate le̝ te̅nez ren-
tez e seruicez ou aut̅ enheritamentes ne fe̅mi̝ q̃ ount Jo̅c-
tura en Dower en asaint le̝ te̅nez ou aut̅ enheritamentz:
Ne le̝ darrainz Volunte̝ de̝ homez de̅ ꝓformie̝ Ne lisse̝ a
e̅me & Bie ou d̅ anz ne Annuitees g̃unte̝ a ausaun pson
ou psonez pur lour seruice̝ pur e̅me & lour Bie̝ ou auter-
ment sont en ꝓfaite suerte ne sanz g̃und trouble e Anik de̝
te̅z per cause de le̝ priuez e disconuz feoffementz Pur le
medye de̝ que̝ Il est ordigne establye e enacte p ladups &
le̝ seignours espirituelz e temporelz e le̝ we̅ns en ast pre
sent parliament assemble̝ e p auctorite diatt . que che̝scun
Estate Feffement Doon Reise Graunte Lesse̝ e Confir-
macions d̝. te̅z. te̅ne̝. re̅te̝. seruice̝. ou enheritame̅
te̝ faite̝ ou eue̝ ou en apres e̅e faite̝ ou eue̝ per asaun pson
ou persones e̅e̅antes de pleyn age & sayn memorie alarge e
miene en duresse a ausaun person ou psones e toute̝ re̅oue̝ e
execucions eue̝ ou faite̝ soient bono e effecuele̝ a celp a qi
il est ency faite̝ esse̝o ou e̅ne̝ e a toute̝ aute̝ a o̅ oeps en-
conter le e̅ndour feoffour e̅nour ou graunt̅our . ene e en
counter le̝ e̅ndours Fiffours Donours ou graunt̅ours
            a ii

ters and became simply a roll of statutes. The journals, however, were prepared with a "businesslike conciseness" that "severely limits the information supplied."

> [W]e can track bills and when a vote is recorded usually get the names of those dissenting from the majority verdict; but about actual goings-on in the House we learn virtually nothing.[26]

Printed Compilations

Private compilations continued to be the main source of statutes for lawyers into the nineteenth century. Such collections were incomplete, only partially collated with official records, with some statutes translated from the original Latin or law French into English, some not translated, and some translations accompanied by the originals, some without the originals.[27] In 1618, Ferdinando Pulton, a venerable lawyer, gained access to the official rolls, and his compilation became standard for more than a century until replaced in 1735 by a compilation by William Hawkins.

The Stuarts (1603–49)

The royal absolutism of the York and Tudor eras was continued by the Stuarts, who succeeded the Tudors after the reign of Queen Elizabeth. The first Stuart, James I, is noted in history for his theory of the "divine right of kings," which left no room for limitations on royal powers. Nevertheless, parliament's gains of the fourteenth and fifteenth centuries proved real when revived in later times.

> The advance and the precedents were recorded in the historical memory and tradition of England and in such records as the Parliament Rolls and the Statutes to be read by future generations who were prepared to convert them into a permanent constitutional scheme.[28]

Sir Edward Coke

The struggles between royalty and parliament climaxed in the seventeenth century. The seventeenth-century leader who did more than anyone to revive the constitutional concepts of the Lancaster era was Sir Edward Coke.

Coke played an active role in public life in all three branches of government. Between 1589 and 1616 Coke spent twelve years as attorney general, ten years as a judge, and five years in parliament. His views emerged most clearly in his judicial role. As judge, Coke defied royal attempts to influence cases and refused to give effect to royal proclamations not approved by parliament.[29] (He also asserted that parliamentary statutes could be invalidated by the judiciary if "against common right and reason"[30]—an idea that did not catch on in England but was reborn in the constitutional law of the United States.)

Coke sought authority for limiting royal powers, combing the sources from the yearbooks to the parliamentary precedents of the fourteenth and fifteenth centuries and weaving these sources into his law reports.[31] His perseverance got Coke fired in 1616. (Among the charges against him were alleged "errors" in his reports—and among those helping to draw up Coke's indictment was his great rival Sir Francis Bacon, who at the time was counselor to the king.)

In 1620, Coke renewed his career as a member of parliament and espoused the powers of parliament so ardently that he was briefly jailed. (Among the emotional high points of this era of confrontation between king and parliament, James I personally entered parliament in 1621 and tore a "Protestation" against some of his actions out of the Commons journal.)

Following the death of James I in 1625 and his succession by Charles I, Coke was instrumental in drafting the Petition of Right of 1628, which has been called "one of the three important constitutional documents limiting the power of the King"[32] (the other two being the Magna Carta and the Bill of Rights, which was to come in 1689).

The Civil War

Coke died in 1634 on the threshold of an era that would see confrontation between king and parliament reach its ultimate limit. In 1639, Charles I found himself in a war with Scotland. The war needed to be funded, and Charles I called a parliament to appropriate the funds. But parliament refused unless Charles I addressed some of the parliament's growing list of grievances. Charles then disolved the parliament (which came to be known as the Short Parliament) and tried to raise the money by force.

Defeated by the Scots, Charles I reconvened a parliament in 1640. (This parliament came to be known as the Long Parliament, since it technically remained in session until 1660.) The parliament proceeded to enact measures limiting royal power, requiring that parliaments be held at least once every three years, and even having the king's closest adviser, the earl of Strafford, beheaded.

In medieval fashion, Charles I then raised an army on his own and called on nobles to support him. His support came largely from Anglicans. His opponents responded with an army of their own, largely made up of Puritans, who dissented from the Anglican state religion. A four-year civil war ensued, from 1642 to 1646, which Charles I lost after an able general, Oliver Cromwell, shaped the dissenters' forces into a disciplined army. In 1648 fighting broke out again. This time, Charles I not only lost but was captured and beheaded in 1649. (The majority of the Puritans in parliament opposed the execution and were dismissed by Cromwell's forces—

leading this portion of the Long Parliament to be called the Rump Parliament.)

The Protectorate (1649–60)

The following decade was the only period in recorded history when England's government was not headed by a king or queen. Oliver Cromwell tried to work through a parliament that he hand-picked (the Barebones Parliament); a written constitution— the Instrument of Government—was tried; and a "Protectorate" was established in which Cromwell's role resembled that of a king. Radical factions called Levellers and Diggers pushed for more sweeping changes but could not agree enough to be effective. Among the projects often proposed, but not acted on, were various schemes for simplifying the law so that the general citizenry could understand it and do away with the need for lawyers.

The Restoration

After Cromwell's death in 1658, no equally able successor emerged, and the country turned to the exiled son of Charles I, who returned and was "restored" as Charles II. After the Restoration, all the legislation of the revolutionary era, from 1642 to 1660, was declared invalid and struck from the statute books. However, the legislation that Charles I was forced to accept between 1640 and 1642 remained in force. Charles II also accepted a form of amnesty for participants in the civil war, and parliament continued to pass further legislation limiting royal power.

Charles II, however, was able to prevail over parliamentary opposition to have his brother, James, a Catholic, succeed him. He became James II in 1685.

The Glorious Revolution

Three years after James II assumed the throne, opposition forces were aroused by his measures favoring Catholics. They turned to James II's Protestant daughter, Mary, and her Dutch husband, William of Orange, who achieved a bloodless victory over James II in 1688 in what came to be called the Glorious Revolution.

William and Mary became joint rulers, but their rule was hedged with conditions imposed by parliament. The conditions were embodied in the Bill of Rights of 1689 and in subsequent statutes that spelled out the required frequency of parliaments, the free-speech rights of members of parliament, and parliament's control over taxation. The royal suspension of laws was prohibited; certain individual rights were recognized, including a limited freedom of religion (for Protestants), and judges were freed from royal control. Thus, at the end of the seventeenth century, parliament "became, to all intents and purposes, theoretically sovereign in England."[33]

Selection 3(B). Codification

B. Shapiro, *Codification of the Laws in Seventeenth Century England*, 1974 WISC. L. REV. 428, 429–65.

In searching for codification in English law, it is necessary to bear in mind that the continental concept of code is composed of three basic ideas. First, the code is the complete body of law within the jurisdiction. Second, the code is the voice of the sovereign and must be enacted by the sovereign, although sovereignty in different polities may be deemed to lie in different places. Third, the code is an ordering, simplifying and systematizing of the authoritative legal materials so that they may be retrieved easily. If we insist that all three elements be present in pure and unadulterated form before we speak of codification, then indeed the history of English and American codification consists of a few relatively isolated incidents. On the other hand, if we will content ourselves with various incomplete and adulterated combinations of the three, then at least in 17th-century England, there is a great deal of commentary, and some government action, that may fairly be included under the codification rubric.

To briefly anticipate, three important strains of codification are evident in England during the early modern period. First is a movement to systematize the statutes, or at least the criminal statutes, purging them of obscure and contradictory provisions and reducing them to a simple and orderly form. Second is a movement to "methodize" the common law; to somehow reduce it to a body of materials from which the fundamental legal rules might easily be retrieved. In some instances these two movements were combined in a call for reducing all the law of England, both statute and common, to a simplified and systematically organized whole. Third there was a radical movement to replace the entire traditional body of English law with a short, simple code derived from the principles of natural justice and/or the Bible. All three of these movements pursued the goal of easy retrievability and the necessity of enactment by the sovereign, but the first two typically put forward less than monopolistic demands for systematization of law.

. . . .

I. Early Sixteenth Century Origins

. . . .

. . . A number of English humanists were interested in social and legal reform. Thomas More, well versed in European intellectual concerns, led the way with his indictment of the English legal system and his advocacy of a system requiring only a few easily understood laws. His Utopians censured nations with "an infinite number of laws and interpretations" and thought it "highly unjust to bind men by laws that are too numerous to be read, and are too obscure to be readily understood." The law, therefore, must be clear and promulgated. But although More obviously found some kind of rationalization and simplification desirable, he did not appear to have used even his short period as Lord Chancellor to implement a reform program centered on codification.

. . . Thomas Starkey, another humanist . . . , favored either the "reduction" of the law to make it more easily accessible or the replacement of the common by the presumably more rational civil law. . . .

. . . [B]ills for "Reformation of diverse Laws and Process in the Laws of this Realm" and for "Reformation of the Common Laws of the Realm" [were] introduced late in 1547. . . . It had been argued, without a great deal of evidence, that although law reform was much in the air in the early decades of the 16th century, the lawyers in Parliament traded their cooperation in other areas for the defeat of law reform bills.

. . . .

II. Elizabeth and Bacon

English interest in codification had a tendency to wax and wane. . . . Beginning in the latter portion of Elizabeth's reign, however, there was a revival of interest and a good deal of activity emanating largely from high administrative circles or possibly from the Queen herself. We can trace a new period of interest in codification schemes beginning in 1584 and running until the outbreak of the revolution of 1640 when the movement began to compete with a radical vision of a rationalized legal system.

In December 1584 . . . a committee was formed to review the "excessive number of penal laws in force," [but] little was accomplished in the 1584 session. . . . Nevertheless, the movement of 1584 set the standard for codification efforts for many years. Until the outbreak of revolution, most calls for codification, simplification, or reduction would concentrate on the penal statutes rather than on the common law as a whole.

The simplification of the law demanded by the Crown came before Parliament again in 1593. . . . Francis Bacon, who would in time become the chief spokesman for codification, . . . urged his parliamentary colleagues forward. . . .

Bacon took the project very seriously. In 1592 he praised the Queen for a "course taken by her own direction for the repeating of all heavy and snared laws, if it had not been crossed by those to whom the benefit it should have redounded." If this suggests opposition from the legal profession, Bacon was willing to try to convince the lawyers on their own ground. His masque *Gesta Grayorum* of 1594 at the Gray's Inn Christmas revels brought his codification proposals directly to a legal audience. In the masque a councillor advises the ruler to "purge out multiplicitie of laws, clear the uncertainty of them, repeal those that are snaring and press the execution of those that are wholesome and necessary. . . ."

The interval between the Parliaments of 1593 and 1597 also saw the inception of Bacon's *Maxims of the Law* . . . [which] contain his attempt to collect the "rules and grounds dispersed throughout the body of the same laws. . . ." The Maxims were only one of many of Bacon's efforts to make English law more comprehensible and retrievable.

. . . .

III. The Early Reign of James I

The desire for codification of the statutes did not die with the passing of Elizabeth. If anything, interest intensified as the new monarch, James I, joined crown officials and parliamentary leaders in the cause of simplification and rationalization of the laws. Early in the reign the proposed union of Scotland and England quite naturally led to discussion of conflicting laws and legal systems. . . .

Bacon took up the new King's challenge. In 1604 his *Articles Touching the Union of the Kingdoms* advised the lawyers of both kingdoms to compose "a digest, under titles, of their several laws and customs, as well common law as statutes; that they may be collated and compared, and that the diversities may appear and be discerned of." The task, he insisted, was not as difficult as doubters might assume. . . . Union thus stimulated English interest in codification.

. . . .

The matter came up again in 1610. . . . In March the King told the Parliament directly of his concern. . . .

James, however, appeared to be asking for a codification program which would include the entire corpus of the common law rather than simply the penal statutes. The House of Commons was quite sympathetic to at least the latter variety of codification. . . . For all the differences between the King and some members of Parliament, one senses agreement in this area.

. . . .

IV. The Baconian Program

A. REFORM PROPOSALS

Bacon noted that the common law had "no Text law," but consisted "in the series and succession" of Judicial Acts set down periodically in the yearbooks or reports. The result was an undesirable degree of uncertainty. He therefore recommended that the common law be "purged and reviewed" and "reduced to fewer volumes and clearer resolutions." By eliminating obsolete and repetitive cases and "idle Queries," by "abridging and dilucidating cases tediously or darkly reported," and by "purging away cases erroneously reported and differing from the original verity of the Record," the Common Law "will be reduced to a corse or digest of Books. . . ." Such a digest would require investigation of the ancient records, comparison of all known cases to eliminate repetition, and thorough analysis of those cases considered to be binding. He also recommended more accurate recording of judicial opinions. In the future, reports compiled by paid reporters would be far superior even to those of the great judges like Dyer and Coke. . . . Bacon's reform program combining statute rationalization and improved reporting indicates that he was not thinking of codification in the sense of freezing the common law at a given point in its development but rather of a variety of means to clarify and systematize the whole body of English law.

Two years later, . . . Bacon offered a new proposal to the King "Touching the Compiling and Amendment of the Laws of England." By 1616, he realized that there might be serious objections to codification from some common lawyers and therefore attempted to anticipate his critics. His strategy was essentially to avoid the appearance of a frontal attack on the common law by resting the practicability of his proposals on the high quality of the existing common law materials. . . . He further contended that his proposals went not "to the matter of the laws, but to the manner of their registry, expression, and tradition: so that it giveth them rather light than any new nature," in order to avoid the current "great uncertainties, and variety of opinions, delays and evasions. . . ."

Although some rationalization was required in the entire corpus of the law, Bacon wished to limit codification to the statutes and specifically rejected the notion that the common law ought to be similarly compiled. He characterized his proposals as suggestions for only modest reform:

> I dare not advise to cast the law into a new mould. The work which I propound tendeth to proyning and grafting the law, and not to ploughing up and planting it again; for such a remove I should hold indeed for a perilous innovation.

. . . .

When the Parliament met in 1621, it was quite willing to consider proposals of this type along with a number of others directed at legal reform. . . . The House . . . appointed a committee which included Sir Edward Coke . . . to draw all the statutes on one matter "into one or more plain and perfect law" and to consider which laws should be continued and which repealed. . . .

Bacon had done a good deal of work on the project in the interval between Parliaments. Coke too was quite anxious to repeal obsolete statutes. While Coke opposed rationalization schemes aimed to "bring of the common laws into better method," and "doubt[ed] much of the fruit of that labor," he outspokenly favored codification and rationalization of the penal statutes. . . .

What is interesting here is that codification was clearly not an "opposition" measure but one on which men as diverse as Francis Bacon, Sir Edward Coke and King James could agree.

The fall of Bacon in 1621 [he was impeached and convicted for bribery] probably slowed the momentum for this and other types of legal reform. Parliamentary concern over more pressing political issues also diverted its attention from codification. Nevertheless the movement continued. Bacon himself was undaunted. Shortly after his loss of power and office, he began work on a Digest of Laws for the King's use. He continued to hope that James would become a "great master in justice and judicature" and an English Justinian.

B. *DE AUGMENTIS SCIENTARUM*

. . . .

The *De Augmentis Scientarum* [by Bacon] contains "the treatise of Universal Justice, or the Fountains of Equity." . . . Bacon found three sources of injustice in society—force, the "malicious ensnarement under colour of law, and harshness of law itself." Certainty was so essential to law that "law cannot even be just without it." Uncertainty, however, was of two varieties: "the one, where no law is prescribed; the other where the law is ambiguous and obscure." . . . Obscurity resulted from "excessive accumulation of laws especially if they be mixed with such as are obsolete," "ambiguity, or want of clearness and distinctness in the drawing of them," "negligent and ill ordered methods on interpreting law," and "contradiction and inconstancy of judgments." The excessive accumulation of laws resulted to a considerable degree from the traditional English method of drafting statutes which "confirm and strengthen former statutes on the same subject, and then make a few additions and alterations." Bacon felt that a preferable method, which would yield "harmony in times to come," would be to adopt a statutory form which "repeals and cancels all former enactments, and substitutes an entirely new and uniform law." He recommended that legislatures review contradictions in the statutes "every three or five years, or as often as it appears good." These should be "examined and drawn up by commissioners appointed for the purpose and then laid before the Parliament" for approval. The commissioners would have the additional duty of proposing the repeal of obsolete and disused laws. In the interim he suggested that the equity courts be empowered "to decree against laws and statutes which are obsolete, and have not lately passed." Relief, however, should not be left to the judge "but to kings, councils, and the Supreme authorities of the state" in the form of proclamations until Parliament reassembled.

If the accumulation of laws is great, or has become confused, they should be entirely remodeled and reduced "to a sound and manageable body." Bacon asserted that this "heroic work" of "expurgation" and digesting the laws required five processes.

> First, let obsolete laws . . . be omitted. Secondly, let the most approved anti-monies [contradictory laws] be received, and the rest abolished. Thirdly, let . . . laws of the same import . . . be erased, and let the one which is the most perfect among them be retained. . . . Fourthly, let such laws as determine nothing, but only propose questions, and leave them undecided, be dismissed in the like manner. Lastly, let those laws which are found to be wordy and too prolix be more compressed and abridged.

Bacon went on to propose creation of a two-fold digest of the laws. The digest would follow the Roman distinction of Digest and Code and would "arrange separately on the one side all the laws received as Common Law" and on the other side the statutes. This was necessary because "in many points, in passing judgment, the interpretation and administration of the Common Law are not the same as the Statute Law." In this "recon-struction of the Laws," the vocabulary and text of the old law and law-books were to be retained as much as possible. The newly modeled body of laws then required confirmation by the legislative body, "lest, under pretence of digesting old laws, new laws, be secretly imposed." . . .

. . . .

V. The Revolutionary Era

A. MIDCENTURY PROPOSALS

. . . .

. . . Codification and simplification of the law was one of the frequently demanded reforms of the revolutionary era. Some of the demands were voiced largely by moderate factions and were similar to those heard earlier in high government circles. Others, more often than not stemming from radicals of one type or another, emphasized the necessity of constructing a simple code. Proposals for a one-volume codification of the entire body of law became one of the hallmarks of Levellers and other radical thinkers. At times, however, the various traditional approaches to reform became so intertwined with radical proposals that it is difficult to distinguish them or precisely specify their origins.

Although codification was discussed in the early years of the Long Parliament [1640–60], it did not begin to attract a great deal of attention until 1647 when radicals began to give the issue new prominence. In 1647 *The Case of the Army Truly stated*, drawn up under Leveller influence, asked that the laws be reduced to a smaller number and included in a simple volume in English. Other Leveller principles included the demand that all laws be reduced "to the nearest agreement with Christianity." Another radical proposal called for a one-volume codification easily understood by laymen. The author assumed that the task was a simple one requiring perhaps three months.

Pleas for codification arose from a variety of sources, with different groups visualizing different types of codes. Some spokesmen, such as the Digger, Gerrard Winstanley, envisioned an entirely new society whose "short and pithy" laws would owe little to those of England. Codification, in his view, was a simple matter. Once complete no judicial interpretation would be permitted. Pamphleteer Hugh Peters also advocated several radical legal proposals, including the substitution of a code inspired by Moses for the common law.

In general the more politically radical envisioned a simple, new society regulated by a few simple laws which might easily be compiled and distributed. Frequently these ideas, which in effect called for the abolition of the common law, were accompanied by proposals for the elimination of the legal profession and many of the existing courts. Since radical law reform plans were based on a nonexistent society (many claimed to be restoring purer pre-Norman institutions), and few if any went as far as actually developing a model code, it is impossible to evaluate the substantive merits of these schemes. Perhaps one should note that the lower and lower middle classes who tended to support such proposals were not very likely to encounter the common law as part of their daily lives. With some frequency the radical reformers cited the example of the American colonists whom they felt were already provided with a simple, easily understood law. The radicals who advocated codification, however, did not make any actual "advances" over their predecessors. For the most part they vociferously advocated creation of a brief code but made little attempt to create one. They tended to be legally naive and assumed that it was the machinations of greedy lawyers, Norman oppressors, or representatives of the Antichrist which prevented realization of their goals.

Not all advocates of codification, however, were naive, anti-common law, or particularly radical. Many of those who envisioned a rationalized and somewhat reformed version of existing law recognized the complexities of any real codification proposal. They tended to think in terms of a difficult and lengthy task to be undertaken by the legal profession. Reformers of this type are in direct line with the efforts of Bacon and other parliamentary reformers of the early part of the century. One proposal of 1649, for example, called for new laws and a new code. A printed English translation would be elaborately annotated by a group of lawyers and laymen to insure certainty and freedom from ambiguity. The commission, not unlike that recommended by Bacon, would sit continuously and make periodic recommendation to Parliament.

. . . .

B. THE BAREBONES PARLIAMENT

. . . [T]he Barebones Parliament [1653], which contained a wider representation from political and religious radicals than any previous Parliament,

... discuss[ed] several concepts of codification during its brief and confused existence. It passed a motion favoring "a new body of the law" which would be easy, plain and short and in accord with the word of God and right reason.... [T]he resolution passed only after "great debate."...

. . . .

Quite in line with past Parliaments, [a] committee first examined the criminal statutes, starting with treason, and proceeding to murder, theft, and so forth. When completed, this project was to be reported to the House and passed.

Evidently there was a good deal of disagreement as to whether the committee was headed in a radical direction inspired by the law of God and "right reason" or in the direction advocated by Elizabeth, James, Bacon, and pre-civil war Parliaments. The creation of the new committee and other actions of the Barebones Parliament were viewed in some quarters as an attack on the foundations of English law and government....

C. CROMWELL AND THE PROTECTORATE

The Barebones Parliament's legal radicalism, either real or anticipated, was among the major reasons for its dismissal and the creation of the more conservative, even traditional, Protectorate government of Cromwell. The desire to use the law of God and right reason as a standard for remodeling the common law apparently frightened the main body of traditional reformers whose basic aim was the better ordering of existing law. The conservative Protectorate government short-circuited radical codification efforts.

Cromwell, now Lord Protector and long an advocate of legal reform, continued to support changes, among which he included the necessity of making the laws plain and short. What specific type of codification he wanted is unclear, though it is likely he favored the more traditional variety. The second Protectorate Parliament offered a program of codification, in a now very familiar vein. A committee was appointed in September 1656 to revise and consider all acts, ordinances, and statutes and to recommend which were to be continued and which repealed. But equally traditionally nothing emerged from the committee....

. . . .

VI. *The Restoration and Sir Matthew Hale*

Despite the tendency of historians to associate law reform and the demand for codification with the civil war period, it is clear that some Restoration thinkers and politicians continued to view codification as a desirable reform.

Sir Matthew Hale was without question the leading Restoration jurist to attempt methodizing and codification. There is no evidence, however, that he ever favored a complete overhaul and codification of the law. He argued that a new model of laws no matter how ably constructed would suffer major disadvantages. It would necessarily be "too strait or too loose," "too narrow or too wide" and would, like all human constructions, require modifications which "disjoint or disorder the fabric." General laws though easily digested were necessarily vague and invited judicial misapplication. Hale, therefore, defended the relatively unmethodical common law as providing greater certainty in specific cases. At the same time he admired the handiwork of Justinian and desired, given the bulk of the books, reports and other sources of the common law and the many contradictory opinions and obsolete items contained in them, "that some complete *corpus juris communis* were extracted out of the many books of our English laws for the public use, and for the contracting the laws into a narrower compass and method." But such a great work required time and the cooperative effort of "many industrious and judicious hands and heads to assist in it."

. . . It would be very dangerous if the task fell into the wrong hands, as it presumably had just a few years earlier. If judges and lawyers refuse the undertaking he warned, it "[s]hall be done by other hands. . . ."

Although Hale was somewhat ambivalent about methodizing, he thought the common law could as easily be reduced to general heads as the civil law. Difficulties of application in specific instances, he reasoned, would affect the common and civil law equally. Despite his many reservations, Hale's own Analysis of the Law attempted to reduce "the Laws of England into a Tolerable Method or Distribution." While he admitted that the complexity of law would not permit reduction to "an exact Logical Method," he felt his volume provided a good starting point. . . . He also hoped his attempt would provide an opportunity for others to improve on his efforts. . . . While methodizing or rationalization is not necessarily codification in the strictest sense, in practice the two are often intermixed or indistinguishable in the writings of this period. . . .

VII. *Late Seventeenth and Early Eighteenth Century*

Parliamentary discussion of codification or reduction seems to have ended after 1666. This development is rather surprising, given the continued legislative interest in other types of law reform in these decades. However, some pamphleteers and other writers continued to advocate codification, though not on the scale of the revolutionary decades.

. . . .

It is unfortunate that these references to common criticism directed against the lack of method, and proposals for systematic and authoritative codification are not more specific. It is interesting to note however that distaste for the civil law based on its allegedly authoritarian predilections are seldom to be heard. For the most part the civil law was viewed as simply an alternative legal system whose advantages either did or did not exceed those of the common law.

. . . .

Most Restoration and early 18th-century demands for codification or rationalization were either pleas for the elimination of conflicting and obsolete statutes or somewhat more boldly for an organization of heads under which relevant common law and more concisely written statutes might be listed.

. . . .

VIII. Conclusion

The decline of interest in codification is puzzling. One explanation has been to . . . view it as part and parcel of Restoration rejection of the revolutionary experience of 1640 to 1660. . . . [However,] there was certainly no immediate reaction after 1660. Indeed at the Restoration relatively conservative authors were most often the sources of the continuing flow of codification proposals. . . .

. . . [I]n accounting for the low level of actual accomplishment even at those points in the century when enthusiasm for one or another form of codification ran high . . . [, p]robably most important were the general weaknesses in English constitutional arrangements. Not only in the area of codification, but in the far broader field of law reform, a recurrent pattern appears. Interest is expressed both by the Crown and the Parliament. Bills are introduced and referred to committees. Then the Parliament is dissolved before legislation emerges. Or Crown and Parliament fall into such conflict over the constitutional issues of their respective governmental powers—issues that led to and then continued after the Revolution of 1640—that they cannot cooperate on the legal reforms that both desire. The same pattern appears during Cromwell's Protectorate. Codification is not an easy task. 17th-century English parliaments simply did not have the continuity or the kind of harmonious relations with the executive branch necessary to accomplish it.

Another aspect of the essentially unstable politics of the period also militated against the success of even limited codification, and here again the pattern recurs. Relatively conservative or moderate forces, well connected to both the Crown or Protector and the Parliament, introduced modest codification proposals usually confined to winnowing and systematizing the statutes. Once the subject of codification was broached in Parliament, however, more radical forces raised the issue of codification of the common law, and this almost inevitably led to, or was perceived as, a radical attack on the common law itself. At that point moderate support for any kind of codification disappeared. The most dramatic instance of this pattern was, of course, the codification proposals of the radical sects during the Interregnum Parliaments which were put forward as part of a program for sweeping away the whole traditional arrangement of English government and society and then rejected by the Protectorate government which itself had been engendered by fear of the radicals.

These political failures should not, however, be allowed to obscure the prominence and continuity of codification proposals during the century. Moreover, the character of these proposals points clearly to the kinds of codification with which common lawyers could be comfortable and which would come to the fore in later centuries. The highest level of 17th-century consensus was on the codification of the criminal statutes, both to eliminate obscure and obsolete provisions that carried the potential for sporadic and arbitrary enforcement and to make the criminal law more understandable to the public. Next came codification of the entire statutory law, not in the sense of writing a complete body of law but of creating an English statute book purged of obsolete and conflicting provisions and ordered so as to simplify the tasks of practitioner and student. Third was some sort of "methodizing" or systematizing of common law materials. Both Bacon's maxims and Hale's outline headings are among the attempts to make the common law more teachable and retrievable by compiling and rearranging it as an alternative to reducing it to statute.

Surely every student of contemporary English and American law will acknowledge the extent to which these proposals have become central features of what we continue to describe as our common law system. To be sure the third has remained largely in the hands of the private compilers of digests, cyclopedias, citators, texts, practice manuals, and reporters rather than flowing exclusively from the sovereign. Yet the quasi-official status of many of them is so clear that it would seem irrelevant to quibble over whether they flowed from Washington or St. Paul printing presses.

Note 3(C). From the Glorious Revolution to Queen Victoria

After the excitement of the seventeenth century, the legal history of eighteenth-century England is tame. According to one commentator, from the beginning of the eighteenth century, "the law remained in its generally static condition" and "stagnation . . . overtook the whole government system" for more than a century.[1]

In 1714, the United Kingdom (the union of England and Scotland) turned to the Hanover line of royalty, who, although German, were closely enough related to England's royalty to make a claim to hereditary succession. The cultural foreignness of the new Hanover ruler, George I, was overlooked in order to keep the Catholic descendants of James II from gaining the throne. George I's lack of acquaintance with the situation in Britain (he did not even speak English) meant that he had to leave governing to others. He did so by accepting the sovereignty of Parliament.

In the eighteenth century, political parties also took root, and the leader of the majority party in Parliament came to be entitled to the position of "prime minister" to the king.

In 1721, Sir Robert Walpole became prime minister and remained in that post until reverses in war forced his resignation in 1742. He is credited with developing the cabinet system of government and guiding the economic development and colonial expansion in which Britain exhibited the dynamism missing from its law and government. Since Walpole, prime ministers rather than kings or queens have been the key individuals in British government.

Jeremy Bentham

Near the end of the eighteenth century, as the French Revolution rocked Europe, interest in legal reform again rose to the fore. The movement for reform was sparked by the philosopher Jeremy Bentham, whose philosophy of utilitarianism had as one of its major aims the development of a simple, all-embracing code of laws. Bentham sought not only the compilation of legislation, and not only the codification of the common law, but the recasting of all legal rules to serve "the greatest happiness of the greatest number"—which was the central tenet of utilitarianism.[2] His philosophy was applicable universally, and he promoted utilitarian codes in the Russia of Catherine the Great, elsewhere in Europe, and throughout the world. His hopes were not fully realized anywhere. The closest approximation to comprehensive codification on utilitarian principles was in a series of codes drafted by John Mill and Thomas Macaulay for India under British rule. On the Continent, Bentham's ideas were contested by German philosopher Friedrich von Savigny, whose "historical" school of philosophy stressed the development of law through the "silent internal forces of national consciousness," rather than through codes imposed by legislatures.[3] In Germany, and throughout continental Europe, however, codes eventually became the core instruments of legal systems, beginning with the French *Code Napoléon* of 1803.

Statutes of the Realm, *1810*

The reform movement sparked by Bentham further bore fruit in a number of legal reforms in England in the first half of the nineteenth century. Among the first was the publication of the *Statutes of the Realm*, beginning in 1810, which compiled statutes to 1714. Though it neither codified the statutes nor even distinguished statutes in force, the *Statutes of the Realm* constituted the first official collection of English legislation ever published.

The compilers of the *Statutes of the Realm* combed through all the official records they could find—the Original Acts, the Statute Rolls, the Rolls of Parliament, and other records held in Chancery. They also scoured England and Ireland for sealed acts and other sources wherever they could be found—courts, public offices, universities, cathedrals, or elsewhere. However, the compilers went beyond official sources and included statutes from private compilations that were considered statutes by "general received tradition." In cases of discrepancies, "various readings" were noted in footnotes. The compilers added: "[A]ny Decision upon the

Degree of Authority to which any new instrument is entitled . . . is entirely disclaimed."[4]

The Age of Reform

In 1830, the reformist Whig party gained a majority in Parliament, ousting the conservative Tory party. Within two years, the keystone of reformist legislation, the Reform Act of 1832, was passed.

Until 1832, voting for Parliament was restricted to the propertied classes. The Reform Act of 1832 extended the vote broadly, assuring a period of Whig domination that lasted until 1860. Another key reform statute, the Municipal Corporations Act of 1835, reformed local governments and created a uniform pattern throughout the United Kingdom. As one historian observed, "it would be hard to imagine a more spectacular break with the past than these two statutes."[5]

In 1837, Queen Victoria was crowned. She reigned for the rest of the century. Her reign marked the height of the British Empire and the continuation of reforms. Perhaps the major breakthrough in the legislative reforms of the Victorian era was the enactment of the Corn Laws of 1846, which eliminated protective tariffs on agricultural imports, a step favored by the emerging commercial and industrial interests, which thrived on foreign trade, and opposed by the propertied aristocracy, which feared foreign agricultural competition.

Reform of the Statutes

The movement for reform included a revival of interest in making the law more accessible. The *Statutes of the Realm* was completed in nine volumes in 1822. A topical index was published in 1824 and a chronological index in 1828. Although this was the first occasion on which dissatisfaction with the availability of legislation in England actually resulted in an official remedial publication, the *Statutes of the Realm* answered only part of the need. The *Statutes of the Realm* has been criticized for stopping at 1714, for including repealed statutes as well as statutes in force, and for emphasizing "received tradition" rather than historical accuracy:

> The vast *Statutes of the Realm* edition incontestably makes good its claim to be the completest collection in existence; in other words, it contains the largest and most varied collection of apocrypha. Its editors were technically competent, but extraordinarily timid. They assembled the materials for a thoroughly critical text, but were so dominated by the tradition of the legal profession that they often printed a corrupt text, because it was the familiar one, and relegated the better readings to the footnotes. Furthermore, our earliest statutes are in French (or occasionally Latin), and so a translation was desirable. This need had been felt since the early sixteenth century, and the early printers had been at pains to provide one. This traditional version was a poor perfor-

mance based upon unsatisfactory texts of the French and Latin. Nevertheless, it was these traditional versions which the editors of the *Statutes of the Realm* decided to print beside their *variorum* text. Once again, they knew the shortcomings of the versions they printed, and put some (but not enough) corrections in their footnotes.[6]

Most important, lawyers needed an accessible source for the current law. The most frequently used source for statute law in the nineteenth century was a privately edited set, Chitty's *Statutes of Practical Utility*. A number of approaches were tried to come to grips with the need for a more comprehensive, reliable source.

Through the first half of the century, efforts to improve access to statutes concentrated on criminal law. In 1816, it was thought that the need could be met by a digest, at least as a step toward the consolidation and reprinting of statues. Legislation was passed calling for such a digest, but a digest was not prepared. Beginning in 1826, some portions of criminal law were consolidated with the support of the prime minister, Sir Robert Peel, but further consolidation was referred to commissions in 1833 and 1845. The 1833 commission issued seven reports—the 1845 commission six. Both concentrated on criminal law, but neither resulted in legislation. Throughout the first half the century, reform was frustrated much the same as in the seventeenth century.

In 1853, hopes were raised anew when the new lord chancellor, Lord Cranworth, announced that he favored reform on a scale grand enough to result in a "Code Victoria." But hopes were to be dashed again.

Selection 3(C). The "Code Victoria"

A. H. Manchester, *Simplifying the Sources of the Law: An Essay in Law Reform*, 2 ANGLO-AM. L. REV. 395, 396–412 (1973).

... [O]n February 14, 1853, the recently appointed Lord Chancellor, Lord Cranworth, announced not only that he was about to attempt a consolidation of the statute law but that he hoped that such consolidation would amount to a Code Victoria. Six years later, however, Cranworth's initiative was spent and the great work which he had set in progress was subject to the strongest criticism. Why did Cranworth fail at the height of the "Age of Reform?" ...

. . . .

Of course, Lord Cranworth was by no means the first to urge the simplification of the sources of the law: that the body of the law should be made more simple, more certain, more available to all the people had been the cry of the law reformer for many years. . . . Towards the end of the eighteenth century, however, it was becoming clear that a reformation of the statutes was necessary. Perhaps the first really decisive step to this end was the enactment of Peel's Criminal Law Amendment Acts of 1826–32. This was a time, after all, during which Bentham's views on the desirability of codification were becoming more well known. Accordingly, there was little cause for surprise when in 1833 the Whig Lord Chancellor, Brougham, appointed a Royal Commission on the Consolidation of the Statute Laws.

The Commissioners reported [in 1835 and] . . . urged the adoption of one of three possible courses. First, there could be a mere reduction of the existing statutes by expurgation. Secondly, there might be a similar reduction together with a classification and consolidation of the remaining enactments. A third and still more radical solution, they reported, would have consisted in a similar reduction, classification and consolidation, with such alterations in the remaining enactments as would make their apparent import correspond with their legal effect.

. . . .

The new Lord Chancellor [Lord Cranworth] announced [in 1853] that he did not propose to renew the Commission of 1835 as he was satisfied that the best chance of completing a general consolidation and digest of the Statute Law would be at once to begin the work without further inquiry as to the best mode of finally accomplishing it. . . .

Bellenden Ker, the only signatory to the Report of 1835 who was still available, was appointed as Head Commissioner. . . . On the face of it his appointment as Head Commissioner seemed an excellent one for here was a man who knew, and had succeeded in, practice: a man, moreover, who was well aware of the processes of inquiry and reform, and a man who both socially and intellectually could hold his own. In 1853 he was about 68 years old. Four other barristers . . . were appointed on a full-time basis as assistants to him. Initially, the Statute Law Board or Commission was to have a life of 12 months.

What did the Board accomplish, then? Certainly no legislation resulted from its labours. [In] 12 months the commissioners did publish three Reports which, with papers attached, amounted to over 600 folio pages in length. Yet the reports themselves are disappointing documents. . . .

. . . .

. . . It was a sorry performance and contemporary magazines recognized it as such: Ker especially was criticized severely. Of course the task was a big one, far bigger than many contemporaries realized. Nor was it a task of the mere scissors and paste variety. Even so, Ker's Board surely revealed a want of method, purpose and means. . . .

. . . [O]n August 5, 1854, Cranworth proposed . . . that a [new] Commission should issue to consolidate the statute law "or such parts thereof as may be found capable of being conveniently and usefully consolidated, combining with that process, if thought advisable, the incorporation of the Common Law; and for the purpose of devising and suggesting rules as may tend to insure simplicity and uniformity, or any other improvement in the form of future statutes". Accordingly, a Commission was issued on August 23, 1854, the members of this large Commission being eminent lawyers and men of affairs.

It was soon evident that the new Commission was neither clearer than its predecessor regarding the scope of consolidation nor more inclined to adopt a comprehensive approach. At its very first meeting the Commission . . . suggested that the only practicable course was to authorize the draftsman employed to recast the entire language of the statutes, and also to introduce amendments within reasonable limits, leaving the exact mode and extent to which the licence should be used to be settled according to the requirements of each individual case. . . . [But] the new Commission was soon persuaded to adopt a different course. For the Commission was advised that it had no general authority to amend. . . . The primary office of the Commission's draftsmen, therefore, as of the Commission, was to present faithfully the substance of the scattered statute law. If such a course were adopted, the Commission was advised, Parliament would have more confidence in the Commission. . . .

Accordingly, the Commission prepared fresh instructions for its draftsmen: now there were to be no amendments beyond the correction of clerical errors and omissions which appeared from internal evidence to be unintentional. . . . However, in June, 1857, the Commissioners inclined towards their earlier view by recommending that the introduction of eight Criminal Law Bills should be made an opportunity for effecting some improvements in the law at the same time. . . .

· ·

Here, then, we have a Commission for the consolidation of the statute laws which is remarkably vague both as to the meaning of consolidation and as to just how it should set about its task. . . .

The [Commission's] second report considered the . . . question of the appointment of an officer or Board whose duty it would be to advise on the legal effect of every Bill which either House of Parliament should think fit to refer to them, and in particular, on the existing state of the law affected by the proposed Bill, its language and structure, and its operation on the existing law; and also to point out what statutes it repealed, altered or modified, and whether any statutes or clauses of statutes on the same subject matter were left unrepealed or conflicting.

Yet all this was little enough to show for three years' work and it was scarcely surprising, therefore, that there should be considerable Parliamentary criticism of the Commission during 1856. . . .

In . . . 1857 the Commission presented its Third Report. It is a slight document. It does list, however, a considerable number of Bills which were said to be in preparation: and the Criminal Law Bills had again been revised and were to be introduced into Parliament once more. This the Lord Chancellor did. In doing so he acknowledged that as yet the Commission had introduced no Bills which had become law—and claimed that they could not possibly have done so in view of the difficulties. Nevertheless, he now believed that they had found their way to doing good service and hoped that in the course of a few years they might be able to reduce the 40 or 50 volumes of statutes then in existence to 10. . . . [But] the heart now seemed to have gone out of the Commission. . . . And in August, 1859, it actually came to an end. . . ." So much, then, for the Code Victoria for which Lord Cranworth had hoped.

. . . .

Why, then, did Cranworth fail . . . ? It is possible to identify five relevant factors, namely: the will and capacity of the legal profession to promote reform in this field, the concern of Parliamentarians that Parliament's legislative role should not be usurped, the reluctance of government departments to proceed with the consolidation of statutes when this might be made a pretext for reopening political arguments concerning the merits of such statutes, the *modus operandi* of both the Statute Law Board and the Statute Law Commission, and the personal qualities of Cranworth and Ker.

Would the lawyers become reformers . . . ? Unfortunately, the lawyers lacked any form of legal education which might enable them to think in terms of broad general principle rather than of slavish adherence to over-literal rules of judicial intepretation of statutes and to their beloved common law.

. . . It was no accident, therefore, that moves for a better form of legal education and for codification went together: and there is some reason to believe that both movements were looked upon coldly by both Bench and Bar. It was a hostility which affected the hopes even of the liberal consolidator for the professional lawyer indeed adhered strongly to precedent and to common law as he knew it. In his view the role of statute was simply to supplement the common law. The Jurist spoke for those lawyers when it referred to [a subcommissioner's] attempt to consolidate the entire statute and common law in the following terms:

> "He could only have made it in forgetfulness of the essential difference between the common law and the statute. The operation is impossible. A code of common law is a contradiction in terms. The function of a statute is to correct and supply the deficiencies of the common law, but not to replace it; and every statute becomes in the course of time the nucleus of a group of common law precedents, by which it is construed and applied. The various clauses of the existing written or statute law may be rewritten with verbal corrections, and in any order of collocation that is thought convenient and the written law will remain unchanged; but the common law would lose in codification every characteristic which gives its peculiar value. No doubt, a code of

statute law could be compiled from the common law, and substituted for it. That would be legislation, not consolidation, and the immediate result would be a prodigious increase in uncertainty."

Now the liberal and practical consolidator knew only too well that any extensive scheme of consolidation amounted to much more than a scissors and paste task. After all how can it be otherwise when the consolidator may be faced with the task of harmonizing the language of Chaucer, Wycliffe, Shakespeare, Congreve and Dickens in a new consolidating statute? . . . Ker realized this at an early stage. The Commission realized it too although, when faced also with the argument that amendments would amount to an improper encroachment upon Parliament's role, it vacillated unpardonably and never really came to grips with the question.

A further obstacle to the consolidator lay in the fact that the rules of the judicial interpretation of statutes were highly technical. Not only did this imply a reluctance voluntarily to adopt a more liberally drafted statement of legislative principle: it could even imply resistance to any simplification at all. . . . It was a line of thought to which Ker returned some years later: " . . . Those really are the rocks which we have. We are induced, on the one hand, to make our Acts of Parliament extremely verbose and extremely precise, to fit them to the principles of judicial decisions, when we have a Judge who decides that a duck in an Act of Parliament does not mean a dead duck, and that ox, cow, calf and other cattle of any kind whatsoever does not mean a bull. A man having all those principles before him, and being employed to draw an Act of Parliament, always draws his Act of Parliament with reference to those principles of construction, and hence in a great degree arises that verbosity which those who frame Acts of Parliament are found fault with for employing. But if you take merely general principles to be worked out by the Judges, you then find that it takes some half a century before the meaning of your abstract law is ascertained. That is the real difficulty of all persons who have either to prepare a code or even to prepare an Act of Parliament." . . .

Moreover, the question of gaining Parliamentary approval to any reforming measure was truly formidable. First, there was Parliament's reluctance to accept any measure as one which went only to simplification of existing law with the consequent unwillingness to forego the opportunity to debate the merits of the measure before it. . . . Secondly, reformers in this field were conscious that if, in introducing a consolidating measure, they included in that measure any change in the existing law this could be said to be an improper encroachment upon Parliament's legislative role. . . .

Neither the Board nor the Commission ever came to grips with this thorny problem. . . . The failure to deal adequately with this problem was surely a potent factor in Cranworth's failure.

. . . .

. . . Was Lord Cranworth suited for such a task? . . . Perhaps the key to his relative lack of success as a reformer lay in his character. A kind and generous man, a leading trait in his character was said to be "his humility and amiability; he was always deferential, and seemed to think that others knew better than himself." His tentative approach had been obvious enough . . . on the inauguration of the Board for which he requested a life span of only 12 months, although he acknowledged that this was quite inadequate for the purposes which he had in mind. Yet such an era of reform above all, was surely a time for boldness. And possibly a Chancellor of less amiability than Cranworth would have required rather more of Ker, the chief agent of his reform, or dispensed with his services. Perhaps a touch of steel and a suggestion of arrogance add something to the reformer's cause. . . .

Note 3(D). Legislation since the Mid-Nineteenth Century

Repeal of Statutes

In the second half of the nineteenth century the logjam blocking reform of the statutes began to loosen. The first successes resulted from the most modest proposals of the Statute Law Commission—the removal of statutes that had lost their validity. In 1856, the first Statute Law Revision Act was passed—dubbed the "Sleeping Statutes Act"; the act repealed 120 statutes. In 1861, a bolder measure repealed 900 "sleeping" statutes. In the same year, portions of the criminal statutes were consolidated, and in 1863, further "sleeping" acts were expunged in a statute that contained a "saving clause" to reassure those who feared that repeal might have a wider ramification than intended.[1] Such clauses were routinely inserted in subsequent acts repealing statutes.

Statute Law Revision (i.e., repeal) Acts continued to be passed in the following decades. To further assure doubters, all such acts have been referred to a Joint Committee of the House of Lords and the House of Commons since 1892.[2] The Joint Committee proceeded to repeal not only statutes clearly no longer in force but also "obsolete, spent, unnecessary or superseded statutes.[3]"

Consolidation of Statutes

The Joint Committee also took charge of the consolidation of statutes in force. A Special Committee of the House of Commons recommended increased consolidation in 1875, but consolidation proposals got off to a slow start. In 1897, such strict limits were enacted for Consolidation Acts that consolidation was suspended for fifteen years. Some Consolidation Acts were adopted in the first half of the twentieth century, but it was not until 1949 that Consolidation Acts were allowed to make "corrections and minor improvements" as well as reenactments of existing statutes.[4]

The Law Commission

In 1965, both statute repeal and consolidation became the duties of a newly created Law Commission. The commission took an expansive view of its role, repealing statutes that "no longer serve a substantial purpose." Sometimes, the Law Commission was overly zealous:

> In 1967, the Riot Act 1714 was repealed on the basis that it was no longer of practical utility, but it was not long before a new offense of riot was enacted in the Public Order Act 1986 in response to the inner-city riots of 1981 and the public disorder associated with the miners' strike in 1984.[5]

The Law Commission also may propose amendments of the substance of the law along with consolidation, provided the amendments are merely designed to effect a "satisfactory consolidation." By 1988, the commission had succeeded in having 175 Consolidation Acts passed, including 31 with substantive amendments.[6]

Codification of the Common Law

Attempts to combine consolidation of the statute law with codification of the common law were less successful. A promising attempt was made to consolidate and codify criminal law in 1882. The attempt failed, but the author of the proposed act, Sir James FitzJames Stephen, created instead a treatise digesting criminal law and criminal procedure. (One commentator has observed that a "good textbook has often been the foundation of a code, and in the meantime is not a bad substitute.")[7]

Successful codification in India and, to some extent, in the United States increased interest in England, especially in the commercial community, and some areas of commercial law were codified—Bills of Exchange (1882), Partnership (1890), Sale of Goods (1893), and Marine Insurance (1906).

In 1925, the law of real estate sales (conveyancing), "the most deeply traditional, history-encrusted" part of English law, was codified.[8] English "codification," however, should be understood as being quite different from the codes in the Roman-law tradition of continental Europe:

> From the point of view of an English lawyer the legislation of 1925 was a revolution, breathtaking. Nevertheless, even this was not "codification" in the Continental sense. Much of the old statute law was left, and still is, in force. . . . But it is the position of the act as regards case-law that really distinguishes it from codification. The re-enactment, for example, of the famous section 4 of the Statute of Frauds (1677)—contracts for land sales to be evidenced in writing—brought with it the incrustation of case-law which it had accumulated. . . And the field is open for future incrustation of court decisions on the new sections of the act. The dualism of case-law and statute law persists. And

case-law plays a very much larger part than it does under the Continental codes.[9]

Codification of the common law is among the duties of the Law Commission, but the commission has proceeded in a much more gingerly fashion in this respect than with statute repeal and consolidation. Since the 1970s the commission has produced studies on the possible codification of contract law, the law of landlord and tenant, criminal law, and family law, but only in a piecemeal fashion. No direct codification measures have resulted.[10]

The relative lack of progress on codification may be attributable to the development of alternative resources for coming to grips with the bulk of statutory and case law. The bulk of case law became more manageable with the publication of a national general digest—Mew's *Digest of English Case Law*—in 1898, followed by the publication of the *English and Empire Digest*, beginning in 1919, and the publication of a national legal encyclopedia, *Halsbury's Laws of England*, beginning in 1907. A digest also accompanied the cases reported in the *Law Reports*. The need for codification was further alleviated by the writers of treatises.[11]

Statutes in Force

The most significant official move to facilitate access to English statutes came in 1868 when a Statute Law Committee was appointed to prepare an official edition of the statutes then in force. The committee's work followed on the heels of the bar's success in reforming law reporting. Like the Incorporated Council on Law Reporting, the Statute Law Committee succeeded in producing a publication that remains alive.

In 1868, a set of all public general statutes consisted of the *Statutes of the Realm*, which stopped at 1714, and individual volumes published year by year since 1714—a total of 118 volumes. Between 1868 and 1878, the Statute Law Committee combed through all 118 volumes and selected the statutes still in force. They found only enough to fill 18 volumes, which were published in a set called the *Revised Statutes*, along with a *Chronological Table* and an *Index of the Statutes*. The set was not arranged by topic but merely reprinted the statutes in chronological order; it also did not do away with the need to consult the complete collection of the statutes; nevertheless, it was a significant advance:

> There are, indeed, two classes of persons whose needs the revised edition will not fully meet, and, it may be added, was not specially designed to meet. The judge who has to decide, the counsel who has to advise, on the construction of an obscure enactment, frequently finds it necessary to refer to the language of Acts, sections, or words, which have been repealed, either as dead law, by Statute Law Revision Acts, or as superseded law, by amending or consolidating Acts. To the historical student the law of the past is even more important than the law of the present. Both these classes of persons require an edition of the

statutes containing everything that has been repealed, either by way of statute law revision or otherwise. But both these classes may derive material assistance from the notes and tables in the revised edition, which show the reasons for each repeal or omission. And to the ordinary legislator, official, lawyer, or member of the public, it is surely an immense advantage to have an edition of the statutes which contains only living law, which is comprised within a reasonable compass, and which may be purchased for a reasonable price.[12]

The *Revised Statutes* was published in a new edition in 1887 and was updated by volumes of current statutes, the *Annual Statutes*, beginning in 1888. The *Revised Statutes* was also updated by supplements and gummed slips that subscribers pasted over amended statutes. A third edition of the *Revised Statutes* was published in 1951, and, beginning in 1972, a new edition appeared in looseleaf binders, under a new title—*Statutes in Force*—containing pamphlet versions of individual acts grouped by topics. The set includes a two-volume subject index. Although the looseleaf format was adopted to allow the timely updating of amended acts, the set has not lived up to its promise of currentness.[13]

Annual volumes of statutes continue to be published as *Public General Acts*. Local acts and private acts are published separately. (The latter are now rare.)

Halsbury's Statutes

Research in the *Statutes in Force* and the *Public General Acts* remains cumbersome, but it matters little, since these sets are seldom used. Instead, statutory research is done most conveniently in a privately published set, *Halsbury's Statutes of England and Wales*, which has been published since 1930.

Like *Statutes in Force*, *Halsbury's Statutes* is arranged topically with an alphabetical index, but *Halsbury's Statutes* has two advantages:

—*Halsbury's Statutes* contains annotations listing enactment and amendment histories of each section of each act, references to related statutes and regulations implementing the statutes,[14] and, most important, references to cases interpreting the statutes.
—*Halsbury's Statutes* is updated in a more timely fashion than *Statutes in Force*, with a Current Statutes Service in looseleaf binders for new acts and bound Cumulative Supplements and looseleaf Noter-up volumes to update annotations.

Subscribers to *Halsbury's Statutes* also have the unusual privilege of being able to receive printouts of the latest statutory information in LEXIS.

LEXIS contains the full text of all public general statutes, and the LEXIS database is more successful than any printed source in keeping statutes up to date. However, LEXIS does not contain the annotations found in Halsbury's Statutes.

Selection 3(D). Legislative History

S. J. Gibb, *Parliamentary Materials as Extrinsic Aids to Statutory Interpretation*, 1984 STATUTE L. REV. 29, 29–37.

In theory at least, the task of a judge is simple: it is "to apply [the] laws made by the people's chosen representative regardless of his opinions."

In practice, however, this is far from simple. Language is a clumsy tool. It is rarely sufficiently precise as to eliminate the need for interpretation. In the words of Justice Holmes: "A word is not a crystal, transparent and unchanged, it is the skin of a living thought and may vary greatly in color and context according to the circumstances and the time in which it is used."

Judicial construction is not a scientific process. This would be impossible by its very nature. A legislature cannot anticipate every potential problem. In any non-totalitarian system it is inevitable that there will be some "residue of free and creative discretion." The difficulty is to determine by what criteria this discretion may be circumscribed.

. . . .

Obviously the starting point is the statute itself. The words used are the single most important evidence of the intent. However, words mean, "in the first instance, what the person to whom they are addressed makes them mean."

True, in some cases there may be no difficulty at all. The words may admit of only the one meaning. This is not always the situation. Essentially the types of problem, which may arise may be divided into four classes:

(i) Words generally possess several shades of meaning and the dilemma may lie in the need to choose as between several equally viable alternatives;

(ii) There may be a conflict between two (or more) provisions of the one statute and the court may be required to select one as prevailing over the other(s);

(iii) The meaning of the words in question may be quite clear but this may be in apparent conflict with the remainder of the statute or productive of an excessively harsh result; and/or

(iv) There may be an apparent lacuna in the statute.

In the past the common law judiciary has demonstrated little sympathy when dealing with statutes. Sir Frederick Pollock suggested that the early rules of statutory construction were explicable only on the premise that: "Parliament generally changed the law for the worse, and that the business of the judges is to keep the mischief of its interpretation within the narrowest possible bounds."

. . . .

Before embarking on any discussion of the materials which may be said to evidence . . . legislative intention a preliminary issue must be addressed. Is there such a thing as the "legislative intention?"

It is by no means certain that a composite body such as a legislature can be said to possess an intention at all. . . . [I]t may be that there is a multiplicity of intentions possessed by the several members of the legislature no single one of which can be ascribed to the body as a whole. Even where it is possible to impute the intentions of the members to the body it may be that the body possesses not one but several, possibly contradictory, intentions.

The notion of the legislative intention is, to some extent, a fiction. . . . However, it is a concept which has been used by the court for some considerable time and remains in use. . . . [I]ts importance follows from one of the fundamental tenets of our constitution: that of the supremacy of the legislature. . . .

Prima facie, the records of the debates and speeches in the Parliament are the most likely source in which to discover evidence of the legislative intention. However, the orthodox position may be stated briefly:

> ". . . What is said by a Minister or by a member sponsoring a Bill is not a legitimate aid to the interpretation of an Act."

The reasons behind this rule are varied. . . . It must be conceded that goals of the sponsor(s) are not necessarily those of the body as a whole.

Lord Halsbury suggested that the result of an examination of the legislative intent might be confusion between what was intended to be done and what was actually done. For this reason he abstained from construing a statute he had drafted. Some writers have extended this argument and express the fear that an examination of the legislative history might be at the expense of the time devoted to the statutory text itself. This view is best encapsulated in the quip that "only when legislative history is doubtful do you go to the statute."

Professor Corry presented one of the most cogent cases against the use of legislative history. His objections stem from the nature of the legislative process which he characterises as less an intellectual exercise in the pursuit of truth than a battle of wits and an essay in persuasion. In his opinion, to appeal from the terms of the statute to the "hurly-burly of parliamentary debate is more like appealing from Philip sober to Philip drunk."

Professor Curtis developed on this theme savagely. In a discussion of the practice of the United States courts in which the use of legislative history is permitted he accused the United States courts of "fumbling in the ashcans of the legislative process for the shoddiest unenacted expressions of intention."

These are not reasons for denying recourse to legislative history as a matter of principle. Rather, these are grounds for proceeding with caution. . . .

Legislative intention is indeed a "slippery phrase." However, the question is not whether legislative intention is discoverable. The question is whether the legislative history is: "relevant and helpful in applying the statute in particular cases."

. . . .

. . . [The] use of legislative history as an aid to the identification of the mischief to be remedied is the least controversial. It is, however, a very fine line between looking to the debates as evidence of the mischief aimed at and looking to that same text as an aid to statutory construction.

The ineluctable conclusion is that legislative history may offer some assistance to statutory construction. However, this is not the end of the matter. As the joint report of the English and Scottish law commissions noted, the courts are merely one part of of the audience to which a statute is directed. It follows from the admission of legislative history into the court room that any lawyer who ventured to advise his clients without having first examined all the relevant legislative history would be acting negligently. . . . To require that they examine the relevant legislative history would add greatly to both the time and the expense involved in preparing cases. Justice Jackson outlined one possible consequence:

> "Only the lawyers of the capital or the most prosperous offices in the large cities can have all the necessary legislative material available. The average law office cannot afford to collect, house and index all this material. Its use by the courts puts knowledge of the law practically out of reach of all except the Government and a few law offices."

. . . .

. . . [A] further problem [is] the "ersatz character of legislative history." . . . If the records of debates were to be regularly admitted into courts, it is probable that the practice of inventing legislature history would increase. At present there is little reason to "cook the books".

. . . .

The objections to the use of extrinsic materials expressed here are essentially practical. There is no objection in principle to the use of extrinsic materials by the courts. Indeed, it is submitted that the reports of law reform commissions and Parliamentary committees should be made available to the courts. These may provide valuable evidence of the general purpose behind the legislation and they may be made as readily available to the general public as any ordinary text.

There has been consideration in Australia of the development of a sophisticated form, of explanatory memoranda. This would be designed to expound the intention and purpose behind the legislation. . . . Ignoring for the present the practical problems inherent in creating such a document, and securing for it some authenticity and/or Parliamentary approval, there seems to be a grave danger of creating . . . a 'split-level statute.' If some additional material is to be relied upon routinely in the interpretation of statutes, . . . the best candidate is the second reading speech by the sponsor of the Bill. If this is to be adopted, however, it is essential that it be made available to the general public and practitioners as freely as is the statute itself. In practice this would mean that the second reading speech would have to be . . . published as an appendage to the Act itself.

Note 3(E). *Travaux Preparatoires*

> England alone in the western world holds rigidly to the rule that *travaux preparatoires* cannot be consulted in order to ascertain the remedy which Parliament intended.[1]

The "orthodox" rule against the use of legislative history for statutory interpretation was first clearly stated in 1769:

> The sense and meaning of an Act of Parliament must be collected from what it says when passed into law; and not from the history of changes it underwent in the house where it took its rise. That history is not known to the other house or to the Sovereign.[2]

More recently, the rule has been attributed to "purely practical reasons":

> It would add greatly to the time and expense involved in preparing cases involving the construction of a statute if Counsel were expected to read all the debates in [Parliament], and it would often be impracticable for Counsel to get access to at least the older reports of debates in Select Committees of the House of Commons; moreover, in a very large proportion of cases such a search, even if practicable, would throw no light on the question before the court.[3]

The rule has been subject to repeated criticism and has been attributed to "the Whigs' mysticism of Parliament."[4] The criticism is summed up in a statement attributed to long time member of Parliament Aneurin Bevan: "[R]ejecting the commentary as evidence of intended meaning of a particular clause [is] like gazing in a crystal ball when you can read a book."[5]

A 1982 study of thirty-four cases involving statutory interpretation concluded that legislative history materials would have been useful to cast light on the "intention of Parliament" if only to indicate that Parliament "either lacked clear objectives, or, had deliberately intended to obfuscate in order to avoid controversy," thus "revealing that the final decision had quite deliberately been left to the judges."[6] The author of the study "strongly recommended that the present exclusionary rule be abandoned."[7] However, legislation recommended by the Law Commission mandating the abandonment of the exclusionary rule failed to pass Parliament in 1980 and 1981.

The orthodox rule does not render all *travaux preparatoires* useless for the purposes of legal research. A long-standing exception to the rule allows courts to interpret statutes in light of their "contexts" or the "mischiefs" that statutes were intended to cure, and that exception has evolved to permit some use of legislative history:

> [W]hat has traditionally been called the mischief "rule" . . . permits evidence of Parliament's intention to be ascertained from material extraneous to the Act, although there are limitations on the kinds of material that may be used and the inferences that may be drawn from them.[8]

The materials that may be used to establish the context of statutes are limited to "pre-legislative documents" such as reports of the Law Commission accompanying recommended legislation.

> By contrast, the explanatory memoranda and notes of clauses prepared by [a government] department to accompany the parliamentary stages of a Bill may not be publicly referred to by a judge for any purpose; and more importantly, the House of Lords has "emphatically and unanimously" affirmed that "recourse to reports of proceedings in either House of Parliament . . . during the passage of a Bill . . . is not permissible as an aid to [the act's] construction."[9]

Nevertheless, even government memoranda, parliamentary proceedings, and other extrinsic aids, such as reports and proceedings of parliamentary committees, remain useful for legal research.

> A judge [and counsel as well] is at liberty to read whatever policy documents he likes in order to arrive at a *private* understanding of the legal effect of a statutory provision.[10]

In fact, English judges have been known to acknowledge consulting sources of legislative history, and some have cited them in opinions, ignoring the orthodox rule.[11]

Moreover, the orthodox rule remains under attack and may be eroded or abandoned in future litigation. Courts have already carved out an exception for the interpretation of international treaties. *Travaux preparatoires* related to treaties are admissible in English courts when two conditions are satisfied: "first, that the material is public and accessible, and, secondly, that the *travaux preparatoires* clearly and indisputably point to a legislative intention."[12]

The key to the future of the exclusionary rule may lie in the publication of *travaux preparatoires*. Since one of the major reasons cited for continuing to exclude legislative history from judicial consideration is the difficulty of gaining access to the materials, even critics of the exclusionary rule concede a need to make the materials more accessible. As one critic of the rule conceded:

[T]he existing ban on the citation of Parliamentary materials should be retained unless and until some means of presenting them in a short and simple form is evolved.[13]

Historical material bearing on the meaning of statutes, however, are of a great variety.

"Pre-natal" Sources

The history of a bill may begin with sources that precede its drafting: government bills may have arisen from commission reports or studies sponsored by the government; they may have been discussed at meetings of the Cabinet; they may have been expanded upon in speeches of ministers and the traditional annual speech of the queen setting forth the legislative program of the government. Some government bills are preceded by "white papers" explaining to members of Parliament the need to enact the bill, and each bill, as a rule, is accompanied by an "Explanatory and Financial Memorandum," which outlines the purposes of the bill and the demands its passage may make on government revenues. Bills may also be responses to requests from outside the government—recalling the ancient practice of Parliamentary petitions.

Government studies, reports of commissions, and white papers are printed in a series called *Command Papers*, which also contains other government publications submitted to Parliament. The speeches of the queen and ministers are printed with other parliamentary proceedings. Explanatory and Financial Memoranda are printed with bills (although not with final statutes). Bills are stored archivally but not published. Deliberations of the Cabinet are not even available in archives; they are kept secret.

Committee Publications

After a bill is introduced in Parliament, it is referred to a committee. The committee may seek further studies, hold hearings, debate, and prepare reports on the bill. Publications of committees are gathered in the House of Commons and the House of Lords into consecutively numbered *Sessional Papers*. Debates of committees are published with the debates of Parliament, although in separate form.

Amendments

Bills are "read" to Parliament thrice and, along the way, may be amended several times. Some bills are accompanied by preambles and long titles, both of which are deleted when the bills are printed as statutes.

Despite their potential usefulness for statutory interpretation, bills are not published. Preambles, long titles, and each proposed amendment can be traced in a printed version, but only at the archive of the Records Office.

Journals

Journals of the House of Commons and the House of Lords have been published since the Elizabethan era. The journals, however, only record the steps each bill has gone through, such as referral to a committee, report by a committee, and vote on the floor. The journals were so limited to shield members of Parliament from the wrath of the king or queen at a time when what was said in Parliament could be used as a reason for political and, not infrequently, even for physical punishment. Resolutions of the Commons in 1628 and 1640 expressly limited journals to the "orders and reports" of each house.[14]

Debates

The recording of parliamentary debates has a colorful history. Debates not only have a low probative value as legislative history (given to variety of views likely to be expressed), but, until the twentieth century, they also have been unreliably reported:

> The exclusion of parliamentary debates could have been justified . . . on the ground that there was no official reporting of those debates, and that the reports which did circulate were highly imaginative . . . and actually unlawful, for the House of Commons regarded them as breaches of privilege.[15]

After Parliament no longer needed to fear the crown, following the Bill of Rights of 1689, Parliament continued to restrict reporting of its debates by what has been called a "curious inversion":

> The prohibition against publishing debates had developed as a shield against the tyranny of the crown. Now it came to be used as a sword to strike down the public demand for information about parliamentary proceedings. Based originally on the possible intimidation the Crown might exercise if debates were reported, the prohibition came to rest on fear of misrepresentation and impatience of the pressure of public opinion.[16]

Nevertheless, journalists defied Parliament and published selections from its debates first in newsletters and then in major newspapers. Such publications, however, were hardly reliable. Among the journalists reporting on Parliament was Samuel Johnson, who admitted:

> I never had been in the gallery of the house of commons but once. Cove had interest with the doorkeepers. He, and the persons employed under him, gained admittance: they brought away the subject of discussion, the names of the speakers, the side they took and the order in which they rose, together with notes of the arguments advanced in the course of debate. The whole was afterwards communicated to me, and I composed the speeches in the form which they now have in the parliamentary debates.[17]

More reliable reporting started in 1803 when the House of Commons assigned reporters a place in the gallery (although the rule against reporting debates remained on the books). From that date, newspaper reporting of debates has come to be replaced by purportedly full transcriptions of proceedings. First a publisher named William Cobbett carried on the work (he also published a compilation of proceedings reported in newspapers in the recent past); then another publisher, Luke Hansard, purchased the business.

In 1889, the set, by then widely known as *Hansard*, was taken over by the government, which used outside contractors to provide the reports of proceedings. The work of the outside reporters was so poor that the government took full charge in 1908. Since 1889, the title page of the set reads "Official Report," but the *Hansard* name was restored in 1943. In addition to proceedings on the floor of Parliament, *Hansard* includes written submissions such as a minister's response to a written question. The full text of *Hansard* is now available in a computer database known as POLIS.

4

Legislation in the United States

Note 4(A). The Colonial Era

The books of statutes accessible to American colonists, like their case reports, largely came from England. English statutory law, like the common law, was applicable to the colonies. However, when it came to legislation, the colonies also had a documentary record of their own. Some of the first printing presses in the colonies were set up in large part to meet the need for publishing the enactments of colonial legislatures.[1]

Prior to the establishment of printing presses, colonial laws were maintained in manuscripts in government offices; they were also distributed to select counties, courts, and sheriffs' offices and were "proclaimed" at public gatherings, as in medieval England. However, the colonists apparently lacked the organizational skills of their ancestors, for the colonial manuscripts were not connected into "rolls" but kept as "loose paper."

Colonists were allowed to have their own legislatures, but they were subject to royal governors and were required to send a copy of each statute enacted by colonial legislatures to London for approval by the Privy Council and the king. Although the colonists found ways to get around the royal veto power (such as enactment of statutes for limited periods), they generally complied with the depository requirement. Thus, the best collection of American colonial statutes is in the Public Records Office in London. In the colonies, ascertaining the law was extremely difficult.

As enough manuscripts of statutes accumulated to cause confusion, attempts were made at compilations even before the introduction of printing. The first attempt was made in Massachusetts. In 1636, John Cotton prepared a compilation of Massachusetts law under the title *Moses and His Judicials* (reflecting the biblical basis of the Puritan legislation of Massachusetts). The Massachusetts legislature, however, rejected Cotton's work and enacted instead another compilation prepared by Nathaniel Ward in 1639 under the less theological title *The Body of Liberties*. The result was confusion, for in the meantime Cotton's work had been shipped to London and printed there in 1641 as *An Abstract of the Laws of New England, As they are now established*. The printed version was shipped back to the colonies and was used as the basis for the law of Connecticut.[2]

In the same period, the first printing press in the colonies was established in Massachusetts. The press apparently never published Ward's compilation, but in 1648 it published another compilation, *The Book of the General Lawes and Libertyes*, which contains a large part of Ward's work. *The Book of the General Lawes and Libertyes* was a work well ahead of its time, as it was not only a compilation but also a topical rearrangement of the Massachusetts statutes. Six hundred copies of this first American law book were printed, but it is now one of the greatest rarities of American bibliography: only one original copy is known to exist; it is at the Huntington Library in California.

Supplements to *The Book of the General Lawes and Libertyes* were printed in the 1650s, and in 1661 a regular pattern of the printing of laws shortly after enactment began with the sessional publication of the Massachusetts *Laws and Orders*. This set continued in an unbroken series until the last days of the colonial era in 1775.

Other colonies were considerably behind Massachusetts. In Virginia, a statutory compilation was prepared in 1662, but it had to be sent to London for printing, as did most other colonial books printed before the eighteenth century. (In London, statutes passed during the Commonwealth period, 1642 to 1660, were omitted from the Virginia compilation, as they were required to be omitted from British books of statutes.)[3] In North Carolina, no printer was available even in the middle of the eighteenth century, and the organization of the laws was described as being in a "shamefull condition."[4] Even where presses were established, shortages of paper, ink, type, and other necessities often delayed publications for years.

Nor was editorial work always reliable. A private compilation from Virginia printed in London in 1684 was condemned by Virginia's legislature as "false and imperfect."[5] A 1710 compilation of New York's laws was described as "not trustworthy," a 1726 compilation as "riddled with errors."[6] Compilations also fell into error when they included statutes that were later disallowed by the Privy Council and king.[7] The poor state of colonial statute law, however, had one beneficial side effect. Owing to the difficulties of public access to the statutes, the compilation and republication of statutory law became "a peculiar American practice"[8]— a practice continued after independence by most states and by the federal government.

THE
BOOK OF THE GENERAL

LAUUES AND LIBERTYES

CONCERNING THE INHABITANTS OF THE MASSACHUSETS
COLLECTED OUT OF THE RECORDS OF THE GENERAL COURT
FOR THE SEVERAL YEARS WHERIN THEY WERE MADE
AND ESTABLISHED,

And now revised by the same Court and disposed into an Alphabetical order
and published by the same Authoritie in the General Court
held at *Boston* the fourteenth of the
first month *Anno*
1647.

Whosoever therefore resisteth the power, resisteth the ordinance of God,
and they that resist receive to themselves damnation. Romanes 13. 2.

CAMBRIDGE.
Printed according to order of the *GENERAL COURT.*
1648.

And are to be solde at the shop of *Hezekiah Usher*
in *Boston.*

The Book of the General Lawes and Libertyes, 1648
(Huntington Library)

Selection 4(A). The Impact of Independence on State Legislation

The Revisal of the Laws, 1776–1786, 2 PAPERS OF THOMAS JEFFERSON 305–324 (J. P. Boyd, ed., 1950).

It is an extremely difficult task to bring into proper focus, to say nothing of fully encompassing, the far-reaching revision of the laws that Jefferson and other leading Virginians embarked upon in the autumn of 1776. This is chiefly because the revision of the laws itself never came into focus. It was a long-drawn-out movement, ending in something of an anti-climax, and never became embodied in a single enactment as in the case of earlier or later revisions in Virginia and in other states. However important for the whole future of society its Bill for Establishing Religious Freedom may have been, the revision as a whole has, for the most part, faded into obscurity against the background of ordinary legislation in the decade from 1776 to 1786. . . .

This resulted partly from its purpose, which was not that of forming a collection of laws then in force but of reforming the entire structure of law so as to strip it of all vestiges of its earlier monarchical aspects and to bring it into conformity with republican principles. . . . Certainly Jefferson's historic decision in the early days of October 1776 to remain in Virginia rather than accept the mission to France was largely determined by his zeal to remake the legal structure of the commonwealth and to remold it both in form and substance so as to coincide more nearly with the leading principles of the Revolution. "I knew," he wrote in his Autobiography, "that our legislation under the regal government had many very vicious points which urgently required reformation, and I thought I could be of more use in forwarding that work. I therefore retired from my seat in Congress on the 2d. of Sep., resigned it, and took my place in the legislature of my state.". . .

. . . Jefferson's achievement as legislator in the years 1776 to 1779 . . . proceeded on a two-fold method.

The first was a singlehanded effort to hasten the new era of republicanism by the drafting of legislative bills on particular subjects—courts of justice, entails, the established church, importation of slaves, naturalization, &c. On these and many other subjects it is safe to say that Jefferson was, as author or chief advocate, responsible for the introduction and adoption of more bills than any other single member of the General Assembly in the years 1776 to 1779. In the variety of subjects touched upon, in the quantity of bills drafted, and in the unity of purpose behind all of this legislative activity, his accomplishment in this period was astonishing. He was in himself a veritable legislative drafting bureau . . . . But

... Jefferson realized that a broader, more systematic revision of the laws was necessary.

His second approach, therefore, sprang from the conviction, as he later expressed it, "that our whole code must be reviewed, adapted to our republican form of government, and, now that we had no negatives of Councils, Governors, and Kings to restrain us from doing right, it should be corrected, in all it's parts, with a single eye to reason, and the good of those for whose government it was framed. Early therefore in the session of 76, to which I returned, I moved and presented a bill for the revision of the laws."...

. . . .

The Bill for the Revision of the Laws was adopted 24 October 1776. On 5 November following, the House of Delegates proceeded to nominate a "committee to revise the laws." ... [T]he majority was in favour of Thomas Jefferson, Edmund Pendleton, George Wythe, George Mason, and Thomas Ludwell Lee, Esquires." ... To be chosen, at the age of thirty three, head of so important a committee and in competition with some of the finest legal minds in America indicates that the suffrage of his colleagues in the legislature agrees with all other surviving evidence as to his leadership and fitness for this work of reform.

The Committee, under Jefferson's chairmanship, met at Fredericksburg on 13 January 1777 "to settle the plan of operation and to distribute the work." ... The first question to be settled, Jefferson stated in his Autobiography, was "whether we should propose to abolish the whole existing system of laws, and prepare a new and complete Institute, or preserve the general system, and only modify it to the present state of things. Mr. Pendleton, contrary to his usual disposition in favor of antient things, was for the former proposition, in which he was joined by Mr. Lee. To this it was objected that to abrogate our whole system would be a bold measure, and probably far beyond the views of the legislature; that they had been in the practice of revising from time to time, the laws of the colony, omitting the expired, the repealed and the obsolete, amending only those retained, and probably meant we should now do the same, only including the British statutes as well as our own: that to compose a new Institute like those of Justinian and Bracton, or that of Blackstone, which was the model proposed by Mr. Pendleton, would be an arduous undertaking, of vast research, of great consideration and judgment; and when reduced to a text, every word of that text, from the imperfection of human language, and it's incompetence to express distinctly every shade of idea, would become a subject of question and chicanery until settled by repeated adjudications; that this would involve us for ages in litigation, and render property uncertain until, like the statutes of old, every word had been tried, and settled by numerous decisions, and by new volumes of reports and commentaries; and that no one of us probably would undertake such a work, which, to be systematical, must be the work of one hand." ...

... The actual scope of the revision seems to lie somewhere between the two extremes of a complete codification or institute advocated by Pendleton and a compilation of laws in force, "omitting the expired, the repealed and the obsolete," that the majority of the Committee, according to Jefferson's remembered account, agreed upon. . . . While the revisal, therefore, did not succeed in "recasting the whole Statutory Code British and Colonial," . . . [t]he General Assembly . . . was well aware that this revisal was not a mere imitation of those that had been made before the Revolution but was indeed a work "which proposes . . . various and material changes in our legal code."

. . . .

[In 1785 Jefferson was in France, and the sponsorship of the reform rested upon James Madison.] Madison pressed for action upon the . . . code that the Committee of Revisors had brought in. At the October 1785 session, as Jefferson expressed it, "by the unwearied exertions of Mr. Madison, in opposition to the endless quibbles, chicaneries, perversions, vexations and delays of lawyers and demi-lawyers, most of the bills were passed by the legislature, with little alteration." . . . This, however, is a generalized recollection that requires modification: it exaggerates the opposition of the legislature and the number of bills approved and minimizes the alterations such bills underwent. The legislature was slow to take up the revisal, but its action in 1785–1786 indicated that its attitude was neither that of indifference nor of hostility. The bills that it selected for approval or for opposition showed that, as legislatures go, its examination of the bills was constructively critical and even discriminating. . . .

On 31 October 1785 Madison introduced one hundred and eighteen of the bills reported by the Committee of Revisors. . . . Only thirty-five of the bills presented by Madison were adopted at this session, though, under the influence of urgent petitions, the legislature did select out of the remainder the greatest of all for adoption—that concerning religious freedom. . . .

The bills that were not acted upon were held over until the October 1786 session and at that time, again under the sponsorship of Madison, twenty-three of them were adopted. . . . By this time, however, it was clear that the General Assembly had no intention of acting upon the revisal as a whole, though the Report continued to be a legislative mine from which particular items were extracted from time to time. . . .

. . . Another Act calling for a revisal of the laws, passed in 1789, asserted that "the great number of laws of this Commonwealth, dispersed as they are through many different volumes, renders it often questionable which of them are in force; copies of those laws are procured with difficulty, and only at high prices; and so many of them have been repealed, wholly or in part, were temporary and have expired; were occasional, and have had their effect; were private or local, or have been reenacted in substance, in the laws, taken from the report of the revisors . . . that scarce a third of them concern the public at large." . . . The Act then appointed a committee of eight to execute this law. The committee was an able and distinguished one. . . . But again nothing resulted. At the October 1790 session another Act was passed appointing . . . a committee to effect a general revision of the laws, with specific directions to ascertain what British statutes there were, if any, that were appropriate but had not yet been enacted in Virginia; to ascertain what general laws should be continued and what discontinued, &c. . . . This Act finally brought about a comprehensive revision, the results being adopted at the October session 1792. . . .

At last Virginia had produced a comprehensive revisal of the laws of the commonwealth. It was narrower in scope and less elevated in purpose than that which Jefferson and his colleagues had attempted, but, at least in respect to legislative approval, its accomplishment was more complete. . . .

Note 4(B). Prelude to Codification

Virginia was the only state to attempt a "complete revision immediately" after independence.[1] In eleven of the thirteen original states, statutes or constitutional measures provided for the "reception" of English law unless expressly changed by specific legislation, or unless "repugnant" to the laws of the new state. In Virginia as well, the piecemeal nature of statutory revision meant a continuing reliance on English precedents and legislation.

Pressure for more sweeping reforms built up soon after independence. Some stressed the desirability of eliminating English influence, especially as relations with Britain continued to deteriorate in the period leading to the War of 1812. Other calls for reform resembled the calls of the Diggers and Levellers during the Commonwealth period in England—calls for radical simplification to make the law accessible to nonlawyers.[2] Such views were especially prominent in the Jacksonian era of the 1820s, which inflamed populist, antilawyer sentiments. The most pervasive reason for dissatisfaction with the law, however, was the charge that it was "inaccessible and uncertain."[3]

The lack of American court reports or texts left the bar reliant on English law books in the years after independence. But uncertainty about the boundaries of the reception of English law threw doubt on the usefulness of English books. Moreover, English books were more scarce than they had been in the colonial era, for "the best of the colonial bar and many of the superior court judges became self-exiled Tories, taking with them not only their knowledge of the law but also their law books."[4]

To remedy the situation, both lawyers and the community at large looked to legislatures. Legislative activity greatly increased until complaints were heard of the "multiplication of statutes."[5] Some states followed Virginia's lead in preparing partial revisions and compilations of their statutes, but, on the whole, "the first postrevolutionary generation was little better at preserving the law they had created than were their predecessors":

> It might be assumed that statute law, being promulgated in a written form, would have been readily available. Such was not the case. In all the colonies,

the statutes passed during the generally annual sessions of their legislatures were published in pamphlet form. But, according to [the editor of] a compilation of New Jersey's provincial statutes in 1776, these pamphlets or session laws came "into the hands of only a few" and were "easily lost." As a result, "a complete set was rarely to be found: Hence it became difficult to know what the law was." A similar situation existed in Virginia, where [it was] claimed in 1803 that session law pamphlets were "extremely difficult" to obtain. "Few gentlemen, even of the profession, . . . have been able to boast of possessing a *complete* collection of its laws." . . . Simple compilations, usually the work of private individuals, were only sporadically printed. A few colonies did undertake to revise their statutes, but nowhere was it an ongoing process, and never was it done at regular intervals.

Even if an individual had a complete set of session law pamphlets or some other collection of colonial statutes, they were difficult to use. Indexes were unknown. Private acts outnumbered public laws, and they were often interspersed chronologically on the same page. Furthermore, . . . "inexperience, inattention, or other accidental circumstances" resulted in "a variety of modifications, provisions, suspensions, and repeals."[6]

In states that compiled and revised their statutes, complaints about the law continued. In Virginia, for example, more than a decade after the revision of 1792, a respected lawyer wrote that the revision was "the parent of new complexities, by the introduction of new law; and the reenaction, omission, or suspension of former acts."[7]

In 1803, France's *Code Napoléon* provided the first realistic alternative to English law for American emulation. The Union's French state, Louisiana, began codifying its laws in 1805. The English translation of the *Code Napoléon* reached the United States in 1812. In the meantime, the ideas of Jeremy Bentham had spread to the United States.[8] The combination of Bentham's rhetoric, dissatisfaction with the law, and the availability of an alternative model resulted in codification becoming one of the hottest topics of public debate.

Selection 4(B). The New York Revised Statutes, 1829

C. M. Cook, The American Codification Movement 131–147 (1981).

. . . [B]y the 1820s, New York was becoming the preeminent commercial center of the nation, and the completion of the Erie Canal in 1825 happily sealed that fate. . . .

This spectacular growth and development placed heavy demands on the legal system and manifested itself in the equally impressive expansion of the size of the objective body of the law. The annual session law pamphlets of New York were rarely less than three hundred pages in length, with some exceeding five hundred pages during the first three decades of the nineteenth century. Each contained a dizzying multitude of separate acts. Following one especially productive session, the New York *American* noted that it had received "a list of laws, 343!!! in number, passed" during the recent session of the legislature. No state had a comparable outpouring of written law. . . .

The enlarged size of the statute book, together with the knowledge that it contained much "useless rubbish," seemingly necessitated relatively frequent revisions. Since the Revolution, New York had undertaken no less than three revisions at intervals of about a dozen years. New York had apparently developed a genuine reform tradition in dealing with its statute law. Only Virginia had made a more concerted effort to insure the accessibility and certainty of its written law.

Even with these almost regular revisions, printers had little trouble selling privately done compilations of the state's session laws. By 1828, nineteen such volumes had been published, some in several editions. With one exception, each was a massive book exceeding five hundred pages, with some approaching a thousand pages. It was only with such tools that the New York attorney could keep abreast of the statutory growth and changes in his state. But the very mass of the law stymied its easy accessibility and certainty. As the idea of codification became popular, New Yorkers began to see its adaptability to their situation.

The growth of the objective body of the decisional law of New York rivaled its statutory counterpart in its own way. Between 1799 and 1823, thirty different volumes of New York common law and seven of chancery decisions had been printed. In no other state was a comparable repository of native case law available.

. . . .

While laymen grumbled a good deal about the law craft, they also had complaints with the law itself and focused their energies on its improvement. It was, after all, the tool with which the legal fraternity exacted their heavy toll from the pockets of the laymen. To remedy this situation, one group of laymen suggested, in a petition to the New York legislature, that the overly technical and highly complex system of laws "copied from English practice" be eliminated and replaced by laws "founded on the plain and simple principles of common sense." The laws, especially those relating to procedure, as they now stood, the petitioners said, "tend to the accumulation of costs, and the discredit of law and its practitioners." . . . A good number of lawyers gave credence to such lay complaints, even acknowledging that lawyers used the defects of the legal system for their own profit. While they probably would have disagreed with any notions that the law could be made simple enough for the average layman to understand completely, lawyers believed that its gross absurdities and artificial technicalities should be removed and the law rendered worthy of the layman's respect and esteem. Codification naturally had a great appeal to these lay reformers. One called it "the *only* reformation worth a moments regard." Lawyers, who essentially determined the course of legal reform, were not deaf to lay demands.

. . . .

Perceiving codification as a danger to the legal order, orthodox common lawyers worked to resist the reform with no less enthusiasm. The fact that they did not take the reform movement lightly is an indication of its apparent strength. . . .

. . . [T]he general codification of the law never came to a clear legislative test in New York in these early years. Rather, codification came to New York only obliquely, through statutory revision. The body of law that emerged from the revision process, known as the Revised Statutes, resulted in a true, if limited, codification of New York law, the first in any common law jurisdiction. Moreover, the Revised Statutes were a clear consequence of the codification movement, manifesting every active element of that reform effort, including the partial codification of selected rules of the common law. It is difficult to say why the New York codifiers did not push the matter of wholesale codification to a decision. Possibly they realized that the powerful opposition within the profession might result in failure, which could do irreparable damage to the codification movement. . . .

. . . .

The legislature assumed that the revision would be no different from those that had preceded it. The laws would be collected, obsolete and private acts would be expunged, and statutes relating to the same topic would be collected in their original form under separate heads. Additionally, the revisors were given special powers to reconcile the statute law with the new constitution [of 1822].

. . . .

At least two of the revisors . . . were . . . sensitive to the need for more comprehensive legal reform. Instead of plunging ahead with their work . . . they believed it was necessary to give "full and deliberate" consideration to how they should best proceed. . . .

[They] expressed their matured conviction to the legislature that the mandate given the revisors was insufficient to attain the best possible results. If they were to have optimum effectiveness, [they] declared they should have the power to "make such alterations in style, in length and structure of sentences, and in arrangements of sections, as will render the statutes more concise, perspicuous, and intelligible." They continued expressing . . . that "our law should be comprised under appropriate titles; and that these titles should be classified in their natural order; and more especially . . . various provisions of each statute should be arranged in the clearest most scientific method, which the nature of the subject will permit." In short, they wanted authorization to codify the statute law of the state, although they assiduously refrained from using the term "codification." While substantive reform was not an important part of their suggestions, it was latent in their desire to rewrite the statutes. Such reform would take on increasing importance as their work progressed.

The two revisors suggested a number of advantages that would accrue from their proposed revision. It would ease acquisition of knowledge of the law by reducing the size of the statute book by half. The law would also be rendered more intelligible and certain by eliminating "the uncertainties and obscurities arising from the long involved sentences, and from . . . intricate and obsolete diction." Once the law were systematically arranged, the necessity for future revisions would be superseded, as changes in the statutes could be easily inserted in their proper place by the legislature. Lastly, once completed, the proposed revision would set an examples for other states to follow. . . .

. . . .

A good number of practitioners expressed strong reservations to the plan or opposed it outright. The crux of their opposition focused on the revisors' request that they be authorized to rewrite the statutes and alter the style and phraseology as they believed necessary. If granted, it was claimed, such power would make the revisors legislators. . . .

. . . [A]n act giving the revisors powers along the lines they had requested was passed by less than commanding majorities. . . .

The new act gave the revisors broad authority to undertake their work. They were empowered to: (1) collect and reduce into one act the different acts and parts of acts relating to the same subject that they believed proper to consolidate; (2) distribute the acts to be consolidated under titles, divisions, and sections; (3) omit all legislation that was repealed, had expired, or was repugnant to the constitution; (4) suggest to the legislature contradictions, omissions, and imperfections in the law and the mode in which they might be ameliorated; (5) designate acts or parts of acts that ought to be repealed; (6) recommend new acts or parts of acts that they believed necessary; (7) complete the revision in all other respects in a manner that they should "deem most proper, to render the statutes more plain and easy to be understood." They were also expressly instructed to make no changes "in the phraseology or distribution of the sections of any statutes, that have been the subject of judicial decision, by which the construction of the statute, as established by such decisions, should be affected or impaired."

In effect, the revisors were given nearly plenary powers to redesign, reformulate, and redevelop the whole body of New York statute law, which had been a century and a half in the making, to say nothing of received British statutes of a longer lineage. The only limitations on their work were the requirements relating to judicial construction and, of course, the need for final legislative sanction. Such a mandate was totally without precedent in Anglo-American legal history. . . .

. . . .

The first report of the revisors, tendered to the legislature in March 1826, showed that they had . . . pursued their mandate zealously. Throughout the report, they expressed a concern for the totality of the statute law in the revision, focusing, not only on the need to create the best possible external arrangement for the whole, but also on what they considered to be a mandatory requirement of the revision—that it have internal integrity. Emphasis on these matters was grounded in the revisors' desire to reformulate the law in such a way as to create optimum accessibility and completeness. This stress on the aggregate of the law was closer to civilian than common law practice, which tended to treat the law as a set of nearly discrete particulars. . . .

. . . .

The legislature warmly endorsed the work of the revisors and did not waver in its support during the three years it took to complete the project. Of course, the lawmakers did not enact the proposals of the revisors uncritically. Frequently, they preserved things that the revisors would have eliminated, or added clauses they deemed necessary. And, on at least one occasion, they directed the revisors to deal more boldly with the law than they had ventured to do. However, if objections were raised or changes made, they were directed at matters of content, not at the format or the general mode of revision.

. . . .

While the Revised Statutes did not result in a revolution in the Anglo-American legal tradition, as would have been consummated by the codification of all the law of the state, they did make a distinct break with the past. This is nowhere more apparent than in the changes made by the revision in the objective body of the law. In other states, the law relating to a given subject could only be found in a variety of books and in a patchwork of statutes that frequently contained extraneous matter that confused the issue. The New Yorker in possession of the Revised Statutes could find the statute law on a given matter in a relatively short section classified with other related topics in one of three volumes. However, as the revisors pointed out, the individual consulting the revised statutes was not to expect to find all the law on the subjects that they treated. Because statutes comprised "but a small portion" of the law of the state, the common law would have to be consulted for comprehensive understanding. But who could deny that a striking improvement had been made?

. . . .

. . . The revisors themselves remarked that statutes that underwent the revision process "have been materially modified. Their details have been perfected; they have been conformed in express terms, to the constructions given them by the decisions of our courts; and in many cases new provisions have been introduced, essentially changing their principles." Moreover, "[i]n numerous instances . . . rules of the common law have been reduced to a written text . . . whilst in other instances those rules have been enlarged, modified, or varied, the more fully to conform them to the nature of our government, and to the habits and exigencies of the people." Significant innovations had been made in the content of the law before. Efforts had even been made on occasion to give some systematic order to portions of the law. But never before had an attempt been made to deal so comprehensively with some of the most difficult problems of the legal structure, both in form and in content.

Note 4(C). Massachusetts, 1835, and New York's David Dudley Field

The New York Revised Statutes of 1829 served as a successful example of partial codification and fueled the codification movement in other states. Successes in other states, however, were largely limited to the compilation and revision of statutes.

Massachusetts

In Massachusetts, the codification of the common law as well as compilation and revision of the statutes was advocated in a report prepared in 1835 by a commission chaired by Joseph Story. Ten years earlier, Joseph Story had written his colleague Henry Wheaton:

> Half our time is now consumed in examining cases. . . . [Codification] would greatly abridge our labours, and exhausting researches of the profession. . . . What a great gain it would be for us to have a starting point—something irrevocably fixed as settled principle.[1]

The 1835 commission report, written by Story, elaborated:

> At present the known rules and doctrines of the common law are spread over many ponderous volumes. They are nowhere collected together in a concise and systematic form, having a positive legislative sanction. They are to be gathered from treatises upon distinct and independent subjects, of very different merit and accuracy; from digests and abridgments; from books of practice and from professional practice; and above all, from books of reports of adjudged cases, many hundreds of which now exist, and which require to be painfully and laboriously consulted in order to ascertain them. . . . A vast deal of time is now necessarily consumed, if not wasted, in ascertaining the precise

bearing and result of various cases, which have been decided touching a particular topic. If the result is at all contested by the adverse party, no counselor would feel safe without a thorough examination of all the leading cases (even though they should spread over centuries), lest he should be surprised at the argument by a loose dictum, a questionable authority, or an ambiguous statement, either distinguishing or controlling the case before him. . . . And yet, it is not too much to say, that often a single page of a Code would contain, in a clear and explicit statement, all that the researches of a week, or even of a month, would scarcely justify them in affirming with an unfaltering confidence.[2]

A decision of the Supreme Judicial Court of Massachusetts, upholding a criminal conviction for the common-law crime of blasphemy, caused public outrage and increased popular sentiment in favor of codification.[3] Joseph Story, nevertheless, was careful to moderate his recommendations: he advised against attempting "the reduction to a Code of the entire body of the common law of Massachusetts." Yet the code resulting from his recommendations was rejected by the Massachusetts legislature in 1844.

New York

By the 1840s, interest in codification had declined throughout the nation. Only in New York did agitation for a code continue, largely because of the delays and expense caused by the state's cumbersome judicial system and system of procedure. The Revised Statutes of 1829 had failed to correct these defects. Among the difficulties was New York's output of case decisions: "The multiple appellate courts of the state boasted an annual output of opinions unrivaled in any other jurisdiction in the common law world."[4]

The standard-bearer for the codification of New York law in the late 1840s was David Dudley Field, a prominent member of the bar who is considered the "hero" of the codification movement.[5] His contribution lay both in his leadership and in his draftsmanship. He not only advocated codification in the abstract but directly worked on drafting concrete proposals for codes of civil procedure, evidence, criminal procedure, penal law, and civil law as well as a political code. His codes were models of clarity.

In 1848, Field's code of civil procedure was adopted in New York. The need for frequent amendments of this code, and the opposition of the bar, led to rejection of his other measures, except for a rewritten penal code passed in 1881. The opposition was led by a New York attorney, James C. Carter.

Codification was wrong, Carter felt, because it removed the center of gravity from the courts. The legislature—the code-enacting body—was comparatively untrustworthy; it was too passionately addicted to the shortrun. . . . Codes impaired the orderly development of the law; they froze the law into semipermanent form; this prevented natural evolution. Carter was impressed by the teachings of the so-called historical school of jurisprudence, founded by German jurists in the early 19th century. They taught Carter that laws were and ought to be emanations from the folk wisdom of a people. A statute drafted by a group of so-called experts was bound to be an inferior product, compared to what centuries of evolution, of self-correcting growth, could achieve.[6]

Field's codes, however, had a second life, as several other states adopted New York's code of civil procedure and new states in the West—Montana, Idaho, the Dakotas, and, most significantly, California—adopted some of Field's substantive codes as well. The impact of codification, however, was blunted by tendencies established during centuries of the common law:

[O]nce the codes were on the books, the results fell far short of the hopes. What happened afterwards would have brought Field to the rim of distraction. Courts and lawyers were not used to codified law; they tended to treat some of the code provisions in accordance with ingrained common-law habits and prejudices. In some cases, the codes' provisions were construed away; more often, they were simply ignored. Nor did the legislature keep its hands off the codes; they tended to let stand the broad statements of principles (they made little difference anyway), but they added all sorts of accretions. It is hard to resist the conclusion that the codes had almost no impact on behavior, either in court or out. Law in action in California did not seem much different from law in action in noncode states, in any way that the codes would help to explain.[7]

Federal Records

While states had a history of colonial legislation to build on, the federal government was a new entity. The federal records began with the Continental Congress meeting in 1774, the Declaration of Independence in 1776, and the Articles of Confederation in 1781. The decision to replace the Articles of Confederation with a new written constitution was preceded by a national discussion embodied in the *Federalist Papers*.

The adoption of a written constitution made the United States unique in the common-law world. The original, hand-written text of the Constitution is under bullet-proof glass in a shrine at the National Archives, but the deliberations leading to its adoption have been poorly preserved.

Selection 4(C). The Constitution

J. H. Huston, *The Creation of the Constitution: The Integrity of the Documentary Record*, 65 TEX. L. REV. 1, 1–39 (1986).

I. Introduction

. . . .

The Constitutional Convention proceedings were conducted in secrecy. No publication of the speeches, resolutions, or votes of the delegates occurred until 1819, when, as the result of a joint congressional resolution of the previous year, the official Journal of the Convention, kept by Secretary William Jackson, issued from the press. Two years later, the Convention notes of New York delegate Robert Yates appeared, covering the debates from May 25 to July 5. Jonathan Elliot began publishing his *Debates* in the state ratifying conventions in 1827. Not until 1840, more than fifty years after Washington took the presidential oath, were James Madison's notes of the debates, a full record of the Convention's proceedings, published.

. . . .

II. The Accuracy and Reliability of Convention Records

A. THE JOURNAL OF THE CONVENTION

. . . .

In 1818, Congress passed a joint resolution ordering the Convention journal printed. The task of preparing it for publication fell to Secretary of State John Quincy Adams, who found the demands of editing exasperating. "The journals and papers were very loosely and imperfectly kept," he complained on June 2, 1818. "They were no better than the daily minutes from which the regular journal ought to have been, but never was, made out."

. . . .

. . . The journal proper . . . was not the problem. The trouble was the seventeen-odd pages, detached from the journal, which recorded the "ayes and noes on the various questions" taken in the Convention. . . .

The real problems arose with a handful of "ayes and noes" in the detached sheets that were accompanied by no contextual information, and which Jackson had keyed to neither questions nor dates. . . . Another trifling problem was that, in a few instances, Jackson may have counted the votes inaccurately. . . . However, the slight probability of error—and the understanding that none of it relates to what the delegates said—

permits confidence in the journal, as published by John Quincy Adams . . . , as a reliable text. No such confidence is possible, however, in Yates' notes. . . .

B. YATES' NOTES

. . . .

The notes were published in Albany in 1821 under the title *Secret Proceedings and Debates of the Convention Assembled at Philadelphia in the year 1787, . . . From Notes taken by the late Robert Yates, Esquire, Chief Justice of New York and copied by John Lansing Jun., Esquire, Late Chancellor of that State, Members of that Convention.* The title page listed no editor. Washington newspapers plausibly but erroneously speculated that Lansing had seen the volume through the press. The identity of the editor would have startled the country's newspaper readers, for he was none other than Citizen Genet—Edmond C. Genet—the tempestuous minister of revolutionary France who convulsed American politics in 1793 [when Genet fitted out privateers in American ports to sail against British shipping in violation of American neutrality]. Fearing the guillotine, Genet refused to return to France when recalled. He married a daughter of Governor George Clinton of New York. . . . Among Clinton's politicial lieutenants were Yates and Lansing. . . . Introduced to the circle of Clinton's friends by marriage, Genet, nevertheless, was distrusted because of the tumultuous scenes he had precipitated in 1793 and because in his occasional forays into political journalism on behalf of his father-in-law, he displayed a penchant for character assassination that produced notorious libels such as one charging Rufus King, a model of probity and a pillar of the New York establishment, with robbing a widow in the settlement of an estate.

Upon Yates' death in 1801, his Convention notes passed to his wife who retained them until 1808. Genet then tried to get them from Mrs. Yates to conduct a political smear campaign. Fearing for their safety in the Frenchman's hands, Lansing intervened and rescued the original manuscript from the widow, promising that she would receive a copy. Lansing completed the copy within a month, making the "transcript verbatim, without the least mutilation or other alteration." Genet then extracted Lansing's copy of Yates' notes from the widow to use in promoting Clinton's political ambitions.

In 1808, Clinton challenged Madison for the presidential nomination on the Jeffersonian Republican ticket. Over the signature of a "Citizen of New York," Genet wrote a polemic against Madison, entitled *A Letter to the Electors of the President and Vice President of the United States.* The raw material for Genet's screed was Lansing's copy of Yates' notes, which Genet edited so drastically and tendentiously that Lansing, who had evidently anticipated just such a reckless manipulation of the sources, later congratulated himself on "getting possession of the original . . . in opposition to some ardent politicians, adverse to the election of Mr. Madison as president."

In his broadside against Madison, Genet promised that the full text of Yates' notes would "soon be offered to the people," but he withheld the document for thirteen years until another set of political ends could be served by its publication. Such an opportunity presented itself on August 28, 1821, when a convention met in Albany to revise the constitution of the state of New York. Genet published what purported to be a complete version of Yates' notes—his *Secret Proceedings*, the version we now have in Farrand[*]—shortly before the convention convened. His purpose was to influence the convention's deliberations, as he admitted in a letter, presenting his *Secret Proceedings* to President James Monroe. . . . Because of the murky nature of New York politics in the 1820s, it is not clear on whose behalf Genet produced Yates' notes. . . . We simply do not know the precise nature of his political agenda in 1821.

What is known is that, in publishing the *Secret Proceedings*, Genet took liberties with Lansing's copy of Yates' notes, liberties that appear to have exceeded those he permitted himself in the anti-Madison polemic in 1808. Lansing's copy of Yates' notes were thought to have been lost until two sheets from July 5, 1787 were discovered recently in Genet's papers at the Library of Congress. By comparing the contents of those sheets— the only ones known to exist—with what Genet actually published as occurring on July 5, 1787, it can be seen that he omitted half of the material on the sheets and altered every sentence that he published. . . . If Genet inflicted similar depredations on the remainder of Yates' notes, those notes as now printed in the *Secret Proceedings* cannot be considered a reliable record of what occurred at the Philadelphia Convention and cannot be consulted as a source of the intentions of the Framers. When Madison read extracts from Genet's publication in August 1821, he protested its "extreme incorrectness." The plaything of an unscrupulous partisan, Yates' notes as published by Genet fully deserved Madison's condemnation.

C. THE DEBATES IN THE STATE RATIFYING CONVENTIONS

. . . .

Our information about the proceedings in the state ratifying conventions comes from a single source: Jonathan Elliot's *The Debates in the several State Conventions, on the adoption of the Federal Constitution, as recommended by the General Convention at Philadelphia, in 1787*. First published in four volumes between 1827 and 1830, Elliott's work is a bibliographical brainteaser, for it was republished in at least seven more editions, in dif-

[*]In 1911, the Yale University Press published the *Records of the Federal Convention of 1787*, edited by Max Farrand. Farrand's edition of the *Records* was published in three volumes and, because of its comprehensive and meticulous scholarship, quickly supplanted all competing editions of Convention records.

fering numbers of volumes, with the contents of individual volumes differing in many cases from edition to edition. Elliot was not a scholar. Rather, he was a Washington political journalist turned editor, whose press was for sale to the highest bidder. John Quincy Adams, who cancelled a government printing contract held by Elliot because he suspected price gouging, described him as "an Englishman, having no character of his own—penurious and venal—metal to receive any stamp." It appears that in the 1830's, Elliot was promoting the political fortunes of John C. Calhoun, although he had opposed the South Carolinian earlier. Some scholars believe that one of Elliot's purposes in preparing his *Debates* was to advance Calhoun's cause, for Elliot supplemented proceedings in the conventions with such states' rights classics as the Virginia and Kentucky Resolves and deleted from the 1836 second edition a letter from Madison, which appeared in the first edition, attacking nullification. Whether Elliot went as far as Genet and doctored the *Debates* to promote the politics of a patron is not clear, but so obvious were their shortcomings that Elliot himself apologized for them in the preface to the first edition, confessing that "the sentiments they contain may, in some instances, have been inaccurately taken down, and, in others, probably, too faintly sketched, fully to gratify the inquisitive politician."

To know why the debates were "inaccurately taken down," it is necessary to know how and by whom they were recorded. Unlike the Philadelphia Convention, the state ratifying conventions were open to the public. Enterprising men recorded the debates in shorthand and then published them as commercial ventures in the newspapers and in book form. Elliot's *Debates* are a collection of these publications, generated in the first instance by shorthand reporters. And precisely here was the problem, for the technique of shorthand was in its infancy in the United States and did not provide the means of recording public discourse accurately.

. . . .

A survey of the records in states for which information is available shows that in some cases insufficient stenographic skills may have been the least of problems. From New Hampshire, Elliot published only a fragment of the Convention debates, the centerpiece of which was a speech by Joshua Atherton. According to the historian of the New Hampshire Convention, Atherton's speech apparently was "written out from tradition, by a hand other than his own, long after the Convention." In fact, it appears to have been composed by parties unknown in 1827, when it was first published as antislavery propaganda in a New Hampshire newspaper.

Elliot reprinted the debates in the Massachusetts Convention from a volume published in Boston in 1788 by Benjamin Russell. In a publisher's note, Russell apologized for " 'some inaccuracies, and many omissions,' due to the 'inexperience' of the reporters." Contemporaries testified that Russell and his colleagues inserted speeches in the published debates that they themselves had written. . . .

Political partisanship in Connecticut and New York, more than the shortage of stenographic expertise, compromised the quality of the record of convention debates in those states. In Connecticut, the *Connecticut Courant* and the *American Mercury*, both Federalist newspapers, hired Enoch Perkins, a young Federalist lawyer, to report the debates at Hartford. The results were egregiously partisan—only one short summary of one Anti-Federalist speech was published, and at least one Federalist speech was said to have been "particularly erroneous." For New York, Elliot published Francis Childs' *Debates and Proceedings of the Convention of the State of New York* . . . that appeared in December 1788. A fledgling stenographer, Childs apologized to the delegates he recorded

> for the imperfect dress in which their arguments are given to the Public. Not long accustomed to the business, he cannot pretend to as much accuracy as might be expected from a more experienced hand,—and it will easily be comprehended how difficult it must be to follow a copious and rapid Speaker, in the train of his reasoning, much more in the turn of his expression.

Childs further impaired his credibility by recording and publishing the debates for only two of the Convention's six weeks, and by allowing speakers to revise their remarks after the event. The most damaging charge against his reliability as a reporter, however, was the accusation that he was a "partyman," a Federalist who manipulated his notes to promote factional interests.

This charge was made with more vehemence against Thomas Lloyd, the reporter of the Pennsylvania and Maryland debates. An ardent Federalist, Lloyd probably had no qualms about taking money from Pennsylvania Federalist leaders to delete all the Anti-Federalist speeches in the Convention, as he in fact did in his *Debates of the Convention of the State of Pennsylvania*, published on February 7, 1788, and reprinted by Elliot. In addition to suppressing the Anti-Federalists, Lloyd eliminated all Federalist speeches except those by Thomas McKean and James Wilson, the latter of which had obviously been corrected and "improved" after the Convention because they were printed with footnotes. The Anti-Federalists correctly charged that Lloyd's *Debates* had been "afterwards altered, dressed and undressed by, and at the pleasure of his benefactors," and were nothing more than Federalist campaign literature. In December and January of 1787–1788, Federalist stalwarts Timothy Pickering and Tench Coxe sent prepublication excerpts from Lloyd's *Debates* to partisans in other states to furnish Federalist orators arguments for ratification. Even Elliot deprecated Lloyd's notes by advising his readers that although he was publishing them, he had sought in vain to obtain better accounts of the Pennsylvania Convention.

The reporter of the Virginia debates, one David Robertson, inspired little confidence in some citizens of the Old Dominion. "The Debates are not Yet published; nor is there any Cause to expect that they will be authentic; the Short Hand Man," wrote George Mason, "being a *federal*

Partizan, [the notes] will probably be garbled, in some such Partial Manner as the Debates of the Pennsylvania Convention have been by Lloyd." *Robertson's Debates and Other Proceedings of the Convention of Virginia*, published in 1788 and reprinted by Elliot, shared the weaknesses of the works of his stenographic colleagues. "I find passages," wrote Madison, "some appearing to be defective, others obscure, if not unintelligible, others again which must be more or less erroneous." John Marshall, whose speeches at the Virginia Convention are frequently cited in the legal literature, was so distressed by Robertson's inaccuracies that he complained that "as to what is given to me . . . , if my name had not been prefixed to the speaches [sic] I never should have recognized them as productions of mine."

The Virginia Convention adjourned on June 27, 1788; Robertson was then hired by James Iredell and William Davie, the Federalist chieftains in North Carolina, to come to Hillsboro and record the action in the ratifying convention in the Tarheel state. Apparently Robertson did not please his employers, for he refused to make a "fair copy" of his shorthand notes. This task then fell to "a little boy the son of Mr. Turnbull," who to no one's surprise, performed the work "most defectively." Various Federalist speakers tinkered with the lad's work before the debates were published by Iredell and Davie. They hoped that the dissemination of the debates "would produce a salutary change in the opinions of the people," whose representatives had failed to ratify the Constitution but were scheduled to try again in 1789. Thus, the North Carolina debates as reported were designed, like those in Pennsylvania, to serve as Federalist campaign literature.

Reviewing the ratification proceedings on the floor of Congress in 1791, Elbridge Gerry asserted that "[t]he debates of the State Conventions, as published by the short-hand writers, were generally partial and mutilated. . . ." . . .

D. MADISON'S NOTES

. . . Although often entreated to publish his notes on the Philadelphia Convention, James Madison never relented in his conviction that they should appear posthumously. At his death in 1836, the notes passed to his widow who sold them to the federal government, which commissioned their publication in 1840; "at once," wrote Farrand, "all other records paled into insignificance." So comprehensive and convincing did the notes appear that most readers accepted them as authoritative. Partisans of Alexander Hamilton, however, challenged their veracity and an undercurrent of skepticism about their accuracy has continued ever since. . . .

The suspicious investigators found their champion . . . in Professor William Winslow Crosskey of the University of Chicago Law School. Crosskey revealed his true feelings about Madison and his notes to his constitutional law classes. According to the reminiscence of a student, Crosskey would begin his class by slamming Farrand's *Records* on his desk and promising "to demonstrate to you that Madison was a forger—he tampered with the notes he kept of the debates at the federal constitutional convention in order to suit his own political advantage and that of his party." Crosskey was more circumspect in the first two volumes of his opus, *Politics and the Constitution in the History of the United States*, published in 1953, merely suggesting "the possibility that his [Madison's] testimony may have been, not inadvertently, but deliberately false and misleading." Elsewhere in the volume, however, Crosskey became more explicit, declaring that Madison, "presented falsely the sentiments of other men" and inserted "spurious" dialogue in his notes. Crosskey argued that Madison's motive in doctoring his manuscript was to play politics—to make his Convention notes support the doctrines of the Jeffersonian-Republican party that coalesced in the 1790s and that Madison helped to lead for the remainder of his career. If we accept Crosskey's account, Madison's notes, no less than Genet's and Lloyd's were the product of political partisanship and were, on that account, corrupt.

. . . .

. . . [I]nsofar as existing evidence permits a judgment, Madison's notes are a faithful account of what he recorded at the Convention in 1787—augmented by motions, resolutions, and votes that he believed to be, and in the vast majority of cases were, accurately recorded by Jackson and accurately printed by John Quincy Adams in 1819.

. . . [U]nlike Yates' notes and the state ratifying debates, Madison's notes and the Convention journal do not suffer from editorial interventions by their authors or others, disqualifying them as sources of information about the Convention. But the question of how accurately these works reveal the intentions of the Framers remains, for although they are faithful accounts of what Madison and Jackson recorded in 1787, it is necessary to know if what Madison and Jackson recorded was a faithful account of what occurred on the floor of the Convention. In short, how good were they as reporters?

. . . The Convention journal consists of little more than a chronological list of motions. It is, in one of Genet's few accurate statements about a constitutional document, a mere "diplomatic skeleton" that needs the discourse of delegates to "fill up . . . its vital parts." Why did the journal lack debates that would explain the objectives of the delegates in making their motions, as well as the meaning they attached to such motions? Secretary Jackson did keep shorthand notes of the debates using his own idiosyncratic system. He was preparing to publish these notes in 1827 to flesh out his skeleton, but no publication appeared and the notes have disappeared. . . .

Madison's notes, then, stand alone as the key to the Framers' intentions. If his notes on any given day are compared to the fragmentary records of debates left by other delegates that Farrand printed or that have been discovered more recently, a rough approximation between the different accounts is evident—demonstrating that Madison was not inventing dialogue, but was trying to capture what was said. Still, there is an enigma about Madison's note-taking methods. The Convention was in session from 10:00 A.M. to mid-afternoon every day except Sunday—"not less than five, for a large part of the time Six and sometimes 7 hours sitting every day," Washington wrote on September 17, 1787. These were full sessions of the Convention; committees, as Madison and others attested, met before or after the day's business, and there is no evidence that the Convention took breaks, although individual members must have excused themselves now and again.

If read aloud, Madison's notes for any particular day consume only a few minutes, suggesting that he may have recorded only a small part of each day's proceedings. . . .

. . . Because Madison's raw Convention notes—his "abbreviations and marks intelligible to myself"—have not survived, it is not known if he recorded all or nearly all of each session and then severely compressed the results or if he followed stenographer Robertson's practice in the Virginia Convention of ignoring everything that seemed "desultory" or "irregular." Whatever the case, much appears to be missing.

Another feature of Madison's notes is troublesome. His own remarks at the Convention occupy a considerable portion of the notes, yet they cannot have been delivered as they are now recorded in print. Madison could not speak and record at the same time. Because he did not prepare his speeches in advance—"having never written one before hand," as he reported late in life—dialogue attributed to him must have been composed after the day's proceedings. After a few hours reflection, Madison may have written a good deal more and a good deal that differed from what he said earlier. . . .

Madison's notes are not a forgery, but they are far from a verbatim record of what was said in the Convention. They omit much of what happened in Philadelphia. . . .

III. A Note on the Documentation of the Bill of Rights

The First Congress under the new federal government, meeting from early April through the end of September 1789, sent twelve amendments to the states for ratification on September 25, 1789. The ten amendments eventually ratified are known, of course, as the Bill of Rights.

In 1789, the Senate did not permit its proceedings to be reported. The documentary record of debates on the Bill of Rights consists, therefore, of deliberations in the House of Representatives. These were published in 1834 by the Washington firm of Gales & Seaton under the title, *The Debates and Proceedings in the Congress of the United States*, known to and cited by scholars as *Annals of Congress*. For the first session of the First Congress, the period covering the gestation of the Bill of Rights, the *Annals of Congress* is a reprinting of a publication called the *Congressional Register*, prepared by none other than Thomas Lloyd, the shorthand reporter of the debates in the Pennsylvania and Maryland ratifying conventions.

Far from improving by 1789, Lloyd's technical skills had become dulled by excessive drinking. In 1940, the Library of Congress acquired the manuscript of Lloyd's shorthand notes of the debates from April 8 to May 15, 1789, and from January 19 to June 3, 1790. These notes were transcribed, insofar as they could be, by a shorthand expert, and the transcription was compared to the debates printed by Lloyd in the *Congressional Register*. It was discovered that what Lloyd published "bears only slight resemblance to the literal transcript of his own notes. Sometimes a speech is printed for which no notes or only very brief notes exist; sometimes a long speech reported in the manuscript is printed very briefly or not at all." Another investigator has reported that Lloyd's reports were frequently "garbled" and that he neglected to report speeches whose texts are known to exist elsewhere. Lloyd's manuscript also demonstrates a wandering mind, for it is periodically interrupted by doodling, sketches of members, horses, and landscapes, and by poetry. . . . It is thus little wonder that on May 9, 1789, Madison condemned the *Congressional Register* as exhibiting "the strongest evidences of mutilation & perversion" and that Elbridge Gerry, after accusing Lloyd of persisting in his Federalist partisanship, complained that "[s]ometimes members were introduced as uttering arguments directly the reverse of what they had advanced." The accuracy of Lloyd's reports "is not to be relied on," Madison advised a correspondent.

> The face of the debates shews that they are defective, and desultory, where not revised, or written out by the Speakers. In some instances, he makes them inconsistent with themselves, by erroneous reports of their speeches at different times on the same subject. He was indolent and sometimes filled up blanks in his notes from memory or *imagination*. I recollect that he put into my mouth, a speech, drawn much from the latter and in its style suited rather to a youthful declaimer than to me in my situation. He finally, became a votary of the bottle and perhaps made too free use of it sometimes at the period of his printed debates.

Some Congressmen did not censure Lloyd quite so severely, but even his apologists admitted that his reports abounded with error.

Therefore, in seeking to ascertain the intentions of the drafters of the Bill of Rights, scholars should know that the *Annals of Congress*—the source traditionally relied upon for that purpose—is the voice of Thomas Lloyd, a voice even less reliable in 1789 than it was at the Pennsylvania ratifying convention.

IV. Conclusion

This Article has examined the most important documentary records surrounding the creation of the Constitution and has found them to be defective in varying degrees. In some cases recorders were incompetent. In others, documents were separated from their compilers and published by editors with partisan agendas who revised and deleted the original material. And in yet others, compilers retained control over their records but still produced alterations and omissions. There were differences in the extent of editorial alteration and in the motives of the editors. But in all cases the resulting documents are not full, reliable records of the debates at the Constitutional and ratifying conventions.

. . . The author will be satisfied if lawyers, judges, historians, and legal scholars are reminded, as they periodically need to be, that the mere fact that a record is in print does not make it reliable.

Note 4(D). Early Federal Statutes

By a statute passed in the first session of the first Congress, the secretary of state was directed to keep an archive of all statutes enacted by Congress and to send "authenticated" copies to members of Congress and to state executives. Authenticated copies could be obtained by the general public for a fee.

Less reliable sources were available to the public in privately prepared compilations of statutes and in newspapers. The latter were the only source for proclamations of statutes to the general public. The secretary of state was directed to have statutes published in at least three newspapers; later, newspaper publication was required in each state.

This system for collection and publication of the acts of Congress continued for the first six years of Congress. No official compilation or index to federal statutes was prepared until 1795.

In 1795, Congress followed the "peculiar American practice"[1] of having statutes collated and printed together with an index. The resulting publication is known, after its editor, as the "Folwell edition" of United States laws. In 1795, Congress also provided for the publication of its laws following each session and the distribution of its published laws to each state. "That was a great step in advance, and the plan worked out was similar, in a general way, to that which has been followed since."[2]

The Folwell edition was continued until 1814. By then, it had reached twelve volumes. A new edition was then commissioned, under dual editorship, and came to be known as the "Bioren and Duane" edition. It had a life of more than thirty years—until 1845, when the *Statutes at Large* began.

Selection 4(D). *The Statutes at Large, Revised Statutes,* and the *United States Code,* 1845 to 1928

R. H. Dwan and E. R. Feidler, *The Federal Statutes—Their History and Use*, 22 MINN. L. REV., 1008, 1009–1022 (1938).

The "Statutes at Large" are today the basic federal statutes available to the public; they have continued in substantially the same form down to the present time and contain, in chronological order, all public acts, resolutions, private acts, and treaties. Publication of those statute books did not begin until 1845. . . . The first five volumes were devoted to public acts and to resolutions from the beginning of the government under the constitution. Volume 6 was devoted to private acts; volume 7, to treaties with the Indians; and volume 8, to treaties with foreign nations. The work through volume 8 was edited by Richard Peters, who had formerly been reporter of the decisions of the Supreme Court of the United States.

. . . .

By an Act approved on August 8, 1846, the [Statutes at Large] edition of the laws and treaties of the United States was declared "to be competent evidence of the several public and private acts of Congress, and of the several treaties therein contained, in all courts of law and equity and of maritime jurisdiction, and in all the tribunals and public offices of the United States, and of the several states, without any further proof of authentication thereof." From the date of that Act on, in searching the statutes, one might accept as final, for practical purposes at least, that which was found in the first eight volumes of the Statutes at Large, unless it had been subsequently repealed, superseded, modified, or amended by another statute or by a treaty. So far as the writers have been able to ascertain, that was the first time that a provision of that kind was made with reference to any published volumes of the federal statutes.

On June 22, 1874, Congress enacted a revision of the permanent public laws of the United States in force on December 1, 1873. . . . Such Revised Statutes of 1873 make up part 1 of the eighteenth volume of the Statutes at Large.

The 1873 revision is the only occasion on which Congress has enacted as law a complete revision of all the federal permanent public statutes. . . . [S]eventeen volumes of the Statutes at Large had accumulated at that time. Much of the material in those volumes was obsolete, much repealed, much superseded, much modified. It was almost a practical impossibility to make a thorough search of the statutes on many subjects. As early as 1848 the House Judiciary Committee had strongly advocated revision.

Finally, acting pursuant to the Act of June 27, 1866, President Johnson appointed a commission to revise, simplify, arrange, and consolidate all statutes of the United States, general and permanent in nature.

. . . From a report made by the commissioners in 1871, it appears that, as a particular part of the revision was tentatively completed, it was sent to various distinguished lawyers who were particularly conversant with the material dealt with in that part for criticism and checking. Finally, in the early part of 1873 the commission made its report to a joint committee of Congress. . . . It was the opinion of the joint committee that the commissioners had so changed and amended the statutes that it would be impossible to secure the passage of their revision. The work was, therefore, handed over to Thomas Jefferson Durant, a District of Columbia attorney, so that he might expunge all changes in the law made by the commission. He devoted about nine months to that work. His completed work was introduced as a bill in the House of Representatives on December 10, 1873. Copies of the bill were sent to many distinguished lawyers throughout the United States, so that the bill might be examined and made as nearly perfect as possible before it was reported to the House.

It can be seen from the foregoing that the work was carefully done by able persons, and that numerous precautions were taken to eliminate errors and inaccuracies. Nevertheless, after the revision had been enacted into law and while it was still on the press, sixty-nine errors were discovered. A statute was immediately enacted making corrections and supplying omissions, which was printed as an appendix in the same volume as the Revised Statutes of 1873. During the next few years one hundred eighty-three other errors plus one error in the corrections were discovered, and another statute correcting errors was enacted. . . . [T]hat experience with errors made Congress reluctant to enact revisions of statutes as law.

. . . .

. . . As a result . . . of the Revised Statutes of 1873, an attorney today need not generally investigate the seventeen volumes of the Statutes at Large antedating the Revised Statutes. Those volumes have, however, great value for interpreting the Revised Statutes when the latter are ambiguous, for the search for treaties with foreign countries, and for the search for temporary, private, local, and appropriation acts.

. . . The 1874 Act directed that at the end of each session of Congress, the secretary of state should cause a *pamphlet* of the statutes enacted at such session to be edited, printed, published, and distributed. At the end of the Congress, the *bound volumes* of the Statutes at Large were to be edited, printed, published, and distributed. The practice of publishing pamphlets of the session laws was discontinued [in 1936]. . . .

On March 2, 1877, a statute was approved authorizing the president to appoint a commissioner to prepare a new edition of the Revised Statutes, inserting the statutes amending, modifying, and affecting the Revised Statutes of 1873 which had been enacted since December 1, 1873. It was provided in the Act that, when published, the new edition should be legal and conclusive evidence of all the laws contained therein. . . .

The following year, . . . an Act was approved amending the . . . 1877 Act . . . and making the new edition only legal evidence. It was also provided that, in case of any discrepancy between the new edition and the original statutes passed since December 1, 1873, the latter should control. The history of that statute . . . shows that Congress, after its experience with the Revised Statutes of 1873, was reluctant to enact as law even a consolidation and revision of the statutes . . . passed during only a four-year period. [The new edition was published in 1878. Supplements followed in 1881 and 1891.]

. . . .

In 1919, Colonel Little of Kansas, Chairman of the House of Representatives Committee on the Revision of the Laws of the United States, commenced the work which eventually became the United States Code. . . .

After eighteen months the compilation or codification was ready. It was introduced in the 66th Congress, passed the House of Representatives unanimously on December 20, 1920, but died in the Senate. . . . The Senate Committee on the Revision of the Laws of the United States apparently gave the compilation and supplement careful consideration. It reported it unfavorably on the ground that there were numerous errors, omissions, and inaccuracies in it. Despite the great care that had been exercised and the unquestionable ability of the revisers, the Senate Committee had discovered six hundred errors.

The compilation or codification bills introduced in the 66th, 67th, and 68th Congresses had provided that the compilation should be enacted as law and, like the Revised Statutes of 1873, that any prior statute, any portion of which was embraced in the compilation, should be repealed.

Between the 68th and 69th Congresses, the House and Senate Committees on the Revision of the Laws devised a new plan for codifying the laws. West Publishing Company and Edward Thompson Company, who published the United States Compiled Statutes Annotated and the Federal Statutes Annotated (private compilations) respectively, were employed to undertake the work of codification. Those companies used Colonel Little's work as a basis. The work was checked by experts in the various government Departments and Commissions. . . .

Despite all the care that had been taken, several glaring errors were discovered when the bill to enact the codification was before the Senate and the House of Representatives. For example, the statutory provision providing for a legislative counsel was omitted in the preparation of the Code, and the bill passed the House of Representatives with that omission. It was discovered in the Senate.

The bill to enact the codification, as it passed the House of Representatives and was reported to the Senate, contained a provision that the Code should not at once repeal all former legislation of a general and permanent character embraced in the Code, but that until July 1, 1927, only prior statutory provisions substantially identical with the matter in the Code should be repealed. Thus, for a period of time, the Code, in cases of inconsistency, was to give way to the provisions in the Statutes at Large and the Revised Statutes of 1873. On July 1, 1927, all statutes of a general and permanent nature not contained in the Code and passed prior thereto were to be repealed. The purpose of that "twilight zone provision" was to allow time to discover and correct errors in the Code.

The Senate, however, after noticing several of the errors in the codi-fication bill, decided that the "twilight zone" provision was not sufficient protection against error. It therefore amended the bill so that it was to be only prima facie the law. The code was approved with that amendment on June 30, 1926. As finally passed, the bill provided specifically that the Code enacted no new law and amended or repealed no old law, and that in cases of inconsistency between the Code and original legislation, the latter was to rule.

. . . .

In 1929, Congress enacted a statute providing that there should be prepared and published, under the supervision of the House of Represen-tatives Committee on Revision of the Laws, not more often than once in every five years, new editions of the United States Code, correcting errors and incorporating the current supplement. The books of such editions were declared to establish prima facie the laws of the United States general and permanent in nature. . . .

. . . In 1928 . . . Congress provided that, beginning with the Seven-tieth Congress, there should be prepared and published, under the super-vision of the House of Representatives Committee on Revision of the Laws, a cumulative supplement to the current edition of the Code at the end of each session of Congress. The books . . . too establish prima facie the law of the United states permanent and general in nature. . . .

Note 4(E). Annotated Codes

Since 1873, no comprehensive code has been enacted by the United States:

> Congress considered other proposals for a comprehensive revision, but the experience with the *Revised Statutes* was considered such a failure, that the Congress hesitated to undertake a similar project.[1]

Instead, since the publication of the *United States Code* in 1926, Congress has been going through it, title by title, to review its contents and, where approved, to enact it into positive law. Twenty-one of the fifty titles have been enacted as of 1990; the rest remain only prima facie evidence of the laws, while the official text remains in the *Revised Statutes* of 1873 and the subsequent *Statutes at Large*.

After West Publishing Company gained a role in the production of the official *United States Code*, it turned its editorial expertise to preparing an unofficial version, on the model of its earlier *United States Compiled Statutes Annotated*, with research aids that would be so useful to lawyers that they would buy the unofficial edition and largely ignore the official edition. West succeeded with the publication of the *United States Code Annotated* in 1927.

The *U.S.C.A.* was not without precedent. As early as 1801, a topical compilation of statutes was privately prepared for Pennsylvania by Alexander Dallas; using his reports of Pennsylvania judicial opinions, Dallas added to the statutory texts notes of cases that interpreted the statutes.[2] In 1811, Charles Smith published another private compilation of Pennsylvania Statutes and appended essays citing cases, in a fashion similar to Wheaton's volumes of the *United States Supreme Court Reports*.[3] Later in the nineteenth century, West Publishing Company's collaborator on the *United States Code*, the Edward Thompson Company, published a number of annotated state codes and, in 1903, published *Federal Code Annotated*, the first "fully annotated" federal code.[4] The title of the *F.C.A.* has been changed to the *United States Code Service*, and it remains a rival to the *U.S.C.A.* The *U.S.C.S.*, now published by Lawyers Cooperative Publishing Company, is often more thorough than the *U.S.C.A.* in its editorial features.

The editorial features of annotated codes most helpful to researchers are:

—amendment histories listing each amendment of each statute and citing to the session laws where the preamendment texts can be found—a necessary feature, since the annotated (and official) codes contain only the language of statutes as currently in force;

—case annotations citing and briefly describing cases that have interpreted each section of each statute;

—cross-references between related statutes, and cross-references to other publications of the company producing the annotated code (e.g., digest key numbers, legal encyclopedias, practice treatises) and to scholarly articles;

—references to administrative and executive rules and regulations promulgated under the authority of each statute and to opinions of attorneys general discussing each statute;[5]

—a thorough word index at the end of each annotated code.

Annotated codes cover not only statutes but also constitutions and the rules of practice enacted by the courts. They also contain a variety of tables designed to link citation changes resulting from statutory compilations, revisions, and codifications. Annotated codes, however, do not provide full preenactment histories of statutes, with citations to committee reports, floor debates, and other "legislative history" documents.[6]

In addition to their editorial features, annotated codes are also updated faster than the unannotated codes published by governments, such as the *U.S.C.*, and updating is more effectively integrated into the body of the annotated codes. Updating of the annotated codes is usually by pocket parts and, when pocket parts get too thick, by replaced volumes, often split amoebalike. Some state codes have adopted a looseleaf format for updating. The *U.S.C.A.*, and many state annotated codes as well, are also updated by "legislative services" publishing new legislation and case annotations. For even more current information, tables of statutes in current reporters may be consulted, but the most up-to-date legislation and case annotations can be found in LEXIS and WESTLAW.

Annotated codes are now published for each state; some states have two rivals sets. Most states, like the federal government, also continue to publish government-sponsored unannotated codes, although some states have adopted the privately published annotated sets as official, and two states have only recently embarked on official compilations—in 1992, Illinois adopted the first official compilation of its statutes since 1874, and Pennsylvania has begun its first official compilation ever.

Selection 4(E). Pennsylvania, 1960

J. B. Fordham & C. C. Moreland, *Pennsylvania's Statutory Imbroglio: The Need of Statute Law Revision*, 108 U. PA. L. REV. 1093, 1093–1121 (1960).

The Commonwealth of Pennsylvania occupies a unique position with respect to the condition of its statute law. The state has an accumulation of session laws which goes back to colonial days; at no time in its history, however, has there been any official bulk compilation, consolidation, codification or revision of the general and permanent legislation of the jurisdiction. It must be readily apparent that to put the statute law of the state in good shape and thus to pave the way for subsequent law-making within a sound framework would be a large undertaking. . . .

. . . It is extraordinary . . . that there has never been any successful official attack on the problem in this, a major state of the Union and one of the original thirteen. It is strange that the legal profession has not pressed for action and demanded the enactment of an official body of statute law upon which reliance might be placed and in which the standing law might be identified readily. The statute law of Pennsylvania is in an untidy mess, a condition which a good lawyer would not tolerate in the case of important private legal documents. . . .

The focus of this Article is not general substantive codification. . . . Nor would any theory of extensive substantive revision fit the case. . . . As a practical matter, substantive revision can be managed effectively only on a topical basis.

Revision in General

Although the official language of a legislative act is to be found in the enrolled bill, usually on file in the office of the secretary of state, each state has always published the acts of each legislative session at the conclusion of the session so that the laws could be readily obtained and consulted. But consultation of the large number of volumes of session laws which accumulate over the years is impracticable, if not impossible. Various methods have been adopted to make the accumulated legislative material available in usable and up-to-date form. The most elementary method— one no longer used—is the republication in chronological order of all general statutes in force. A more common method today is the republication of all sections of the general statutes in force, arranged by broad general subjects. Such a publication is properly referred to as a compilation, although this usage is not uniform throughout the United States.

Compilations, even when prepared under the direction of the legislature, are only prima facie evidence of the law inasmuch as they are not enacted as the law. The most familiar example of such a compilation is the first edition of the *United States Code*. Unofficial compilations, such as *Purdon's Pennsylvania Statutes Annotated*, have no authority other than usage, although a state may "legalize" such a work as was done, for example, in Maryland.

A third and much more effective method is the one frequently referred to as a codification or revision, although here again usage in this country is not uniform. As used in this Article, revision refers to enactment of the entire body of general and permanent statute law in improved, simplified style and in orderly arrangement. It involves the harmonizing of the language of the entire body of statutory law and the elimination of duplications, contradictions, obsolete provisions, redundant and verbose expressions, acts or parts of acts judicially declared invalid and provisions of law impliedly repealed. It does not make changes in the substance and effect of existing law, but merely provides a well-organized and clarified statement of the complete body of the effective legislation of the state. It requires enactment by the legislature to become effective and upon enactment becomes the law. Any pre-existing general and permanent statutes which are neither included nor preserved by saving clause are repealed.

What we have been describing is, in substance, a process of consolidation of laws, whose function is to bring together the existing general and permanent legislation which is to be continued in force and not to achieve substantive changes. Such is the problem of language, though, that some changes may be wrought unintentionally in an effort to improve style and expression. This is not likely to be a matter of substantial moment, especially if the revisors exercise restraint and care and if the revision expressly declares that no changes in substance are intended.

The Pennsylvania Situation

UNOFFICIAL COMPILATIONS

For 275 years the colonial and state legislative bodies of Pennsylvania have been enacting statute law. . . . [N]ot once in that long period has the accumulation of legislation ever been subjected even to a complete official compilation, let alone a consolidation, codification or revision. In this respect Pennsylvania stands alone among the states of the nation. How have its judges, lawyers, public officials and others managed?

· ·

The early chronological collections of session laws were not satisfactory; they simply reproduced the accumulation of statutes in the order of enactment without other classification. A more helpful method of presenting the statutory law of the state was inaugurated by Collinson Read in 1801 and by John Purdon in 1811. These publications were "digests" or abridgements of the existing laws of the state, arranged by broad general subject. Purdon published three more editions during his lifetime, and subsequent to his death this work has gone through ten more editions. The current edition, . . . published by the West Publishing Company . . . is a typical set of West annotated statutes, divided into seventy-seven main titles with subdivisions and elaborate annotations and histories of each section. But despite the merits of the editorial work on the present edition of *Purdon*, the compilation cannot be any better than the statutory material with which the editorial staff must deal. The publisher may have done a good job of lining up its selection of general and permanent laws in a rational order, but it could not have done any legislative pruning or shaping.

INADEQUATE LEGISLATION

Most of the inadequacies of the current *Purdon* are the result of faulty work in the legislative process. The legislature in passing amendments has frequently failed to make appropriate changes in earlier enactments; as a result the current Purdon is replete with outmoded or ambiguous sections, simply because the original acts or sections have not been amended, as they should have been. . . .

· ·

During the past seventy-five years or so, the legislature has seen fit to "codify" the law with respect to particular subjects; when it has done so, however, it has frequently failed to make logical changes or corrections, with the result that the editors of the current *Purdon* have been forced to make a place outside the "code" for miscellaneous material which should have been taken care of by the code itself. . . .

. . . The legislature itself is frequently confused; it has been known to amend repealed acts, or to refer to nonexistent sections of acts, or wrong sections. Surely one explanation for this legislative ineptitude is the confused and incoherent state in which the statutory law of the Commonwealth is to be found. But perhaps the most serious criticism of the unsatisfactory condition of the statute law is that, for all practical purposes, it is left to a private publishing house to determine what is the controlling statutory law of the state. Although the official source of statutory law is the enrolled bills, deposited with the Secretary of State and published by him at the end of each session of the legislature, it is clear that no one can use this great mass of material effectively or economically. . . .

The problem has been dealt with for the past 145 years by the use of *Purdon* and similar publications. The difficulty with such a solution is not so much the question of the correctness of the text of the unofficially printed versions of the "general and permanent" laws as it is the entirely unofficial determination of what legislation falls within that category and the absence of an official statutory framework for orderly change. Since the volumes of session laws cannot be used with any practicality, reliance must be placed on the unofficial compilation. But here are found only those laws or parts of laws which the *publisher's editors* have determined to be in effect. It is *they* who decided what laws have been repealed by implication or are not general or permanent. That their task is not made easy by the methods employed by the legislature is beside the point. The fact remains that for a century and a half, the courts, lawyers and citizens of a great state have been dependent for the conduct of their business on entirely unofficial compilations of a ragged and bulky accumulation of legislation. If there ever were a clear case for cleaning up and putting in good order the "statute book" of a state, Pennsylvania presents it.

. . . .

Experience in Other States

IN GENERAL

The experience of other states with respect to the official treatment of general and permanent legislation can provide useful information on the process and mechanics of revision. The two new members of the Union aside, all of the states except Pennsylvania have made some type of official codification or revision at one time or another; many have done so within relatively recent years. Thirty-two states have enacted codes or revisions which have the force of law, and eleven have adopted official compilations. California and New York occupy a distinct position in the present connection. California has a system which, in the composite, amounts to general codification. Its general and permanent legislation is found in several major codes which have been separately enacted. The New York Consolidated Laws, which have been separately enacted over a period of a good many years, are in both design and effect a consolidation of the substantive statute law of the state.

The only two jurisdictions which are in a posture at all comparable to that of Pennsylvania are Illinois and Indiana; while the former did achieve a revision in 1874 and the latter in 1852, neither of these states has produced an official compilation, codification or revision since those early efforts.

. . . .

PUBLICATION

Vital to the success of statute law revision, and therefore demanding attention in the development of the basic revision plan, are first, the initial publication which facilitates the finding of the law, and second, a followup publication which will preserve the advantages of the revision despite the enactment of subsequent legislation.

There are at least five well known approaches to the publication problem. Wisconsin, the birthplace of continuous revision, uses biennial publication of all its general and permanent legislation, with new matter fitted in by the revisor of statutes. In order to preserve a convenient two-volume size, the Wisconsin practice is to publish separately cumulative annotations prepared by the revisor. A second method is to publish individual or cumulative supplemental volumes as the session laws are ground out. A third, used in several states, is the issuance—as the extent and importance of legislative developments dictate—of replacement volumes embodying new legislative material.

A fourth method is the use of pocket-parts. Ordinarily, pocket-parts are prepared on a cumulative basis and contain all legislative developments intervening between the publication of the original volume and that of its supplement. Colorado and Tennessee employ an interesting variation of the pocket-part plan as a device to keep their statutes up to date. At the beginning of each regular session of the legislature, the revision agency submits bills to codify the acts of the previous session as they appeared in pocket-parts during the interval between sessions. The enactment of these bills makes the new legislation the law of the state in codified form, just as if it had appeared in a code in the first instance. This device also provides a solid, rational basis for uniformly enacting the law by reference to code sections.

Finally, a new method, originated in Oregon and embraced by Kentucky and Nevada, is the loose-leaf plan. This method is not carried to the point of substitution of individual pages, as is common in the law services, but rather involves the reprinting of an entire chapter in which there has been any change and the substitution of the fresh printing for the chapter as it previously appeared. The chapter reprintings are designed to obviate the evils of mistake and carelessness with respect to the insertion of particular pages and to provide the substitute material in a manageable unit without blank pages. The cost of reprinting is kept down by preserving the original type and changing it only to the extent required by new legislative action. The Oregon plan is a rather attractive one; it keeps all the general and permanent statutes up to date and does this in a way which minimizes the risks of carelessness and error in the substitution of new material.

Note 4(F). National Access to State Statutes

Until recently, one of the major gaps in the legal literature of the United States has been the lack of a national statutory index. Although most litigation involves only the laws of individual states, the need to consult out-of-state statutes has long been recognized: "[T]he laws of other states, especially neighboring states, may be involved in a case, or other states may have comparable laws."[1]

A proposal for a " 'National Statutes System' paralleling the deservedly successful 'National Reporter System'" was published in 1930.[2] In the 1960s one of the earliest applications of computer technology to legal information was an attempt by the American Bar Foundation to develop a national index to current state statutes,[3] but the project was eventually discontinued.

Other topical compilations of state statutes on a national basis were made in conjunction with various publications. Citations to such compilations are collected in an irregularly supplemented reference book—*Subject Compilation of State Laws* (1981–).

The only national source for state legislation on all topics in paper is a one-volume state-law summary published as part of the leading national directory of lawyers—the *Martindale-Hubbell Law Directory*. However, the best source for national access to state statutes has come to be the two national legal databases, LEXIS and WESTLAW. Both databases have all state statutes in full text, with historical notes and annotations. For the texts of repealed statutes and earlier versions of amended statutes, it remains necessary to consult the session laws, which are also being added to LEXIS and WESTLAW.

National access is also available to a limited number of statutes that have been enacted by state legislatures from a uniform prototype. Uniform laws have been proposed since the late nineteenth century by a national organization, the National Conference of Commissioners on Uniform State Laws, which has one representative from each state appointed by the state's governor. The uniform laws adopted by states are published not only in the states' codes but also in a national set—the *Uniform Laws Annotated*—which has the text of each uniform act with notes on variations in the texts and interpretations of the act among the states that have adopted it. Uniform acts have played a large role in the piecemeal codification that has been characteristic of United States law since the mid-nineteenth century; they have also played a role in the relationship of states and the federal government.

Selection 4(F). Uniform and Model Laws

J. J. White, *Ex Proprio Vigore*, 89 MICH. L. REV. 2096, 2096–2133 (1991).

Introduction

The National Conference of the Commissioners on Uniform State Laws (NCCUSL) is a legislature in every way but one. It drafts uniform acts, debates them, passes them, and promulgates them, but that passage and promulgation do not make these uniform acts law over any citizen of any state. These acts become the law of the various states only *ex proprio vigore*—only if their own vitality influences the legislators of the various states to pass them.

. . . .

The Conference, of course, is different from conventional legislatures in more than one way. Although the Commissioners are technically public officials, they are an elite group. Most of the Commissioners are prominent lawyers not chosen on the same basis used to choose a legislator, but chosen because they have a more intellectual interest in uniform law than would a typical legislator. They are elected not by a vote of the electorate but by the single vote of the governor. This mode of election doubtless removes the Commissioners farther from the people than the typical state legislator; it also produces a group that is much more sophisticated in the law and more interested in long-range questions than they would be if they had to stand for reelection every two or four years.

For the purpose of this article, I assume that the product of such an elite legislature is technically superior to the product of most state legislatures and at least the equivalent of what Congress itself could produce. Of course, technical competence is far down the list of things that commend particular legislation to state legislatures and even further down on the list of the public at large. Yet the principal argument that the Commissioners can make on behalf of a uniform law when it is considered by a state legislature is its technical and substantive superiority over a law born in the back room of a state legislature and sired by a lobbying organization.

. . . .

History of the Conference

The exact origin of the NCCUSL is somewhat obscure, but it is clearly tied to the American Bar Association (ABA) and to its founding in 1878.

One of the purposes of the ABA was to prompt "uniformity of legislation throughout the Union." Other bar associations took up the call for uniform legislation and doubtless had an impact on the formation of the NCCUSL. In 1888 a proposal was introduced in the legislature of New York to create "commissioners for the promotion of uniformity of legislation in the United States." Shortly thereafter the American Bar Association passed a resolution recommending that each state adopt an act similar to that proposed in New York. In 1890 the New York legislature approved the proposal, and in 1892 the NCCUSL's first meeting was held in Saratoga, New York.

Eventually all of the states, the District of Columbia, and Puerto Rico appointed Commissioners and have taken part in the acts of the National Conference. Even from the earliest time, however, people differed about the appropriate and feasible form of uniform legislation. The original New York law contemplated uniform laws on "marriage and divorce, insolvency and the form of notarial certificates." The American Bar Association resolution added laws dealing with descent, distribution of property, acknowledgment of deeds, execution and probate of wills. All of these topics were then thought to be uniquely state law questions, beyond the interest, ken, and the constitutional reach of Congress.

Originally the Commissioners held the naive assumption that the law could be "found" and stated. The original plan contemplated "put[ting] in statutory form . . . established principles to be found in a long line of cases" on "all subjects where uniformity is deemed desirable and practicable." Where authority differed, the NCCUSL was to follow the greatest authority. Repeatedly the Commissioners have drawn the distinction between law reform—a topic not within the authority of the NCCUSL—and codification of existing principles.

As any student of modern law knows, even the modest business of choosing between divergent authority is a reform and a change in the law at least in the state whose common law is rejected. But more fundamentally, any attempt to codify a body of common law necessarily presents the drafter irresistible opportunities to state rules that had been only vaguely articulated or deeply buried in the cases. In one sense, each of these statements of the law is more than a mere codification of existing principles. Notwithstanding that fact, now so obvious, the bar associations, either out of willful ignorance or because they had not thought about it, insisted on the more limited goal for the NCCUSL: "It is exclusively the province of this committee to make uniform, so far as it may, the existing laws of the various states on the subject of interstate application. . . . [I]ts duty does not lie at all in the direction of promulgating new statutes."

Although the NCCUSL occasionally made self-conscious decisions to "reform," the admonitions against novelty have continued. For example, in 1929 the Committee on Scope and Program reiterated: "As a rule the Conference should avoid entirely novel subjects with regard to which neither legislative nor administrative experience is available." The issue again arose in 1958 where the NCCUSL proposed new "model" acts. The

Commissioners contemplated model acts as those where wide adoption would be impossible because of the local notions of the question addressed or for other reasons.

Even the most recent pronouncement of the Conference published in 1988 states that as a general rule the Conference should avoid acts on subjects that are "entirely novel and with regard to which neither legislative nor administrative experience is available." While one no longer sees the assertion that the Conference should merely codify, novelty is still forbidden, at least in circumstances where there is no track record (and presumably where novelty cannot be hidden in disguise of codification).

The expansion of the power of the federal government . . . and the subsequent congressional exercise of that power in areas formerly reserved by law or custom to the states has intensified the Commissioners' uncertainty and anxiety about their role. . . . Initially the need for the Conference arose because Congress was constitutionally foreclosed from enacting laws concerning a number of matters thought to influence only a state or citizens of a particular state. Any nineteenth-century lawyer would have said that such matters as private tort claims, private contract, rules on bills of exchange, security interests, insurance, and a host of other matters were beyond the power of Congress. . . .

. . . [T]he constitutional barriers that had excluded the Congress from these areas were torn down. Today it is difficult to imagine an event so local or so remote from interstate commerce that the Congress could not enact a law concerning it. To the extent Congress chooses to exercise this new power, it will have extinguished the need for the NCCUSL.

. . . The original constitutional division of legislative power between the states and the federal Congress arose to some extent out of fear of centralized government and of the power that such a government would wield. That idea was well expressed at the time of the drafting of the Constitution and was frequently on the lips of nineteenth-century politicians and statesmen. With the removal of the constitutional barriers against federal laws governing most elements of a private citizen's life, the same fear that caused the constitutional barriers in 1789 should again trouble the citizens, now exposed to federal power.

Ironically, the NCCUSL may find this new-found fear of federal power to be a reason for their organization. Conceivably the Commissioners can be a rallying point for the states against federal encroachment. In 1910, . . . a news account noted that President Taft had suggested as much:

> The cry against overcentralization of the government would be hushed if the states worked in harmony with each other in their law making; otherwise, as Senator Root predicted two years ago, Congress will be urged to effect for the whole country the laws which conditions demand and the state statutes fail to supply.

That the Commissioners' role might be to fill the void that would otherwise be filled by federal law has not gone unnoticed by the Commissioners themselves. Commissioner Allison Dunham made the point twenty-five years ago: "From the very beginning, including the early reports of the American Bar Association, it has been a theme that uniformity of law by voluntary state action was a means of removing any excuse for the federal government to absorb powers thought to belong rightfully to the states."

. . . .

History of Uniform Legislation by the NCCUSL

Since 1892 NCCUSL has promulgated over 200 uniform acts. . . . [M]uch of the Commissioners' seed has fallen on barren land. Of the more than 200 uniform acts, 107 have been adopted by fewer than ten states; seventy-seven of those have not made the grade in even five states, and a number of the uniform acts have earned zero adoptions. Many of the unsuccessful acts have been withdrawn or superseded by other acts; these are no longer included in the listing of uniform laws.

The Commissioners have had great successes as well. Twenty-two acts have been adopted by more than forty states. Because the Uniform Commercial Code superseded three of these previously successful acts and is itself counted as at least three acts, . . . the number twenty-two slightly exaggerates the number of successes.

. . . [T]he successful acts, those passed by more than forty states, . . . [are]: commercial acts, lawyer and court acts, and descent and estate acts. The first category includes nine acts. It contains the queen of all uniform acts, the Uniform Commercial Code. Also included are such important acts as the Uniform Partnership Act, the Uniform Limited Partnership Act, and the Uniform Arbitration Act.

Under the rubric "lawyer and court acts" we list things such as the Uniform Criminal Extradition Act, the Uniform Act to Secure the Attendance of Witnesses from Without a State in Criminal Proceedings, Uniform Durable Power of Attorney Act, and the Uniform Reciprocal Enforcement of Support Act. These categories are not perfect; for example, one might include the Uniform Arbitration Act in the list of lawyer matters and exclude it from the commercial law list. Finally are acts having to do with distribution of decedents' estates; the Uniform Anatomical Gift Act and the Uniform Simultaneous Death Act fit here. . . .

. . . .

[T]he future of the Commissioners as an influential elite legislature is in doubt. Conceivably the fear of a more powerful centralized government will enhance their power. It is just as likely that Congress and the federal agencies will snatch more and more power from the Commissioners and from the states by enacting statutes and adopting regulations. We may see the day when the federal government will rule not only traditional state areas of worker's compensation, torts, and insurance, but even the treasured commercial law. . . . [O]thers will see the National Conference of Commissioners on Uniform State Law as a wise and conservative alternative to federal regulation and federal legislation.

Note 4(G). Legislative History

Unlike the courts of England,[1] courts in the United States generally admit extrinsic evidence that may throw light on how statutes should be read. The receptiveness of United States courts to legislative history materials has spawned a specialized publishing enterprise to deal with congressional legislative history publications. The enterprise is known as the Congressional Information Service (CIS).

The sources of congressional legislative history are so voluminous that CIS makes extensive use of microfiche to keep the sources within physically manageable bounds. CIS provides microfiche copies of the following congressional sources from the earliest available to date:

—all bills and resolutions in original and amended version;[2]

—all published hearings held by subcommittees, full committees, and conference committees of the Senate and House;[3]

—all committee reports and House and Senate documents (which include messages from the president or from government agencies proposing legislation);[4]

—all committee prints (which report on research sponsored by committees or subcommittees);[5]

—transcripts of debates on the floor of Congress and supplementary materials;

—slip laws and the *Statutes at Large*.

In short, virtually the entire documentary output of Congress is assembled and republished in microfiche by CIS. Moreover, CIS has developed thorough indexes by subjects, names, and citations, with abstracts summarizing publications, and citations to legislative histories for all statutes.

The feat accomplished by CIS serves as a model for organizing a vast and complex body of information. CIS indexes, abstracts, and legislative history citations are also expected to become available on compact discs.

Another publication—a looseleaf service published by Commerce Clearing House—the *CCH Congressional Index*, traces the progress of bills during a congressional session. Even more current is the LEGIS library of LEXIS. (WESTLAW is developing a similar service.) LEXIS has also developed full-text legislative histories of selected statutes in its specialized topical libraries. Precompiled legislative histories are also available from a number of sources on microfiche or paper.

Without access to the CIS indexes/abstracts and fiche, or a ready-compiled legislative history, preparing a legislative history from scratch can be quite difficult and time-consuming.

Bills are published in microfiche by the Government Printing Office (GPO), but only as introduced and as reported by committees. Other versions are fully available only in archival copies.

Committee reports are published in the *U.S. Serial Set* by the GPO and indexed in the *Monthly Catalog of United States Government Publi-*

cations, also published by the GPO. But the quality of indexing in the *Monthly Catalog* is very much inferior to the CIS indexes, and the *Monthly Catalog* contains no abstracts. Selected reports are reprinted in the *United States Code Congressional and Administrative News*, published by West Publishing Company (in paper and on WESTLAW).

Committee hearings, committee prints, and House and Senate documents are also published by the GPO and indexed in the *Monthly Catalog*. The *Monthly Catalog*, however, only indexes these documents by general subject headings, whereas the CIS index includes names of committees or subcommittees, committee chairpersons, witnesses at hearings, titles, bill numbers, and House and Senate report and document numbers as well as subjects.[6]

Debates on the floor of Congress have been published with relative accuracy in the *Congressional Record* since 1873. Prior to that date, privately published sets—the *Annals of Congress*, the *Register of Debates*, and the *Congressional Globe*— varied in quality:

> The reports for the first eighty-four years are by no means comprehensive, nor could they be called accurate. This is due to the fact that there was during that period no systematic method of recording them.[7]

The introduction of shorthand transcription in the middle of the nineteenth century noticeably improved the quality of reporting congressional debates, but reporting was limited to briefs of speeches, and members of Congress were invited to submit full texts, which were published in an appendix. Members of Congress were thus free to embellish their remarks and submit "speeches" that were not delivered at all. This tradition persists in the practice of allowing members of Congress to submit "extensions" of their remarks for the *Congressional Record* and to make "corrections" to the transcriptions of their remarks.

The *Congressional Record* also includes presidential messages accompanying proposed legislation and presidential statements made when signing or vetoing statutes. Presidential messages and statements can also be found in the *Weekly Compilation of Presidential Documents*, which has compiled presidential publications of all sorts since 1965. The compilations are cumulated in *Public Papers of the Presidents*, which also includes papers of several presidents prior to 1965.

Presidential statements relating to legislation can also be located through the House and Senate journals. The journals contain only notations of legislative action, not texts of bills, amendments, committee hearings or reports, floor debates, or statutes.

Legislative journals take on more importance on the state level. They constitute the most commonly published source of state legislative history. Bills and their amendments are usually traceable only at a few document depositories at state libraries or other leading libraries or at state document archives. Some state agencies—especially legislative drafting bureaus and legislative counsels' offices—can also be useful sources. New Jersey, California, and some other states publish selected hearings and reports of legislative committees; Illinois and some other states make audio recordings of selected committee deliberations and make copies of tapes or transcriptions available for sale. Some states, such as Illinois, publish floor debates in microfiche. Published state documents can be traced in the *Monthly Checklist of State Publications* published by the Library of Congress, but only for documents known to the Library of Congress.

The use of legislative history for statutory interpretation remains controversial—both because of its high cost and because of its questionable utility. In the 1920s Justice Holmes warned: "It is delicate business to base speculations about the purposes or construction of a statute upon the vicissitudes of its passage";[8] in the 1970s a leading scholar condemned the use of legislative history as "expensive perfectionism";[9] and in the 1990s Justice Antonin Scalia has raised the issue anew.

Selection 4(G). Challenging the Use of Legislative History

W. N. Eskridge, *The New Textualism*, 37 U.C.L.A. L. REV. 621, 621–85 (1990).

An analytical conundrum besets a court's interpretation of a statute: The statute's text is the most important consideration in statutory interpretation, and a clear text ought to be given effect. Yet the meaning of a text critically depends upon its surrounding context. Sometimes that context will suggest a meaning at war with the apparent acontextual meaning suggested by the statute's language. How should the judge proceed? Is contextual evidence even admissible in such cases? How can it be excluded? The Supreme Court's traditional resolution of this conundrum has been to consider virtually any contextual evidence, especially the statute's legislative history, even when the statutory text has an apparent "plain meaning." This traditional approach has been challenged by a few commentators and, now, from within the Court itself. . . .

. . . .

Since . . . a decision handed down early in his first Term with the Court, Justice Scalia has criticized the Court for relying on legislative history to confirm or rebut the apparent plain meaning of a statute. . . . These opinions, . . . and a speech he gave in 1985, have developed the outlines of . . . "the new textualism." The new textualism posits that once the Court has ascertained a statute's plain meaning, consideration of legislative history becomes irrelevant. Legislative history should not even be consulted to confirm the apparent meaning of a statutory text. Such confirmation comes, if any is needed, from examination of the structure of the statute, interpretations given similar statutory provisions, and canons of statutory construction. It is not clear that Justice Scalia would eliminate consideration of legislative history altogether, but his approach would severely curtail its use.

. . . .

I. The Traditional Approach . . .

. . . At least rhetorically, the Court views its role as implementing the original intent or purpose of the enacting Congress. In this endeavor, legislative history is usually relevant, either to supply meaning for an ambiguous statute or to confirm or rebut the plain meaning of a clear statute. The relevant legislative history runs the gamut from footnotes and appendices in committee reports, to legislators' statements on the floor or in committee, to statements by bureaucrats and law professors, to proposals rejected in committee or on the floor, to significant legislative silences. In short, almost anything that casts light upon what Congress attempted to do when it enacted a statute is potentially relevant. The Court does, however, consider certain evidence to be more significant than other evidence.

. . . .

[A] IMAGINATIVE RECONSTRUCTION AND VARIETY IN LEGISLATIVE HISTORY

Often, the Court's inquiry into legislative history is a brief foray, in which the Court quotes from one or two legislative sources to buttress its interpretation. On other occasions, however, the Court actually does a serious documentary history of a statute, what Judges Learned Hand and Richard Posner have called "imaginative reconstruction." In this mode, the Court will trace the evolution of the statute and its debating history, from early legislative proposals to enactment, obviously with a focus on the interpretative issue in the case. The goal of the inquiry is not only to retrieve specific legislative consideration of the issue (if such occurred), but also to recreate the general assumptions, goals, and limitations of the enacting Congress. Through this imaginative process, the Court seeks to "reconstruct" the answer the enacting Congress would have given if the interpretive issue had been posed directly.

. . . .

. . . In an inquiry to reconstruct Congress' original intent or purpose, much of what passes for legislative history is obviously relevant, including the text of proposed bills, changes made in the bills by committee, the committee's report on the bill, discussion of the bill by Members of Congress at the committee hearings and on the floor of the House and Senate, votes rejecting amendments or amending the bill, and the conference report reconciling differences between the Senate and House versions (if necessary). Other materials have been found relevant by the Court sometimes, based upon conventions or inferences it has made about probable legislative intent.

1. Statements of Nonlegislators

Initially, it might seem anomalous for an inquiry about probable legislative intent or purpose to consider statements by nonlegislators. Yet much legislation is actually drafted by people outside the Congress, which is then persuaded to enact it, often without much discussion or alteration. Hence, what these nonlegislative drafters have to say about legislation is often of interest to the statutory interpreter, and indeed much of this evidence is preserved in hearings and letters where the drafters explain the statute to the legislators who are called to vote on it. To take an obvious example, the President often proposes legislation, and presidential transmittal letters and addresses may be useful in discerning the original point of a statute. Presidential veto messages may sometimes be useful, especially when Congress passes legislation over the President's veto, implicitly rejecting the President's policy preferences. The Administration of President Reagan believed that presidential signing statements should be given weight in statutory interpretation.

The President is not often personally involved in advising Congress about drafting legislation, but executive departments and the independent agencies often are, and their opinions about bills they have drafted or supported are often noted in the Supreme Court's discussion of legislative history. The Department of Justice, as the main legal arm of the executive branch, often has a strong voice in drafting and pressing for legislation, especially civil rights and criminal statutes. Consequently, in these areas especially, the Court often stresses the views of Attorneys General or other Department of Justice officials.

Finally, the Court will consider the views of private persons and groups that draft or lobby for legislation. Occasionally, law professors' testimony is important evidence, especially if they originated or drafted the legislation, and the Court has also considered the views of private interest groups that advocated particular legislation. Most commonly, however, the Court will rely on shared understanding of competing interest groups. Many statutes reflect carefully crafted compromises among the various groups, and the Court sometimes finds documentary records of such compromises useful when interpreting the statutory result.

2. Legislative Silence

The silence of legislators can be as significant as their utterances. Sherlock Holmes once solved a case by making inferences from the fact that a dog did not bark. . . . Using similar logic, the Court has created a principle of continuity: Every time Congress enacts or amends a statute, it is acting against an established background of legal rules and interpretations, which Congress is presumed to know. . . . [If] no one says anything, . . . [the] strong inference [is] that the pre-existing rules are left in place. . . .

. . . In many . . . cases, the Court presumes from Congress's silence over time that Congress "acquiesces" in judicial or agency interpretations of a statute, or presumes from Congress' silence when reenacting . . . a statute that Congress wants to carry forth previous interpretations. . . .

3. Subsequent Legislative History

Perhaps most peculiar of all is the Court's occasional willingness to consider "subsequent legislative history" (something of an oxymoron), that is, the interpretation of a statute expressed by Members of Congress after the statute has been enacted. Such statements are sometimes found in floor debates, committee reports, and even affidavits or amicus briefs in statutory cases. Given the Court's focus on the original legislative intent or purpose and the possibility of manipulation, it has often iterated that "the views of a subsequent Congress form a hazardous basis for inferring the intent of an earlier one." . . .

Nonetheless, the Court sometimes has considered subsequent legislative history when interpreting statutes. The Court's stated reason is usually the dearth of other interpretive guides. Also, subsequent Congresses often rely on certain assumed interpretations of previous statutes. When it is apparent that the legislature has relied on an interpretation that is not clearly incorrect, it makes a good deal of sense for an intentionalist to credit subsequent legislative interpretation. Indeed, the Court will give some weight to statutory interpretations accepted and relied on by regulators and the regulated community. Should it not give at least as much weight to legislative reliance on its interpretations of prior statutes, as on private or agency reliance?

[B] HIERARCHY OF SOURCES IN THE COURT'S USE OF LEGISLATIVE HISTORY

Given the foregoing discussion, the Court is not at a loss in having much material from which imaginatively to reconstruct a legislative history. Sometimes all the sources point to the same interpretive answer, which makes the Court highly confident of its resolution. Other times the different sources will point in different directions. As a result, the Court has worked out a rough hierarchy of evidence to resolve conflicts. The hierarchy is based upon the comparative reliability of each source: How likely does this source reflect the views or assumptions of the enacting Congress? Is there a danger of strategic manipulation by individual Members or biased groups seeking to "pack" the legislative history? How well-informed is the source? The figure below . . . reflects this hierarchy.

. . . .

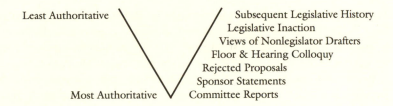

Least Authoritative — Subsequent Legislative History / Legislative Inaction / Views of Nonlegislator Drafters / Floor & Hearing Colloquy / Rejected Proposals / Sponsor Statements / Most Authoritative — Committee Reports

1. Committee Reports

. . . Committee reports are the most frequently cited and relied-upon sources of legislative history, and in the Court's traditional view the most authoritative source. "A committee report represents the considered and collective understanding of those Congressmen involved in drafting and studying proposed legislation. Floor debates reflect at best the understanding of individual Congressmen. It would take extensive and thoughtful debate to detract from the plain thrust of a committee report. . . ." Committee reports are often the best evidence of bicameral agreement, either because the House and Senate reports are identical, or because a conference report explicates the chambers' resolution of differences.

2. Sponsor Statements

. . . Next only to committee reports in reliability are statements by sponsors and/or floor managers, and the Court relies on their statements routinely. "[R]emarks . . . of the sponsor of the language ultimately enacted, are an authoritative guide to the statute's construction," because the sponsors are the Members of Congress most likely to know what the proposed legislation is all about, and other Members can be expected to pay special heed to their characterizations of the legislation. "While the views of a sponsor of legislation are by no means conclusive, they are entitled to considerable weight, particularly in the absence of a committee report."

3. Rejected Proposals

. . . " 'Few principles of statutory construction are more compelling than the proposition that Congress does not intend sub *silentio* to enact statutory language that it has earlier discarded in favor of other language,' " the Court remarked. This is a slight overstatement of the Court's practice. Oftentimes, the rejection of proposed language by the committee, on the floor of the House or Senate, or in conference is quite probative, since it is direct evidence that Congress considered an issue and agreed not to adopt a specified policy. But other times it is unclear that the rejection was truly a referendum on the issue later before the Court. . . .

4. Floor and Hearing Colloquy

"In construing laws [the Court has] been extremely wary of testimony before committee hearings and of debates on the floor of Congress save for precise analyses of statutory phrases by the sponsors of the proposed laws." Thus, statements by legislators at hearings or on the floor are not as authoritative as those of sponsors and floor managers, unless the speakers can be identified as "players" on that particular bill. According to the conventional wisdom, nonplayers are less likely to know what the consensus view is on the bill, and are more likely to behave strategically (engaging in the famed "planned colloquy"). Further, the views of those unsupportive of the proposed legislation "are no authoritative guide to the construction of legislation. It is the sponsors that we look to when the meaning of the statutory words is in doubt." This conventional wisdom has been relaxed somewhat in the last twenty years, for the Court frequently looks to legislative colloquy, especially to discern the general assumptions made at the time a law was enacted. Moreover, where the sponsor's statements are either too general or suspicious, the Court will rely on more specific colloquy instead. Even the views of opponents have sometimes been considered.

5. Nonlegislative Drafters and Sponsors

. . . The Court will usually invoke . . . statements [of nonlegislative drafters and sponsors] as further evidence in support of conclusions gleaned from the statutory text, committee reports, and sponsor's statements. Nonlegislator evidence will be most important in cases where it is clear that the statute was a careful compromise reached outside the legislative process and merely ratified by the legislature, and sometimes in cases where there is virtually no other evidence.

6. Legislative Silence and Subsequent History

. . . [E]vidence of legislative silence and subsequent history is usually too ambiguous to count as legislative history, but in some contexts the sources are considered by the Court. "[W]hile the views of subsequent Congresses cannot override the unmistakable intent of the enacting one, such views are entitled to significant weight, and particularly so when the precise intent of the enacting Congress is obscure." Much the same can be said of the dog that doesn't bark argument: Legislative silence will usually be supporting evidence of legislative intent and will be the main evidence only when there is virtually no other evidence of legislative intent.

II. The New Textualism: Justice Scalia's Critique of the Traditional Approach and the Court's New Direction

The traditional approach . . . has been well received by judges, lawyers, and even law professors in the generation weaned on the legal process philosophy of the 1950s [which] is skeptical of claims that words are self-defining. . . . The Court's ability to establish its case through historical as well as textual evidence makes its opinions seem more authoritative and reliable.

The traditional approach is in trouble. Because of several theoretical developments in the 1980's, an increasing number of scholars and judges are questioning the traditional approach. Justice Scalia's critique . . . has found a receptive audience, including an audience on the Supreme Court. Although the Court has hardly abandoned the traditional approach, its practice in statutory cases . . . has been influenced by the new textualism. There is little reason to believe that the new textualism is a fad . . . and its influence may expand.

. . . Three different types of criticisms render the traditional approach vulnerable: (1) the realist criticism that legislative intent is an incoherent and indeterminate concept; (2) the historicist criticism that present interpreters can never completely reconstruct a hypothetical historical intent; and (3) the formalist criticism that the traditional approach is inconsistent with the structures of our constitutional democracy [by giving too much discretion to unelected judges].

. . . .

There has been some evolution over time in Justice Scalia's critique of the traditional approach. His initial attack (while a court of appeals judge) focused mainly on the extensive judicial use of committee reports as authoritative evidence of statutory meaning, and seemed to accept other legislative history as authoritative in some cases. . . . According to Judge Scalia, . . . committee reports are scant evidence of even a probable or made-up legislative intent, because they are crafted by staff, are not necessarily even read by the legislators themselves, and are subject to packing at the behest of interest groups and other legislative insiders. This line of attack, including the specific evidence adduced by Judge Scalia, has been persuasively criticized. . .

Since his elevation to the Supreme Court, Justice Scalia's critique has been both more radical and more formalist. . . . [I]n his first year, Justice Scalia distinguished himself for a reluctance to rely on legislative history in his opinions, concurrences, and dissents. In his second year, he generally questioned the use of any kind of legislative history. "Committee reports, floor speeches, and even colloquies between Congressmen, are frail substitutes for bicameral vote upon the text of a law and its presentment to the President." . . .

. . . .

Nowhere does Justice Scalia demonstrate that one can never show that the President and virtually everyone in Congress "very probably" shared a collective understanding not clearly revealed on the face of the statute. Nonetheless, he seems to lean toward the view that legislative history should not be consulted (except in cases of absurd results and, possibly, of ambiguity), as something of a prophylactic rule to cabin the discretion of judges *and* to encourage Congress to enact clearer statutes. . . .

Justice Scalia is aware of the familiar precepts that words do not interpret themselves and that their meaning depends upon their context. He probably would agree that a dictionary definition will not always answer the difficult interpretive issues and would admit that context is necessary. Like the defenders of legislative history, therefore, Justice Scalia admits "coherence" arguments, that is, arguments that an ambiguous term is rendered clear if one possible definition is more coherent with the relevant legal authorities than other possible definitions. But, unlike defenders of legislative history, Justice Scalia admits only arguments based upon textual, or horizontal, coherence (this meaning is consistent with other parts of the statute or other terms in similar statutes), and not based upon historical, or vertical, coherence (this meaning is consistent with the historical expectations of the authors of the statute). Consider the clearest statement to date of his approach:

> The meaning of terms on the statute-books ought to be determined, not on the basis of which meaning can be shown to have been understood by a larger handful of the Members of Congress; but rather on the basis of which meaning is (1) most in accord with context and ordinary usage, and thus most likely to have been understood by the whole Congress which voted on the words of the statute (not to mention the citizens subject to it), and (2) most compatible with the surrounding body of law into which the provision must be integrated—a compatibility which, by a benign fiction, we assume Congress always has in mind.

. . . Justice Scalia also has claimed functionalist advantages for his approach. Textualism will curtail opportunities for judicial lawmaking by limiting the tools available to judges seeking to escape plain statutory meaning. It will prevent the Court from being misled by manipulative legislative history and will remove incentives for legislative actors to create such history. And it will obviate the need for practitioners and judges to engage in the needless, and often very expensive, search through legislative histories before they can be sure of statutory meaning.

. . . .

The Supreme Court has not thrown over its traditional approach to legislative history in favor of the new textualism, yet. In each year that Justice Scalia has sat on the Court, however, his theory has exerted greater influence on the Court's practice. . . .

. . . .

III. Evaluating the New Textualism: Should the Court Ignore Legislative History?

. . . .

Indeed, the new textualism is a very attractive formalist theory. By focusing on the plain meaning a statute would have for the ordinary, reasonable reader, the new textualism has the intuitive appeal of looking at the most concrete evidence of legislative expectations and the material most accessible to the citizenry. The statutory text is what one thinks of when someone asks what the "law" requires. In its focus on statutory logic, structure, and analogies, the new textualism also appeals to the sophisticated legal analyst. By asking the interpreter to consider the textual analysis as a rigorous "holistic" enterprise, the theory poses exciting analytical possibilities.

. . . Once the statutory text is unencumbered by evidence of original legislative expectations, it is free to evolve dynamically, especially where the statute is open-textured. Moreover, Justice Scalia's holistic approach opens the door for statutes to evolve over time "in the light of surrounding texts that happen to have been subsequently enacted. This classic judicial task of reconciling many laws enacted over time, and getting them to 'make sense' in combination, necessarily assumes that the implications of a statute may be altered by the implications of a later statute." The new textualism permits the updating of old statutory policies as new statutory policies are adopted and new constitutional limitations developed.

Notwithstanding these formidable advantages, the new textualism has provoked public controversy. Two types of criticisms have been made to date. . . . First, some criticize Justice Scalia and the new textualists for having a "hidden agenda," to wit: By deferring to Republican-controlled agencies and narrowly construing the liberal laws of the Democrat-controlled Congress, the new textualists (mainly conservative Republicans) seek to reduce the power of government to do good in our society. The reconstruction of the intellectual background of the new textualism [casts] doubt that this is the whole story, even if it is partly true. . . .

Second, traditional legal process theorists and judges criticize Justice Scalia for ignoring context, which is necessary to give meaning to the bare language of statutes. . . . Justice Scalia . . . differs with the traditional legal process writers in what he will consider as context. The new textualism considers as context dictionaries and grammar books, the whole statute, analogous provisions in other statutes, canons of construction, and the common sense God gave us. The only context not normally considered is legislative history, and most of the new textualists will consider legislative history if the other aids still leave the statutory meaning truly unclear. Not only does Justice Scalia escape the no-context objection, but he urges a more efficient use of context: Do not engage in the potentially exhausting review of legislative history unless necessary. . . .

. . . [However, although] Justice Scalia considers a great deal of context, . . . the context he emphasizes is just as manipulable as the context emphasized by the traditional approach. That is, Justice Scalia's approach requires choices among competing evidence just as much as the traditional approach does. . . .

. . . .

[Nevertheless,] Justice Scalia . . . has a rather good functional case: The traditional approach relies too much on legislative history, much of it obscure, for too little payoff. The "cost" of this research into legislative history is borne not just by the Court and its litigants, but by litigants at all levels and, most of all, by counsel rendering predictive advice to clients. "It is hard enough to search a long, heterogeneous and often conflicting legislative history as relates to a particular issue in a current controversy," Professor Dickerson writes. "It is vastly harder and impracticable to search all aspects of the legislative history as they relate to the myriad of potentially troublesome problems that the lawyer would like to anticipate."

Traditional legal process theory tries to solve the problem of excessive legislative history by trimming away certain types of history (such as anything but committee reports and sponsor statements). This is a difficult strategy to follow because of the legal process emphasis on context: In many cases, as the new textualists argue, committee reports will be misleading (by design), and the most reliable evidence of a true legislative deal will be testimony at hearings, presidential statements, or even legislative silence. In short, once you open the door to consideration of legislative history, it is hard to exclude any type of evidence without viewing it in the context of the whole story. The new textualists suggest another strategy for dealing with excessive legislative history. This approach advocates prophylactic rules to exclude legislative history altogether in certain types of cases and to treat legislative history more critically in all cases. . . .

III

ADMINISTRATION

The King and His Council (From Fitzherbert's *La Grande Abridgement*, 1565)

5

Administrative Publications in England

Note 5(A). Early Royal Documents

"What we now call 'Administrative Law' is as old as government itself."[1] Royal records for administrative purposes exist from Anglo-Saxon times. Since the seventh century, royal charters have been preserved, assigning privileges and rights—usually grants of lands, sometimes grants of governing rights to local communities—with some charters, such as the "Great Charter" of 1215, recognizing wide-ranging rights and privileges. Charters granted to individuals or communities are often preserved not in government archives but in the archives of recipients—such as church or municipal archives.

Royal charters were first written in a cumbersome fashion as "diplomas":

> In the Anglo-Saxon period both royal and private charters generally took the form of a diploma written in Latin and describing in a very solemn and artificial manner the creation or transfer of an estate of land. Modeled at first upon the private deeds of the later Roman Empire, the charter gradually acquired a pronounced ecclesiastical flavor. The preamble containing the grantor's reason for the donation abounded in pious references proving the blessedness of giving, and in references to classical mythology. The dispositive proper set forth in minute detail the boundaries of the land. Lastly came the sanction, which appealed to any and all ecclesiastical penalties should the will of the grantor be thwarted.[2]

The Norman Conquest introduced a new form of royal charter—the writ—which was used for a wide range of administrative purposes, including the commencement of legal actions in royal courts. Written "in the form of a simple letter," the writ was one of the devices most responsible for gaining Norman rulers their reputations as effective administrators:

> Compared to the cumbersome diploma, the writ was an amazingly efficient document, able to do in a few lines what a diploma could scarcely do in scores. Unknown to the Continent before the Normans adopted it, the writ became one of the chief instruments of the strong Norman-Angevin administration both in England and on the Continent. [T]he charters allow us to see how the law operated in civil cases, to reconstruct legal procedure in court, and to learn of royal rights and of the relation between king and local administrative officers.[3]

The crowning administrative achievement of the Norman rulers was the *Domesday Book,* which recorded the resources of England as a basis for levying the "Danegeld"—the tax to finance war against the Danes. The *Domesday Book* "provides our surest description of finance, central and local administration, and the status of rural and urban inhabitant."[4]

> The making of Domesday, the great rate book of the kingdom, is a magnificent exploit, an exploit which has no parallel in the history of Europe, an exploit only possible in a conquered country. Under Henry the First national finance becomes an orderly system, a system of which an orderly written record is kept. The sheriff's accounts for 1132 are still extant on what is called the Pipe Roll . . . ; this is one of our most valuable sources of information. It has been casually preserved; it is not until the beginning of Henry II's reign that we get a regular series of such records.[5]

From the middle of the twelfth century, an unbroken stream of pipe rolls has been preserved from the Exchequer, recording the reports of the sheriffs to the king accounting for money collected, debts owed, and expenses incurred in the performance of their legal duties. In addition, financial accounts of the royal household, the "chamber" and "wardrobe," and documents relating to taxation are preserved in the Exchequer.

In the second half of the twelfth century, the Chancery began producing a variety of records. In addition to writs, "assizes" were issued by the Chancery as public declarations to implement royal policies, such as assizes defining judicial procedures and jurisdiction (an assize of 1179 substituted jury trials for trials by battle), or establishing a national militia, or setting rules for administration of royal forest lands, or setting standards for weights, measures, and money; less formal administrative pronouncements were issued as "constitutions" or "ordinances," or informal instructions such as those given to justices setting forth on eyres, or commissions charged with investigations of local officials.[6]

Beginning in 1199, the Chancery started keeping copies of charters in a charter roll. Early in the thirteenth century, copies of other documents issuing from the Chancery began to be recorded in "patent rolls," if public declarations or open instructions to royal officials, or "close rolls," if private communications.

In the late thirteenth century, during the reign of Edward I (1272–1307), lawmaking by royal charter began to give way to lawmaking by statute. As the statutory record began in the Statute Rolls and the Rolls of Parliament near the end of the century,[7] a distinction came to be drawn between statutes, which were enacted with the consent of the "estates of the realm"—that is, parliament—and "mere ordinances" issued by royal authority without parliament.

Selection 5(A). Statutes and Ordinances

W. S. HOLDSWORTH, SOURCES AND LITERATURE OF ENGLISH LAW 45–54 (1925).

. . . [T]he Great Charter . . . had made it clear that the council of the nation ought to be consulted as to the passing of laws. But this was then but a vague restraint upon the crown, because the manner and form in which the nation should be consulted was uncertain; and so, . . . the line between legislative and merely administrative acts was not clearly drawn. It is the growth of the legislative power of Parliament which gradually draws a distinct line between these two kinds of acts. But this was a gradual process. . . . As late as 1349 it was said . . . that 'the king makes the laws with the assent of the peers and the commons, and not through the instrumentality of the peers and commons'. . . .

Since it was the king, acting on the advice of his council or of Parliament, who initiated legislation and framed the laws, it did not appear anomalous that he should act upon the information of any considerable body of his subjects, such as, for instance, the merchants and the clergy. And in fact we find that laws were made on the petitions of both these classes. And, as the king was clearly the executive authority, we get ordinances, the legislative force of which it is difficult to estimate. Thus, at the beginning of the fourteenth century, though Parliament had definitely made its appearance, it would have been difficult to give a very precise answer to the whereabouts of the legislative power in the state. We might say, as was said in 1322, that a statute ought to be enacted with the common consent of the estates of the realm. But this leaves very much at large the question what is common consent, and the question of the manner in which a statute differs from a mere ordinance. It is the action of Parliament in the fourteenth and fifteenth centuries which gradually clears up these difficulties. In the first place, it gradually separates those enactments to which it has consented from those to which it has not consented. In the second place, it gradually asserts a right to the initiation of legislation, and a control over the manner in which a statute is framed.

(i) Parliament gradually separates those enactments to which it has consented from those to which it has not consented, by preventing ordinances enacted on the petition of outside bodies, such as the clergy or the merchants, from being reckoned as statutes, unless they received its approval. . . . This, however, did not completely distinguish statutes from mere ordinances. . . . The difference between statutes and mere ordinances did not turn solely upon the question whether they were assented to by all the estates of the realm. A good deal depended upon the question whether the enactment was intended to make a permanent and deliberate change in the law, or whether it was intended to be somewhat in the nature of an experimental provision. In fact, it is difficult to be quite sure of the exact contents of the medieval statute book, because much depended upon the intentions of king and Parliament; and their intentions were not always expressed.

(ii) Some of these difficulties were solved by the assertion on the part of Parliament of a claim to the initiation of legislation, and to a control over its form. In the fourteenth and at the beginning of the fifteenth century it was, . . . the king and his council who framed and enacted the statute upon the petition of Parliament. But, as the [fifteenth] century advanced, the initiation of legislation gradually passed from the crown to the commons, and sometimes to the lords. . . . Statutes are made not by the king, at the request of the lords and at the petition of the commons, but 'by the authority of Parliament'. This phrase first appears in 1433, and, from the year 1445, it becomes a regular part of the enacting words. . . .

The machinery of legislation had thus reached its final form at the close of the medieval period. But though it had become quite clear that the king could not make a statute, he had not lost all his legislative power. He still possessed the power to make ordinances or proclamations. In fact this subordinate legislative power was not peculiar to the king. It belonged to many medieval communities—manors, hundreds, or boroughs— all of which then performed various governmental functions. The fact that Brooke in his Abridgement could class together cases relating to the by-laws of these communities, and cases relating to royal proclamations, is very significant of the effect of the rise of the legislative power of Parliament upon the king's power to legislate. But though royal proclamations had become comparable to by-laws in respect of their subordination to statute law, they were of vastly greater importance. The power to issue them was a jealously guarded prerogative. . . . But all through the Tudor period the extent of this prerogative was very ill defined. This was due to two causes. In the first place, the vague powers of the medieval king had never been expressly curtailed. No doubt the logical consequence of the rise of the legislative power of Parliament was a limitation upon the king's power to legislate; but it was an indirect and therefore a vague limitation. In the second place, the growth of the modern state necessitated a constant and minute regulation by the central government of the activities, both of the individual, and of various parts of the body politic; and this obviously necessitated an extensive use of royal proclamations. 'When the common state or wealth of the people require it,' it was said . . . 'the king's proclamation bindes as a lawe and neede not staye a Parliamente.'

Thus the question of the king's power to legislate by proclamation was one which needed definite settlement. On the one hand, no one desired to give the king power to overturn by proclamation the existing machinery of law and government, and to alter radically the rights and duties of the subject. On the other hand, it was clearly necessary that the king's proclamations should be obeyed. The existing law was obscure; and the inconvenience of this obscurity was not likely to be overlooked by Henry VIII, who was remarkable for his political prescience. His statute of Proclamations [1539] was a very able attempt by king and Parliament to deal with the problem in a manner which commended itself to the public opinion of the day. The safeguards by which the Act was accompanied, and the use which Henry made of it, prevent us from regarding it as anything in the nature of a 'lex regia'. Rather it was an attempt to deal with a constitutional problem in a manner satisfactory to the king and the subject. The king got his large powers to legislate by proclamation recognized, and put upon a firm basis. But his proclamations must have the consent of his council; the death penalty could not be inflicted for their breach; and the range of subjects with which they could deal was limited by the proviso they were not to affect rules of the common law, existing Acts of Parliament, or rights to freehold. The Act was repealed in the first year of the following reign [1547]; and this meant that the king's power to legislate by proclamation again relapsed into its old obscurity. Proclamations were somewhat more extensively used by Henry's successors than by Henry himself. But no large changes in the law were made by their means. In fact, the extent to which they could be legally used was never finally settled in the sixteenth century, because the Tudors made so tactful a use of their powers that no demand for the settlement of this question was raised.

The clear-cut theories of the first Stuart king [James I] as to the extent of his prerogative, and the attempts which he made to carry his theories into execution, brought this, amongst other constitutional questions, to the front. In 1610 the Commons complained that 'proclamations have been of late years much more frequent than heretofore, and that they are extended not only to the liberty, but also to the goods inheritances and livelihood of men . . . by reason whereof there is a general fear conceived . . . that proclamations will by degrees grow up and increase to the strength and nature of laws'. Coke was consulted as to the answer to be given to this remonstrance; and his answer . . . permanently settled the sphere in which they were operative. They could not vary statute or common law; and, by means of them, the king could only effect those things which by his prerogative he was allowed by law to effect.

Note 5(B). The Tudor-Stuart Proclamations

The reigns of Henry VIII and his Tudor and Stuart successors constituted
a period when royal lawmaking by "proclamation" flourished. The period
has been criticized as being one of "unparliamentary government."[1] The
excesses of royal power were exemplified in the enforcement of proclamations through the infamous "star chamber" courts that functioned outside the established common-law courts. However, the Tudor/Stuart era
may also be interpreted as a period when executive powers were defined
and distinguished from legislative powers. Following the reign of Henry
VIII, statutes and proclamations seem to have found their respective roles.

> After 1547 statute and proclamation seem to have gone happily hand in hand.
> Early Tudor statutes had delegated authority to proclamations in matters that
> could not easily be regulated by parliament, such as price controls, and the
> whole field of economic legislation came to rest upon this double foundation.
> Sometimes statutes authorized control by proclamation, as in the case of price
> fixing and wages limitations. Sometimes proclamation was used to clarify or
> expand statute. . . . Sometimes proclamations were used to reconcile the dif-
> ferent claims of various pressure groups which had been overlooked by the
> statute-drafters. Sometimes, too, proclamations were used to suspend a statute
> in an emergency, or if problems arose over its implementation: the 1536 act
> for the true making of woolen cloth, for instance, caused difficulties and was
> suspended by proclamations more or less annually until a new statute of 1542
> amended the earlier one.
>
> Only very occasionally did proclamation "create" law, except in the spe-
> cial case of control of the coinage, which was universally recognized as a part
> of the royal prerogative. . . . In general, the neglect of recognized constitu-
> tional limits occurred only in an emergency, or when the proclamation was
> meant to be backed up rapidly by a statute: thus, the 1580 proclamation
> against new buildings in London was intended to be supported by a statute in
> 1581, but a series of accidents held it up until 1593. Proclamations were used
> in the sixteenth century, therefore, primarily to back up statute, to declare that
> the monarch wanted a specific statute particularly carefully observed—or, con-
> trariwise, temporarily suspended.
>
> Certainly contemporaries seem to have voiced few anxieties about their
> use. The only major discussion of the matter after the passing of the 1539 act
> and its repeal in 1547 was in the course of a debate in 1576 on a bill that
> would have allowed the monarch to appoint by proclamation the kind of cloth-
> ing every degree of person within the realm should wear. The main constitu-
> tional objection then expressed appears to have been that the bill would have
> required publication of the proclamation in one place only, and not in every
> county, as was normal. However, some members did object that "a procla-
> mation from the prince should take the force of law, which might prove a
> dangerous precedent in time to come. For tho' we live now in the time of a
> gracious sovereign", what might happen in the future? The bill did not suc-

ceed. . . . [T]here was no major outcry about [proclamations] until the reign of James. Even then, it appears that the complaints voiced so forcibly in the 1610 petition against proclamations arose out of the tactless way in which James was using them to promulgate policies which had already been rejected by parliament—most notably Scottish union—rather than because the Commons believed that proclamations were of themselves an evil.[2]

The proclamations of the Tudor and Stuart eras, like the royal documents before them, were recorded in the patent and close rolls of the Chancery. Publication was by public readings and postings of broadsides, but no historical collection of proclamations was available to the public. In 1910, a private collector published an extensive bibliography of Tudor and Stuart proclamations that remains the most thorough source.[3]

Selection 5(B). The Eighteenth and Nineteenth Centuries

C. K. Allen, Law and Orders 26–33 (3d ed., 1965).

Beginnings of Legislation

. . . .

[A] celebrated enactment of Henry VIII was his Statute of Sewers, and it is particularly interesting as the first example of the creation of a statutory body entrusted with wide delegated powers of a mixed kind. It appointed Commissioners with "full power and authority to make, constitute and ordain laws ordinances and decrees, and further to do all and everything, mentioned in the said Commission . . . and the same laws and ordinances so made to reform, repeal and amend, and make new from time to time as the cases necessary shall require in that behalf". The rules made by the Commissioners were given the full validity of statutes, subject to their being certified into the Chancery and receiving the royal assent, and in addition the Commissioners were invested with powers to levy rates on landowners and to adjudicate on cases of non-payment and to impose penalties. Here, then, was a remarkable blend of delegated powers, legislative, administrative and judicial. The statute remained in force for four hundred years. . . .

Types of Delegated Powers

In the next two hundred years subordinate legislation for the most part took one of two forms; it was designed to meet emergencies, in which the ordinary Parliamentary processes would have been too tardy, or to confer a variety of powers of local government. In the first category are such things as the import and export of various commodities both at home and in the Colonies, or quarantine regulations for a sudden outbreak of plague or smallpox; these matters were generally governed by royal proclamations and were dictated by sudden economic crises or by epidemics in face of which the public were, as a rule, singularly ignorant and helpless. In the second class . . . the powers of the Commissioners of Sewers; law-making powers, in such matters as the regulation of gaols and beerhouses, and even the manufacture of cloth, were constantly added to the miscellaneous administrative duties of the Justices of the Peace; and a long list of ad hoc authorities would include the . . . bodies of commissioners for the regulation of such public concerns as the safe-guarding of cliffs, navigation on the Thames, drainage of the fens, hackney coaches, rules for the Port of London, and many others.

The Stuarts

Under the Stuarts, the question of the ultimate governmental power, including the legislative power and the claim to suspend or dispense from the law, passed into a phase of acute conflict between prerogative and Parliament. It does not fall within our present purpose to recall the pretensions of James I or to repeat the well-known and tragic story of the causes and events which brought Charles I to the scaffold. In the sequel of the Commonwealth England made its only experiment in government by decree, which was rejected, with an almost excessive degree of reaction, by the Restoration. No great constitutional development took place during the lax period of recovery under Charles II, but with the last of the Stuarts the old issue of the prerogative, now exacerbated by religious dissension, flared up anew and precipitated a second revolution, this time bloodless, yet more decisive than the first; for with the [Glorious Revolution] the doctrine of Divine Right was once for all displaced by statutory succession to the throne—in short, by limited monarchy as it has been understood ever since. The legislative supremacy of Parliament, and the subordination of the prerogative to the law, have not thereafter been in doubt.

The Eighteenth Century

In the eighteenth century, however, Parliament was still smarting from the encounters of the preceding age and still suspicious of the executive. It was therefore chary of putting its legislative powers in commission, even in matters of pure administration. There was a certain amount of emergency legislation for the safety of a sorely-threatened realm, and much decentralised administration in the squirearchical rule of the Justices of the Peace. But the public general statutes of this period tend to be either overloaded with detail or to be directed to specific instances rather than to general rules. Parliament, writes Maitland, "seems afraid to rise to the dignity of a general proposition; it will not say, 'All commons may be enclosed according to the general rules', 'All aliens may become naturalised if they fulfil these or those conditions', 'All boroughs shall have these powers for widening their roads', 'All marriages may be dissolved if the wife's adultery be proved'. No, it deals with this common and that marriage." In short, Parliament was attempting to conduct the whole business of government by its own machinery, and it is interesting to speculate exactly what that machinery was, for there must have been an active administration, of which we hear little in history, within the legislative framework. One result of this attempt to monopolise the powers of government . . . was that the eighteenth century was barren both in important legislative principles and in broad developments of the common law. It was a period of social stagnation. Fortunately, however, the absorption of powers was not carried to a dangerous extreme and it diminished throughout the century as the memory of former conflicts receded and as Parliament felt more assured of its constitutional status. It was, for one thing, offset by the powerful counterweight of the independence of the judiciary, a principle which had been permanently established and which was jealously maintained.

Also, even in this era of Parliamentary supremacy not a few extensive powers were delegated to certain authorities of great constitutional importance. Chief among them were the Commissioners of Customs and Excise, whose powers, very considerable in extent, were regarded with some uneasiness . . . by Members of the House of Commons. . . . Again, early in the century, by the Mutiny Act of 1717, the Crown was given (not without protest) almost exclusive disciplinary powers over the Army, both at home and abroad—though, curiously enough, Parliament insisted on retaining its right to enact the Articles of War for the discipline of the Navy. Altogether, despite a tendency to lopsidedness in Parliament's insistence on the pre-eminence of its own power, the balance of the constitution was preserved.

The Nineteenth Century

Thus there was a continuous tradition of the delegation of powers, though it developed unevenly in different ages; and it is to the nineteenth century that its great and rapid extension belongs. The causes were many. After 1832 we entered upon a period of social and legal reform unprecedented in our history. It is the fashion nowadays to speak as if our own age were the first and true inventor of "social legislation". To the eyes of our generation, many of the reforms of the nineteenth century seem so elementary and obvious that they are hardly recognised as reforms at all—if, indeed, they are not sneered at as part of the "mess of centuries". But in their day there were bold and often revolutionary measures, and hardly any of them was achieved without patience and determination. Every aspect of social life, and a great many aspects of what the *laissez faire* philosophy regarded as private life, came under review in the era of growing collectivism. Public health, education, local government and municipal reform, poor law, labour law and especially child labour, criminal law, company law, judicature and procedure, matrimonial and family law, land law—all these were the subjects, not of a few isolated Acts, but in most instances of a whole course of legislation. There were also great consolidating and amending statutes in different branches of the technical law, criminal, commercial, and the law of property real and personal. In addition, Parliament grappled with all the highly technical questions arising from the development of many scientific inventions and discoveries, such as railways, electricity, gas, therapeutics and many others. At no time and in no country has there ever been such a huge and varied volume of constructive legislation, and it is to be remembered that most of it was framed by a staff of Parliamentary draftsmen which would today be regarded as absurdly inadequate.

The Civil Service

It would, however, be a grave misrepresentation to suggest that all this activity was the work of Parliament alone, or that the House of Commons was attempting to govern as it did in the eighteenth century. The work would not have been possible without the assistance of an able, loyal and imaginative executive. The Civil Service expanded so rapidly that in the course of the century it multiplied itself twelve times, whereas the total population of the country multiplied itself by four. And the Civil Service was not only reinforced in numbers but transformed in spirit. No doubt a good many of the old elements of inertia and patronage lingered on for many years. . . . But a new breed of energetic civil servants had grown up— men with an enthusiasm for their task, and with ideas not merely about means and methods, but about plans and policies. . . . [T]hey all left the imprint of personality on the unromantic labours which they were called on to perform. Chief . . . and earliest among these Whitehall missionaries—with the failings as well as the virtues of most missionaries—was Edwin Chadwick, the protege of Bentham and the pioneer of public health. . . . Chadwick gave the public a strong dose, which turned out to be an overdose, of the Benthamite medicine of compelling people to be happy. The Poor Law Amendment Act, 1834, for which he was largely responsible, is generally regarded as a remarkable early example of delegation by way of centralisation, for at one sweep it took away the powers of some 1,500 local authorities and placed them in the hands of a triumvirate with almost unlimited authority over pauperdom. It proved intensely unpopular and was abolished in 1874 in favour of a Poor Law Board with a President capable of sitting in Parliament—*i.e.,* in effect a Government Department subject to the ordinary rules of Ministerial responsibility. The same fate befell the General Board of Health, in which Chadwick was also deeply interested, and which was again an extraordinary example of centralised executive powers. It disappeared in 1854, and it was not until sixty-five years later that a Ministry of Health grew out of the Local Government Board. The centralising tendency continued throughout the century, despite the replacement of the Justices of the Peace by new local administrative authorities in 1888, many of whom complain today of the increasing restrictions imposed upon them by the overriding powers of Whitehall.

Growth of Delegation in the Nineteeth Century

It is not surprising, then, that delegation is frequent in the statute law of the period, though it varies considerably from year to year. . . . The Formulas, which have led to difficulties in later times, for reinforcing the authority of rules and orders appear at an early stage. Thus in 1825, a statute confers on justices a general power to make rules and orders "for carrying into effect the provisions and purpose of this Act", but adds the proviso, which has not always been inserted in recent statutes, "such rules and orders not being inconsistent with the express enactments or conditions herein contained". The great Reform Act of 1832 itself, giving power to appoint certain days and times in substitution for those specified in the Act, provides that such substituted days and times shall "be deemed to be of the same force and effect as if they had in every instance been mentioned in this Act". An Act of the following year provides that rules and orders made under it "shall be binding and obligatory . . . and be of the like force and effect as if the provisions contained therein had been expressly enacted by Parliament". Instances begin to occur of powers being given to subordinate authorities to alter or dispense with the minor provisions of existing statutes. . . . An Act of [1871], the Lunacy Regulation (Ireland) Act (s. 118), furnishes an early example of a provision that either House might by resolution annul orders made under the Act—an expedient which . . . was later to become common.

Thus the practice and the range of delegated legislation constantly grew throughout the century. From 1890 onwards the Statutory Rules and Orders were published in annual volumes under expert editorship. Between the year 1894 and the end of the century the average annual total Orders made was just over a thousand; from 1901 to the outbreak of war in 1914 it was 1,349; and in the war years, 1914 to 1918, 1,459. In the years 1919, 1920 and 1921 it reached the unprecedented figure of 2,275 and in the inter-war period it remained in the neighbourhood of 1,500. . . . The whole growth was wayward and unsystematic. No consistent principle governed this huge extension of powers, which were most unevenly distributed among different authorities. Departments and draftsmen and Parliament itself acted by mere opportunism, without any common or correlated policy. When, on top of this sprawling luxuriance, came the exigencies of two wars, what had been a thicket grew into a forest, in which it became increasingly difficult to find the path or direction.

Note 5(C). Limitations on Delegated Legislation

The reluctance of Parliament to delegate legislative authority during the eighteenth and early nineteenth centuries may be attributed not only to the residual effects of the historical contests between Parliament and the crown. It was also a result of the prevailing "mercantilist" opinion of the times, influenced by the laissez-faire concepts of economist Adam Smith, which led to a general antagonism toward government regulation. The legislative reforms begun in 1832 signaled the end of the mercantilist era.

Increasing government regulation after 1832 was fueled not only by reformist zeal but also by the increasing complexity of the areas needing regulation. With the growth of railroads and mass labor employed in factories, Parliament had neither the time nor the expertise to deal with the technical details that required regulatory attention. Regulation needed to be applied on a daily basis and frequently amended to meet changing conditions.

By the early part of the twentieth century, especially after the First World War had caused a leap in government regulation, some felt that the pendulum had swung too far:

> At present there are signs of a reaction from that process of multiplying departments and departmental regulations which was developed by the special conditions of a great war. If liberty is felt to be imperilled, it is no longer the Crown which can be attacked, for the Crown no longer runs counter to the wishes of Parliament. It is the department which is regarded as the enemy. It is the department which has been heard to justify its actions by pleading the prerogative in a tone which has not been used since Stuart times.[1]

Part of the opposition to delegated legislation was reminiscent of the opposition to statutory codification—delegated legislation, like codification, was not considered "English":

> In Continental countries, as is well known, the delegation of legislative powers is far more extensively exercised than in England or in English-speaking countries. In France, statutes are often couched in general terms and enunciate a principle which the executive is to carry out in detail. . . .
>
> In Italy the power of the executive officials to make regulations is even more extensively used. The constitution declares that "the king makes the decrees and regulations necessary for the execution of the laws without suspending their observance or dispensing with them." But the interpretation put upon this provision is so broad that the Government is practically allowed to suspend a law subject to responsibility to Parliament, and even to make temporary laws which are submitted to Parliament later. And Parliament uses very freely the power of delegating legislative power to the Ministers. . . .
>
> Such extensive delegation of legislative powers would not be tolerated in England. . . . Englishmen have a deep-seated distrust of official discretion, a

deep-seated scepticism about bureaucratic wisdom. . . . Therefore, although [an Englishman] acknowledges the impossibility of providing for every detail in an Act of Parliament, and the consequent necessity of leaving minor matters to be regulated by statutory rules or by executive discretion, he scrutinizes with a jealous eye provisions which delegate the power to make such rules, or which leave room for the exercise of such discretion, and insists that they should be carefully expressed and limited, and be hedged round with due safeguards against abuse.[2]

Safeguards against administrative excess fall under three headings—parliamentary scrutiny, judicial review, and publicity.

Parliamentary Scrutiny

Parliamentary scrutiny prior to the creation of statutory rules is exercised only if statutes authorizing the statutory rules specifically require that the rules be "laid" before Parliament for a specified time prior to becoming operative. Such provisions may require parliamentary assent, or, more commonly, they may become operative after the passage of the specified time period if no objection is raised in Parliament. In either case, Parliament may only accept or reject the rules; it may not amend them.

Parliamentary scrutiny has not been considered very effective in limiting the creation of statutory rules. In practice, the "laying" requirement is generally satisfied by placing a draft of proposed rules in Parliament's library, where it is seldom if ever consulted. Moreover, few statutes require draft rules to be laid before Parliament:

> Such a provision . . . is in fact very rare. It is probably not to be found in as many as one per cent of the statutes conferring legislative powers, and in the great majority of such statutes there is no provision for parliamentary control of any sort.[3]

More effective parliamentary control over statutory rules is exercised by the practice of ministerial responsibility to Parliament. Since cabinet ministers, who are in charge of the most important administrative agencies, are members of Parliament, the rules and orders issued by their departments are open to questioning in Parliament, no less than their other actions:

> Whether or not he signs it or sees it personally, the Minister is personally responsible for the instrument when it is publicly issued. From this personal responsibility for its issue comes the political responsibility of the whole Cabinet for it. And the Minister, like the other members of the Cabinet, is himself a Member of Parliament—not by law, but by custom and political necessity. In the moment of issuing the instrument therefore there is a certain democratic control over delegated legislation.[4]

Judicial Review

The most effective parliamentary control over statutory rules and orders
may lie in the drafting of the statutes that authorize them. Such statutes
are the sole sources of authority for administrative rules and orders, and
the conformity of rules and orders to their authorizing statutes is subject
to judicial review. Judges may invalidate administrative actions of all sorts
as *ultra vires* if they exceed the authority granted by statute.

From time to time it has been suggested that special administrative
courts be set up to supervise administrative agencies, but this suggestion,
too, has been generally considered un-English as well as a threat to the
tradition of judicial review. (Administrative courts are common in continental Europe.) An even greater threat to judicial review of administrative
action lies in the power of Parliament to bar judicial review:

> Expedients have . . . in many cases been resorted to for the purpose of ousting
> this power of judicial review and rendering statutory rules and orders unchal-
> lengeable as Acts of Parliament themselves; and, of course, no Court can ques-
> tion the validity of an Act of Parliament.[5]

Publicity

Prior to 1893, agencies were not required to publish their rules or orders
in any form. Most, however, were published in the *London Gazette,* a
government publication published since 1665 for miscellaneous government announcements (including royal proclamations) and commercial
notices (such as the winding up of companies). In 1893, Parliament
enacted the Rules Publication Act requiring the publication of certain proposed rules in the *London Gazette* for forty days prior to their effective
dates.

> Perhaps the most practical of the statutory safeguards against hasty and insuf-
> ficiently considered legislation under delegated powers is the obligation
> imposed by the Rules Publication Act, 1893, to publish a preliminary draft for
> criticism. This obligation applies, subject to some very important exceptions,
> to all rules which are required by statute to be laid before Parliament.[6]

The act, however, has been criticized for its "very important exceptions."
Among the exceptions, the act did not apply to some important agencies,
including the Local Government Board (later the Ministry of Health), the
Board of Trade, the Revenue Department, and the Post Office. The coverage of the act could also be limited by other statutes, and even those
agencies covered by the act could evade its application by a "certificate of
urgency."

The purpose of the forty-day preenactment publication requirement
was not only to inform the public but also to give any interested "public

body" the opportunity to make "representations and suggestions" concerning the proposed rules. The act specified that

> any representations or suggestions made in writing by a public body interested to the authority proposing to make the rules shall be taken into consideration by that authority before finally settling the rules.

The act did not create any further right for participation in agency rule making.

Section 3 of the 1893 act governed the publication of statutory rules and orders subsequent to enactment. Section 3 itself called for statutory instruments by authorizing the Treasury to make "regulations" for the numbering, printing, and sale of statutory rules. The section also required notice (but not full text) of new statutory rules in the *London Gazette*. Section 4 of the act allowed differing treatment of "public" and "personal or private" rules.

The Treasury regulations enacted by authority of the 1893 act required the printing of statutory rules in an individually numbered series and in an annual compilation. The publication of such a compilation had begun in 1890, before it was required by statute.

As the second edition of the *Revised Statutes*[7] was completed in 1887, the editors turned their hands to bringing order to the statutory rules and orders. They collected all statutory rules and orders they could locate, up to 1890, and published them in alphabetical order in eight volumes called *Statutory Rules and Orders Revised*. Thereafter, the set was kept up to date by annual volumes, called *Statutory Rules and Orders* (in 1946 the title was changed to *Statutory Instruments*). In 1891, the first index to rules and orders was published. The *Statutory Rules and Orders* became the vehicle for compliance with Section 3 the 1893 act. However, Section 3 also was weakened by exceptions.

Selection 5(C). Section 3 of the Rules Publication Act, 1893

C. T. CARR, DELEGATED LEGISLATION 44–47 (1921).

The documentary form in which statutory rules and orders are officially published is governed by section 3 of the Rules Publication Act [1893] and by the Treasury regulations made thereunder. Before that Act was passed, delegated legislation was almost undiscoverable. Part of it was buried in the pages of the "London Gazette" . . . ; the rest was scattered over Parliamentary Papers or other departmental documents or files without any definite system.

Since 1893 statutory rules and orders have been printed on a methodical plan. . . . All are classified and labelled under their general heading of
law and are usually prefaced with a brief summary stating by whom they
are made, at what date, and under what Act of Parliament. As the documents are printed in uniform octavo size and thus placed on sale, it has
ceased to be necessary to print them also in the different type and setting
of the "Gazette."

The creation of this official system of publication has removed the
reproach that the law embodied in statutory rules was less well known and
less easy to find than the law embodied in Acts of Parliament. Nevertheless
the title Statutory Rules and Orders is not synonymous with delegated
legislation, for the official system of publication does not cover the whole
field. . . . The . . . Act of 1893 . . . was not dealing with all delegated
legislation but with the legislation made by certain "rule-making authorities." . . .

Many of the bodies to which Parliament has delegated legislative
power are excluded by this definition. A railway is not a "rule-making"
authority nor is a municipal corporation; their bye-laws are therefore not
statutory rules and orders.

There are other classes of secondary legislation which also escape the
net of section 3 of the Rules Publication Act.

A large number are ruled out because they are merely confirmatory
[for example, the rules of colleges at Oxford and Cambridge that are
enacted by the colleges themselves and merely confirmed by a rule-making
authority], others because they are of an executive rather than a legislative
character. This latter distinction corresponds roughly with the distinction
between general and particular commands. . . . [A general command] is a
rule, not a transient sudden order from a superior to or concerning a
particular person but something permanent, uniform and universal. Confidential rules are also excluded; so also, subject to the direction of the
Treasury with the approval of the Lord Chancellor and Speaker, are annual
or periodically renewed rules such as the militia regulations or the education codes. The editor is allowed a discretion; if doubts arise, questions
are decided by the Treasury, Lord Chancellor and Speaker.

Not every document which is officially registered and numbered is
printed. Many which are of local interest are not printed, but are tabulated
in a classified list at the end of the annual volumes of Statutory Rules and
Orders. If departments think it unnecessary to have their orders printed,
their wishes are considered. And not every Statutory Rule and Order is put
on sale. . . .

Finally Statutory Rules and Orders have been interpreted as being only
those which are descended immediately from Acts of Parliament. If a rule
or order is made by virtue of a previous rule or order, then the result is
not the child but the grand-child of an Act of Parliament; it is not statutory
but sub-statutory, and therefore it has strictly no right to be published in
the series. This distinction between child and grand-child did not greatly

matter until August, 1914, but during the war the Defence of the Realm Act had numbers of grand-children: the Defence of the Realm Regulations were the immediate parents, the Act was the grand-parent. . . . [A] set of manuals of emergency legislation . . . introduced these grand-children to the public.

From what has been said, it also follows that the official series does not include orders made by virtue of the prerogative instead of by virtue of an Act of Parliament. These prerogative orders, which deal with such matters as the constitution and currency of parts of the Empire overseas, are however gathered up by the Editor of the annual volumes of Statutory Rules and Orders and printed by him in an Appendix thereto.

If ever the Rules Publication Act were amended or replaced, opportunity would no doubt be taken to review the scope of section 3. The distinction between statutory and sub-statutory rules and regulations is too artificial to bear explanation to the public which is concerned to know what laws it must obey. . . .

The resolutions of Parliament sometimes have legislative effect; for example they could reduce the hours of work underground in collieries from seven hours to six under the Coal Mines Act of 1919, and they can amend regulations under the Emergency Powers Act of 1920. Not being formal Acts of Parliament, the resolutions of Parliament do not appear in the statute book, and Parliament not being a "rule-making authority," they are not statutory rules and orders. There should be some recognised uniform system of publishing all secondary legislation of this kind which is of public importance.

Note 5(D). The Statutory Instruments Act, 1946

Although the Rules Publication Act of 1893 was much criticized, it remained in force for more than fifty years. In 1932, a Committee on Ministers' Powers, which included such notables as legal historian William Holdsworth and the socialist intellectual Harold J. Laski, held hearings on the deficiencies in the publication of delegated legislation. C. T. Carr, who was editor of the *Statutory Rules and Orders* and the *Revised Statutes,* testified and recommended that "no rule or order should have validity until registered" for publication.[1] The Second World War intervened, and the matter did not receive Parliament's attention until 1946.

During the war, however, a new factor was added to Parliament's scrutiny of proposed administrative rules. Near the end of the war, the home secretary neglected to lay before Parliament some regulations of his department that were required to be laid, and the validity of the regulations were therefore questioned. In the ensuing discussion, it was widely acknowledged that the requirement of laying regulations before Parliament was largely meaningless, since members of Parliament very rarely took the opportunity to scrutinize the regulations. As a result of the discussions, a Select Committee was established to provide greater scrutiny for regulations without taking up the time of Parliament as a whole.

> To assist [Parliament] to be vigilant, the House . . . delegates powers to a committee . . . officially known as the "Select Committee on Statutory Instruments" and, colloquially, as "the Scrutiny Committee". This committee has been set up in every session since that of 1943–4. It is, by a firm convention, presided over by a member of the opposition—though the Government has a majority in the committee—which indicates that its functions are not party-political in the narrow sense, and it is assisted by an officer of the House of Commons, the Counsel to the Speaker. . . . The fact that Mr. Speaker's Counsel is not the servant of any Ministry is important. The Scrutiny Committee considers all instruments laid before the House, and reports whether they comply with certain formalities, and also whether they appear to make an "unusual" use of the powers delegated by the act. The committee also examines witnesses from the departments, if necessary, and it issues Reports at intervals during the session—Reports which are public and which are generally noticed in the Press.[2]

The Select Committee's report "has no effect on the instrument" it examines;[3] it is simply a report to Parliament usually concentrating on the revenue implications of any proposed instrument, whether the instrument is subject to judicial review, the retroactive effect of the instrument, whether the instrument contains provisions that may be *ultra vires*, defects in the drafting of the instrument, and whether "there appear to have been unjustifiable delay in the publication [of the instrument] or in the laying of it before Parliament."[4] In practice, "[v]ery few instruments are reported . . . in proportion to the total output of subordinate legislation."[5]

The 1893 act was repealed and replaced by the Statutory Instruments Act of 1946. The 1893 act's requirement for the publication of proposed rules in the *London Gazette* is not repeated in the 1946 act.

> There is therefore no general requirement of prior publicity, and an ordinary member of the public has little chance of getting to know about proposed statutory instruments. But by an almost universal practice, the department proposing to make a new statutory instrument takes steps to ensure that the various interests particularly affected by the proposal are consulted. Some Acts of Parliament make this obligatory.[6]

The 1946 act also provides more uniform procedures for laying regulations before Parliament than did the 1893 act. When a statute requires regulations to be laid before Parliament without specifying when and for how long, the 1946 act provides that the laying shall be for twenty-one days before the regulations come into operation. The 1946 act, however, does not answer all the criticisms that were leveled against the 1893 act:

> Convenient though these reforms are, it should be noted that they do not touch one central problem, for whether a statutory instrument does or does not need to be laid depends on the terms of the Act under which it is made.[7]

The 1946 act also broadened the requirement for publication of statutory instruments. Section 2 of the 1946 act provides, as a general rule:

> Immediately after the making of any statutory instrument, it shall be sent to the King's printer. . . [C]opies thereof shall as soon as possible be printed and sold by the King's printer.

However, the regulations for the implementation of the 1946 act (the Statutory Instrument Regulations, 1947) contain several important exceptions—including:

> (a) Any "local" instrument, i.e., one which is "in the nature of a local and personal or private Act", and certified by the "responsible authority" (i.e., the Minister by whom the instrument is made or, in the case of an Order in Council, the Sovereign in Council) to be such . . . .
>
> (b) Any "general" instrument . . . certified by the responsible authority (above) to be
>
> > "of a class of documents which is or will be otherwise printed as a series and made available to persons affected thereby".
>
> (c) Any instrument which the responsible authority (above) considers to be temporary in nature,
>
> > "having regard to the brevity of the period during which that instrument will remain in force and to any other steps taken or to be taken for bringing its substance to the notice of the public," . . .
>
> (d) Bulky schedules or other documents referred to or identified in a statutory instrument need not be printed if the responsible authority (above) certifies this to be unnecessary or undesirable. . . .
>
> (e) Also if the responsible authority (above) considers that printing and sale of copies of any particular instrument would be "contrary to the public interest", the authority may so certify; there is no power in the Regulations for any such certificate to be overruled. . . .[8]

Moreover, the 1946 act, like the 1893 act, does not apply to instruments issued under royal prerogative rather than under a statutory power. (Although royal prerogative has become severely limited, it continues to have force in some areas, including regulation of the civil service, the military, colonial affairs, and other foreign affairs.) Nor is the 1946 act applicable to subdelegated instruments (the "grand-children" of statutes), which often take the form of "circular letters" and other administrative documents that cannot be classified as "statutory instruments" but "may have important legal consequences."[9] In this century, both royal prerogative and subdelegated powers were used increasingly in times of war.

Orders issued by royal prerogative have been collected annually and published at the end of the *Statutory Rules and Orders* and its successor, *Statutory Instruments*. However, subdelegated instruments and other forms of "quasi-legislation" are available only in a spotty fashion.

Regulations issued under the 1946 act provide for a Reference Committee with power to review the application of exceptions to the act's requirement of publication. Perhaps the Reference Committee is responsible for the fact that, despite continuing exceptions to the general requirement of publication, the 1946 act, as applied, seems to meet with general acceptance:

> There is now no serious difficulty, as there once was, in obtaining knowledge of recent Statutory Instruments (older ones are sometimes found to be "out of print", but can generally be consulted in the annual volumes, now well indexed).[10]

Improved compliance with the publication requirement of the 1946 act may also be due to Section 3(2) of the act, which provides:

> In any proceedings against any person for an offence consisting of a contravention of any such statutory instrument, it shall be a defence to prove that the instrument had not been issued by His Majesty's Stationery Office at the date of the alleged contravention unless it is proved that at that date reasonable steps had been taken for the purpose of bringing the purport of the instrument to the notice of the public, or of persons likely to be affected by it, or of the person charged.

Selection 5(D). Administrative Tribunals

W. A. ROBSON, JUSTICE AND ADMINISTRATIVE LAW 573–76 (3d ed., 1951).

The advantages of administrative tribunals are . . . the cheapness and speed with which they usually work; the technical knowledge and experience which they make available for the discharge of judicial functions in special fields; the assistance which they lend to the efficient conduct of public administration; and the ability they possess to lay down new standards and to promote a policy of social improvement.

But these tribunals, like other human institutions, have defects as well as merits. . . . Many of these drawbacks are not inevitable or inherent in the very nature of administrative law, but could without difficulty be remedied.

One great disadvantage is the lack of publicity which attends the work of administrative tribunals. In the exercise of judicial functions by great departments such as the Ministry of Health and the Ministry of Education, there is usually no oral hearing, though each side must of course have an opportunity of stating its case in writing; and even where there is a hearing it is not open to the public. The rules of procedure laid down for the local appeal tribunals under the National Insurance Act specifically exclude both the general public and the press from being present. Reports of decided cases are seldom published, except by a few tribunals, such as the National Insurance Commissioner in regard to claims for insurance benefits. . . .

Even when decisions are published, they are widely scattered in obscure documents which may easily escape the knowledge of persons or interests affected. The decisions are usually given in an abbreviated form and the reasons are seldom disclosed. Moreover, only a few selected cases are published.

These are real disadvantages. Without publicity it is impossible to predict the trend of future decisions, and an atmosphere of autocratic bureaucracy is introduced by the maintenance of a secrecy which in the ordinary course of events is quite unnecessary. There is no inherent reason why these disadvantages should attach to administrative justice. There can be no objection to permitting the public to attend hearings when they are given or to requiring all administrative agencies which perform judicial functions to publish reports of their decisions, at regular intervals, giving reasoned arguments for the conclusions. The public could without difficulty be made to understand that the reported cases were not to be regarded as immutable precedents to be followed inflexibly on all future occasions, but taken merely as indications of the direction in which the mind of the tribunal was moving—a direction which would be subject to change if circumstances so demanded. In this way it would be possible to obtain a body of informed criticism on the work of the tribunal which would have a beneficial effect not only on those sections of the public coming under its jurisdiction, but also on the tribunal itself.

Very little improvement in the practice of administrative tribunals in regard to the publication of reports and the obligation to give reasoned decisions has taken place . . . despite frequent . . . criticism from many quarters and recommendations on the subject by the Committee on Ministers' Powers. There is in general an increasing tendency on the part of government departments to cloak their activities, however harmless or beneficial, in a thick mist of secrecy, and this general inclination has helped to encourage unnecessary mystery-mongering on the part of administrative tribunals.

The tribunals for conscientious objectors normally sit in public, and the press and interested persons can attend the meetings. But . . . one of the defects of these tribunals is their failure to give reasoned judgments, publish precedents and observe uniform standards. The local tribunals sometimes furnish applicants with only a brief and inadequate note of the reasons for their decisions. . . . These documents apparently received such confidential treatment that even members of the tribunals were not always aware of their contents, so that different tribunals were giving inconsistent decisions on such a vital question as whether a British subject with Italian parents could be regarded as having a valid conscientious objection to fighting in the war on the side of the Allies. . . .

There are occasional signs, however, that Parliament is beginning to be aware of the desirability of imposing a duty on administrative tribunals to afford publicity to their proceedings and to publish reasoned decisions. The Minister of Transport, in hearing appeals under the Restriction of Ribbon Development Act, 1935, was required not only to publish a summary of the facts which he found, but also of the reasons for his decision. Under the National Health Service Act the Minister of Health must provide by regulations for the publication of the decisions of the special tribunal which hears complaints against medical practitioners. These are only straws in the wind, but they are blowing in the right direction. One would like to see a strong Parliamentary gale sweep away the refusal of many administrative tribunals to publish their more important cases, to provide oral hearings, to have public sittings and to give reasons for their decisions. There is much to be said for the suggestion of a uniform method of official publication in a series entitled 'Administrative Notifications and Decisions'.

Note 5(E). Administrative Publications since 1946

Following the enactment of the Statutory Instruments Act of 1946, statutory instruments still in force were compiled and published in 1949 as *Statutory Rules and Orders and Statutory Instruments Revised to December 31, 1948*. The compilation was thereafter kept up by annual volumes of *Statutory Instruments;* no subsequent compilation has been published. The latest annual update consists of six volumes, two for each four-month period. For more current updating, individually published instruments must be consulted, and, for occasional instruments missed by *Statutory Instruments,* resort may also be had to the *London Gazette:*

> Occasionally, there are lapses. Thus, the *Territorial Waters Order in Council 1964* was printed in full in the *London Gazette,* but was not reprinted in the *Statutory Instruments* series until the final volume of 1965, because it was not brought to the editor's attention until then. Hence, it is necessary to subscribe to the *London Gazette* as well as to the *Statutory Instruments* series to be absolutely certain that you have complete coverage of all of this type of material.
>
> One or two more mundane regulations, also have from time to time missed inclusion in the *Statutory Instruments* series or its predecessor the *Statutory Rules and Orders* series, whether through accident or design. Two noteworthy absentees, which are both still in force, are the Electricity Supply Regulations 1937 and the Children Act (Appeal Tribunal) Rules 1949. More recent absentees are the various statements of Immigration Rules, which have been issued as House of Commons Papers in 1973 and 1980.[1]

Until 1960, each annual *Statutory Instruments* was arranged by subject. Thereafter, the arrangement became chronological to reduce the work of the editors and allow for speedier publication. Access to the 1949 compilation and the subsequent annual volumes is available by subject through the *Index to Government Orders in Force,* which is compiled biennially and supplemented in alternate years. The *Index* also contains a chronological table of statutes listing, under each, the subject headings under which its instruments are indexed.

Access to all statutory instruments since 1671 (including nonstatutory instruments and instruments no longer in force) is available by citation number through the *Table of Governmental Orders,* which is published annually. The *Table* indicates the amendment history of each instrument. Instruments still in force are printed in dark type. Both the subject *Index* and the numeric *Table* are updated monthly in the *List of Statutory Instruments.*

The 1949 compilation, the annual *Statutory Instruments,* the *London Gazette,* the *Index,* the *Table,* and the *List* are all official publications, published by the Royal Stationers Office. Although they can be used as a self-sufficient system for locating statutory instruments, they are cumbersome. More than four decades of annual volumes plus current instruments must be consulted through three distinct reference sources.

As with case reports and statutory codes, the shortcomings of official publications provide opportunities for private publishers. Consequently, the publishers of *Halsbury's Laws of England* (the leading English legal encyclopedia) and *Halsbury's Statutes of England* (the most convenient printed source for English Statutes) also publish statutory instruments in force in *Halsbury's Statutory Instruments* (published since 1951).

Halsbury's Statutory Instruments, however, is not a self-sufficient source for English statutory instruments. It is a more convenient source to consult initially than the official sources, since it is thorough, arranged by subject, with an annual index volume, and frequently updated, but *Halsbury's Statutory Instruments* contains only selected instruments in full text; others are merely summarized.

The use of summaries keeps *Halbury's Statutory Instruments* conveniently short, but it necessitates resort elsewhere for the full texts of summarized instruments. Fortunately, this no longer requires access to a full set of the official *Statutory Instruments.* Statutory instruments in force are now also available in full text on LEXIS. LEXIS, in fact, is more complete than the annual volumes of Statutory Instruments, since the annual volumes omit instruments that cease to be operational during the year. But *Statutory Instruments* has some advantages over LEXIS: both *Statutory Instruments* and LEXIS omit local instruments, but the annual volumes of *Statutory Instruments* contain tables listing the year's local instruments. (The text of the local instruments can only be secured from the archives of the Public Records Office.) The annual volumes of *Statutory Instruments* also contain indexes by subject and tables linking instruments to their related statutes.

Statutory instruments are also available in a variety of looseleaf services. In fact "it might be quicker to look [statutory instruments] up in [a] looseleaf . . . than in the official *Statutory Instruments* series, because there the possible field of search is so much narrower."[2] Looseleaf services, however, are not available in all fields. The field best served by looseleaf services is taxation; other fields include labor relations, motor vehicles, planning law, local government, housing, and environmental law.

Looseleaf services have the virtue of unifying statutes, statutory and nonstatutory instruments, case decisions, and editorial commentary in one source, usually linked in a convenient arrangement by tables, indexes, and other editorial aids. Looseleaf services also include regulatory information from circulars, manuals, and other sources not widely available as well as references to encyclopedias, treatises, and periodical articles.

Looseleaf services are also one of the few sources where the decisions of administrative tribunals can be found. Although some tribunals publish selected decisions, there are now more than two thousand such tribunals in England, and no attempt has yet been made at systematic publication beyond a few individual tribunals.

A few tribunals publish their own decisions, and these are usually highly selective; some receive only limited circulation. Only one set— *Immigration Appeals*—is considered authoritative and may "be cited before the superior courts of record."[3] Some, such as *Lands Tribunal Cases,* are published by commercial publishers. Selected decisions of administrative tribunals are also published in a number of topical court reports and specialized periodicals. Decisions of tribunals on taxation, land valuation, immigration, and employment are also available on LEXIS, including some not published elsewhere.

Neither *Halsbury's Statutory Instruments* nor the official volumes link statutory instruments to cases that have interpreted them. This is another function served by looseleaf services for those regulatory fields that are remunerative enough to have one. Tables of statutory instruments considered in judicial opinions are also included in each volume of the *Law Reports* and the *All England Law Reports* but are nowhere cumulated.

6

Administrative Publications in the United States

Note 6(A). From Independence to the First World War

In the years immediately following the independence of the United States, the era governed by the Articles of Confederation (1775–89), Congress attempted to administer through its own committees rather than through an executive. This was one of the causes for the failure of the Articles. In the Constitution, the organization of the executive branch is left vague and largely subject to the control of Congress. The authority of the president to issue proclamations and executive orders was yet to be defined.[1]

In 1789, Congress established four major executive departments—the Department of State, the War Department, the Treasury Department, and the post of Attorney General. The Post Office was established in 1794; the Navy Department in 1798. Specific agencies dealing with customs, veterans' pensions, patents, and Indian affairs were also established before 1800. The Treasury Department's General Land Office was set up in 1812 and became the busiest federal agency, giving rise to the popular use of its name to denote a booming business. The Land Office also gave rise to the first report of administrative decisions.[2]

Relatively few new federal agencies were created in the first half of the nineteenth century. The major new department of this era was the Department of the Interior, established in 1849.

Most areas of regulation were left to the states. Public works (roads, waterways), the protection of consumers (by the regulation of banks, insurance companies, the professions, industry, and commerce), public schools, and the protection of public health and safety were largely governed by state law. However, publication of state administrative materials prior to the Civil War was rare.

In the late 1830s, the federal government gave an indication of its ability to assume administrative responsibility when state regulation appeared insufficient. Following a number of tragic boiler explosions on steamboats, the federal Steamboat Inspection Service was established in 1838.

During much of the 1800s, federal positions were filled by the corrupt "spoils system" initiated in the administration of Andrew Jackson. To "democratize" government service, federal jobs were awarded not on the basis of merit, experience, or seniority but on the basis of political connections and, often, political payoffs. For more than half a century, the spoils system was unchecked. It was ended in 1883 by the creation of the Civil Service Commission, which instituted a merit system for hiring and promotions and job protection for federal employees.

At the same time, government regulation of industry, whether by states or the federal government, met with considerable public opposition. This was the era of laissez-faire. Nevertheless, near the end of the nineteenth century, regulation was imposed first to control the railroads and, later, other industries.

As a growing web of railroads spread throughout the nation in the late nineteenth century, the railroads, and the grain elevators that accompanied them, had farmers at their mercy—and they were not merciful: "[E]xploitation of the farmer by high freight rates had been particularly rapacious."[3]

Farmers in the Midwest were especially vulnerable to exploitation. Their common interests led them to organize. Their Populist movement gained control of state governments in Illinois, Iowa, Minnesota, and Wisconsin. Populists, however, did not prove to be effective regulators. Populist-dominated legislatures passed laws limiting freight rates and set rules for the conduct of railroads, but many of the laws were poorly written or overturned when challenged in courts.[4]

The Populists did succeed in one key Supreme Court case. In 1876, the Supreme Court upheld the constitutionality of government regulation of private businesses affecting the "public interest."[5] However, state regulation was not an effective way to deal with the national phenomenon of railroads. State regulation was also severely restricted in 1886 when the Supreme Court prohibited state regulation of railroad rates as an interference with interstate commerce.[6] In response, in 1887, the Interstate Commerce Commission was created to regulate common carriers nationally.

The Populist movement in the Midwest connected with the Progressive movement in the East. Progressive reformers advocated government regulation of big business, the breakup of monopolies, and improved measures for public health and the protection of workers.

The conditions of American workers and farmers received attention in the following years with the creation of the Department of Labor in 1888 and the Department of Agriculture in 1889. In 1890 the Sherman Anti-trust Act was enacted, with enforcement powers in the attorney general, to extend regulation to monopolistic businesses beyond the common carriers. In 1906, the Pure Food and Drug Act led to the Food and Drug Administration. In 1903 the Department of Labor became the Department of Labor and Commerce, and in 1913 the Department of Commerce came into its own, followed in 1914 by two other agencies to regulate business and banking—the Federal Trade Commission and the Federal Reserve Board. The year 1914 also saw the publication of the first looseleaf service in federal taxation to control the growing body of laws and regulations generated by the federal income tax, enacted in the previous year, and its offspring, the Internal Revenue Service.

The First World War brought increased administrative regulation. During the war, two publications attempted to keep track of the special rules and regulations of the time: an *Official Bulletin* was published, but "this was by no means complete [and] no provision was made for its continuance";[7] and a privately prepared compilation was published in 1918 but was also incomplete and was never updated.[8]

Selection 6(A). At the End of the First World War

J. A. Fairlie, *Administrative Legislation*, 18 Mich L. Rev. 181, 181–200 (1920).

. . . .

Important as . . . executive regulations have been, even in time of peace, they are of much greater importance in time of war; and during the recent emergency regulations of this kind have been brought to the attention of many outside the circle of government officials.

. . . .

Perhaps the earliest recognition of the general significance of this field of governmental action, is in a pamphlet entitled "Remarks on Army Regulations," by G. Norman Lieber, Judge Advocate General of the Army, which was originally printed in 1897. In this pamphlet General Lieber stated:

> "It is difficult to form a true conception of the vastness and importance of all this great body of executive regulation law, controlling, as it does, the administration of all the executive departments with its rules of action. And when we consider that these rules of action are in general made, construed, and applied by the same authority, thus combining quasi-legislative, quasi-judicial and executive authority, we cannot fail to be very much impressed with the extent of jurisdiction covered by them."

There are indeed, besides presidential proclamations and executive orders, many elaborate systems of executive regulations governing the transaction of business in each of the executive departments and in the various services both within and without these departments. These include organized codes of regulations for the army, the navy, the postal service, the consular service, the customs service, the internal revenue service, the coast guard, the patent office, the pension office, the land office, the Indian service, the steamboat inspection service, the immigration and the naturalization bureaus, and the civil service rules. In addition to long established types of regulations, there have been many new series of regulations issued in recent years both before the war, and more recently by the new war agencies, such as the Food and Fuel Administrations, the War Industries Board, and the War Trade Board.

.   .   .   .

In addition to the systematized and codified regulations, there is perhaps an even more extensive body of more specialized rules, orders, and instructions issued by the various departments, bureaus, commissions, and local agents, knowledge of which is often limited to the persons who have to apply them and to those whom they affect.

Types of Regulations

. . . Most regulations are issued to supplement statutes, in many cases under express provisions in the statutes, and in other cases as an implied power of interpretation or application. But there are also important regulations issued as an exercise of the constitutional executive power of the President.

Thus the army and navy regulations were for a long time issued by virtue of the President's constitutional authority as commander in chief of the army and navy. In other cases the President has issued proclamations and executive orders without reference to any statute or congressional authorization, as in some instances of reservations of public lands.

Regulations issued in accordance with statutory provisions are much more common. Thus the President is now specifically authorized to make regulations . . . in relation to the duties of the diplomatic and consular service, and for admission to the civil service. He may issue regulations as to the treatment of alien enemies in time of war, rules for the operation of the Panama Canal, and regulation relating to Indian affairs. He . . . has explicit power to establish internal revenue districts, pensions agencies, and forest reservations. Under some tariff acts he has been authorized to suspend tariff duties on imports from countries which entered into reciprocity agreements with the United States. Under the tariff act of 1890, he was even authorized to suspend certain clauses of the act permitting the importation of certain commodities free of duty, with reference to goods imported from countries which imposed duties on American products deemed by the President to be reciprocally unequal and unreasonable. By this provision, the imposition of duties was made to depend on the action of the President; and this grant of power to the President was upheld by the Supreme Court. . . .

The war legislation of the past two years made further extensive grants of power to issue administrative regulations and orders. The Selective Service Act authorized the President to make regulations relating to the draft, the time of registration, and the organization and procedure of local boards. The Food and Fuel Act of 1917 vested the President with sweeping powers of control over food and fuel supplies; and further authorized him to exercise this power through such agency or agencies as he might establish. . . .

Heads of the executive departments are also definitely authorized by statute to issue administrative regulations; and most executive regulations are in fact issued in the name of a department, bureau or commission rather than that of the President.

. . . .

Various boards and commissions outside of the executive departments have also power to prescribe administrative regulations. The Interstate Commerce Commission is authorized to make general rules or orders for the regulation of proceedings before it; and has also been authorized to establish safety appliance standards. . . . Rules and regulations are also authorized to be made by the Federal Trade Commission, the Federal Reserve Board, the Farm Loan Board, the United States Shipping Board and the Copyright Office in the Library of Congress.

. . . .

Judicial Rulings

A definite line of demarcation between administrative regulations and the provisions of statutory legislation is not easy to draw. Indeed cases can be cited where analogous, and almost identical, rules are to be found both in the form of statutory provisions and in administrative regulations. Thus the customs collections districts were for many years established by acts of Congress; while internal revenue districts were subject to change by executive regulation. Even more striking are the provisions of the Overman Act, under which it is stated that the President may, by executive act, alter temporarily, the provisions of acts of Congress establishing and organizing the administrative agencies of the national government.

Such instances give point to the questions which have arisen as to whether administrative regulations are not substantially legislation, and so beyond the power of the executive (except in the case of constitutional authority), and beyond the power of Congress to delegate. . . .

. . . The line of distinction is not, and probably cannot be made, exact. Whatever the logical difficulties, the fact remains that there is a broad twilight zone between the field of what is distinctly and exclusively legislative and what is necessarily executive in character; that courts have recognized that matters within this "no man's land" may be at times included in statutory legislation, and at other times may be expressly authorized by statute for administrative action; and if neither of these steps is taken such action has been, under some circumstances, assumed as an inherent executive or administrative power.

. . . .

The power to make executive rules to interpret statutes and to aid in the administration of laws, even when not expressly authorized, appears also to be clearly established by long practice.

At the same time the power to issue administrative regulations is not unlimited; and certain restrictions have been laid down by the courts. An executive regulation not authorized may be declared void; and a regulation interpreting a statutory provision may be overruled as erroneous. The power conferred to make regulations for carrying a statute into effect must be exercised within the powers authorized, that is it must be confined to provisions for regulating the mode of proceeding to carry into effect the law as it has been enacted; and it cannot be extended to amending or adding to the requirements of the statutes nor to subverting the statute. Thus, when the Interstate Commerce Commission, under a provision in the original act of 1887 to prevent discriminating and unreasonable railroad rates, undertook to fix a schedule of maximum reasonable rates it was held that this was exercising a legislative power which had not at the time been clearly conferred on the commission. When this authority was expressly named by Congress, it was accepted by the courts.

. . . .

Preparation and Publication

Notwithstanding the variety and volume of administrative regulations, and their importance in the work of the government, comparatively little attention has thus far been given to the methods of their preparation and publication. This is perhaps due in part to the fact that very few, if any, even of the government officials have any adequate appreciation of the scope and significance of such regulations in the governmental service as a whole. There has been a good deal of discussion of the need for improvement in legislative drafting; yet legislative bills receive a good deal more careful consideration than most administrative regulations. In the matter of publication, acts of Congress and state legislature are promulgated in well known and accessible ways; but it is a difficult and almost impossible task to keep track of the multifold variety of administrative regulations.

In the case of the highest class of such regulations—the proclamations and executive orders of the President—there appears to be no definite agency charged with their preparation. Drafts for proposed measures of this kind seem to be prepared in the departments specially concerned with the subject matter; and after receiving the approval of the President, they are issued by the Department of State in separate leaflets, countersigned by the Secretary of State. Proclamations are afterwards reprinted in the volumes of congressional statutes and treaties; but there is no official publication of the series of executive orders except in the original detached leaflets. During the war a good many proclamations and executive orders were reprinted, along with other administrative regulations, in the "OFFICIAL BULLETIN"; but this was by no means complete, and there is as yet no provision for continuing even this form of publication as a permanent arrangement.

Nor is there any general system for the preparation and publication of regulations issued by departments, bureaus, commissions and other agencies. These are issued in the name of the head of the department or other government agency; but in very few cases can they receive his personal attention, and even if personally signed by him, the actual work of drafting the regulation has been done by others. Moreover the drafting of such regulations is no less, and in some respects it is more technical and difficult than the drafting of legislative measures. . . .

. . . Most of the departments have a division of publications; but these have no responsibility for the preparation of regulations, and in many services there is no organized machinery for this work, and important regulations may be issued on the basis of memoranda prepared in haste and without careful study and consideration.

In the matter of publication there is a maximum of variety and confusion. Not only is there no general system, but no department has developed a system for itself. Each bureau, and often each local office, has its own methods, or more often lack of method. There are in some cases, considerable bodies of more or less permanent regulations, such as the consular regulations and the army regulations. Yet even these are subject to frequent change and amendment; and a serious problem for the subordinate official is to keep posted on the latest changes. But there are also more numerous volumes of rules, instructions, and orders, not part of the permanent regulations, often making what prove to be continuing changes from the provisions in the main body of regulations. Still further, special instructions may be issued in the form of mimeographed circulars, or circular letters, or even in telegrams sent to certain officials which may never be reissued in any of the regular series.

There is no approach to uniformity in nomenclature. Rules, Regulations, Instructions, General Orders, Orders, Circulars, Bulletin, Notices, Memoranda and other terms are given to different series of publications by different government offices, with no clear distinction as to the meaning of these terms. In some cases an attempt seems to be made to separate regulations which impose mandatory orders from circulars of information or advice; but even this distinction often breaks down in practice. Further difficulties arise from the frequency of changes and modifications; and here again there is no uniformity in the form and methods of issuing such amendments.

Subordinate officials may ordinarily be supposed to receive the official publications from their own superiors bearing on their own work. Yet even here, there is sometimes a failure to prepare or to carry out an adequate system of distributing orders and regulations. In some cases the number and variety of instructions issued are more than can be taken care of by individual officers, especially in the absence of regular and frequent indices, digests and summaries. More difficult is the problem of one branch securing publications issued by another branch which may have an important bearing on its work.

For the citizen outside the government service, the problem of securing and keeping track of the administrative regulations which may affect his affairs is even more difficult. It is not easy to learn which of the government services are responsible for particular matters. One would not expect the Commissioner of Internal Revenue to issue regulations for the sale of narcotics, nor the Secretary of Agriculture to regulate importations of certain commodities. Large business enterprises need to keep in touch with many of the numerous government services, which may issue duplicating or even conflicting orders. There is also, sometimes, the difficulty of securing regular distribution for important regulations which affects subordinate officials.

These criticisms are not directed at the present administration. They represent conditions that have existed for a long time, and have been accentuated in recent years with the increasing mass of legislation and administrative regulations affecting others than government officials. They have been further emphasized by the great extension of government control and the enormous pressure of work in the government during the war. But the fundamental difficulties are of long standing; and even after some relaxation since the close of the war, the permanent difficulties demand attention.

There is need first, within each department and in the government service as a whole, for more systematic and uniform methods in the preparation and publication of administrative regulations. There should be in each department an agency for supervising the preparation and issue of all such regulations within the department. The number of classes of publications should be reduced, and a more uniform terminology established. Finally there should be an official publication which will record all regulations and instructions issued by all branches of the government service.

Note 6(B). The New Deal

Following the First World War, new agencies came into being to regulate the progress of technology—the Federal Power Commission in 1920, the Civil Aeronautics Administration in 1926, the Federal Radio Commission (later renamed the Federal Communications Commission) in 1927.

The stock market crash of 1929 and the subsequent economic depression led to President Franklin D. Roosevelt's New Deal program, which relied on administrative regulation as the primary technique for remedying the nation's economic ills.

Among the first measures of the New Deal was the National Industrial Recovery Act of 1933, which established the National Recovery Administration (NRA), a body charged with drafting a series of codes to govern industrial competition and labor relations. After two years of work with mixed results, the Supreme Court invalidated the NRA's mandate as an unconstitutional delegation of legislative authority to an administrative agency.[1]

The first year of the New Deal (1933) also saw the creation of the Farm Credit Administration, the Federal Deposit Insurance Corporation, and the Tennessee Valley Authority; in 1934 came the Securities and Exchange Commission, in 1935 the Social Security Administration and the National Labor Relations Board.

To keep track of all the new and old federal agencies, the *United States Government Manual* was published in 1935 and has been reissued annually ever since. This directory describes the function and basic organization of each agency, with names of principal officers, but provides little detail on the subordinate units of agencies.

The constitutionality of a number of New Deal agencies was challenged, but the challenges subsided as the act establishing the NLRB— the Wagner Act of 1935—was upheld by the Supreme Court in 1937.[2] Prior to this "switch in time," President Roosevelt had threatened to "pack" the Supreme Court by enlarging its membership and appointing justices favorable to the New Deal.

Some administrative agencies, beginning with the Civil Service Commission and the Interstate Commerce Commission in the 1880s, were established as "independent agencies"—free of presidential control. In 1937, a President's Committee on Administrative Management criticized the independent agencies as a "headless fourth branch" of government and recommended presidential control.[3] The committee's recommendation, however, was not adopted.

The 1937 committee also recommended the establishment of an independent administrative tribunal at each formerly independent agency.[4] This recommendation, too, was not acted on.

Administrative proceedings, however, were and remain subject to judicial review. Initially, most federal judges had little reluctance to review the details of administrative opinions. In time, however, courts adopted a deferential attitude toward the "expertise" of regulators.

Within a few years, the New Deal's zealous regulatory approach resulted in a wealth of agency regulations. As the number of agencies multiplied, little attention was paid to uniformity of procedures, much less uniformity of publications. The result, for the public, was chaotic.

Selection 6(B). Following the Example of England

E. N. Griswold, *Government in Ignorance of the Law—A Plea for Better Publication of Executive Legislation,* 48 HARV. L. REV. 198, 203–212 (1934).

Congressional enactments are readily available to the profession. The bound volumes of the Statutes at Large provide a uniformly understood mode of citation, while private initiative has supplied a number of independent compilations, complete with tables, by which the status of any legislative enactment of the past may be told quickly and accurately— whether it has been amended, repealed, superseded, or is still in force. But what do we find as to the form of that most important group of legislative pronouncements, the administrative rules and regulations? It seems scarcely adequate to say that what we find is chaos. If a pamphlet is discovered which purports to contain the rules and regulations in question, there is no practicable means of telling whether the entire regulation or the article in question is still in force, or, as is so often the case, has been modified, amended, superseded, or withdrawn. There is no feasible way of determining whether or not there has been any subsequent rule or order which might affect the problem. The rules and regulations are most often published in separate paper pamphlets. Many of them, including most of the Executive Orders of the President, are printed on a single sheet of paper, fragile and easily lost. An attempt to compile a complete collection of these administrative rules would be an almost insuperable task for the private lawyer. It seems likely that there is no law library in this country, public or private, which has them all. Even if a complete collection were once achieved, there would be no practicable way of keeping it up to date, and the task of finding with requisite accuracy the applicable material on a question in hand would still often be a virtual impossibility. The officers of the government itself frequently do not know the applicable regulations. We have recently seen the spectacle of an indictment being brought and a appeal taken by the government to the Supreme Court before it was found that the regulation on which the proceeding was based did not exist.

   And yet these ephemera have the "force and effect of law". Such a situation is none the less intolerable because we have never known anything better. Is there no alternative? On the contrary, the solution is amazingly simple. All that is needed is an official publication, analogous to the Statutes at Large, in which all rules and regulations shall be systematically and uniformly published. In such a publication lawyers could readily find the full and complete text of any regulation. Regulations could be readily cited and could be made just as accessible as the statutes of Congress are now. Moreover, with the help of indices and tabulations (such as are now included in the United States Code and its supplements, and in several private publications) one could readily determine whether a particular rule or regulation was still in force, and if not, the extent to which it had been changed or modified or superseded.

The condition in which we find ourselves is not novel, nor is the solution suggested original. As long ago as 1890, the same difficulty was faced in England. . . .

. . . .

Beginning in 1890, statutory rules and orders of a public and general nature were collected and published in England pursuant to a direction made by the Lord Chancellor and the Treasury. Shortly afterwards the Rules Publication Act, 1893, was enacted. Pursuant to that Act regulations were prescribed by the Treasury with the concurrence of the Lord Chancellor and the Speaker of the House of Commons. Under this authority rules and regulations in England are published separately in systematic form as soon as issued, are collected annually into one bound volume uniform with the statutes, and indices and cumulations are published at frequent intervals, showing quickly and accurately the exact state of the regulations on any problem.

Such a systematic scheme for the publication of administrative rules and regulations is in force in other English-speaking jurisdictions. Statutes similar to the English model have been enacted in Australia and in Northern Ireland. There is a statute to the same effect in Canada. Annual compilations of rules and regulations are published by government authority in India, New Zealand, and South Africa, though apparently without statutory sanction. Similar publications are common in the Latin countries. Indeed, apart from the United States, it would be very difficult to find a nation of importance which does not use some method to make available and accessible a record of the acts of its executive authorities.

The cost of such a publication would obviously not be prohibitive. It would readily command a considerable sale, for all law libraries and many law offices would find it essential to be on the regular subscription list. Moreover, there would be a substantial saving in that rules and regulations so published would not require publication in separate pamphlet form as is now the case. In other words, the adoption of a systematic scheme of publication would not mean more printing but simply the introduction of some semblance of order into the printing which is now done.

If such a project should be adopted, numerous subsidiary questions would require attention. It would be necessary to determine the form and content of the publication, and the "Official Gazette" of other countries might be offered as a model. The establishment of a publication in that form would, indeed, be a great step forward, but it would likewise have its drawbacks. An "Official Gazette" might tend to be no more than a federal newspaper, puffing the activities of the Federal Government; and, in any event, its pages would be cluttered up with a great many items of no permanent importance, such as notices, lists of pending bills, new items, and so on. The result would be that purchasers and libraries must fill their shelves with pages of materials for which they have no use, and the task of searching for rules and regulations is made that much more difficult. More-over, a publication in the form of an "Official Gazette" would have to appear at regular intervals, while the material with which we are concerned does not lend itself to regularity in its natal days.

These objections may be met by providing not for a heterogeneous publication like an "Official Gazette" but simply for the systematic and uniform publication of the rules and regulations themselves as they are issued, just as the acts of Congress are now printed in slip form immediately after becoming law. It should be made the duty of every government department or official who exercises the power to make rules and regula-tions to send a copy forthwith to the Public Printer, and that official should assign it a definite number and print it in a series, all in the same type and general style, including all rules and regulations. At the end of each cal-endar year, the rules and regulations so published should be gathered together in a bound volume or volumes, arranged systematically, with a complete index and proper tables showing the effect of the rules and reg-ulations issued during the year on the statutes and on other regulations. So far as rules and regulations are of an interpretative nature, the require-ment of prompt publication would seem to be a reasonably adequate safe-guard to the public. But where a rule or regulation establishes or defines a criminal offense or provides for a penalty, there should be a provision under which such a rule or regulation would not be effective until actually published.

Considerations of some difficulty are encountered in the obvious fact that all rules and regulations cannot feasibly be published. Many of them are of purely private concern, as for instance, Executive Orders exempting an individual from the civil service acts or allowing an individual to remain in the government employ after the retirement age. Other regulations relate solely to the internal administration of the government departments. There is no need to make these public, and it is appropriate that many of them should not be. With respect to so-called "local" regulations, how-ever, this is not wholly true. Any regulation which might affect the public as such, or any considerable body of it, should be published, even though it is not of general concern. The proper selection of rules and regulations for publication can be more readily left to administrative action than to exact definition in the statute. The English Act gives the authority to make rules on this question to the Treasury with the concurrence of the Lord Chancellor and the Speaker of the House of Commons; but if a legislative officer were given such authority in this country, there might be some question of an unconstitutional interference with the separation of powers. Such power might better be given to the Secretary of State and the Attor-ney General, acting with the approval of the President. . . . And approval of the regulations by the President would be appropriate because of the great importance of the subject matter.

. . . .

Finally, the adoption of a scheme of publication for the future would solve only part of the problem. There would still remain the great mass of regulations in force when the new system went into effect. Provision should therefore be made for the compilation of a comprehensive collection of all such regulations. The preparation of such a compilation might well be entrusted to the Library of Congress. That organization has recently produced an admirable index of the federal statutes, and it could be expected to handle the difficult task of gathering together all past rules and regulations in a wholly satisfactory manner.

A complete index of all rules and regulations in force should also be published at frequent intervals. Such an index should include references not only to the regulations themselves but also to the statutory authority under which the regulations are made. The index now published at three-year intervals in England furnishes a useful model for a similar publication here.

Note 6(C). The *Federal Register* and the *Code of Federal Regulations:* 1936 to 1939

Proposals for a government publication resembling an official gazette were rejected by President Roosevelt, who wanted to avoid the appearance of imposing a "government newspaper" on the nation.[1] The matter, however, came to a head in 1934 in the case of *Panama Refining Co. v. Ryan,*[2] popularly known as the *Hot Oil* case.

The National Recovery Act had imposed limits on oil drilling and authorized regulations to enforce the limits. Defendants in the *Hot Oil* case were charged with violating the regulations embodied in an executive order, and the case reached the Supreme Court before it was discovered that the executive order at issue was no longer in force when the violation was alleged to have taken place. Embarrassed government prosecutors moved to dismiss the case, but the Supreme Court did not let the government off easily. Some years later, Justice Jackson recounted:

> [I]n Panama Refining Co. v. Ryan, . . . the Government was obliged to admit that the Executive Orders upon which it had proceeded below had been repealed by another Executive Order deposited with the State Department. . . . . At the argument . . . the Court, led by Mr. Justice Brandeis, subjected government counsel to a raking fire of criticism because of the failure of the Government to make Executive Orders available in official form.[3]

The American Bar Association also joined the cause. At its 1934 annual meeting, the A.B.A. endorsed the following conclusion of its Special Committee on Administrative Law:

> (a) Rules, regulations and other exercises of legislative power by executive or administrative officials should be made easily and readily available at some central office, and, with appropriate provision for emergency cases, should be

subjected to certain requirements by way of registration and publication as prerequisite to their going into force and effect.

(b) Decisions of those administrative tribunals which do not now publish their decisions should similarly be made easily and readily available at such central office and should be periodically published.[4]

The publication of an official gazette had been under study since the beginning of the New Deal. As a result of the *Hot Oil* case, the A.B.A.'s stand, and the article by Harvard Law Professor (later Dean) E. N. Griswold,[5] the process was accelerated, and Congress passed the Federal Register Act in 1935.

The act established the *Federal Register* as the government's official gazette for the publication of presidential proclamations and executive orders, and the regulations, rules, orders and other instruments of federal agencies of "general applicability and legal effect." The act provided that deposit of an agency document in the office of the *Federal Register* would constitute constructive notice of its contents, but a "document required . . . to be published in the *Federal Register* is not valid as against any person who has not had actual knowledge of it" unless made available for publication and public inspection by the issuing agency.[6] Exempt from the publication requirement were documents "effective only against Federal agencies or persons in their capacity as officers, agents, or employees thereof"; but the act required publication of "every document or order which prescribes a penalty."[7] To accommodate President Roosevelt's aversion to a government newspaper, the act specified that "comments or news items of any character" may not be published in the *Federal Register*.[8]

The publication of administrative materials proved to be a much more demanding task than the publication of statutes. Whereas statutes originate from one source and are tied to the schedule of annual or biennial sessions, administrative materials originate from a multitude of agencies and can be issued, repealed, and amended at any time. Thus, the *Federal Register* is published five days a week, Tuesdays to Saturdays, throughout the year, except days following holidays.

The *Federal Register* began publication on March 14, 1936. At the end of one year a "permanent" edition compiled the year's issues. The Federal Register Act also required federal agencies to prepare

a complete compilation of all documents which ha[d] been issued or promulgated prior to the date documents [were] required or authorized . . . to be published in the Federal Register and which [were] still in force and effect and relied upon by the agency as authority for, or invoked or used by it in the discharge of, any of its functions or activities.[9]

The agencies had six months to prepare their compilations, but they had trouble complying:

Publication of regulations in force encountered serious delay. Eighty to 90 percent of the "compilations" originally submitted by the agencies consisted of obsolete provisions, disorderly amendments and useless formal headings. Therefore, the act was amended in 1937 to require that each agency submit a "codification" by July 1, 1938, and every fifth year thereafter, to be published as a "supplemental edition" of the *Federal Register*.[10]

Presidential proclamations and executive orders were also to be compiled. The task was relatively easy for proclamations, since they were required to be deposited with the secretary of state and had been published in the *Statutes at Large* since 1854 (although publication has been called "haphazard" and was not required by law until 1895).[11] As for executive orders:

> Although as early as 1907 the State Department had attempted to initiate a numbering system for executive orders, apparently many of them, both prior and subsequent to that date, were transmitted directly to agencies or individuals affected thereby with the result that even today there is grave doubt that all executive orders have been rescued from the Stygian darkness that enveloped them over a period of years.[12]

Available proclamations, executive orders, and agency codifications were finally brought together and edited into a *Code of Federal Regulations* in 1939. The first edition of the *C.F.R.* contained regulations in force as of June 1, 1938. It arranged agencies by broad topics in fourteen volumes, plus a one-volume index. It was kept current by annual supplements and the daily *Federal Register*.

Legal scholar John Henry Wigmore called the *C.F.R.* and the *Federal Register* "a reformative revolution in federal administrative law."[13] But some problems remained. Executive orders and proclamations were treated differently than the regulations of agencies:

> Executive Orders and Proclamations . . . are not usually given an index number when originally published in the *Register;* and the indexing for the *Code* has to be taken care of later. Moreover, they often cover several subjects in one document; so that the *Code* must show them *both* in their complete original text and also as distributed into the appropriate title, etc. Hence they form a special problem.[14]

Proclamations and executive orders have been published as the first substantive section in each issue of the *Federal Register* and in title 3 of the *C.F.R.* with its own index and tables listing contents, changes, and statutory authorities. Title 3 has been compiled periodically since 1936. The compilations, however, have been considered unsatisfactory:

> These compilations are . . . unsatisfactory because they do not offer a means of determining, *with assurance,* which presidential regulations are at present in force and which of them at present bear on a given question of administrative regulation. . . . [In place of cumulations,] the text of each presidential regulatory provision must be integrated into the appropriate agency codification.[15]

The *Federal Register* received further criticism:

> Under the present scheme a table of contents [of the *Federal Register*] is printed in each daily issue; monthly, quarterly and annually cumulative indexes are published, but they suffer from inadequate headings. A comprehensive cumulative index, amply furnished with cross references, is essential. . . .
>
> The form of the daily issues of the *Federal Register* indicates that by a little editing, much improvement could be made. No headnotes appear in connection with the various items and only by reading them through can their contents be ascertained. No uniform set-up has been adopted. For example, a Presidential order concerning tariff duties was printed in the form of a letter to the Secretary of the Treasury.[16]

It was also suggested that the statutes authorizing each regulation be cited in the *Federal Register* (they were footnoted in the *C.F.R.*), that the committee in charge of publishing the *Federal Register* had too much discretion on what to publish, and that "[i]t would have been better had the Act conditioned constructive notice not only upon filing, but upon publication as well."[17]

In 1941, the attorney general appointed a Committee on Administrative Procedure to investigate the need for procedural reform in various administrative agencies. As part of its report, the committee recommended that more information from federal agencies be published than called for by the Federal Register Act.

Selection 6(C). The Committee on Administrative Procedure, 1941

ADMINISTRATIVE PROCEDURE IN GOVERNMENT AGENCIES: REPORT OF THE COMMITTEE ON ADMINISTRATIVE PROCEDURE 25–29 (1941).

An important and far-reaching defect in the field of administrative law has been a simple lack of adequate public information concerning its substance and procedure. . . . There are comparatively few works on "administrative law," and even fewer which deal with administrative procedure as such. The publications of the agencies themselves are in a number of instances found to be out of date or of too generalized a character. To all but a few specialists, such a situation leads to a feeling of frustration. Laymen and lawyers alike, accustomed to the traditional processes of legislation and adjudication, are baffled by a lack of published information to which they can turn when confronted with an administrative problem.

Such a state of affairs will at least partially explain a number of types of criticisms of the administrative process. Where necessary information must be secured through oral discussion or inquiry, it is natural that parties should complain of a "government of men." Where public regulation is not adequately expressed in rules, complaints regarding "unrestrained delegation of legislative authority" are aggravated. Where the process of decision is not clearly outlined, charges of "star-chamber proceedings" may be anticipated. Where the basic outlines of a fair hearing are not affirmatively set forth in procedural rules, parties are less likely to feel assured that opportunity for such a hearing is afforded. Much has been done in recent years to alleviate these difficulties. But much more can readily be done by the agencies themselves.

. . . .

After thorough studies had been undertaken in 1933 at the direction of the President, provision was made, for the first time in the history of the United States, for the publication of administrative regulations in the manner of other laws. As a result the Federal Register now provides for the daily publication of new "rules, regulations, and orders" having "general applicability and legal effect." The Code of Federal Regulations is a codification of the same documents. While this important step made it possible for the citizens to discover what rules, if any, had been made, it did not provide affirmatively for the making of needed types of rules or for the issuance of other forms of information. Rules and regulations are not the only materials of administrative law. . . .

A primary legislative need . . . is a definite recognition, first, of the various kinds or forms of information which ought to be available and, second, of the authority and duty of agencies to issue such information. . . . Without attempting to exhaust the subject, it is possible to list at least [five] forms of vital administrative information [not required to be published in the *Federal Register*]:

1. *Agency organization.*—Few Federal agencies issue comprehensive or usable statements of their own internal organization—their principal offices, officers, and agents, their divisions and subdivisions; or their duties, functions, authority, and places of business. The United States Government Manual is not sufficiently detailed to fill this gap. Yet without such information, simply compiled and readily at hand, the individual is met at the threshold by the troublesome problem of discovering whom to see or where to go—a problem sometimes difficult to solve without irksome correspondence or unproductive personal consultations.

2. *Statements of general policy.*—Most agencies develop approaches to particular types of problems, which, as they become established, are generally determinative of decisions. Even when their reflection in the actual determinations of an agency has lifted them to the stature of "principles of decision," they are rarely published as rules or regulations, though sometimes they are noted in annual reports or speeches or press releases,

as well as in the opinions disposing of particular controversies. As soon as the "policies" of an agency become sufficiently articulated to serve as real guides to agency officials in their treatment of concrete problems, that fact may advantageously be brought to public attention by publication in a precise and regularized form.

3. *Interpretations.*—Most agencies find it useful from time to time to issue interpretations of the statutes under which they operate. These interpretations are ordinarily of an advisory character, indicating merely the agency's present belief concerning the meaning of applicable statutory language. They are not binding upon those affected, for, if there is disagreement with the agency's view, the question may be presented for determination by a court. But the agency's interpretations are in any event of considerable importance; customarily they are accepted as determinative by the public at large, and even if they are challenged in judicial proceedings, the courts will be influenced though not concluded by the administrative opinion. An agency's interpretations may take the form of "interpretative rules." More often they are made as a consequence of individual requests for ruling upon particular questions; but as "rulings" they are often scattered and not easily accessible.

. . . .

[4] *Forms.*—A most useful type of information is found in forms for complaints, applications, reports, and the like. Most agencies issue these in connection with their rules of practice. They are helpful to the individual because they simplify his task and make it unnecessary for him to speculate concerning the desired contents of various official papers.

[5] *Instructions.*—Some agencies operate wholly, or for the most part, through examinations, statements, or reports. In such agencies, instructions for such examinations, statements, or reports are the important form of administrative information and are, to all intents and purposes, an essential type of rule-making.

. . . .

Interpretations and policy instructions to the staffs of administrative agencies are now available to the public to a limited extent, especially where interpretative regulations are formally adopted and promulgated. In addition, some agencies have expressed their instructions to their agents in available printed form. To some extent, however, the officers of some of the agencies are controlled in their dealings with outsiders by instructions or memoranda which they are not at liberty to disclose. Rarely, if at all, is there justification for such a practice. Not only does it seem unfair to the individual to compel him to meet unseen regulations, but it is inefficient to encourage representations to an agency which might be stilled if the adoption of a definite policy were known. The Committee is strongly of the opinion that, with possible rare exceptions, whenever a policy has crystallized within an agency sufficiently to be embodied in a memorandum or instruction to the staff, the interests of fairness, clarity, and efficiency suggest that it be put into the form of a definite opinion or instruction and published as such. The extent to which the publication should be separate from that of statutory regulations will vary from agency to agency, but in general it would be wise to distinguish the two. In any event, the publication of the settled policies of each agency which affect outsiders should be complete.

Note 6(D). The Administrative Procedure Act and the Second Edition of the *C.F.R.*: 1946 to 1949

In 1944, the first quintennial edition of the *C.F.R.* was to be published, but because of wartime conditions, publication was postponed. Instead, only a cumulated supplement was issued. Action on the recommendations of the 1941 committee report was likewise postponed.

Following the war, in 1946, Congress enacted an Administrative Procedure Act (APA) to respond to the 1941 report and to revamp the *Federal Register* and the *C.F.R.* The APA required each agency to make available to the public not only its "substantive rules of general applicability" but also:

—"statements of general policy,"
—interpretations "for the guidance of the public,"
—descriptions of "central and field organization," and
—"statements of the general course and method" by which "functions are channeled and determined."[1]

Three exceptions were allowed to the publication requirements of the APA:

—rules "requiring secrecy in the public interest,"
—rules relating to "internal management," and
—rules relating to "named persons."[2]

The APA also required that a new regulation be published at least thirty days prior to the effective date, allowing the public time to comment. However, this requirement could be dispensed with "for good cause found."[3] In response to this requirement a new section for "Proposed Rule-Making" was started in the *Federal Register* with the first issue of 1947.

The broadened requirement for agency publications, however, did not still criticism. Agencies continued to be accused of not publishing all that the public needed to know, but the failure was attributed less to gaps in the legislation than to laxness in agency compliance:

There are thousands of rules meeting [the APA] definitions—rules that create and interpret law, that state policy, and that describe agency organization and procedures—which do not appear in the *Federal Register*. On occasion the responsible officials seem to have been careless. . . . In most instances, however, failure to publish seems to result from a refusal to believe that Congress really intended what it said. In effect, there has been an unwitting conspiracy to exclude from the *Federal Register* a huge quantity of documents that have general applicability and legal effect . . . [especially] interpretations, policy statements, and Government forms.[4]

Criticism also extended to the practice of incorporating unusually bulky documents by reference in the *Federal Register*:

[W]hat real reason is there for denying to people the guaranty that they can find in the Federal Register all general rules that affect them or their clients? The Preface to Volume I recites such a guaranty. . . . In 1941 the Attorney General's Committee called for such a guaranty, and Congress, by enacting the APA in 1946, believed it had ensured the necessary reform. Why, then, continue to deny the guaranty on the ground of mere bulk? . . .

. . . [I]t is ostrich-like to argue that our aim should be ignorance—to argue that, by letting agencies withhold rules from our only centralized repository, we somehow cure the evils of bigness. Is not the sensible course rather to accept bigness, and then to focus on the tasks of editing and publishing?

The mushrooming of administrative rules has been paralleled by a similar growth of other sources of law, and there is much complaint, for example, about the quantity of judicial opinions. Fortunately, the complainers have not impeded the processors, and we are witnessing marked gains in the reporting, headnoting, annotating, and digesting of cases. It is imperative that there be comparable gains in the reporting, classifying, cross-referencing, and indexing of rules.[5]

At the same time, the *Federal Register* was accused of including material that unnecessarily increased its bulk:

To make room for more rules we could cull from the Federal Register a great volume of documents that are not rules and ought not to be there. The fact that Judge Bowen of Seattle has to send "greetings" to a federal marshal, in litigation involving Andy Hardy's life insurance policy, hardly merits an entry of six full-length columns. And legislative draftsmen usually do harm when they stuff the Federal Register with such items as corporate charters and notices to purchasers and unknown claimants of war assets and alien properties.[6]

Criticism extended to the *C.F.R.*, both for its "indices and tables [being] inadequate"[7] and for failing to include all that it should:

[S]everal kinds of rules . . . are excluded from the CFR even though they have been published in the Federal Register.

First, there are the "descriptions of agency organization." . . .

Second, there are miscellaneous rules that seem to have been excluded from the CFR for budgetary and other reasons unrelated to publication needs. Thus, innumerable rules of certain war agencies were included by reference only, the alleged justification being that they were not "permanent" in nature.

. . .

The third group of rules published in the Federal Register but not in the CFR includes the interpretations and policy statements that often precede the text of a rule, in the form of preambles or recitals.[8]

By 1948, the *C.F.R.* had also become unwieldy, requiring the use of seven separate parts

I.e., the original edition, the 1943 cumulative supplement, and the annual supplements for the years 1943–47. The whole set, through 1947, comprised 48 separate volumes.[9]

In 1950, the ten-year-old *C.F.R.* was replaced by a new edition codifying the rules in force as of January 1, 1949, into fifty "titles," with some of the titles paralleling the *United States Code*. This remains the basic organizing scheme of the *C.F.R.* Each title groups agencies dealing with one topic. For example, title 37 of the *C.F.R.*, dealing with patents, trademarks, and copyrights, covers:

—the Patent and Trademark Office of the Commerce Department,
—the Copyright Office of the Library of Congress,
—the Copyright Royalty Tribunal,
—the Assistant Secretary for Technology Policy, and
—the Under Secretary for Technology of the Commerce Department.

Upkeep was no longer to be by annual supplements but by pocket parts to each volume that could be issued whenever major additions or revisions warranted.

By substituting pocket parts for bound supplements, the editors of the 1949 edition of the *C.F.R.* may have created gaps in the historical record of agency regulations. Libraries generally retain bound volumes but discard pocket parts.[10]

The 1949 edition was generally considered a step forward, but dissatisfaction with the *Federal Register* and the *C.F.R.* continued. The *Federal Register* continued to be criticized for being published on cheap, perishable paper,[11] and the indexing of the *C.F.R.*—and, by implication, the *Federal Register* as well—remained a problem. A leading law librarian remarked:

[T]he Index to the *Code of Federal Regulations* [is] the worst possible index of any publication I know. It is so highly analytical by agency and subagency that it is most difficult to find anything you are after.[12]

The criticism became especially pronounced at the end of the 1950s, as the *Federal Register/C.F.R.* system reached its twentieth anniversary.

Selection 6(D). A Looseleaf Proposal, 1959

N. J. Futor, *Searching the Federal Regulations: Forty-seven Steps Are Too Many,* 45 A.B.A. J. 43, 43–46, 99–101 (1959).

. . . If, at the time of receiving the *Federal Register* issue of Wednesday, February 17, 1957, one had attempted to locate the official version of the latest regulations issued by the Federal Communications Commission or Civil Aeronautics Board, forty-seven steps would have been necessary [to check the bound volumes and the pocket parts to the *C.F.R.* and the quarterly, monthly, and daily indexes to the *Federal Register*].

. . . .

. . . After going through the forty-seven steps, one would still not be current. . . . [T]he issue of Wednesday, February 27, 1957, would presumably have reached the subscriber on February 28 or March 1, containing no documents submitted by the agencies later than Thursday, February 21. . . . The *Federal Register* is not a current daily publication in the sense of the *Congressional Record* and the morning newspapers, which report the events of the previous day. . . .

. . . .

There is a growing recognition of the fact that the present system is fundamentally unsound. The American Bar Association has sponsored an administrative practice bill which, while not dealing affirmatively with publishing, displays enough concern for the problem to indicate that consideration should be given to

> the feasibility of making the Code of Federal Regulations current by some loose-leaf system and making the whole service or any part or subpart thereof available nation-wide on subscription.

The present system should be replaced with an integrated system designed to provide a compact set of current agency regulations, something that is not now available. . . .

The present method of official publication was authorized by the Federal Register Act in a provision for publication of all regulations in force, and a provision for the publication of all notices and new regulations in a gazette. The intention of the former provision was to parallel English publication of regulations in force, which was governed by the Rules Publication Act, 1893. The intention of the latter provision was to establish a gazette corresponding to the *London Gazette*. Thus, the system adopted pursuant to those provisions was patterned after an English system developed in the Victorian era.

. . . .

By 1935, the adoption of an official system for publishing federal agency regulations was long overdue. As early as 1920, Professor Fairlie had pointed out that every bureau or local office had its own system or lack of system, that there was no uniformity in nomenclature, that the various levels and branches within an agency had no adequate system of distributing orders and regulations to one another, and that the citizen outside the government service had even more difficulty in keeping informed.

In 1934, an article by Dean Griswold, while questioning the desirability of a gazette, pointed out that publication on the order of the English system would be preferable to the haphazard practices which obtained in the United States. Congressman Celler, who introduced the measure which became the Federal Register Act, acknowledged his indebtedness to that article.

In attempting to persuade Congress to pass the act, proponents of the measure had a powerful argument in the precedent of the English system in operation since 1893. That argument would not have been available in behalf of a new and untried system. Proposal of a new system, no matter how logical or efficient, might have meant delay or defeat. And, in 1935, it appeared that neither delay nor defeat should be risked. . . .

. . . In an earlier day, an administrative agency was considered to function more or less as a clerical automation which prepared regulations for deposit in the interstices of a comprehensive statutory structure. Accordingly, the English—in the 1890's—disregarded the individual identity of the agencies and blanketed all regulations under an omnibus designation, with artificial major divisions called "titles", corresponding to the titles of the statutory code. In other words, regulations were viewed as little more than footnotes to the statutes. That approach was adopted in the Federal Register Act and the publications issued pursuant thereto. In 1935, the full implications of the expansion of federal functions which began in 1933 had not yet become apparent. But that expansion led to federal agency activity of an impressive level of volume and significance, and regulations developed a new order of importance. With the advantage of more than twenty years of experience, it is now clear that the nature of regulations should be reappraised, and that a different mode of organization should be employed. As the Supreme Court said in 1950:

> . . . It must not be forgotten that the administrative process and its agencies are relative newcomers in the field of law and that it has taken and will continue to take experience and trial and error to fit this process into our system of judicature.

. . . Such foundation as the "footnote" concept may ever have had, has now crumbled away. The late Mr. Justice Jackson observed that administrative agencies "have become a veritable fourth branch of the Government, which had deranged our three-branch legal theories much as the concept of a fourth dimension unsettles our three-dimensional thinking." As a result, "within the limits of their respective competences, the administrative departments and agencies resemble a group of special legislative bodies". It is, therefore, unsound to organize administrative regulations as if they were footnotes to the statutes. There is hardly more justification for doing so than there would be for blanketing the statutes of Congress with those of the state legislatures under an omnibus designation with major divisions corresponding to the titles of the United States Code. . . .

Conditions have changed since the 1890's, and it cannot now be considered that an administrative agency is ordinarily confined to the filling in of nooks and crannies in a three-dimensional statutory framework. More often the statute is merely an enabling act, constituting a one-dimensional point of departure, and the subject takes on significant dimensions only as categories of regulations are developed by the agency.

. . . .

. . . The statutory titles simply [do] not constitute an appropriate mode of organization for the varied categories of regulations.

. . . Nine of the CFR titles average about twenty pages each, while five of the titles run to thousands of pages each. Some of the most important categories of regulations thrown into those five titles do not even get a chapter—these are jammed into a subchapter. When a lengthy and important body of regulations is crowded into a subchapter the section numbers tend to be longer and there are certain inconveniences in organization. . . .

. . . The present system requires that a regulation be reprinted in a new format over and over again:

(1) An old regulation is printed in a bound volume of the *Code of Federal Regulations;* and
(2) A new or amended regulation is printed
(a) first in the *Federal Register* then
(b) reprinted *every year* in a supplement to a bound volume of the *Code of Federal Regulations;* and
(3) When the supplement gets unduly large, the regulations in force contained in the bound volume and in the supplement, are reprinted in a replacement volume. . . .
(4) In addition to all this official reprinting, unofficial reprinting is carried on by the agencies.

. . . .

. . . It is impossible to use the *Federal Register* and *Code of Federal Regulations* as normal legal materials. No one can afford to take the "forty-seven steps". Not only would it require an inordinate amount of time;

there would be too great a possibility of oversight in the hurried examination of such a myriad of indices. . . .

. . . Agency personnel and members of the public often desire to have a convenient manual of an agency's regulations. In general, this is not possible with the officially published regulations. The regulations of a single agency tend to be scattered among various titles and many of those titles embrace the regulations of more than one agency. For one whose interest is limited to a single agency, or segment of that agency, this is not convenient. But even if one were willing to suffer the inconvenience, he is still met with the fact that many of these titles are not separately published. For the most part, under the official system, there is no separate availability of regulations: whether by category, by title, or by agency. Because of this, the agencies are driven into wasteful unofficial publishing in order to serve the needs of government personnel and the public.

The Proposed New System

In General. Under the proposed system, the *Code of Federal Regulations* and the *Federal Register* would be discontinued, but centralized publishing, through the Division of the Federal Register, would be retained. Each category of regulations (as well as the statutes pursuant to which they were issued) and notices related thereto, would be separately available for purchase. Each category of statutes and regulations, together with a subject matter index, would be published in the form of loose-leaf sheets. Thus, they could be kept up to date by means of replacement sheets; *i.e.*, a replacement sheet would supplant an old sheet whenever any part of the old sheet was modified by amendment or repeal. If an amendment called merely for supplementing rather than modifying existing regulations, it might be possible in some cases to add new sheets while leaving the old sheets undisturbed.

Numbering of Sheets. The sheets containing the regulations in force would be numbered on one side only. Each sheet number would be followed by a dash and the number of its edition; thus, "35–1" would indicate "sheet 35, first edition" and, if an amendment required issuance of a second edition of sheet 35, it would be designated as "35–2." . . .

Check List. A Check List would be published at appropriate intervals, listing the numbers of the sheets then currently effective. . . .

. . . .

Locating Earlier Versions of a Regulation. Filed in a loose-leaf binder would be the superseded sections of the regulations (in numerical order), and the superseded Check Lists (in order of their date). Thus, for any given date, it would be simple to locate the then effective version of the sections of a regulation. After turning to the section numbers in question, one could—if necessary—be guided by the Check List applicable to the desired date. . . .

Note 6(E). The 1960s and 1970s

The proposal to publish the *C.F.R.* in looseleaf form was dismissed by the director of the office of the *Federal Register:*

> No loose-leaf system yet devised has [absolute reliability]. Every user of a loose-leaf publication is at the mercy of those who inserted the leaves. No matter how good the filing instructions, no matter how pressing the need for accuracy, and no matter how conscientious the person filing, the user has no absolute assurance of completeness and accuracy. There are simply too many chances for human error involved.[1]

A note in the *Harvard Law Review* also concluded:

> [I]t seems that a bound publication may be more appropriate for a formal government publication which is intended to be not only a current source of information but also a permanent and official record of the regulations issued.[2]

The note also favored the existing arrangement of the *C.F.R.* by topic rather than proposals for its rearrangement by agencies.[3]

The editors of the *Federal Register* and *C.F.R.* responded to some of the other public suggestions. The indexes and tables in the *Federal Register* were more frequently cumulated, reducing the forty-seven steps needed for updating to at most seven; the paper of the *Federal Register* was not improved, but the set was microfilmed to provide archival copies; and the upkeep of the *C.F.R.* was enhanced by "piggyback" supplements issued in addition to pocket parts.

By the late 1960s, as the *Federal Register* passed its thirtieth anniversary, criticism over its organization and the organization of the *C.F.R.* subsided. However, regulatory agencies continued to be criticized for withholding information or announcing new policies through channels other than the officially mandated *Federal Register*—through regulatory hearings, internal memoranda, letters to private individuals, and press releases.[4] Earlier, in 1953, a report to the American Society of Newspaper Editors called for increased legal protection for the right of access to a wide range of government information.[5] The report was published as a book and became a best-seller. A decade later, public access to government information became one of the leading social causes of the 1960s.

The 1960s and 1970s experienced growth in administrative regulation comparable to the New Deal era. Unlike the New Deal, the new regulatory activity of the 1960s and 1970s was not a response to a national economic crisis but a result of an era of social activism:

> The themes of this period have included federal assistance to depressed geographical areas; commitment to a cleaner environment; massive support for vocational and for primary and secondary education; "economic opportunity" for the poor; housing and community action programs; federally supported medical insurance for the poor and the elderly; enforcement of legislation outlawing discrimination in accommodations, hiring, and voting; federal aid to

local law enforcement and the criminal justice system; organization for voluntary action; the development of new energy resources and the conservation of existing ones; the promotion of consumer interests; and a host of others.[6]

The establishment of the Department of Health, Education, and Welfare in 1953 foreshadowed the new agencies to come. Among the agencies started in the 1960s and 1970s are:

The Department of Housing and Urban Development
The Transportation Department
The Department of Energy
The Environmental Protection Agency
The Occupational Safety and Health Administration

The increase in the number of agencies was compounded by an increase in the amount of information each agency was required to make public. The movement for greater access to government information culminated in the passage of the Freedom of Information Act of 1967 and the Sunshine Act of 1976. Both acts, however, have been limited by exceptions and by periods of restricted enforcement. Among the competing considerations, concerns about government invasions of privacy have resulted in laws limiting access to government information regarding individuals.

Selection 6(E). Freedom of Information, Privacy, and Sunshine

B. ROSEN, HOLDING GOVERNMENT BUREAUCRACIES ACCOUNTABLE 131–139 (2d ed., 1989).

Freedom of Information Act

. . . .

On July 4, 1966, President Johnson signed the Freedom of Information Act (FOIA) with a ringing declaration about the importance of openness in government for our freedom and independence. The Justice Department was given responsibility for administering the law. The department's guidelines to agencies made clear that disclosure of government documents was to be the general rule, not the exception. The law identified specific exemptions from disclosure which relate primarily to personal data on individuals, business and trade secrets, classified information affecting the national security and foreign policy, and certain inter-and intra-agency memoranda.

In announcing the Justice Department's guidelines, the attorney general said, "If government is to be truly of, by, and for the people, the people must know in detail the activities of government. Nothing so diminishes democracy as secrecy."

This represented nothing short of a revolution in government information policy. Less than ten years earlier, hearings held by a Special Subcommittee on Government Information of the House Government Operations Committee revealed a "none-of-your-damned-business" attitude on the part of federal agencies. For example, such routine information as names and salaries of federal employees would not be released except when a responsible reporter wanted the information for a reasonable purpose; and the government would decide who was "responsible" and what was "reasonable." The names of cattle companies which had been given permits to graze their stocks on government owned land were held secret. Similar secrecy surrounded the amount paid by the government to rent an office building in a major city inside the United States.

By the early 1970s it was apparent that the high expectations of the 1966 law were not being fulfilled. Many agencies engaged in stalling tactics in response to requests for information, since there were no deadlines for compliance and no penalties for violations. Some agencies charged excessive fees for copying and document searches to discourage inquiries. Numerous exemptions concerning investigatory files and internal memoranda were interpreted so broadly as to defeat the purpose of the legislation; and the courts were not authorized to review such cases de novo and examine records in camera to decide whether all or any part of the records could be withheld under the exemptions.

To address the weaknesses, Congress passed a bill in 1974 to amend the law. President Ford vetoed the bill for constitutional (encroached on executive authority) and operational (too burdensome) reasons. The veto was overridden largely because of Watergate abuses and other government misdeeds that were kept secret, and partly because there was a widely held belief in Congress that executive agencies did not try hard enough to achieve the intent of the 1966 law.

In 1986, on the recommendation of the Reagan administration, the FOIA was again amended to deal with two persistent problems: (1) the need to adequately protect law enforcement records, and (2) the need to reduce the cost of administering the program. To meet the first need, the amendments increase significantly the authority of federal agencies to refuse to release law enforcement records. Prior to the amendments, only "investigatory" records could be withheld. Now potentially all "records or information compiled for law enforcement purposes" can be withheld.

With regard to costs, it is undeniable that FOIA has added to the cost of government. A 1980 bulletin from the Department of Justice stated that in 1978 alone, federal agencies spent a total of $47 million to administer that law. To lower the cost, the 1986 amendments authorize agencies to charge the full costs of reviewing documents and otherwise processing requests for information under FOIA when those requests are made for commercial purposes: for example, requests by organizations that resell government records or information. There are special fee limitations applicable to non-commercial requesters. The amendments also tighten the standards for waiving charges. Only if disclosure is in the "public interest" because it is likely to "contribute significantly to public understanding of the operations or activities of the government" may the charges be waived.

The Freedom of Information Act as amended gives any person the right to ask for any government record that she or he "reasonably describes" in writing. The agency must furnish the record unless there is a specific exemption in the law that permits the agency to refuse. In the latter circumstance, there is a right to appeal within the agency and a further right to appeal to a federal district court. District courts may enjoin agencies from withholding information, punish employees who fail to carry out the orders of the court, award attorneys' fees and costs to successful litigants, and call on the U.S. Office of Personnel Management to consider disciplining agency employees who deliberately and improperly withheld information requested. At all stages, including action by the court, the law specifies short time limits for action.

To help individuals and organizations make use of the law, each agency is required to publish in the Federal Register:

a description of the agency organization and where to submit requests for information;

statements about how the agency conducts its business; and

its rules of procedures, substantive rulings, and general policies.

Agencies must make available for public inspection and copying, [with current indexes]:

statements of policy not published in the Federal Register;

decisions on cases (to protect privacy of individuals, identifying details may be deleted);

administrative staff manuals and instructions to staff that affect the public; and

any reasonably segregable portion of a record after deleting portions that are exempt.

Early in the Carter administration, the Department of Justice advised agencies that it would not defend them in FOIA suits unless disclosure of the information is demonstrably harmful, even if documents do legally fall within exemptions of the act. In other words, the government would not withhold information unless it is important to the public interest to do so; agencies should lean to public disclosure when making decisions on access to federal records. Many states have enacted similar laws and have adopted a similar attitude in applying them to specific requests.

In 1981, the Reagan administration presented a different attitude in applying the act. The Department of Justice revoked the "demonstrably harmful" doctrine and advised agencies that "current policy is to defend all suits challenging an agency's decision to deny a request submitted under the FOIA unless it is determined that (a) the agency's denial lacks a substantial legal basis; or (b) defense of the agency's denial presents an unwarranted risk of adverse impact on other agencies' abilities to protect important records.

Apparently responding to this change in attitude, many agencies have shown little concern about complying with some of FOIA's affirmative disclosure requirements. In a review conducted of components of 13 cabinet-level departments and the Veterans Administration in 1986, [the General Accounting Office] found numerous instances where agencies did not publish or keep current and available to the public required information about the organizations and their record systems. This diminishes the ability of the public to deal effectively with those agencies on FOIA matters.

While the benefits are not quantifiable, there is no doubt that the Freedom of Information Act has had a significant qualitative impact on the accountability of government agencies. Tens of thousands of individuals and hundreds of issue-oriented organizations have made use of the FOIA to find out what the bureaucracies are doing and why. In many cases, agencies have changed their policies and practices as a result of these disclosures. All large agencies now employ full-time people whose professional commitment is to carry out the law properly. The federal experience has encouraged over 40 states and several foreign countries to adopt the freedom-of-information concept. Opening up the processes of government and reducing secrecy are making governments behave more often in ways that are acceptable to the citizens. This is no small achievement in democratic societies.

Right to Privacy Laws

The Freedom of Information Act reflects the conflicting values of openness in government and personal privacy. Specific provisions in the act exempt from release personnel, medical, and investigatory records about individuals other than to the one requesting the information. The Right to Privacy Act, passed in 1974, the same year that the Congress amended the Freedom of Information Act, goes beyond these provisions and enhances accountability by

1. permitting people to know what records government has about them;
2. allowing individuals to add information to their own records in order to correct them; and
3. prohibiting agency officials from revealing to others any information about an individual without that individual's permission. (Intentionally releasing such information can subject the official to a $5,000 fine.)

The Right to Privacy Act sharply limits the authority of agencies to maintain information on religious and political activities; such information may be maintained only when specifically authorized by law or the individual or required in law enforcement. The law also restricts the authority of agencies to sell or rent government mailing lists. Federal officials who violate the act are subject to civil and criminal penalties.

Both the FOIA and the Privacy Act limit administrators' discretion: the former by severely restricting the authority to keep government information secret, and the latter by sharply limiting authority to disseminate information about individuals. . . . In considering the relationship of these two laws, it is useful to keep in mind that the exemptions on access to information in the FOIA are discretionary, not mandatory. Before passage of the Privacy Act, an agency could, but was not required to withhold information that would, if disclosed, constitute a clearly unwarranted invasion of personal privacy. With passage of the Privacy Act, an agency no longer has that discretion.

This change is quite clear, but problems in administration remain because there are conflicting interpretations about congressional intent regarding the key phrase "clearly unwarranted invasion of personal privacy." The Report of the Senate Governmental Affairs Committee calls on administrators to balance the opposing interests: "protection of an individual's private affairs from unnecessary public scrutiny, and the preservation of the public's right to government information."

Balancing these interests would seem to require the exercise of considerable administrative discretion. The Report of the House Government Operations Committee appears, however, to allow no such administrative discretion. . . . When administrators' decisions are challenged, the courts decide.

. . . .

The benefits to the individual and to society generally of the Privacy Act, properly implemented, are obvious. One major problem has developed which is not beneficial to society: the Privacy Act denies access to records that would provide information on the results achieved by certain government programs. For example, it has discouraged longitudinal research on the effectiveness of federally funded programs in such areas as drug treatment, work training, and criminal rehabilitation, because they require periodic contacts with those who participated in order to note their progress. . . . New ways are being sought to obtain this information without infringing on the privacy rights of individuals concerned.

. . . .

Sunshine Laws

. . . .

The independent regulatory commissions such as the Securities and Exchange Commission, Interstate Commerce Commission, Federal Power

Commission, Federal Trade Commission, and other . . . agencies, totaling about 50, are now governed by the Sunshine Act approved in 1976. It prohibits ex parte communications, that is, private communication between a person having an interest in a decision of the body and a member of the decision-making body. The law requires these agencies or parts of agencies to give notice in advance of their business meetings of top officials, and to hold them open to public observation, unless agency officials vote to close a session for a specific reason permitted by law. Such reasons may include discussions of information dealing with the national security, personnel problems, information that invades the privacy of individuals, and commercial and financial information that could damage a company's competitive position.

When meetings are closed, agencies are required to make and keep a verbatim transcript. The reason for closing a meeting can be challenged. Ultimately a federal . . . court decides, based on a review of the transcript, whether the agency was justified in closing the meeting. The burden of proof is on the agency. If the court finds the agency's decision was not justified, in whole or in part, then the transcript or that part that should have been open is made available to the public.

All 50 states and many local jurisdictions have some kind of sunshine laws. In all jurisdictions, open decision making spells less influence for special interest groups—but it also creates problems. It is more difficult to deal rationally with conflict in a public arena. Compromises are harder to work out, particularly where representatives of groups whose positions may need to be modified are themselves under attack by hard-liners from within their own organizations. Some decision makers in . . . agencies also complain that sunshine laws prevent useful, informal discussion and speculation with colleagues that could lead to better decisions in formal public sessions. Others disagree.

In the federal government, fewer publicly announced meetings of decision makers appear to be one consequence of the sunshine law. A Congressional Research Service survey of 59 agencies covered by the law revealed that over a five-year period the number of meetings dropped by 31 percent, from a high of 2,297 in 1980 to a low of 1,596 in 1984. Some agencies have substituted nondecisional staff briefings for public meetings to facilitate informal discussion with policy makers. Later, publicly announced meetings are held to take formal action. These agencies may be complying with the letter of the law, but the spirit of the law appears to be suffering.

Note 6(F). Contemporary Administrative Publications

Updating

To keep up with the growing volume of regulatory information in the 1960s, the format and updating of the *C.F.R.* were changed once again in 1967. The entire *C.F.R.* was reissued in pamphlets (about 120 of them). Since 1967, about one-quarter of the pamphlets have been updated every three months.

To update the *C.F.R.* pamphlets, the number of steps required has been reduced to, at most, three through a separate pamphlet entitled *LSA: List of C.F.R. Sections Affected,* and a "List of CFR Sections Affected" in the *Federal Register.* Updating can then involve a great many additional steps to look up and collate the references gleaned from the *LSA* and the "List of CFR Sections Affected."

Indexing

Although the updating of agency regulations was simplified, its indexing remained so poor that an attorney, John Cervase of the New Jersey Bar, brought suit in 1976 to compel the government to publish an improved index.[1] At the time the suit was brought, the *C.F.R.* index volume consisted of 164 pages, which, the suit alleged, constituted a "table of contents" rather than "an analytical subject index."[2] The suit was dismissed by the district court but was reinstated on appeal by the circuit court. The suit was then settled in 1979 as a new *Index and Finding Aids* volume of the *C.F.R.* was published and the government agreed to pay the plaintiff's appeal costs.[3]

The new *Index and Finding Aids* volume of the *C.F.R.* included an expanded index and a list of the agencies that included indexes of their own in individual title pamphlets. A revised *Index and Finding Aids* volume has been issued annually since 1979.

The *Index and Finding Aids* volume of the *C.F.R.* can be updated in a monthly *Federal Register Index* and in the table of contents in each issue of the *Federal Register.*

The indexing of the *C.F.R.* and the *Federal Register* continued to receive criticism after the 1979 improvements:

> Mr. Cervase may be pleased with the results of his lawsuit, but problems still exist. Much of the greater length of the 1979 *C.F.R.* index is the product of the use of larger type and wider spacing between lines. Compared with the quantity of indexed material, the index remains pitifully short and general. Users of *C.F.R.* will find that it is still exceedingly difficult to research U.S. regulations.[4]

The indexes also lack specificity; they refer to parts of the *C.F.R.* rather than specific sections. And the upkeep is slow.

In 1981, a private publisher, the Congressional Information Service (CIS), came to the rescue with an *Index to the Code of Federal Regulations,* which is superior to the government-produced index in detail and comprehensiveness. The CIS index is updated quarterly and indexes geographic locations as well as agencies and subjects.

In 1984, CIS also started an index to the *Federal Register.* The *CIS*

Federal Register Index is an ambitious undertaking with a "calendar" section (for the effective dates of regulations and deadlines for public comments on proposed regulations), lists of *C.F.R.* sections affected, and docket numbers of agency files, as well as a thorough index.[5] Updating is weekly, but the weekly issues are usually published two to three weeks after the latest issue of the *Federal Register* included in their coverage.

On-line Access

The most current and most thorough indexing to the *C.F.R.* is available in LEXIS and WESTLAW. Both databases include the *C.F.R.* as well as the *Federal Register,* within at most a week of publication. Coverage began in 1981 on LEXIS and 1984 on WESTLAW, but the *Federal Register* is available on both databases back to 1980. WESTLAW also has executive orders back to 1936.

Perhaps the next step in the evolution of the *Federal Register* and the *C.F.R.* will be direct on-line publication, freed from the limitations of paper publication. Such a database could provide instant access to the current texts of regulations with one lookup.

On-line access to the regulations of government agencies could also provide links to the histories of the regulations and to court cases interpreting the regulations. Such information is provided for statutes in annotated codes, but no publisher has yet attempted a "C.F.R. Annotated."

Archival Research

Limited history notes in the *C.F.R.* cite the statutes, proclamations, or executive orders that authorized each regulation along with "source notes" citing the latest *Federal Register* in which the regulation appeared. Reference to the original appearance of a regulation in the *Federal Register* can be valuable to trace the substance of amendments and for various "Supplementary Information" explaining the regulation and summarizing comments received prior to its finalization, none of which is republished in the *C.F.R.*

Authority notes can also be found in the annual *Index and Finding Aids* volume of the *C.F.R.,* updated in the monthly *LSA* volumes.

However, there is no convenient source for tracing the history of regulations beyond the authority and source notes. Histories of amendments, transfers, and repeals can only be researched by the cumbersome process of tracing back through the replaced issues of the *C.F.R.,* the *LSA,* and the archival set of the *Federal Register.* For this purpose, replaced *C.F.R.* volumes have been republished on microfiche.

"Annotations"

Cases reviewing agency regulations can be researched through *Shepard's Code of Federal Regulations Citations,* started in 1949, and in several topical units of *Shepard's*. Cases listed in the *C.F.R. Citations*, however, are only from federal court cases and *ALR* annotations from 1949 to 1977. Since 1977, citations from state courts and selected law reviews have been included as well, and *Shepard's* topical units generally include citations from both federal and state courts as well as agency opinions and law reviews.

Agency Opinions

The Federal Register Act of 1935, the Administrative Procedure Act of 1946, the Freedom of Information Act of 1967, and other measures have imposed on federal agencies a uniform method for the publication of their regulations. No such uniformity has been imposed on the publication of agency opinions. Instead of a uniform set of reports for all agencies, each agency is free to adopt its own pattern of publication.[6]

The Administrative Procedure Act requires agencies to make their final opinions "available for public inspection and copying," but publication is not required.[7] As a result, practices among agencies vary widely.

Some agency opinions are published in advance sheets and cumulated in bound volumes with indexes, much like court reports; others are published only in pamphlets or typescript or microfilm. Some, such as the *FCC Record*, one of the most frequently cited, include not only opinions but regulations, notices, and other agency materials as well. As a general rule, most are well behind date.

Thirty-five series of reports are published steadily enough to be included in a citator unit—*Shepard's United States Administrative Citations*. Some agencies have more than one series included, and some of the series are from specialized courts (the Customs Court, the Court of International Trade). Also included is the *Opinions of the Attorney General*, which consists of advisory opinions issued to guide other government agencies. Other agency reports are included in topical units of *Shepard's*, such as *Shepard's Federal Labor Law Citations*, which includes the decisions and orders of the National Labor Relations Board.

Other publishers of legal reference sources have shied away from regulatory material. Legal encyclopedias, *ALR* annotations, digests, annotated codes, and other general sources usually ignore not only agency opinions but regulations as well, although the *U.S. Code Annotated* and, especially, the *U.S. Code Service* include citations to *C.F.R.* and include selected agency opinions in their annotations.

The variety in the publication of official federal agency opinions has given commercial publishers opportunities to republish the opinions in more carefully controlled formats. Several topical reports include agency opinions. Examples are *American Maritime Cases* and *Public Utilities Reports*. Most topical reports are by-products of looseleaf services—a form of publication that has become popular in fields subject to administrative regulation.

Looseleaf Services

Despite many adaptations and improvements since 1936, the *Federal Register/C.F.R.* system remains cumbersome and difficult to use. Lawyers avoid using them if possible.

It is possible to avoid using the *C.F.R.* and *Federal Register* in specialized fields served by commercial looseleaf services. "[T]he loose-leaf reporting service originated because of the inaccessibility and complexity of the vast bulk of Federal and State administrative regulations."[8]

Topical looseleaf services started with a tax service in 1914, the year after the imposition of the federal income tax. The creation of the Federal Trade Commission and the Federal Reserve Board, also in 1914, led to new looseleaf services, as did increasing regulatory activity during the New Deal, when services in labor law, securities, and social security began. New looseleaf services were begun in the 1960s in environmental law, energy regulation, and other fields newly subject to extensive regulation.

The characteristic looseleaf service is limited to a specific topic that involves significant regulatory activity. Each looseleaf service reprints in full the texts of authorizing statutes, applicable regulations, and agency opinions together with full texts of the court opinions—federal and state—dealing with the topic. Thus, looseleaf services offer one-stop access to all primary sources in fields that, without looseleaf services, would be the most difficult to research. Looseleaf services also include occasional court or agency opinions not reported elsewhere and information on proposed legislation, other pending developments, and news items.

Moreover, the primary sources are usually organized in a convenient manner (often with the governing statutes as the frame) and indexed thoroughly in a variety of ways and according to specialized terminology. Tables for finding, updating, and cross-referencing are generally provided by the editors along with explanatory commentary and references to law reviews and other sources. Most looseleaf services contain a section at their beginning entitled "How to Use This Service."

Most significantly, looseleaf services provide prompt updating. Most services mail updates weekly. Currentness, however, comes at a price. Looseleaf services are among the most expensive legal publications.

Looseleaf services are also expensive in terms of the time required to file updates. In some services updates are filed cumulatively, creating chronological cumulation in the bodies of the services with subject access provided by indexes; others are interfiled, with the bodies of the services arranged by topics (with indexes) and with updates replacing individual pages. The cumulative services are easier to keep up, are less prone to error in filing, and preserve the archival record more thoroughly than interfiled services; but interfiled services provide greater simplicity for research.

To preserve archival records, some looseleaf services include "transfer binders" for storing replaced pages that may be of continuing interest. After a time, court and agency decisions are generally removed from the looseleaf binders and replaced by bound volumes, creating a separate set of topical reports.

The leading looseleaf publishers—Commerce Clearing House (or CCH), Prentice-Hall, and Bureau of National Affairs (or BNA)—have turned to computers to help them meet the challenge of coordinating information from a diverse array of sources and preserving archival records while providing exceedingly prompt updating. Several BNA services have become available on both LEXIS and WESTLAW; Prentice-Hall has developed its tax database, PHINet, which is available through WEST-LAW; and CCH has developed its own database—CCH Access—and has begun to make its tax service available on compact discs. In the meantime, both LEXIS and WESTLAW have developed specialized "libraries" designed to serve much the same functions as looseleaf services—prompt, unified access to legislation, regulations, court opinions, and agency opinions—although without the indexing, the commentary, and the extraneous news items contributed by the looseleaf editors.

State Regulation

As federal regulatory activity increased, regulatory activity at the state level followed. But as the *Federal Register,* the *C.F.R.,* and commercial publishers brought some order to federal regulatory information, the states lagged behind. In 1946, the National Conference of Commissioners on Uniform State Laws and the American Bar Association approved a Model State Administrative Procedure Act that included provisions for the publication of administrative regulations, but only a handful of states took action until the late 1960s. In 1966, it was written: "The battleground may now shift to the states [owing to] their failure, in large part, to make adequate headway in publishing their regulations."[9]

In the mid-1960s, only twelve states had requirements for the publication of administrative regulations.[10] In other states, the prevailing practice was to have a copy of each administrative regulation filed at the office of the secretary of state and available for public inspection:

> The old-time system still in effect in more than half of the states is that of filing regulations in a central state office, usually that of the secretary of state. This means that a lawyer or a party may have to look to the state capital in order to know the effective law. Even when he goes or sends to the state capital, he may find that clerks are unable or unwilling to dig out the materials he seeks, for the regulations often remain unclassified or poorly classified, the indexes are often inadequate or nonexistent and piles of uncodified material may be either still effective or long superseded.
>
> The only reason that the system of uncodified accumulations has been at all tolerable is that the official system has been so widely supplemented by informal distribution of regulations by the agencies to parties affected. Those lawyers or parties who are constantly in touch with a particular agency are normally

well enough informed; the inconvenience is to those who are only sporadically affected. That the main reliance is on informal arrangements for distributing regulations is shown by the apparent fact that the accumulations in central state offices are so rarely consulted.[11]

By 1989, forty-one states and the District of Columbia were publishing an administrative code, and thirty-five of them were backing them up with weekly or monthly publications similar to the *Federal Register*.[12] Four additional states were publishing periodic registers but not compiling them into codes.[13] The remaining five states were still in the dark ages with neither code nor register.[14]

Although the looseleaf format was rejected for the *C.F.R.*, it has become popular for state administrative codes. A number of state administrative codes are also available in microform and are becoming available on LEXIS and WESTLAW.

Virtually all states publish manuals of state organization ("Blue Books") and opinions of attorneys general. A few states also publish opinions of various administrative agencies dealing with such matters as public utilities, banking, insurance, and state taxation.

IV

SCHOLARSHIP

Fee simple.

Enant in fee simple is he which hath Lands or Tenements to hold to him and to his heires for euer : and it is called in Latine, Feodum simplex : for Feodum is called inheritance, and Simplex is as much to say as lawfull or pure, and so Feodum simplex, is as much to say, as lawfull or pure inheritance : for if a man will purchase Lands or Tenements in fee simple, it behoueth him to haue these words in his purchase, To haue and to hold unto him and to his heires : for these words (his heires) make the estate of inheritance Anno 19. Henrici 6. fol 38 for if any man purchase Land in these words: To haue and

First Page of Littleton's *Tenures* (c. 1481)

7

Secondary "Authorities"

Note 7(A). Glanvill and Bracton

Predating the first yearbooks, older than the earliest plea rolls, the seminal document of the common law is a treatise. Attributed to Ranulph de Glanvill, justiciar during the reign of Henry II, the treatise was written about 1187, as a practical guide to practice in the courts of the king. Having such a guide helped the king's courts eclipse the local courts of England's nobility. Thus Glanvill's book has been called "the true beginning of the common law."[1]

Written at a time when revived interest in Roman law was reshaping the laws of continental Europe, Glanvill's book served both to absorb the influence of Roman law and to set English law apart from Roman law.

> [Glanvill's] book shows that Roman law has supplied a method of reasoning upon matters legal, and a power to create a technical language and technical forms, which will enable precise yet general rules to be evolved from a mass of vague customs and particular cases.[2]

At the same time, Glanvill identified and strengthened the central feature of the common law—its system of writs:

> In the law of procedure we see one very permanent feature of the common law—its dependence upon writs—the common law already knows a number of writs which corresponds to the various causes of action of which the King's court takes cognizance. But as yet there is no fixed number of causes of action, for the King is very free to issue new writs as he pleases.[3]

Glanvill's compilation of writs has been followed by a tradition of compiling forms to aid lawyers in practice before courts. The earliest such compilation, known as the *Registrum Brevium*, dates from 1227. Modern collections of forms include contracts, deeds, leases, and wills as well as practice forms.

About fifty years after Glanvill, a far more ambitious work was written by one of the king's justices, Henry de Bratton, known as Bracton. Bracton began by turning to the plea rolls and compiling what could be viewed as one of the earliest of court reports. He collected about two thousand cases from the decisions of the best judges represented in the plea rolls of 1216 to 1240. The collection came to be called his *Note Book*. He then wrote a treatise that, like Glanvill's, was modeled on Roman law but organized the rules of the common law, using the cases he collected:

> The treatise shows us that English law has already acquired two of its permanent characteristics. As in Glanvill's book, it is clear that it depends on the writs and the forms of action. But Bracton's book makes it clear that it depends also on decided cases. Wherever possible Bracton vouches a case, and he criticizes decisions of which he does not approve. As yet there are no reports, and so the cases are taken from the rolls. But in his citation and reliance on cases Bracton is in advance of his age.[4]

Although Bracton's use of cases represents a significant advance since the time of Glanvill, Bracton's use of cases was vastly different from the use of cases in modern times:

> It is manifest that [Bracton] had no notion of the modern system of using cases as a source of law; nor does he use cases as the data from which he ascertains the law by a process of induction. . . . He uses them, not because he feels bound by them, but because he feels the need of authority in the intellectual, rather than the legal, sense. The fact that English law is not "written" gave him a good deal of difficulty. . . . Our original writs did not go far enough—indeed, they only reached the threshold of legal proceedings, and left one there. . . . Bracton . . . sought authority in cases. Not any cases, but carefully selected cases; not the latest cases, but what seemed to him the best cases.[5]

Bracton used Roman law not only as a model for the arrangement of his treatise but also to fill gaps in the substance of the common law. In this respect, his treatise was not emulated by future authors. The generations of lawyers following Bracton relied more and more exclusively on the common law and largely ignored Roman law, which was largely relegated to the universities. But the doctrines incorporated by Bracton continued to be cited, and his treatise remained influential.

> [Bracton's] treatise upon English law . . . had no competitor either in literary style or in completeness of treatment till Blackstone composed his commentaries five centuries later.[6]

The treatises of Bracton and Blackstone are sometimes referred to as "institutional treatises," since they deal with the entire body of English law. Although no other noteworthy institutional treatise was written between the thirteenth and nineteenth centuries, some elementary manuals written for justices of the peace attempted to encompass the whole of law—a form of literature that became quite popular in the American colonies and, later, the United States, where justices of the peace were numerous and performed many of the functions of trial courts.[7] More significant, a number of specialized treatises appeared following the introduction of printing in the late fifteenth century, beginning with the classic work of Littleton on land law.

Selection 7(A). The History of the Treatise

A. W. B. Simpson, *The Rise and Fall of the Legal Treatise: Legal Principles and the Forms of Legal Literature,* 48 U. CHI. L. REV. 632, 634–79 (1981).

I

For considerable periods of its history the common law system produced hardly any treatises at all. In the medieval period the only one of any significance is Littleton's *Tenures* (ca. 1481), a work whose origin is mysterious; it is possible—though there is no evidence of this—that it originated in lectures. The *Tenures* was hardly more than a tract, comprising approximately 80,000 words of law-French text. . . . Dividing the subject matter into three books, it sets out in a systematic arrangement the basic definitions, principles, and distinctions that constituted the substantive law of real property. . . . There is no sense in which the work merely systematizes or digests cases; what the books purport to provide is the theory that enables the reader to understand "the arguments and the reasons of the law." Littleton stated his understanding of the "common learning" of the tiny coterie of lawyers whose views constituted the common law. Actual cases are rarely discussed, though many hypotheticals are, and the author is quite uninterested in providing authority for his propositions—a feature that strikingly differentiates the *Tenures* from many later treatises. Littleton had no imitators in the fifteenth or sixteenth century, in spite of the enormous success it enjoyed. The failure of the work to generate a tradition suggests that it was anomalous. . . .

II

It was the fate of Littleton to become the subject of a distinct literary form, the gloss; the best-known example is Coke's *First Institute,* or *Coke on*

Littleton. The text came to be treated as though it were itself law; it was regarded with a reverence approaching that accorded an actual statute. Although there were other works of authority, no other treatise ever achieved this status. It was no doubt Littleton's unique character that explains Coke's extravagant praise: "This book is the ornament of the Common Lawes and the most perfect and absolute Work that ever was written in any humane science. . . ." Placed in its historical context, the *Tenures* is indeed a remarkable work. Not only was it the most successful attempt ever made in the history of the common law to state a single branch of the law as a systematic body of definitions, principles, and distinctions, it was also virtually the first such attempt, and did not rely upon an earlier scheme of arrangement.

In the long period between the publication of the *Tenures* and the beginning of the eighteenth century there was a massive increase in the quantity and variety of legal literature. The introduction of printing, coupled with the growth in the size of the legal profession, assisted this development. . . . But while attempts were made to write treatises, practically nothing was achieved. The great books of the law in this period . . . are not treatises. In particular, Coke's chaotic writings do not fall into this category, and their success depended not on their literary form, but on the personal authority of their immensely learned author. The typical forms of literature were collections of statutes and cases, the two authoritative forms. Parasitic upon these were systematizing abridgments of cases and statutes, indices, formularies of various types, glosses on authoritative texts, and expositions of [terms]. . . .

. . . This reflects a persistent problem of status that confronted the treatise writer in a legal world in which the modern concept of authority, attached peculiarly to judges, had begun to emerge; the text writer, unless he himself is a judge, possesses as an individual no authority derived from office. Consequently his views are important only if they are unoriginal . . . and if their authority derives solely from their substance. The . . . treatise essentially evolved out of the abridgment tradition. . . .

Lawyers and critics were, of course, fully aware of the disorderly and unmethodical appearance of the common law system. . . . From the fifteenth century onwards lawyers had been attempting to reduce the unwieldy mass of legal materials, sometimes for their own personal use and sometimes cooperatively, by digesting it under titles arranged, for the want of any better system, alphabetically. This generated the abridgments and common-place books, which remained dominant forms of legal literature until the nineteenth century. The systematizing efforts of the compilers of abridgments could make possible the production of treatise literature based upon an analysis of the material abridged. This was a process quite distinct from that which produced Littleton's *Tenures,* a work that is unrelated to any form of digest or abridgment. Littleton stated the law in a systematic form; he imposed a rational arrangement for which no earlier model existed. . . .

An alternative to the attempt to refine the crude structure of the earlier alphabetical abridgments was to react against it and try to construct, by rational analysis, a new comprehensive scheme for systematizing the whole of the law. This feat was first attempted by Hale, and the resulting scheme, his *Analysis of the Laws of England* [published posthumously in 1713], made Blackstone's *Commentaries* possible, for Blackstone built his work more or less exactly on Hale. Hale's *Analysis* in its turn was much influenced by the structure of Justinian's *Institutes*, which were themselves based on Gaius's *Institutes*.

Hence Blackstone's *Commentaries* are based on a scheme of arrangement dating back some fifteen hundred years, one designed to give structure to . . . works of a kind foreign to the common law system.

III

The practical approach to the disorderly condition of the law, then, was to tidy it up, to systematize it; no particular theoretical view of the nature of the common law was involved. An alternative and essentially theoretical approach was to maintain that the law was already systematic, however improbable this claim might appear to the uninitiated. This generated a peculiar form of legal literature that predated the rise of the treatise. . . .

. . . [T]he chief literary expression of the theory of principles produced a form of literature very different from Littleton's *Tenures*, and one that is now quite extinct. . . . [C]ommon lawyers set about the task of making and publishing and, inevitably, commenting upon, collections of legal maxims. The best-known early example of this form of literature is Bacon's collection of twenty-five maxims, originally submitted to Queen Elizabeth I in 1597 as a specimen of a general scheme to make the common law more coherent and intelligible to both lawyers and laymen. Bacon had in mind a general plan for the restatement of English law, but he did not wish to turn the system into a codification or, as he put it, into "textlaw." A collection of maxims, together with a book of *Institutes* and a book of Terms of the Law, was to operate principally at an educational level; the main body of the restatement was to consist of abridgments. . . .

. . . .

In theory, collections of maxims could be arranged not by an alphabetical scheme, but by some more rational substantive method, and thereby produce a structure for ordering the law. Indeed, to this day there are portions of legal treatises that could as well be presented as commentary upon maxims. . . . The most notable product of this process was Finch's *Law,* posthumously published in 1627. . . . Finch's methodical scheme for expounding the "body of our Lawes"—what we would call substantive law—was workable and, until Hale produced a better one, the best to be found; nevertheless, the schematic division of maxims by sources, although interesting jurisprudentially, was a dead end and could never have formed the basis for . . . expositions of the law. . . .

. . . [A]lthough maxims still feature in legal exposition, argument, and justification, they are now regarded as slightly comical, and the form of literature directly related to them is dead. It is noticeable that in modern English theoretical works they are hardly ever mentioned as "sources of law." The decline in popularity of this form of literature is partly explicable in terms of the rise of the treatise, which expounded the law in a way more coherent than was possible by any rearranged scheme of maxims. Three other factors may have been significant. First, it came to be thought improper to invent maxims; one could only collect them like zoological specimens. By their nature they ought to be as established and antique as possible. Hence, the collector was inhibited from attempting a more elegant and satisfactory exposition of the law; he was condemned to unoriginality. Second, maxims had to be in another language, normally Latin, and a text built upon them could not continue to command respect after the fall from dominance of the traditional classical education; stylistically, the use of Latin maxims, once thought elegant, is now a subject for ridicule. Third, the tradition enshrined in collections of maxims was that the entire common law system possessed an intellectual unity. This view gave way to the idea that branches of the law form coherent wholes. Even this latter view is now doubted. Maxims have come to seem not just antique but archaic. The form of literature associated with them had died out, but the legal theory upon which they rested came to find a different form of expression in the treatise.

IV

. . . . [A] considerable number of treatises were written in the eighteenth century, and it was then that the treatise tradition became established. Yet the new form of legal literature, though it came to supplant the collections of maxims, was nevertheless based on the same theory of the nature of law.

The great legal publishing event of the century was of course the appearance of Blackstone's *Commentaries* in 1765–69, preceded by his *Analysis of the Laws of England* in 1756. The *Commentaries* originated in lectures delivered at Oxford from 1753 onwards. After 1758 Blackstone delivered these lectures as Vinerian Professor; the endowment of the chair was derived in part from the other major legal publication of the century, Charles Viner's twenty-three-volume abridgment (1741–57). Blackstone['s] . . . success and . . . resulting fame . . . must have encouraged the production of [treatise] literature. Certainly, before his work appeared few [treatises] of any substance were published. . . .

. . . .

Blackstone . . . wrote not for lawyers, but for what is now called the intelligent layman—a concept that includes law students at the beginning of their course of study. Now Blackstone, it must be remembered, was essentially a civilian and an academic; his disappointed ambition was to become Professor of Civil Law at Oxford. His principal contact with legal practice dates from after the publication of the *Commentaries,* not before; had he never become Vinerian Professor and published his great work, I think it is safe to say that no one would ever have heard of him as a common lawyer. The *Commentaries* do not arise from the common law. Though the scheme dates back to Hale, nothing remotely resembling them in execution had appeared in the English language before.

We should not forget, however, that in the eighteenth century quite a number of very substantial legal works, presumably intended for educated laymen rather than specialists, were published in English and appear to have been well received. These works belong to the civil and natural law tradition. . . . The thinking behind [these] publication[s] was that . . . "all the fundamental maxims of law and equity . . . must be the same in all countries." This is the essential credo of the natural lawyers. . . . All these were scholarly, substantial works, written in stylish prose and available in handsome editions. Nothing comparable had emerged from the common law tradition since Bracton's monumental work five centuries before, which itself had been written with a degree of civilian influence.

After becoming the first Vinerian Professor of English Law in 1758, Blackstone set himself the task of doing for the common law what had already been done for the civil law, and vindicating his new charge as a rational system "built upon the soundest foundations, and approved by the experiences of ages." Indeed, while extolling the virtues of the civil law he sounded a note of caution: "[W]e must not carry our veneration so far as to sacrifice our Alfred and Edward to the manes of Theodosius and Justinian. . . . [I]f an Englishman must be ignorant of either the one or the other, he had better be a stranger to the Roman than the English institutions." A spirit of nationalistic self-satisfaction permeates the *Commentaries,* and it is striking that once English law had been expressed in the language of the scholar and the gentleman, as civil law previously had been, common law legal writing took on a literary character it had previously lacked. The success of Blackstone encouraged the writing of more detailed studies of branches of the law that had been treated only in outline form by the master. Furthermore, the discursive literary style of the *Commentaries,* which sharply differentiated such a work from glosses or lists of maxims, must have furthered the idea that this was the better way to expound the principled science of the law.

. . . .

In nineteenth-century England the treatise came to be the typical form of creative legal literature. Although legal periodicals had been in existence for some time, they did not provide an outlet for scholarly writing until the *Law Quarterly Review* was inaugurated in 1885, and it is only in our century that they have become quantitatively significant. The other innovation in nineteenth-century legal writing was the collection of leading cases. . . . This type of literature enjoyed considerable favor, and numerous collections appeared before the idea of relating the casebook to a particular method of legal instruction was conceived by Christopher Columbus

Langdell at Harvard in 1870. Later in the century an attempt to produce a casebook without commentary, directly modeled on Langdell's *Cases in Contract* and intended for the same pedagogical purpose, failed in the sense that the case method never really caught on in English legal education. The dominance of the treatise was not affected by these experiments, and to this day in England there is no indication of any decline in the vogue for treatise writing. The continual production of such works, even in fields such as contract law that have been worked over and over for nearly two centuries by a multitude of writers, must reflect a curious stagnation in English private law, or at least in certain parts of it.

Many of the authors of the nineteenth-century treatises are still, in name at least, familiar to all English lawyers (however forgotten they may have become in America), because their works have lived on in "editions," or are still consulted on occasion, or are mentioned in later works that are still consulted. . . .

The authors of the nineteenth century were men of varied backgrounds. Some few, such as Archbold, appear to have been primarily legal writers, while others, such as Chitty, were practitioners who were also involved in legal education. Some wrote as young men to advertise themselves, or simply to make ends meet. More curious explanations exist with regard to why some lawyers turned to authorship. Leake apparently was encouraged to write after his deafness had ruined his law practice. Woodfall, it is said, broke his leg. In the later nineteenth century the tradition of treatise writing by academics began with Pollock and Anson, though it is only in recent times that academics have tended to predominate. This is hardly surprising; only since the Second World War has university-based legal education existed on any considerable scale in England.

Nineteenth-century treatises vary greatly in quality, and at their worst are disorderly, rambling works of condensation. . . . At their best they are elegantly written and highly systematic. . . . Treatises produced in this self-consciously selective and methodizing spirit have come to be distinguished from others that offer a more comprehensive treatment of the case law, the latter being known in England as "practitioners' books." More fundamentally, however, the distinction reflects a contrast between a concept of law rooted in reason, and one rooted in authority. Plainly, treatises written in the spirit of the former offer the treatise writer a more elevated status in the scheme of things. . . . So the treatise writers of the nineteenth century, insofar as they consciously embraced a theory of law, inherited and claimed to express the belief that private law consisted essentially of a latent scheme of principles whose workings could be seen in and illustrated by the decisions of the courts, where they were developed and applied. The text writer set out to expound these principles in a rational, coherent manner, as was appropriate to a science.

So far as the form of the treatise is concerned, the most interesting development in the nineteenth century belongs to the history of the codification movement. A number of treatises were written in the form of codes, the code being the next logical step in the process of systematization beyond the discursive treatise. . . . The development is in a sense an obvious one. Once the law had been set out in a discursive manner as a methodical scheme of principles, rules, and exceptions, the idea developed that it would be possible to replace the bulk and complexity of these treatises with more concise statements of the main principles, similar in brevity to the old maxims of the common law. Further exposition could be supplied by commentary. . . . With the decline in the interest in codification this form of literature has not increased in popularity, though examples survive in England. . . .

. . . .

Though the legal theory associated with the treatise tradition is still expressed to this day, there has been, I suspect, a significant decline in the belief that legal principles (or at least some of them) are of universal validity; hence, the link between the treatise and the belief in natural law has become attenuated. This development may be subtly related to the formal status of the treatise in the English theory of precedent, which is that the opinion of a treatise writer generally is not authoritative. There is a convention of formal legal argument that normally excludes the citation of treatises as a mode of justifying assertions about what the law is. Although practice is not uniform in the English courts and is becoming more flexible, it is generally said that the arguments of a treatise writer can be adopted as part of an argument, but not offered as a warrant that the argument is correct; there are exceptions to this in the case of certain "works of authority." . . . Although this convention is irrelevant to any assessment of the general influence of treatise writers upon the form and substance of the law, it does reflect the notion that only holders of high judicial office enjoy the power to issue authoritative statements of the law.

One can also point to the generally low status of law schools and legal academics in England as a partial explanation for the English attitude toward treatise writers. Furthermore, many authors were young men and not prestigious figures when they published their treatises (though some became celebrated later in life, either through success in practice, or through a reputation for learning acquired by means of their writings). To writers who claimed to be formulating universal rational principles, the lack of personal authority was not particularly significant; it was what they wrote, not the identity of the author, that mattered. But with the decline of this spirit the treatise writer's formal status inevitably declines as well, for what he says then appears to matter only to the extent that it can be supported by judicial authority, or is accepted as correct by the judiciary. He who has no authority himself comes to rely on authority and not on pure reason. . . . This is the spirit of positivism, which is of course antithetical to that of the natural lawyers.

V

In America the history of the legal treatise took a different course. Law publishing for lawyers began in the late eighteenth century . . . and already by the end of the century several English treatises had appeared in American editions. . . . Blackstone's *Commentaries* were enormously successful in America; there were American editions in 1771–72 and 1790. In the early nineteenth century the practice of relying on English texts, whether imported or produced in special editions, continued. . . . Thus Joseph Story began his career as a text writer by editing English texts. . . .

Aside from statutory material and books intended for laymen, the earliest steps toward an indigenous legal literature took the form of publication, in the late eighteenth and early nineteenth centuries, of law reports. The first significant expository work was Zephariah Swift's *System of the Law of Connecticut* (1795–96), making Swift the first American treatise writer. Nathan Dane's *Abridgment,* published in eight volumes between 1823 and 1829, facilitated treatise writing in America. It was the first attempt to offer American lawyers an alternative to the English abridgments (particularly Bacon's *Abridgment*) on which they had previously been forced to rely. This work, on which Dane had labored for nearly half a century, was a deliberate attempt to supply the want of an American statement of post revolutionary law, and to prevent the fragmentation of the law: "The evil to be feared in our country is, that so many sovereign legislatures, and as many Supreme Courts will produce too much law, and in too great variety; so much, and so various that any general revision will become impracticable." The publication of James Kent's *Commentaries* between 1826 and 1830 provided an indigenous alternative to Blackstone that was hugely successful. In 1829 Joseph Story, who had been appointed to the Supreme Court in 1811, became the first holder of the chair endowed by Nathan Dane at Harvard, and from 1832 until his death in 1845 he published his remarkable series of treatises, covering Bailments (1832), the Constitution (1833), Conflicts (1834), Equity (1835), Equity Pleading (1838), Agency (1839), Partnership (1841), Bills of Exchange (1843), and Promissory Notes (1845). Had his health not broken down (his death was caused partly by overwork), further treatises might well have followed. Thereafter in America the treatise tradition was firmly established, and such works were produced on an extraordinary scale.

From Story's time onwards, the production of treatises was associated with organized, systematic legal education, which of course developed much earlier in America than in England, and on a much more impressive scale. This does not mean that the typical treatise writer was a cloistered academic, as the law schools until Langdell's time employed practitioners as professors. But the writing of treatises became the appropriate activity for law professors. With the development of an indigenous treatise literature, often of higher quality than anything available in England, reliance upon imported books, or American editions of such books, became less necessary. Indeed the quality of American treatises produced a reverse movement: not only were they exported to England, but there were in some instances specially produced English editions.

The establishment of the treatise-writing tradition in America took place in an intellectual climate entirely different from that in England. The treatises dealt of course with the common law, but there had, after all, been a revolution in America, and there was a certain incongruity in the continued use and further reception of a disorderly body of essentially English law, many aspects of which were regarded as extremely objectionable. There was also a deep-seated dislike and distrust of lawyers as a professional class, and the evolution of a legal profession in America was in any event a recent development—one that was by no means generally welcomed. The early American legal writers were, in a sense, on the defensive, and for this reason they were anxious to demonstrate that the enterprise in which they were engaged, the exposition of the American common law, was a respectable one. Obviously it would not do for them to present the common law as English judge-made law that Americans for some bizarre reason should continue to respect in spite of the revolution. The Americans wrote in a nationalistic spirit, and inevitably stressed the American character of the law they were expounding, and the degree to which English common law had been rejected or modified in America. On the other hand, the amount of available indigenous material was limited, and they therefore made extensive use of English materials that could not be presented as possessing any authoritative character in America.

The theory of the law that was appropriate to their writings was essentially that of the natural lawyers. The claim that law was a science was a characteristic refrain. . . .

As law was a science based on principles, the function of the jurist was to expound these principles in a systematic manner; in his search for them he might appropriately use any juridical material that came to hand, as sources both of illumination and of illustration. . . . Story in particular wrote in this eclectic spirit, and quotes in the preface to his treatise on Agency the assertion by Sir William Jones that "[w]hat is good sense in one age must be good sense, all circumstances remaining, in another; and pure unsophisticated reason is the same in Italy as in England, in the mind of a Papinian and of a Blackstone." . . .

In this spirit it was possible to ransack not only the English and American sources, but also those of the civilians and natural lawyers for the best law, an enterprise that had the additional advantage of demonstrating the author's erudition, thus contributing to the prestige both of the author and of the task on which he was engaged.

Later in the century Joel Prentice Bishop, a Boston lawyer who abandoned practice to devote himself wholly to treatise writing, at which he was both prolific and extremely successful, wrote a book, now forgotten, in which he expounded a general theory of the function of the treatise writer. This, *The First Book of the Law* (1868), was cast in the form of advice to students: it was subtitled "Explaining the Nature, Sources, Books and Practical Application of Legal Science, and Methods of Study and Practice." Unlike the writer of digests, the treatise writer is not concerned merely to catalogue the multifarious "points adjudged"—"deemed by idiots to be the law." Instead, his task is to "unfold the rules, the principles, the reasons, which not only governed former decisions, but are to govern subsequent ones." These include "inner principles which perhaps not even the judges saw when they decided the cases." Indeed the true treatise writer may find, in dealing with a particular topic, that "in all the cases the judges had confused ideas, and their observations are not worth anything." The writer must then *discover* the true rule, "and he is just as much entitled to the credit of the discovery, as was Sir Isaac Newton for the *discovery* of the law of attraction in nature." In conformity with this theory, which elevates the status of the text writer (and Bishop was an enormously vain man), he ridicules the English attitude toward treatise writers that links authority with judicial status. The similarity between Bishop's views and those of Langdell is obvious enough and suggestive of derivation.

And so, firmly based on a theory, the American treatises poured forth, culminating in the vast works—or the ultimate treatises, as they have been called—of Wigmore, Williston, Corbin, and Scott.

VI

The great enterprise in which the treatise . . . writer is engaged is the methodizing of disorderly traditional or customary law; once the job has been done competently by a Blackstone or a Story, much of its intellectual excitement disappears. Later treatise writers are relegated to the laborious task of reworking the same materials or refining matters of detail, and this is particularly true when the branch of law involved is relatively static. It requires some dramatic change to give rise to a distinguished new treatise. . . . Good treatises will indeed tend to have a conservative effect on the law to the extent that they are successful; thus much of the conceptual structure of modern contract law was fixed by the early nineteenth-century treatise literature. In this way, treatises contain the seeds of their own destruction.

This destruction may also come about in another way. After private law (or indeed any branch of law) has been systematized, the obvious next step is codification, which will confer a special authoritative status upon a particular succinct statement of the principles of the law. In the nineteenth century, both in England and America (but more particularly in the latter), there was a powerful movement for codification but it was largely a failure. In England there remain some flickers of life in the corpse. In America, the most recent expressions of this natural evolution out of the treatise have been the Restatements and uniform legislation such as the Uniform Probate Code.[*] Neither in England nor in America, however, can the decline of the treatise tradition be explained by reference to the enactment of comprehensive codes of private law or the natural resultant development of forms of legal literature expounding the codes.

[*See *infra*, Note 7(B), and *supra*, Selection 4(F).]

Yet in America, where the common law treatise reached perhaps its ultimate point of development, the genre has by now declined rather markedly from its preeminence. . . . From the beginning, the treatise in America had to contend with the considerable number of different jurisdictions in which the law was administered, each state potentially possessing its own common law. This obviously presented an obstacle to the exposition of a universal common law by the text writers. Perhaps it was not a fatal obstacle; the writers could still aim to present a rational scheme of private law and hope that it would be received in the various state jurisdictions by virtue of its very intellectual force. The jurisdictional variations were exacerbated by another phenomenon, however: the rising bulk of legal material, particularly law reports. This development in turn went hand in hand with an increased significance attached to reported decisions. As reports became available, they were bound to be used. Even in the early nineteenth century, when the problem hardly existed, the sheer quantity of legal books was a source of continual alarm and complaint. Joseph Story, back in 1821, spoke eloquently of the groaning shelves of the jurists, and lamented that "the mass of the law is, to be sure, accumulating with an almost incredible rapidity." Over a century later, when the problem had become much more severe, Samuel Williston was to voice the same complaint. All this threatened the treatise tradition—how could the systematic writer reconcile his presentation of the law as a coherent set of principles with the shambles accumulated in the law libraries?

A possible reaction to this situation is associated with Christopher Columbus Langdell. Langdell did not invent the idea of legal science, which had been a commonplace of legal thought long before his time, nor did he invent the casebook. He has, however, two achievements to his credit or discredit that can be viewed as relevant to the history of the treatise. First, his version of legal science was one in which, although the principles of the law were to be found in decided cases, "the cases which are useful and necessary for this purpose at the present day bear an exceedingly small proportion to all that have been reported. The vast majority are useless, and worse than useless, for the purposes of systematic study." This theory, which, as we have seen, may have been derived from Bishop, and is in any event implicit in the belief in leading cases, enabled the treatise writer to purvey a sort of higher or better law. . . . Such a theory enabled the systematizer to cope with bulk and thrive on diversity. On the other hand, one might maintain that Langdell's other achievement, the case method of legal instruction, was likely to have the opposite effect. The case method created a need for a type of literature that generations of American academics have spent their energies producing: the casebook, or today the collection of cases and materials. Lectures can readily be turned into treatises; casebooks cannot. But although after Langdell's time the production of casebooks and the writing of law review articles (it was during his deanship that the *Harvard Law Review* was founded) came to absorb a considerable output of creative energy, the great American treatises—multivolume works such as Wigmore, Williston, Corbin, and Scott—are products of this century; there is no sense in which Langdell's ideas can be said to have destroyed the treatise.

What appears to me to have had the greatest negative effect on the treatise-writing tradition in America is the realist movement. This movement, ill-defined though it may have been, involved a scepticism and even a cynicism about the significance of legal doctrine in the determination of cases, and it has profoundly affected the attitudes of both those who practice law and adjudicate, and many of those who teach at American law schools. Judicial opinions cease to be regarded as the expression of some rational scheme of principles, but rather as material to be used to justify and cover with a veneer of respectability arguments or conclusions reached on other grounds. A system of ready access to such material is all that is needed. The professional services, and more recently the on-line computer systems such as LEXIS and WESTLAW, have arisen to meet this need.

A movement that minimizes the importance of legal doctrine is hardly likely to generate enthusiasm for the work of analyzing doctrine and expounding it as the principled science of the law. So influential has the realist movement been that today it is possible for lawyers to express genuine incomprehension at the activities of those who, in earlier periods, believed in the validity and importance of such work. . . .

This school of thought, which adopts a somewhat cynical approach to the claim that the common law consists of a body of principles, and which sees common law adjudication as an arbitrary process, has a long history in both England and America. There is nothing really new about the iconoclasm of the American realists. What is new, however, is the reception of their notions among lawyers, and in this sense the great significance of the realist movement for legal history lies in the recognition that it is possible to have lawyers, and flourishing lawyers, without law in the sense that law traditionally has been understood. Whether this state of affairs is to be regretted or welcomed is debatable, but it is clear that it offers no hospitality to the legal treatise.

Note 7(B). Treatises, Encyclopedias, Restatements

Treatises

Although "institutional" legal treatises have not been written since Blackstone and Kent, and new, specialized, multivolume treatises have also become rare, several existing specialized treatises have become standards in their fields and have been kept up to date by their publishers. Among the most well known are *Corbin on Contracts, Williston on Contracts, Wigmore on Evidence, Scott on Trusts,* and *Fletcher on Corporations.* Treatises on the law of individual states—such as B. E. Witkin's *Summary of California Law*—are also published for most states.

Some treatises, such as those by Samuel Williston and John Henry

Wigmore, have received great respect not only in academic circles but also among practitioners and judges. Such works are not infrequently cited in judicial opinions, but their status as "authority" remains questionable.

> The treatise is ordinarily the work of one or two men and consequently represents their views. If law were merely a set of mechanical determinations based on manipulation of agreed quantitative data in operations governed by universally valid hypotheses it might be possible to rely on an individual author in determining "what the law is." But since law is not at all like that, only a sampling of the views of all scholars can lead to a reliable picture of what formulations of problems and what processes for solution are available to the court. The real value of such treatises (and the same is true of articles in the major legal periodicals) is to provide the judge with a broader, more considered, more fully understood basis for consideration and decision, not to tell him what the law is.[1]

In addition to the multivolume standard treatises, the legal profession is served by several publishers producing shorter specialized treatises and by a variety of publications from the continuing legal education programs of state bar associations, the American Bar Association, and the American Bar Association–American Law Institute Joint Committee on Continuing Legal Education. The largest number of legal treatises, however, are produced by legal academics.

Critical legal scholarship is largely centered in the law schools. With the exception of the American Bar Foundation, (the research arm of the American Bar Association) and a very few other research organizations, very little institutionally sponsored research is carried on in law. Government-sponsored legal research is also rare.

The development of reference works to keep track of legal treatises also receives very little institutional or government support. Nor have commercial publishers taken the lead. While cases, legislation, and administrative regulations are kept track of (however imperfectly) by national sources published by government and commercial publishers, keeping track of treatises has been left largely to individual libraries through their catalogs. National access is achieved by pooling the catalogs of individual libraries in national computer networks.

Most libraries in the United States follow a standard format for catalog records and a uniform system of subject headings. The subject headings are provided by the Library of Congress, which also developed the most widely used system for the classification of books by subject-oriented numbers on library shelves.

Some specialized libraries, however, have rejected the Library of Congress subject-heading system and classification numbers as not adequate to deal with their specialized literature. For example, medical libraries have developed their own specialized systems through their own National Library of Medicine. Law has no "national library," no specialized subject headings, and some legal classification schemes developed in the past have been generally abandoned for the sake of the uniform application of Library of Congress numbers.

Some commercial publishers have provided information sources dealing with legal treatises in limited ways. While "in print," treatises are kept track of in a number of sources, including *Law Books in Print* and its upkeep service, *Law Books Published,* and *Law Books and Serials in Print.* Current legal treatises can also be traced in the *Catalog of Current Law Titles,* which is a composite of the "current acquisitions" lists of a substantial number of law libraries.

In addition, many specialized bibliographies have been prepared by scholars of individual topics or eras. A classic scholarly bibliography, listing English law books published prior to 1600, is J. H. Beale's *Bibliography of Early English Law Books,* published in 1926 and supplemented in 1943 by R. B. Anderson. The most ambitious American legal bibliography, modeled on Beale's and listing law books published prior to 1870, is in preparation by M. L. Cohen and B. Halevy. Other bibliographies are so numerous that bibliographies of bibliographies have become available. W. S. Chiang and L. E. Dickson have published five-year cumulations listing legal bibliographies in *Legal Bibliography Index* since 1978.

Library catalogs, in-print lists, and bibliographies generally publish only information regarding the author, title, subject, publisher, date, and pagination of treatises with some additional notes that may provide further information on the contents of treatises.[2] Some "annotated" bibliographies provide further comments, but evaluative information is usually difficult to find. Lists of law books recommended to law school libraries have been published by the Association of American Law Schools[3] but are now out of date; and a committee of the American Bar Association has from time to time published lists of law books recommended to lawyers.[4]

The most thorough evaluations of treatises are in book reviews published in legal periodicals, but most book reviews appear a considerable time after the publication of the books reviewed. With the automation of periodical indexes, it is becoming increasingly easy to locate such information.[5] As the automation of card catalogs and periodical indexes advances and converges, citations to book reviews may one day be linked to cataloging records.

Technology may also expand the information available in cataloging records. With the huge storage capacities available in computers, cataloging records may be expanded to include the tables of contents, indexes, and perhaps the texts of introductions as well—all to be searchable by keywords. And technology is bringing about a new form of the treatise— a treatise combined with a looseleaf service on compact disc. Experimental products are beginning to reach the market, using a treatise as the framework and attaching to it an entire topical "library," allowing the reader by means of "hypertexting" to jump from citations in the treatise to full texts of the cases, statutes, regulations, or other material cited.

Encyclopedias

Like some treatises, *Halsbury's Laws of England* and the two legal encyclopedias of the United States—*American Jurisprudence 2d* of the Lawyers
Cooperative Publishing Company and *Corpus Juris Secundum* of West
Publishing Company—are designed to state "what the law is." Their
authority, however, rests on the work of anonymous editors employed by
the publishers. The statements of law in encyclopedias are also limited by
their concentration on cases to the relative neglect of statutes and administrative regulations.

Although legal encyclopedias are on occasion cited by courts, their
main value lies more in marshaling case citations[6] than in their textual
statements.

> Most critical discussions of law books as authority distinguish the two major
> functions of encyclopedias—as digests and as authoritative texts—and assess
> their value separately with relation to each function. The general opinion is
> that these works are useful as digests, but that the text and documentation are
> frequently of such uncertain quality as to make reliance on them without prior
> consultation of the cases and other more reliable authorities a questionable
> practice.
>
> . . . .
>
> The . . . emphasis on reconciling decisions, . . . on rationalizing conflicts,
> . . . the obvious intent to simplify that which can never be simple, the deter-
> mination to rationalize "apparently" inconsistent ideas, the promise of cer-
> tainty with reference to matters that can never be certain, all these and many
> other aspects of . . . encyclopedias . . . indicate an approach to the judicial
> process which is mechanical and superficial.[7]

Restatements

Another attempt to state "what the law is" is embodied in the *Restatements* of the American Law Institute. The *Restatements* constitute a
unique project designed to gather the views of a group of leading scholars,
along with leading judges and practicing lawyers. The aim of the *Restatements* is not merely to sample those views but to boil them down into one
clear statement carrying the authoritative endorsement of the ALI.

The ALI was organized in 1923 and has published and updated the
Restatement of the Law ever since. Individual volumes have been published
for *Contracts, Torts, Property,* and seven other topics. Each topic contains
the "black letter" rules, "comments" with "illustrations" as approved by
the institute, and "notes" added by the reporter, who is always a leading
scholar in the field. "Notes" include citations to cases, statutes, treatises,
and other sources.

Although, in rare instances, a *Restatement* may go beyond attempts to distill the law from judicial decisions, statutes, and other sources and venture to state what the law should be,[8] the chief aim of the institute has been "the clarification and simplification" of the law.[9] "Many lawyers felt that the 'growing indigestible mass of decisions' threatened the continuance of our common law system."[10]

Thus, the impulse that gave rise to the American Law Institute is the same impulse that motivated the movement for codification. (The ALI, in fact, has drafted several proposed model acts for legislative enactment in addition to its work on the *Restatements*.) The *Restatements*, however, have not become the basis for codification proposals. Their aim, rather, has been to simplify the common law so as to make codification unnecessary.

The *Restatements* lack any government sanction. They carry only the force of a consensus of knowledgeable individuals—a persuasive force probably greater in fact, but no different in kind, than the force of any individual author.

The influence of the *Restatements* is acknowledged by the fact that a unit of *Shepard's Citations* is devoted to tracing each citation of a *Restatement* by courts and in twenty leading legal periodicals. The ALI itself also carefully monitors citations of the *Restatements* and publicizes the data in each *Restatement*. Moreover, various drafts of the *Restatements* are preserved, and the proceedings of the ALI are published, and both are used to interpret the *Restatements* in a manner akin to statutory legislative history materials.[11] Cases applying the *Restatements* are also digested in an extensive appendix to each *Restatement*. But despite the level of authority achieved by the *Restatements*, some have considered the concept of the *Restatements* itself misguided:

> They [the authors of the *Restatements*] took fields of living law, scalded their flesh, drained off their blood, and reduced them to bones. The bones were arrangements of principles and rules (the black-letter law), followed by a somewhat barren commentary. . . . The restatements were, basically, virginally clean of any notion that rules had social or economic consequences. The arrangements of subject matter were, on the whole, strictly logical; the aim was to show order and unmask disorder. (Courts that were out of line could cite the restatement and return to the mainstream of common-law growth.) The chief draftsmen, men like Samuel Williston and Austin W. Scott of Harvard (contracts, trusts), were authors of massive treatises. . . . They expended their enormous talents on an enterprise which, today, seems singularly fruitless, at least to those legal scholars who adhere to later streams of legal thought. Incredibly, the work of restating (and rerestating) is still going on.[12]

The attack on the *Restatement* concept came largely from a group of scholars who have come to be known as "legal realists." The *Restatements*, in fact, have been viewed as specifically aimed at the realists:

[T]he Restatement project can be taken as the almost instinctive reaction of the legal establishment of the time to the attack of the so-called legal realists. What the realists had principally attacked, savagely and successfully, was the essentially Langdellian idea that cases can be arranged to make sense—indeed scientific sense. Such an idea, the realists demonstrated, was purest moonshine and nonsense. By the 1930s, at least in the law schools, the Langdellian position had become untenable—and, in an unkind reversal, the case method of teaching had been turned on its head and used to disprove everything its inventor had held dear. But in the 1920s there was still hope that the revolution could be put down, that unity of doctrine could be maintained and that an essentially pure case law system could be preserved from further statutory encroachment. The radical solution to the breakdown of the case law system, which the realists had perceived, would, no doubt, have been statutes all around—a universal, Benthamite codification. The conservative response, which, looked on as a delaying action, was remarkably successful, was the provision of Restatements.[13]

Selection 7(B). A Realist Critique

J. H. Merryman, *The Authority of Authority*, 6 STAN. L. REV. 613, 613–73 (1954).

. . . .

The citation of authority in judicial opinions, briefs, articles, texts, annotations, encyclopedias, and other forms of legal writing is often an uncritical unreflective process carried out without conviction or understanding about the purpose of citation, the nature of authority or the function of precedent. Presumably a citation means something to the person citing, and presumably he anticipates that it will have some meaning to a reader. . . .

. . . .

Traditionally any discussion of the merits of authority begins with a distinction between primary and secondary authority, the former being statutes and decisions and the latter anything else a court cites in its opinion. Between them important differences are supposed to exist. Thus it is said that only statutes and cases are produced by the authority of the government, by legislators and judges who are aware that they are engaging in a lawmaking process and who are in some sense responsible to those to whom the law will be applicable. This difference is supposed to be sufficiently great to justify classification of secondary authority in such a way as to suggest that it is clearly inferior as "law" to statutes and cases. It is obvious however that given the judicial practice of citing secondary authorities in opinions these works can and do play a part in the total legal process which is not greatly different from that played by primary materials. It is possible for cases to be decided, rules of law to be stated, lines of decision begun and perpetuated, solely on the authority of a textual treatment having its origins outside the judicial or legislative process. Citation of the secondary authority makes it part of the judicial process, and ultimately it becomes impossible to draw clear distinctions between primary and secondary authority except in terms of origin. Clearly the statute and the authoritative decision are the most obvious and probably the most important types of authority, but anything cited by a court is for that reason alone, if for no other, authority in the same sense if in lesser degree.

It is sometimes said that primary authority is binding, but that secondary authority is at most "persuasive." Any realistic view of the judicial process must make it clear that no authority can ever be binding in this sense. The most that can be said is that a court may feel more strongly persuaded by some authority than by some other, and that cases are undoubtedly more persuasive than *Corpus Juris.* But the subjective and accidental factors involved in the choice of possibly applicable decisions, formulation of what they have to say which is applicable to the instant case, and actual application to the facts regarded as significant leave so much room to avoid being "bound" that it is not very realistic to speak of authority in terms of absolutes. This is especially true where, as in many jurisdictions in the United States, the courts can expressly overrule their own prior decisions. In practice it is quite possible for a secondary authority to be more authoritative than primary authorities, since the judge has so much discretion in determining what is applicable to his case and how it is to be applied that he can, if he wishes to support a conclusion he has reached in the case, find that which supports it applicable and that which does not inapplicable.

. . . .
. . . Actually the application of authorities to cases to arrive at decisions is not nearly as simple or mechanical a process as the layman thinks it should be. It is no easy matter to reach general agreement on just what a case says or does not say; the infirmities of the linguistic processes involved, the uncertainty as to what the prior judge meant by way of dictum and what he considered as going to the heart, or close to the heart, of the case, the difficulties of determining whether the prior decision is or is not applicable to the instant case, and on what basis applicability should be considered, the problems involved in actual application of prior doctrine to the new and different situation, these are all very great. To this should be added that the prior case occurred and was considered in its own factual context by a different person with different views about the nature of law and laws, the function of the judicial process, the sources of authoritative

doctrine, the ends of litigation, operating in a different society, and operating from a different cultural and social background than the present judge. The number of these variables, and the impossibility of ever approaching anything like constancy with relation to them, make it clear that the judicial process is one of constant approximation, of making judgments on hosts of imponderables, of applying one's own views, biases, predispositions—all held within varying limits—to problems which are never the same as previous problems, to issues which are always new, in which litigants and society exert new pressures. To this process everything available to the judge is consciously or unconsciously relevant. If he is a good judge he recognizes the value of a realistic view of . . . stare decisis . . . ; he will wish to deal properly with the new problem, recognizing that in doing so he "changes" the law, but he will try to do it in such a way as to preserve the proper continuity with the prior law. In this way he will do what he can to resolve the ever-present conflict between rest and motion.

Further, if he is a good judge, he will recognize that to do this well he needs to be a very learned and able man, and that he should get all the help it is possible for him to get, wherever available. It is here that the function of the really good secondary authority is most obvious—in helping the judge to shape the precarious course of decision from precedent through application. A group of judicial opinions in prior cases gives the judge a raw material with which to work, a point from which to depart, and occasionally some insight into the course of decision, but ordinarily little more. A study of the problem by an able scholar, with time to devote to it, with an inclination toward research and reflection, may provide the judge with additional insights into the problem and its appropriate judicial solution. This is as valuable a tool to the judge as the stuff of earlier decisions on related problems and there is a growing tendency to consult secondary authorities for assistance in shaping decisions. But the quality of a secondary authority will vary with respect to the ability and application of its authors and editors; and its utility as a salutary aid to judicial decision in the always difficult, ever unclear type of case with which the appellate judge is presented will depend to a great extent on the purposes for which the work was prepared and the premises on which it is based. A work prepared by authors and editors who view the judicial process (if they think about it at all) as a mechanical search for the appropriate rule will probably tend to create and perpetuate the same view among those who use it. Works which ignore social interest, the data of the behavioral sciences, the facts of political life, which are unwilling to look beyond legal concepts to the actual conflicts of interest involved in litigation, encourage a similar attitude in the lawyers and judges who read them. By frequent judicial use and approval the easy philosophy of such works tends to permeate the judicial process and thus to make consideration of a more realistic, but more difficult, jurisprudence less likely. Consider:

The Restatement

The Restatement, as is generally known, has been prepared by men of the greatest ability, working in the finest tradition of careful, thoughtful scholarship, in a noncommercial enterprise conducted under the auspices of an organization of unimpeachable integrity known as the American Law Institute. The product of their work has become familiar to all law students, lawyers, and judges and has become an important part of the judicial process through repeated citations and quotations in the decisions of state and federal courts. The Restatement is a work of the highest quality, standing well up in the scale of secondary authorities, and deserving the respect of the bench and bar.

However, it is too easy to lose sight of the fact that the Restatement does not have the unqualified approval of legal scholars—that it embodies an approach to problems of law and the legal order, a set of juridical assumptions and preconceptions, which represents only one group of legal thinkers. Opposed to this group are other equally respectable and respected scholars to whom the Restatement is, in many of its aspects, objectionable. The fact is that there is an ideological schism among legal thinkers along lines which tend to divide them into pro- or con-Restatement. The latter group, most of whom may be described as the legal realist, have well expressed their views about the Restatement in published criticisms of it.

Thus Green criticizes the *Restatement of Torts* for stating black letter rules instead of describing processes for decision of tort problems and for trying to state substantive law only, rather than substance and procedure together, "with the inevitable result that the product is a sort of dehydrated something, drained of nearly all the vitality found in such abundance in this, one of the most dynamic fields of government." He states that by failing to work out a comprehensive and careful tort analysis and classification the Reporter and his associates made an "initial and irredeemable" mistake which explains "much of the unrealiability" of the Restatement. He accuses the authors of "overelaborated generalizations" which warp traditional legal terms and concepts into shapes unrecognizable to judges. He finds the formulations of the Restatement useless to judge, to jury, to advocate, to law student: "In short, the trouble I find with the Restatement is to discover any purpose for which it can be used which is not already better served by some other form of legal literature." He expresses fear that by virtue of the important names connected with it and with the Institute and the attractive form in which it is published it will be given a sanctity to which it is not entitled on the merits. He accuses it of not being a restatement of any existing recognizable law, but rather a statement of something new and different—something which might be called "classroom" law—which carries with its operation almost certain or automatic judgment, and which leaves no question unanswered. This automatic process ignores the realities of what goes on in the courthouse, where cases are subjected to trial court functions, jury participation and perhaps appellate review before anyone knows what the outcome will be.

. . . .

In speaking of volumes one and two of the *Restatement of Property* McDougal states:

. . . .

> To elaborate upon the now commonplace criticism of the earlier restatements would be futile. Some reviewers have pointed to naivete in fundamental assumptions—assumptions that certainty is obtainable and obtainable by high abstractions, that certainty is more important than flexibility, that "substantive law" is all-comprehensive and designed to govern human conduct in and out of courts, that the defects of "the law" can be cured by restating it as it is, that a restatement of the law as it is is a restatement of it as it ought to be, and so forth; others have deplored the omission of historical, economic, and sociological backgrounds and of studies of comparative experience in other countries, the ignoring of, except by indirection, consideration of what "the law" ought to be, a failure to study the social consequences of institutions and doctrines, the omission of supporting authorities, reasoned discussion, and contrast of conflicting opinion, the use of "doctrinal" rather than "factual" classifications and of the blackletter-comment-illustration formula of expression, and so forth. . . . [I]n a world where funds and capacity for research are limited it seems not unfair to criticize a great research organization for its choice of aims—especially when the announced aim is a will-o'-the-wisp that can lead only to subsidized snark hunting. To assume that the judicial handling of property problems in contemporary America can be made more predictable by an authoritative canonization and rationalization of ancient, feudal-conditioned concepts and doctrines—of, for example, the distinctions between legal and equitable, divesting ("cutting short") and normal expiration, conditions subsequent and conditions precedent, remainders and executory interests, rights of entry and possibilities of reverter, and so forth—is little short of fantastic.

The later volumes of the *Restatement of Property* have been subjected to even more intense and searching criticism, . . . even attack . . . not only on the validity of the approach taken to statement of the law of covenants but on the tactics of the Reporter and the nature of the procedure within the Institute with reference to its adoption and promulgation. . . .

The *Restatement of Contracts* ("the summary of Williston on Contracts which is called the Restatement") has been carefully reviewed by Patterson, who raises numerous valid questions about it, characterizes it correctly as an expression of only one of two basically opposed jurisprudential schools, and places it in proper perspective as "the oldest and most respectable of contract analyses, the most widely accepted among law professors and among the *cognoscenti* of bench and bar"—but still only one analysis. "Other types of analysis of legal problems have received the attention of many legal scholars. . . . This batch of intellectual ferment has got labelled 'functional approach' or 'legal realism.' The names are trite and undefined because the movement itself, unlike its older rival, lacks a concerted effort at definition. Yet rival it is."

The most widely criticized of all Restatements undoubtedly is that on conflict of laws. The differences in fundamental assumptions between the Reporter and his critics are very great, and the consequences of these differences in terms of actual proposed solutions or methods of solution of legal problems are frequently more obvious than in other fields. As a result the body of critical writing about this part of the Restatement has been large, and almost any discussion of legal problems in the conflicts area includes some contribution to one side or the other of the controversy. . . .

. . . What the Restatement represents at best are the considered views of one group of legal scholars, to the exclusion of those of another group of comparable reputation and ability. The published criticism of the Restatement is sufficient to indicate that these differences in thinking about law have practical consequences for cases. . . .

. . . [The Restatement and] the great bulk of the published [secondary] works available to judges . . . are written in such a way as to overemphasize the role of stated authoritative doctrine and submerge the role of the processes of decision in the solution of social problems in the courts. By emphasizing "the law" to the exclusion of "the legal process," by perpetuating the illusion that all there is to decision of a case is location of the appropriate rule, by ignoring what cannot be rationally ignored about modern linguistic theory, by assuming that judges are not subject to the same psychological processes as other humans, by refusing to talk about how a raw case is split up into "legal issues," by omitting any mention of how one determines whether a given authority is applicable to one of these issues, by failing to discuss what really is involved in applying the authority to the issue . . . these works perpetuate an unsophisticated concept of the legal process in which the actual bases of decision are concealed not only from the society he serves but from the judge who decides.

A first step in freeing himself from this view of law is that the judge recognize that headnotes from previous decisions, no matter how carefully arranged, how accurately copied, how smoothly run together into text, no matter how carefully weighed, distilled and condensed into higher abstractions, do not of themselves decide cases. They are at best data. If the judicial process is to be a conscious, meaningful process the judge must be aware that he *selects* data, that he *formulates* questions, that he *applies* doctrine in his own way, that he *achieves* results, and that the decisions in earlier cases play only a small part in the total process. This consciousness on the part of the judge will then make it possible for him to ignore the false front of mechanical jurisprudence and get to the heart of the matter— the personal and social values which have always played the larger part in decision, however unconsciously employed.

8

Legal Periodicals and Sources Beyond the Law

Note 8(A). Legal Periodicals in England

The idea of a periodical publication began with the publication of the first news sheets in seventeenth-century England. The era was also rich in broadsides and pamphlets addressing the divisive issues of the turbulent period of the Civil War, the Commonwealth, and the Restoration. But such ephemeral publications were unsatisfactory forms of communication from the perspectives of the authors as well as the would-be readers—printers had to be found; distribution was haphazard; copies were difficult to locate. Much of the broadside/pamphlet literature of past centuries has been irretrievably lost.

Combining short essays into a composite work and issuing such composite work at preset periodic intervals reduced the difficulties of publication, distribution, and preservation. Moreover, periodicals provide a forum for other forms of communication that could not stand alone—news items, comments on current cases and legislation, biographical notes, book reviews, advertisements.

Nevertheless, the first periodicals other than newspapers did not appear until the middle of the eighteenth century, and the early history of periodicals is littered with failures. The first distinctly legal periodical, the *Lawyers' Magazine* of London, lasted less than two years, from 1761 to 1762.

The matter for surprise is that publishers persisted in the attempt to issue law periodicals when the fate of most of them is recalled. During the 76 years from 1761, when the Lawyers' Magazine was first published, until 1837, twenty-nine legal periodicals were launched. Most of them died in from one to six years. Only six lived more than ten years, and at the end of the period only five were still being published.[1]

The number of legal periodicals increased in the 1830s and 1840s, fueled by the general interest in law reform and codification. A number of periodicals were inspired by Jeremy Bentham and devoted their pages to explorations of the "science of jurisprudence."[2]

In general, however, legal periodicals were aimed at the practical interests of the practicing bar. Serious scholarly articles did not find a regular periodical outlet until the publication of the *Law Quarterly Review* in 1885. In this respect, the United States was ahead of its mother country:

> There were few outstanding English legal periodicals prior to the 1885 publication of the *Law Quarterly Review* in London. . . . Yet by that year, America could boast of scores of legal journals, several of which were being edited with a high degree of professionalism. The *Law Quarterly Review,* moreover, imitated the approach of the earlier *American Law Register* and *American Law Review.* The *Quarterly Review* was distinguished by the intellectual superiority of many of its lead articles and the leadership of its esteemed editor, Sir Frederic Pollock.[3]

The *Law Quarterly Review* is published by a commercial publisher, Stevens and Sons. In 1937, a similar periodical, the *Modern Law Review,* was started and was also eventually taken over by Stevens and Sons. These two remain the leading scholarly legal periodicals of England, although they have been joined by law reviews published at the two leading law schools of England—the *Cambridge Law Review* began in 1921, and the *Oxford Journal of Legal Studies,* a latecomer, began in 1981. In recent years, several less influential law schools have also started to publish law reviews. In this, the law schools of England appear to be following the example of the United States.

Selection 8(A). Legal Periodicals in the United States

M. I. Swygert and J. W. Bruce, *The Historical Origins, Founding, and Early Development of Student-Edited Law Reviews,* 36 HASTINGS L. J. 739, 739–91 (1985).

. . . .

Most accredited law schools in the United States publish a student-edited law review containing scholarly writing about recent court decisions, unresolved issues of law, and other topics of interest to the legal community. Begun a century ago by law students as an academic experiment, law reviews have achieved a prominent and influential position in the legal profession. Much has been written both praising and criticizing these periodicals, particularly with respect to the unique phenomenon of law students managing and editing journals to which academic and practicing professionals submit articles for evaluation, revision, and publication. This process stands in stark contrast to that employed in most other disciplines, in which scholarly journals are edited by recognized authorities in the field and works are selected for publication by a panel of expert referees.

. . . .

Historical Origins

All the earlier forms of legal writing—treatises, law reports, and periodicals—influenced the founders of law reviews, but the growth of legal journalism in America during the nineteenth century provided the groundwork upon which law reviews were built. The "concise and casual" legal writing found in legal periodicals introduced during this period contrasted sharply with the tedious and encyclopedic treatises of Blackstone, Kent, and Story.

. . .

. . . .

EARLY AMERICAN LEGAL PERIODICALS

In the early 1800's, the current news of the day in America was provided mainly by general circulation newspapers, which frequently reported recent court decisions. These journalistic accounts, however, often contained inaccuracies and inevitably were incomplete. Hence, members of the legal profession "demanded a medium of their own." The publication and growth of case reports was one response to this demand. Yet the case reports failed to meet all the needs of the bar. Practitioners desired a publication devoted specifically to bar-related matters.

By the early 1800's, American lawyers had settled throughout the nation. Unlike England, in America the practice of law was largely decentralized. The decentralization resulted in a disjointed body of common law. The development of the American common law along different paths was due not only to the vast geographic distances involved, but also to differences among the court systems in each state. Consequently, the treatises, which tended to be national or universal in scope, did not fully meet the needs of practitioners, whose law practice was primarily local or state oriented.

Furthermore, the treatises and commentaries discussed law developed decades in the past, but the states were rendering new decisions daily. Although the newly published case reports contained accounts of recent decisions, there were so many cases being decided in so many jurisdictions that one could hardly keep up. Moreover, the reporters rarely analyzed or commented upon these cases.

Finally, although the competent practice of law required knowledge of numerous and specific legal principles, rules, and procedures, it also involved dealing with judges, lawyers, and clients—people about whom it was expedient to be informed. Lawyers needed publications that would set out "the literature of the bar, especially its biographical and statistical material, questions of legal reform, chit-chat, and gossip, and [even] an enlivening anecdote." Thus, "concise and casual" legal publications devoted to the American practitioner became inevitable.

First American Legal Periodicals

The first legal periodical in America was the *American Law Journal and Miscellaneous Repertory,* published in 1808 at Philadelphia. . . .

The *American Law Journal and Miscellaneous Repertory,* like many journals to follow, was in essence a transitional publication between the earlier case reporters and the later legal magazines that developed in the mid-nineteenth century. . . . It primarily contained long excerpts of judicial opinions. Hence, to a degree it was another "reporter." But unlike the reporters, it also contained a short biography, some notices and brief descriptions of recent law books, and a commentary or editorial section. . . . It was issued irregularly in six volumes through 1817.

. . . .

. . . Three other short-lived journals were published during these years. First, . . . The *Carolina Law Repository* [began] in 1813. It survived until 1816. . . . The inclusion of speeches and commentary by nonlawyers led one reviewer to conclude that *The Carolina Law Repository* was "only partially a law magazine."

In 1818 another legal periodical appeared: *The New York Judicial Repository,* published in New York City. This monthly magazine consisted almost exclusively of reports of trials, especially criminal trials and those thought to have a mass appeal. The published reports included cases dealing with assault and battery on a wife, assassination, conspiracy, a duel challenge, grand larceny, libel of a son-in-law, swindling, and rape. This journalistic venture into legal sensationalism lasted only six months. . . .

The final effort at publishing a legal periodical during this period was also short-lived. . . . Like the earlier *New York Judicial Repository,* the *United States Law Journal* apparently tried to be a magazine for the general populace. And like the *Repository,* it failed.

Each of these early legal periodicals was unable either to define or to carry out its mission. By featuring case reports, these publications were similar to the numerous established reporters. And, by attempting to attract a wide audience, at least two of these periodicals were too general for practicing attorneys yet overly technical for the general readership.

Although none of the legal periodicals published in the first quarter of the nineteenth century attained a position of literary distinction or last-ing influence, they represent the first step toward a new form of legal publication. The next move in that direction was taken in 1829. . . . *The United States Law Intelligencer and Review,* a legal journal . . . has been properly described as the "first publication displaying the distinctive fea-tures of the law magazine" as it exists today. *The Law Intelligencer and Review* was distinctive because it included what came to be called "lead articles," a writing format which eventually produced some of the most significant legal scholarship of the times and foreshadowed the mainstay of modern law reviews. In particular instances, these articles approached the treatise in stature, respect, and influence.

The United States Law Intelligencer and Review also contained case reports and general news, but the lead article, "well considered, upon live subjects," was its hallmark. Unfortunately, this periodical ceased publica-tion in 1831 after only three volumes. Its demise may have been due to financial difficulties rather than deficiencies in its content.

Many early journals failed because publishers were either unable or unwilling to extend the necessary financial support. . . . By 1850, approx-imately thirty law journals had been attempted in America, but only about ten survived. Nonetheless, the phenomenon of legal journalism was spreading across the United States, and a more sophisticated, nationally oriented law journal evolved. Two journals founded during the mid-1800's—the *American Law Register* in 1852 and the *American Law Review* in 1864—qualitatively advanced legal journalism in this country.

American Law Register and American Law Review

. . . The monthly issues of the *Register* were distinctive because they con-tained more scholarly articles than the other journals. Roscoe Pound described the *Register* as the prototype of the "academic-professional type of periodical" which became the "characteristic American type." In the *Register,* "along with popular articles and addresses there were more sci-entific articles from a general, even . . . a comparative law standpoint." This scholarly emphasis no doubt contributed to the *Register*'s most sig-nificant achievement—its survival. Indeed, it exists today under the title of the *University of Pennsylvania Law Review.*

. . . .

. . . The *Register,* like all previous American law journals, began as a commercial venture not associated with a university. Beginning with Vol-ume Ten, however, various boards of editors consisting of practicing attor-neys, jurists, and law professors operated the *Register.* . . .

[An] editorial board member, William Draper Lewis of Philadelphia, . . . [was appointed] as dean of the University of Pennsylvania Law School in 1895 . . . [and] arranged for the *American Law Register* to be published by the law school he headed, apparently because he believed "that an important attribute of a good law school was a law journal." This conclusion reflected developments in legal education at the time; by 1895 Harvard and Yale already had established successful law school periodicals.

In 1896, law students at Pennsylvania began to edit the *Register*. The name of the publication was changed in 1908. . . . The *University of Pennsylvania Law Review* goes on, . . . making it the oldest continuously published legal periodical in America.

Another prominent legal periodical that emerged during the mid-1800's was the *American Law Review,* which was first published in Boston in 1866. . . . Unlike the monthly schedule of the *Register,* the *Review* was issued quarterly. This schedule may have allowed for more careful writing, selection, and editing of its contents. Certainly, that was the result; the first issue of the *American Law Review* was a breed apart. There were five substantial lead articles dealing with conceptual and institutional issues of national interest. The editors . . . successfully appealed to the intelligentsia of the nation's legal profession. . . .

By including scholarly lead articles, honestly critical book reviews, news of legal events having regional and national interest, and contributions from the best available legal minds, the *American Law Review* quickly became and arguably remained the most important American legal periodical of the nineteenth century. Its role as a model for the later student-edited law reviews made the *American Law Review* an important link in the evolutionary chain of American legal periodicals. . . .

At this stage, however, in the latter half of the nineteenth century, many developmental paths were still open in the field of legal journalism. If the *American Law Review*'s birth in 1866 heralded a more "academic" future for the American legal periodical, the emergence of other law journals suggested the continuation of a more "professional" orientation.

Professional Journals

Lead articles in the *American Law Review* usually had an academic orientation. They were written primarily to educate. . . . Most legal periodicals published in the 1870's, however, were designed primarily to inform— to discuss recent decisions, developments in the law and in legal education, efforts at codification, and news in a journalistic rather than in a scholarly style. These practitioner-oriented journals typically began with comments or editorials, followed by brief articles, case reports, digests, and concluded with book notices. The few "articles" typically did not "lead" the issue, but were buried in the middle. Yet, as mediums of information about legal matters of interest to lawyers and judges, a few of these publications performed superbly.

One journal in particular understood its informational function and successfully performed it for nearly forty years. This publication, *The Albany Law Journal* commenced on January 8, 1870. . . . Although an academic review might publish only quarterly, an informational magazine must appear more frequently to be of value. *The Albany Law Journal* commenced as a weekly. . . .

. . . .

The *Albany Law Journal* often raised its voice in behalf of better education of lawyers and for higher standards for entry into the profession. The *Journal's* continuing concern for improving the public image of lawyers was typified by its reaction in its initial issue to a letter in the New York *Independent* newspaper that criticized the legal profession for producing "so few saints, so few martyrs, so few moral heroes." The *Journal* responded that "[nearly] every trace of social and religious liberty on earth is due to lawyers," adding that it was "high time that the vulgar notions about lawyers were done away with."

In certain ways, the *Albany Law Journal* of the late nineteenth century resembles the *American Bar Association Journal* of the mid-twentieth century. For example, each reportedly had the largest circulation of any legal periodical of its time. In addition, both journals sought the support of the entire legal profession. One important distinction is that the American Bar Association, a professional organization, publishes the *American Bar Association Journal,* but the *Albany Law Journal* was not affiliated with any bar organization. As might be expected, these publications did not coexist; the American Bar Association began publishing its *Journal* in 1915, seven years after the demise of the *Albany Law Journal.*

. . . .

The success of the *Albany Law Journal* spawned a score of other professional journals during the early 1870's. One of its better "imitators" was the *Central Law Journal,* located in St. Louis, Missouri, and published weekly. . . .

Other similar regional periodicals soon sprang up throughout the country; no longer was the publication of legal periodicals centered in the northeast. . . . Several specialized periodicals also appeared by 1875. They included the *Insurance Law Journal,* the *Medico-Legal Journal,* The *Bankrupt Register,* the *Internal Revenue Record and Custom Journal,* and the *American Civil Law Journal.* More would soon follow. The number of legal periodicals published in this country leaped from seventeen in 1870 to forty-two in 1886.

Several factors contributed to this explosion of commercial ventures in legal periodical publishing. The success of the *Albany Law Journal* was one. Another was the deprofessionalization of the bar. As . . . barriers to entry into the profession were lowered, more persons began to practice law. Many of these new, often unschooled lawyers probably were concerned less with the universal principles of law found in the treatises than with cases and news of their particular region or state. The new legal periodicals fulfilled their need.

. . . .

Thus, American legal periodicals paved the way for the student-edited law reviews by developing formats for legal writing, by demonstrating that legal periodicals could be useful to the profession, and by creating a wide-spread audience for articles combining scholarly insights with a professional focus. Although English authors originally dominated doctrinal writing . . . , the Americans blazed the new path of legal journalism that eventually led to student-edited law reviews.

The Founding of Student-Edited Law Reviews

Student-edited law reviews emerged in the late nineteenth century. Contrary to popular belief, the *Harvard Law Review* was not the first student-edited law review. Law students at two other institutions, Albany and Columbia, produced short-lived law journals prior to the publication of the first volume of the *Harvard Law Review* in 1887. . . .

INITIAL VENTURES AT ALBANY AND COLUMBIA

With publication of the *Albany Law School Journal* in 1875, the American law periodical was no longer exclusively in the hands of "professionals." This journal . . . did not last long. Apparently, it survived only one academic year. . . . [I]t was started and edited by students of Albany Law School. . . .

. . . .

This "novel experiment" consisted of a few short articles, reports of moot courts dispositions, news items, and information about the law school's clubs. The *Albany Law School Journal* attempted to be a chronicle of law school events and a magazine of general interest to graduates and members of the profession. This concept was unique in the history of English and American legal periodicals.

. . . .

Despite the failure of the first student-edited legal periodical, other efforts were made. In February 1885, almost ten years after the demise of the *Albany Law School Journal*, six young men at Columbia Law School started the second student-edited legal periodical—the *Columbia Jurist*. . . . The Columbia law students modeled their effort after other periodicals being published by some academic departments in Columbia College. . . .

The editors declared that the weekly *Jurist*'s greatest value would be as a reference work for students and that it would include notes from class lectures, moot court decisions, plus "all news that can interest Law Men.". . .

Like the editors of the earlier *Albany Law School Journal*, the student editors of the *Jurist* did not focus solely on internal matters of the law school. They also took note of developments in the law and, in imitation of the successful commercial law journals, published casenotes of recent decisions and lead articles by "persons of acknowledged merit." By calling on contributors from both inside and outside the college, the student editors of the *Columbia Jurist* "made their magazine the forerunner of the modern university law review."

. . . .

The *Columbia Jurist* was not received with open arms by its commercial brethren. The second volume of the *Jurist* contained five separate articles concerning "Mr. Dudley Field's Civil Code," and the student editors became embroiled in a journalistic controversy with the *Albany Law Journal* and the *American Law Review* over the proposed Field Code. The commercial publications had endorsed the codification effort and asserted that the *Columbia Jurist* editors, who espoused the opposing view, had "indulged themselves largely in an intemperate" reaction. . . .

Weekly issues of the *Jurist* continued to appear for only another year. After Volume Three, Number Eighteen had been published in 1887, the *Jurist* died. The *Albany Law Journal* commented that the *Jurist:*

> ha[d] succumbed after a long disorder, manifested by an inveterate hatred to codification. The disease lately took a bad form, and with a gasp the *Jurist* expired on January 29th last. . . . The *Jurist* died penitent, and by a singular fact made a public confession of its wicked life and its unholy antipathy to codification. With its last breath it feebly murmured, the need of codification is confessed on all sides, and then it died. May so die all enemies to codification! We don't want them to die, but when they die, we want them to die penitent.

The real reason for the demise of the *Columbia Jurist* notwithstanding the *Albany Law Journal*'s romantic belief to the contrary, was the inability of the new student editors to meet the grinding task of putting out a weekly publication.

Despite its short duration the *Columbia Jurist,* unlike the earlier *Albany Law School Journal,* had a significant impact on the development of student-edited law reviews in this country. A copy of the *Jurist* attracted the attention of Harvard law student John Jay McKelvey in the fall of 1886. The Columbia venture motivated McKelvey and other Harvard students to start a student-edited law review of their own. Indeed, the initial issue of the *Harvard Law Review* appeared in the spring of 1887 with McKelvey as editor-in-chief. . . .

HARVARD LAW REVIEW

During the 1880's, student clubs were common at Harvard Law School. Their principle function was to organize "Moot Courts," which were an important part of the curriculum. In the fall of 1886, eight third-year students formed a new club, the Langdell Society, "for the serious discussion of legal topics and for other serious work on law." In addition to conducting mock trials, the members planned to write legal essays to be read at meetings. The intention of writing essays only for their own use soon gave way, however, because "it was felt that the . . . writers deserved a wider circulation than was originally proposed and the founding of the *Harvard Law Review* was the result."

Of course, it was not quite that simple. The prospective editors presented the plan to the faculty, who displayed "differing degrees of warmth in support offered." In particular, the students consulted Professor James Barr Ames. . . . Ames was a likely consultant because his general availability for counseling made him the students' "best friend" during this period. As Joseph Beale, a student founder and later a Harvard law professor, recounted: "Ames approved [the idea for the review] without reserve, wrote the first leading article, and became the chief advisor and helper of the editors throughout his life." . . .

The faculty played no role in managing the review, although apparently the students had invited them to do so. With the exception of Ames, they may not have had high hopes for the new venture because faculty minutes initially referred to the periodical as a "paper" rather than as a "journal" or "review."

. . . .

The students were also inspired by the heady times at Harvard in November 1886. The occasion was the 250th anniversary celebration of the founding of the university. . . .

. . . [John Henry] Wigmore [one of the student founders], later discussing the birth of the journal, bluntly stated that the celebration of the 250th anniversary "put pride into our hearts, and the conviction that the Harvard Law School had a message for the professional world."

This conviction became the key to the eventual success of the daring, perhaps even rash, student experiment in legal journalism. The mission of the publication was to be a vehicle for the "faculty's scholarship, . . . not so much as an organ for ourselves."

Indeed, the founding of the *Harvard Law Review* gave the faculty, and Ames in particular, a new outlet for their scholarship. Prior to the *Review*'s birth, Ames and Professor James Bradley Thayer had begun research on legal history topics, but did not publish the results until the *Review* was in existence. The *Review*'s editors unabashedly relied on such faculty articles to justify the new venture in legal publishing. [According to Wigmore:] "We *knew* that our faculty comprised scholars of the highest standards and accomplishments in their fields. . . . We *knew* that their pioneer work in legal education was not yet but ought to be appreciated by the profession. We yearned to see the fruits of their scholarship in print."

A problem of funding remained. The project was not an official part of the law school program, and it needed outside support. At the suggestion of Ames, the student editors sought assistance from alumnus Louis Brandeis, secretary of the newly created Harvard Law School Association. Brandeis gave the editors money and placed them in touch with other members of the Boston bar who were likely to support the project. Student editor McKelvey also solicited alumni in the New York City area for subscriptions, which were reportedly numbered around 300 by the first issue.

The stage was set. It was time for the student editors to produce an enduring, first-rate academic journal. Although the result was not radically different from leading legal periodicals of the time, the review clearly reflected a law school orientation.

The initial issue of the *Harvard Law Review,* published in the spring of 1887, consisted of two lead articles, notes about the happenings at the school, reports of moot court arguments, summaries of class lectures, case digests and comments, book reviews, and a list of books received. The editors declared that their goal was to be a vehicle for the publication of research centered at Harvard Law School, to furnish news about the school to alumni, and to spread the word of the new method of instruction introduced at Harvard.

The reference to the "Harvard system of instruction," of course, concerned the "case method:" the use of casebooks, rather than textbooks, and Socratic, rather than lecture, pedagogy. The person most responsible for instituting this system at Harvard was Christopher Columbus Langdell, who became dean of Harvard Law School in 1870 and transformed the institution into a model of the modern law school.

. . . Certainly the intellectual excitement produced by the effective use of casebooks and Socratic dialogue played a critical role in the founding of the *Harvard Law Review.* The student editors thus were not mere purveyors of Harvard's "message for the professional world," they were a part of it because they were the products of the new casebook method. They had been taught to analyze, not merely to recite from rote memory like schoolboys. And they wanted the legal profession to take notice.

. . . .

Student editor Wigmore was in charge of the recent cases department. Although established commercial journals all had similar departments run by well-respected editors, Wigmore and his fellow students did not hesitate to become "criticasters of judicial decisions." The primary objective was to select cases "which bore directly upon topics discussed" in the classroom. Wigmore also was involved in writing notes about law school news. On occasion these notes were "calculated to induce in . . . [the students] a complacent feeling that . . . Harvard Law School . . . was achieving things."

. . . .

A final feature of the publication deserves mention. United States Supreme Court Justice Felix Frankfurter wrote that the *Harvard Law Review* was a democratic institution "permeated by ethical presuppositions and assumptions and standards." Students became members of the *Review* if they excelled academically; there were no other considerations.

. . . .

Early Development of Student-Edited Law Reviews

The *Harvard Law Review* rapidly developed influence in academic and professional circles. The impact on the academic world of the first successful student-edited law review is reflected in the creation of similar periodicals at other institutions. In the legal world at large, its articles soon began to affect judicial decisions and legislative deliberations.

EXPANDING ROLE IN LEGAL EDUCATION

In a twenty year period following the founding of the *Harvard Law Review*, five of the nation's then most prestigious law schools—Yale (1891), Pennsylvania (1896), Columbia (1901), Michigan (1902), and Northwestern (1906)—modeled legal periodicals after the Harvard prototype. During the next two decades, the law review tide swept the country as many other law schools started and nurtured student-edited periodicals.

The phenomenon of the early growth of law reviews did not occur solely because other institutions modeled one aspect of their programs after the country's leading law school. To be sure, an element of "keeping up with Harvard" motivated the establishment of law reviews at other law schools. Other factors, however, contributed significantly to the increase in the number of law reviews. Most important, the law schools recognized the educational benefits of such student-run operations. In addition, the existence of a law review was, and still is, considered to be the mark of a mature educational institution, one whose reputation is partially based upon the students' academic product. Moreover, law schools made a positive statement about their commitment to legal scholarship by including a law review in their curricula.

. . . Thus, once these institutions adopted the Harvard model, the die was cast for legal education. Thereafter, a law school without a law review was considered a lesser institution.

. . . .

The efforts of . . . Michigan and Northwestern, are noteworthy for reasons other than their early entry into the field of law school publication. First, the creation of law reviews at these institutions marked an emergence in the midwest of what previously had been largely a northeastern phenomenon. Second, and more important, the journals at Michigan and Northwestern were initially operated by the faculty.

. . . .

It is unclear why the Michigan law faculty chose to operate the publication themselves. Possibly they believed that such control was necessary for the success of the venture. . . . The students, of course, were involved, but only as "editorial assistants." As the *Michigan Law Review* became firmly entrenched in the school's program of legal education, however, the situation changed. "Over the years, the Law Faculty tended to turn over more and more of the editorial work of the *Review* to the student editors. . . ." By the late 1930's, the students had "taken over a much larger share of the total responsibility, with the faculty serving primarily in an advisory capacity."

Northwestern was the next law school to produce an enduring law review. The publication at Northwestern, founded in 1906, followed the format of the *Harvard Law Review,* but was more closely aligned to the *Michigan Law Review* in two respects. First, it was designed to fill a need of the legal community in a particular area of the country—Illinois. Second, it was initially edited by the faculty with some student assistance.

The relatively narrow focus of the Northwestern publication is explained in its first issue. There the editors commented:

> Undoubtedly, the field for law reviews of a general character is already over-crowded. Moreover, it must be conceded that such reviews, however excellent, enlist the interest of but a small minority of the practicing lawyers in Illinois. It is believed, however, that there is genuine and widespread need of a live periodical primarily devoted to the discussion and exposition of Illinois law, and of matters of special practical value to the Illinois bar. In that belief, and with the purpose of supplying that need, this *Review* is launched.

Given this perspective, it is easy to understand why the Northwestern faculty chose to call its journal the *Illinois Law Review.* The local orientation of the review also was the reason that the University of Chicago and the University of Illinois law schools united with Northwestern for several years in the late 1920's and early 1930's to produce this publication. Although the cooperative editorship apparently was successful, Northwestern resumed sole control of the *Illinois Law Review* in 1932. Two decades later the review's name was changed to the *Northwestern University Law Review* to reflect the identity of its publisher and the expanded scope of its content.

As in the case of Michigan, it is difficult to determine why the Northwestern Law faculty assumed control of the review and initially permitted only limited student involvement. The dean of the school at the time was John Wigmore, who had been one of the student founders of the *Harvard Law Review.* Nevertheless, Wigmore apparently did not advocate an entirely student-edited journal, but supported the concept of a faculty managed publication involving only a few student associate editors.

Perhaps the limited use of student talent in the early days of the review was due in part to the involvement of a Chicago attorney in the establishment of the *Illinois Law Review.* The attorney, Nathan MacChesney, had attended the University of Michigan and was aware of the *Michigan Law Review.* . . . His involvement may also explain the inclusion of alumni on the review as associate editors.

. . . [O]ver time the law students at Northwestern played an expanding role in the publication of the *Illinois Law Review.* Following a quarter of a century of faculty control, "complete responsibility for the *Review* was turned over to the students of the law school and in 1932 the first student editor-in-chief was chosen."

Although six years intervened between events at Northwestern and the development of the next enduring law review, the trend was established. Once law reviews emerged at the leading law schools described above, it was a foregone conclusion that the remaining institutions would

join the movement. This proved to be the case. By 1930, forty-three law
schools featured law reviews, although "the division of work and responsibility between the faculty and the students of the law-review-publishing
schools varie[d] considerably." Whatever their editorial makeup, law
reviews already had assumed significance in addition to their educational
value to the students. Almost from the beginning, election to an editorial
position proved to be a ticket to attractive placement opportunities. . . .

INFLUENCE ON THE LEGAL PROFESSION

It is difficult to assess precisely how the early reviews influenced the legal
profession. Certainly some commercial law journals did not think very
highly of these competitive journalistic efforts by law students. Nonetheless, there is substantial evidence that law reviews had an almost immediate
impact on the development of the law in the courts and the legislatures.

The best known example of an influential early law review article is
The Right to Privacy, written by Samuel Warren and Louis Brandeis, which
appeared in the *Harvard Law Review* in 1890. Shortly after its publication,
the article was cited by a judge, who apparently based his opinion on its
contents. Eventually the article produced a broadbased change in the law.

. . . .

. . . The members of the Supreme Court, as well as other judges, gradually increased their reliance on law review articles over the years until by
the mid-1920's the impact of law reviews on judicial decision-making was
well recognized. In this regard, one commentator noted: "When a
Supreme Court Justice was first told by some friend that the *Harvard Law
Review* declared his latest decision *wrong,* he may have pretended to scorn
the disapproval as the theoretical conclusion of an immature student, but
it hurt just the same."

Early law review articles also influenced the thinking of legislators.
Many articles contained the recommendation that a certain legal problem
could best be solved legislatively. Consequently, the law reviews served "as
a mine for legislative drafting bureaus;" numerous statutes resulted from
the suggestions of authors of law review articles. One authority has even
suggested that the National Conference of Commissioners on Uniform
State Laws was created in response to law review criticism of existing law.

. . . .

Conclusion

. . . .

The early law school reviews imitated the format, style, and content of the
more influential commercial publications. Even so, the student-edited law
periodicals that appeared near the end of the nineteenth century and in
the early years of the twentieth century were unique in three respects. First,
"not one iota of commercialism" inspired the commencement of any of

the student-edited law reviews. They were designed instead to facilitate academic scholarship. Second, the student-edited reviews began as a "medium of extracurricular training." The editors were not paid, nor did they receive academic credit for their law review work. And third, the student-edited reviews were managed, edited, and at least partially written by nonprofessionals.

The idea that individuals who have not yet graduated from law school select, edit, and publish critical writings for the legal profession still causes concern among critics. Yet few voices are raised scorning the efforts of students who edit law school reviews today. . . .

Note 8(B). Legal Periodicals—Quality, Quantity, and Indexing

A half-century after the founding of the *Harvard Law Review,* as law reviews spread throughout the law schools of the nation, they came under severe criticism. The classic blast at law reviews came from a law professor, Fred Rodell of Yale Law School:

> There are two things wrong with almost all legal writing. One is its style. The other is its content. That, I think, about covers the ground. And though it is in the law reviews that the most highly regarded legal literature . . . is regularly embalmed, it is in the law reviews that a pennyworth of content is most frequently concealed beneath a pound of so-called style. The average law review writer is peculiarly able to say nothing with an air of great importance.[1]

The criticism continues after another half-century.[2]

Much of the criticism of the quality of law reviews may be due to their sheer quantity. Law is the only discipline that ties the publication of much of its scholarly literature to its educational institutions. In other disciplines, scholarly journals are generally sponsored by professional associations or published by commercial publishers. In either case, the articles published in the scholarly journals of other disciplines are generally subject to review by panels of scholars ("peers" of those submitting articles). Thus, in other disciplines, the number of periodicals published is likely to be determined by the amount of scholarship deemed worthy of publication, whereas the number of law reviews published is determined simply by the number of law schools. With nearly two hundred law schools in the United States, and with many law schools publishing more than one periodical,[3] it is not surprising to read charges that the quantity of legal writing published is running "amok" and that much of the material published is of questionable quality. The lack of quality is also frequently attributed to the lack of peer review at all but a few law school periodicals.[4]

Despite the artificially large number of law school periodicals, the lack of variety among them is remarkable. Only occasional sparks of originality can be found—such as an annual issue of the *Michigan Law Review* devoted to reviewing the year's new law books, and the University of Utah's *Journal of Contemporary Law*, designed to address a lay audience as well as lawyers. In format, law reviews are almost uniform—containing articles (usually by faculty), notes and comments on recent cases and legislation (written by students), and book reviews, in regimented order.

The lack of attempts at differentiation among law school periodicals may in part be due to their lack of reliance on market forces. Almost all law school periodicals are run at a loss and are subsidized by law schools. The subsidies keep subscription prices low.

In addition to law school reviews, a number of law periodicals are published by commercial publishers. These tend to be relatively costly, specialized, and practice oriented.[5] Also aimed at practitioners are a number of expensive newsletters on specialized topics. Such newsletters are primarily valued for their currentness and are seldom consulted for research; as a result they are generally not indexed.[6]

The United States also has two national legal newspapers—the *National Law Journal*, published in New York, and the *Legal Times*, published in Washington. In addition, a number of local legal newspapers are published carrying news largely of interest to the local practicing bar.

Practitioners' journals are also published by national, state, and local bar associations. These have been characterized (by a law professor) as running "from the mediocre to the atrocious," with few exceptions.

> They reflect a profession interested in penny-ante legalism. . . . Perhaps the best of the worst is the *American Bar Association Journal*. It . . . publishes brief articles and other commentary—mainly by practitioners—which on the whole suggest that lawyers care little about the larger social questions of the day.[7]

The low esteem of most bar journals is also evident in many law libraries. Collections of state and local bar journals are often kept only on microfiche. However, some bar publications are well respected—among them periodicals published by individual sections of the American Bar Association.[8] All but a few bar periodicals have had their contents indexed since 1980.

The Indexing of Legal Periodicals

By the time the *Harvard Law Review* began publication, the need for an index to legal periodicals was evident. Although much in the contents of legal periodicals was only of passing interest, journals of the caliber of the *American Law Register* and the *American Law Review* contained much of lasting value.

In 1888, an index to legal periodical articles from the colonial days to 1887 was published. It was entitled *An Index to Legal Periodical Literature* but became known, after the names of the editors, as the "Jones-Chipman" index. It indexed articles selectively based on merit rather than length:

> In many instances brief articles have been referred to because they seemed to be of value, while others of . . . length . . . have been omitted because they seemed to be of merely temporary or local interest.[9]

The Jones-Chipman index was updated after 1888, but it faced financial difficulties, and publication was suspended in 1899. No other publisher dared to risk a legal periodical index, and the profession was again without an index for nearly a decade. Finally, in 1908, the fledgling American Association of Law Libraries took on the job and began to produce the *Index to Legal Periodicals,* using the volunteer labor of law librarians largely at Harvard Law School—one of the very few times a professional association in the United States undertook a project to improve the control of legal literature. The first volume of the *ILP* indexed legal periodicals from 1898 to 1908.[10]

As the *ILP* became financially viable, it was taken over by a commercial publisher—the H. W. Wilson Company—in 1961. The AALL remained as sponsor of the *ILP*, and an AALL committee served as advisers to the publisher. The relationship, however, became strained, as the *ILP* was the subject of repeated criticism. The criticism crested in the 1960s and 1970s.

> The criticisms historically leveled against the *ILP* fall into three categories: (1) the scope of its coverage; (2) the quality of its indexing; and (3) the timeliness of its updating.[11]

According to criteria drawn up by the AALL advisory committee, indexing in the *ILP* was limited to periodicals "regularly publish[ing] legal content of high quality and permanent reference value."[12] The AALL advisory committee applied these criteria in recommending the indexing of journals, but the H. W. Wilson Company was at times reluctant to follow the committee's advice, for cost considerations. Between the demanding terms of the standard and the publisher's pressure to keep the list of indexed periodicals down, many legal periodicals were not indexed—among them were a substantial number of bar journals and a number of others that arguably satisfied the indexing criteria. Moreover, beginning in 1961, artificial page limitations were imposed. Rather than rely on the judgment of editors, as in the Jones-Chipman index, articles of fewer than five pages were omitted. For book reviews and bibliographies, the threshold was lowered to two pages.

Throughout the 1960s and 1970s, book reviews and student case notes received separate treatment in the *ILP*, and their indexing was abbreviated. Although there was a table of cases, there was no table of statutes. And finding an entry under some subject headings was not an easy task.

> The most frequently heard criticism of the *ILP* subject headings relates to the "broad" headings which result in pages upon pages of entries with no subdivisions or any other device to help the researcher except the opening words of titles. . . .
>
>   . . . The subject headings used in the *ILP* were originally based on the key numbers of the *American Digest System*. Since their adoption they have gone their own way, with piecemeal revisions made almost continuously since the Second World War. Maintaining control over such an evolutionary development is an extremely difficult task under the best of circumstances. It requires the maintenance of an "authority file" to avoid synonymous entries and to coordinate each heading with each related heading through a network of "see" and "see also" references. Moreover, related headings must be carefully defined through "scope notes" to avoid unnecessary overlapping and duplication. In a situation involving a multitude of editors over several decades, repeated revisions from a Committee with constantly changing membership, and, perhaps, an inappropriate list (one designed for case law rather than periodical literature) to begin with, it is not surprising that the requisite control has not been kept. The problem reaches nightmare proportions when a researcher tries to wind through topics such as civil rights, discrimination, equal protection, human rights, minorities, races and segregation. To search all of the above headings (not to mention other relevant headings dealing with education, employment, housing, public accommodations, voting rights, etc.) would require [in one volume] going through over 25 pages of listings with no breakdowns by subheadings.[13]

On top of its other shortcomings, each monthly issue of the *ILP* appeared nearly three months after the publication of the articles it indexed. To make up for this time lag, a weekly index to law reviews was started by the law library of the University of Washington under the title *Current Index to Legal Periodicals*. The *Current Index* has been marketed nationally, but it has never been cumulated; it is designed simply to be perused weekly and then discarded.

By the mid-1970s the cumulative effect of the unhappiness with the *ILP* was straining relations between the AALL advisory committee and the H. W. Wilson Company. In 1978, the H. W. Wilson Company rejected a number of periodicals the committee recommended for indexing, and the AALL withdrew its endorsement of the *ILP*. The AALL then invited publishers to submit proposals for a new AALL-sponsored index and endorsed the proposal of Information Access Corporation.

IAC began publication of a new legal periodical index in 1980 in three formats: a printed index called the *Current Law Index* and a microfilm index in a "rapid reader," called *Legal Resources Index*, which also became available on-line. The contents of the on-line and microfilm indexes were identical; the *CLI* was nearly identical but excluded a list of legal news-papers indexed in the *LRI* (the two national newspapers and local news-papers from New York, New Jersey, Pennsylvania, Chicago, and Los Angeles).

Even without the newspapers, the *CLI* indexed a substantially longer list of periodicals than the *ILP,* including the journals of many state and local bar associations. Moreover, the *CLI* and *LRI* have no artificial min-imum page limitations, and they use much more detailed subject headings, with subheadings and cross-references, than the *ILP.* The headings used in the *CLI/LRI* are based on the *Library of Congress Subject Headings*[14] used for library catalogs, leaving open the possibility that the index-ing of periodicals will one day be combined with the cataloging of books.

The subject headings devised for books, however, may not be specific enough for periodical articles. The headings have also been criticized for inadequate, and sometimes insensitive, treatment of issues dealing with minorities, women, and a variety of social issues. Moreover, articles on controversial legal topics such as critical race theory or feminist writings are often difficult to find in the indexes.[15]

In the mid-1980s, IAC began to phase out the microfilm *LRI* in favor of a compact disc version, renamed *LegalTrac,* which is replaced monthly with an updated disc. The *LegalTrac* database has also become available on LEXIS and WESTLAW, where it is updated daily.

Under the stimulus of competition from the *CLI/LRI,* the *ILP* made significant improvements in the 1980s. A table of statutes was started in 1980; and subject headings have been brought under control by the 1988 publication of a *Thesaurus* volume containing a list of *ILP* subject headings with extensive cross-references.

The *ILP* also has become available on LEXIS and WESTLAW as well as through the publisher's own Wilsonline database, along with a disc version, *WilsonDisc,* which is superior to *LegalTrac* in search capability. *WilsonDisc* allows keyword searches to the titles of articles and to multiple-word subject headings, whereas *LegalTrac* can be searched only by initial words.

The searching of a periodical index by keyword is a rather limited advantage. Article titles often do not reveal adequately the contents of articles. Keyword searching would be more advantageous if titles of articles were supplemented by descriptive words or if legal periodical indexes, like indexes in some other fields, contained abstracts of articles.

A growing number of legal periodical articles are also becoming avail-able on-line in full text. Both LEXIS and WESTLAW have been adding legal periodicals to their databases, although their approaches differ some-what. Each database has selected a list of leading periodicals for full inclu-sion; WESTLAW has been including the texts of selected articles from other periodicals as well.

Foreign and Nonlegal Periodicals

The *ILP,* the *CLI/LegalTrac,* and the articles available in LEXIS and WESTLAW in full text leave two significant gaps—foreign periodicals and nonlegal periodicals.

Both *ILP* and *CLI/LegalTrac* index periodicals not only from the United States but also from Canada, the United Kingdom, Ireland, Australia, and New Zealand. Legal periodicals from other nations were not indexed (in the United States or in their home countries) until 1961, when, having given up the *ILP,* the AALL decided to launch an *Index to Foreign Legal Periodicals.*

The *IFLP* continues under AALL sponsorship. In recent years, the *IFLP* has been thoroughly overhauled and made available on-line. A disc version is also under discussion. The *IFLP,* however, indexes only slightly more than three hundred legal periodicals from among the thousands available worldwide. Included are legal periodicals specialized in international or comparative law published in the United States and the other five nations, which are also indexed in the *ILP* and *CLI/LegalTrac.*

The *ILP,* the *CLI/LegalTrac,* and the *IFLP* index periodicals that contain predominantly, if not exclusively, legal articles. Legal articles, however, are also published in many periodicals that are not predominantly legal—including the leading scholarly journals in the social sciences, history, and philosophy and in popular periodicals, such as *Harper's, New Yorker,* and the *New York Times Magazine.* Since the legal-periodical indexes miss such articles, another index—the *Index to Periodical Articles Related to Law*—was created by two law librarians, R. M. Mersky and J. M. Jacobstein. The *IPARL* continues to be published but has not been added to any database. In its early years, the *IPARL* also indexed selected legal periodicals excluded by the *ILP,* but these periodicals were dropped in 1980 when the *CLI/LRI* began to index a more inclusive list of legal periodicals.

Shepardizing Legal Periodicals

Although the concept of tracing citations was initially developed to evaluate the current validity of judicial opinions and statutes, the concept has also been applied to scholarly articles not only in law but in other fields as well.[16] Citators can thus be used for locating related articles and for measuring the influence of articles.

A special unit of *Shepard's Citations* devoted to law reviews has been published since 1947. For the first ten years of its existence, the unit existed merely to trace "who cited whom" in the pages of law reviews. Since 1957, the citation of law reviews in judicial opinions is also included.

The editors of *Shepard's* have also selected twenty legal periodicals for special treatment—the *ABA Journal* and nineteen law school reviews.[17] Whenever any of these periodicals cite a case, statute, federal regulation, or certain administrative decisions, the citation is included in the state (but not the regional) citators or in a special volume of *Shepard's* federal unit or in the *CFR* or *Administrative* and/or topical units. Among the twenty periodicals, *Shepard's* editors seem to give top priority to the *ABA Journal;* it alone is cited in the standard federal units of *Shepard's*. In each state unit, the list of twenty is expanded by the addition of reviews from all the state's law schools.

Selection 8(B). The "Brandeis Brief"

A. T. Mason, *The Case of the Overworked Laundress,* in QUARRELS THAT HAVE SHAPED THE CONSTITUTION 176–90 (J. A. Garraty, ed., 1964).

Nearly half a century separates *Muller v. Oregon* (1908), a judicial landmark unscarred by criticism, from the Supreme Court's unanimous decision of May 17, 1954, outlawing racial segregation in the public schools. The latter ruling, the most controversial judicial pronouncement since *Dred Scott,* has stirred mixed reactions. Certain Southern lawyers and lawmakers denounce the decision as based "solely on psychological and sociological conclusions," instead of on law and "factual truths." A few social scientists, noting Chief Justice Warren's sympathetic reference to the findings of modern sociological and psychological authorities, are ecstatic. The Warren Court had provided "the greatest opportunity ever accorded sociologists to influence high level decisions." Louis D. Brandeis' novel briefmaking technique, introduced in the Muller case, had at long last, it was thought, paid off.

Ex facto jus oritur—out of facts springs the law—must prevail, Brandeis pleaded, if we are to have a living law. Justice David J. Brewer, speaking for a full bench in the Muller case, had apparently nodded his approval. The Warren Court, in language strikingly similar to Brewer's, had also yielded, it seemed, to the imperatives of authentic empirical data. Chief Justice Warren, like Justice Brewer, had responded favorably to Brandeis' blunt caveat: "A lawyer who has not studied economics and sociology is very apt to become a public enemy."

. . . Prior to 1908 the constitutionality of statutes restricting working hours had been argued almost entirely on their legal merits. Briefs of counsel had been confined chiefly to the states' authority, under the police power, to enact such measures . . . despite interference with "freedom of contract" guaranteed by the Fourteenth Amendment. . . .

. . . *Lochner v. New York* in 1905, known as the Bakeshop Case, [was] far-reaching in its power-crippling implications. . . . In the Lochner case the Court was confronted with a New York statute limiting the working hours of bakers to ten a day or to a sixty-hour week. "Is this law," Justice Rufus W. Peckham asked, "a fair, reasonable, and appropriate exercise of the police power of the state . . . ?" Five justices answered "No." "There is," they said, "no reasonable ground for interfering with the liberty of persons or the right of free contract, by determining the hours of labor in the occupation of a baker." . . .

By 1907 events had taken place which were destined to undermine Justice Peckham's assumptions. In that year Curt Muller, an obscure laundryman of Portland, Oregon, was arrested for violating the state's ten-hour law for women. Muller tried unsuccessfully to build a defense on Justice Peckham's predilections in the Bakeshop Case. . . . Muller naturally appealed his conviction to the United States Supreme Court, where Brandeis, as counsel in defense of the Oregon statute, had a chance to demonstrate by recourse to facts that the Oregon legislators could reasonably have believed their ten-hour law to be an appropriate remedy for a probable evil. The dragon to be slain was judicial preference, the rugged dogma of *laissez-faire*.

. . . .

. . . More than the Oregon statute was at stake, for similar legislation had been passed in nineteen other jurisdictions. Massachusetts had earlier sustained an hours-of-work law for women, but the courts of Illinois had found its own legislation in conflict with both the state constitution and the Fourteenth Amendment. . . .

. . . Realizing that the crux of the matter lay in human facts, in diverse medical and sociological data, [Brandeis] enlisted the services of nonlawyers, amassed the authoritative statements and testimony of medical and lay experts. He would need, Brandeis told [his sister-in-law and research collaborator,] Miss Goldmark, "*facts,* published by anyone with expert knowledge of industry in its relation to women's hours of labor, such as factory inspectors, physicians, trade unionists, economists, social workers." Aided by ten readers, Miss Goldmark delved into the libraries of Columbia University, the Astor Library, and the Library of Congress. A young medical student devoted himself solely to research on the hygiene of occupations. Meanwhile, Brandeis constructed the legal argument.

The finished brief contained only two scant pages of "law" and over a hundred of extralegal sources. Besides the testimony of scholars and special observers, here and abroad, the brief included extracts from over ninety reports of committees, bureaus of statistics, commissioners of hygiene, and factory inspectors. A generation of experience in Europe and America had not only demonstrated widespread evil, but also the physical, moral, and economic benefits of shorter working hours. "Production not only increased but improved in quality. . . . Regulation of the working day acted as a stimulus to improvement in processes of manufacture. . . . Factory inspectors, physicians and working women were unanimous in advocating the ten-hour day. . . ." Some experts considered ten hours too long.

"Long hours of labor are dangerous for women primarily because of their physical organization."

No one knew whether the Court would notice a brief so unconventional. In all previous cases in which social legislation had been invalidated, the judges, by recourse to abstract logic, had confidently denied any "reasonable" relation between the legislation and its stated objective of improved public health. In 1905, Justice Peckham had asserted categorically that "it is not possible, in fact, to discover the connection between the number of hours a baker may work in a bakery and the healthy quality of the bread made by the workman." One could not be sure that the Court would recognize the factual relation even if it were shown.

No lawyer, except Brandeis, had this faith either in the justices or in himself. Shrewdly playing down the revolutionary aspect of his brief, he tried to show that the Court had practically asked for a convincing demonstration of public health needs, not merely a logical array of precedents. The legal portion of his argument listed five rules established in the Bakeshop Case. He accepted them all, including Peckham's insistence that "No law limiting the liberty of contract ought to go beyond necessity." Brandeis diverged from Justice Peckham only in contending that in the determination of necessity, logic is not enough. "There is no logic that is properly applicable to these laws except the logic of facts," he said.

Brandeis appeared in oral argument January 15, 1908, before a Court dominated by superannuated legalists. . . . Rattling the dry bones of legalism, William D. Fenton, counsel for Muller, argued that "Women equally with men, are endowed with the fundamental and inalienable rights of liberty and property, and these rights cannot be impaired or destroyed by legislative action under the pretense of exercising the police power of the state. Difference in sex alone does not justify the destruction or impairment of these rights."

. . . .

"We submit," Brandeis told the justices, "that in view of the facts of common knowledge of which the Court may take judicial notice and of legislative action extending over a period of more than sixty years in the leading countries of Europe, and in twenty of our states, it cannot be said that the Legislature of Oregon had no reasonable ground for believing that the public health, safety, or welfare did not require a legal limitation of women's work in manufacturing and mechanical establishments and laundries to ten hours in one day."

The justices listened with interest and admiration. In what Brandeis said they could discern no wholesale erosion of established principles, no "creeping socialism." Taking the Brandeis brief in stride, the Court's spokesman, Justice Brewer, mentioned the Boston lawyer by name and commented on his very "copious collection of material from other than legal sources." Continuing, the Justice struck a cautious note, observing that "Constitutional questions are not settled by even a consensus of present public opinion." Yet, he added, "when a question of fact is debated

and debatable, and the extent to which a special constitutional limitation
goes is affected by the truth in respect to that fact, a widespread and long-
continued belief concerning it is worthy of consideration."

· ·

For the moment, the Court had at least recognized the usefulness of
facts in establishing the "reasonableness" of social legislation. The mighty
laissez-faire barrier had been penetrated. Requests for the Brandeis brief
poured in from lawyers, economists, college professors, and publicists. The
Russell Sage Foundation reprinted it in quantity, and the National Consumers' League aided in its distribution. Brandeis, the National Consumers' League, and the American people had taken an important step toward
a living law. *The Outlook* of March 7, 1908, called the Muller decision "a
victory for posterity," "unquestionably one of the momentous decisions
of the Supreme Court," "immeasurable in its consequences, laden with
vast potential benefit to the entire country for generations to come." . . .

. . . Brandeis was immortalized in a way that transcended his famous
factual briefs. It was January 28, 1916. The nation's capital was relatively
serene. Suddenly Washington and the country was stunned as if struck by
a salvo from an unseen Zeppelin. That day President Wilson nominated
Louis D. Brandeis Associate Justice of the United States Supreme Court.

· ·

. . . [T]he Brandeis way caught on. In recent years his type of brief
has become the lawyer's stock in trade, particularly in cases involving racial
discrimination. As part of the effort to induce the courts to create a new
legal rule in the enforcement of restrictive covenants based on race, sociologists were called in as expert witnesses and queried about population
patterns, availability and condition of housing, and the effect of racial ghet-
tos on health, crime, and juvenile delinquency. The special sociological
memorandum introduced in these cases was the precursor of the Social
Science Statement appended to appellant's brief in the School Segregation
Cases in which more than a score of psychologists and sociologists
appeared as expert witnesses. In opposition Virginia called two psychologists and a psychiatrist. Prior to this dramatic development, government
lawyers, using statistical and related data, were markedly successful in law-
suits against private corporations. Opposing lawyers soon began to file
briefs of the same kind. The results, however, were not altogether satisfying
for those promoting the factual brief as the champion of social advance.
"There are ways of rigging your statistics," Charles Edward Sigety, teacher
of statistical method, observes, "so that almost any conclusion can be
reached from the same basic information."

The point was illustrated in the Supreme Court case of *Jay Burns
Baking Co. v. Bryan* (1927). In 1926 the Nebraska Legislature, in an effort
to prevent fraud, prescribed the maximum and minimum limits for the
weight of bread. When this act came before the High Court, counsel on
both sides, employing the Brandeis method, flooded the justices with special reports of chemists and others dealing with the technical phases of

bread making. Faced with conflicting expert testimony, the Court collected "facts" of its own. Seven justices, after exhaustive research, sustained the contentions of the plaintiff; two, presumably as well versed in the science of baking, were convinced that the state had proved its case. Justice Brandeis, dissenting, then set in clearer focus the role of social and economic statistics in the judicial process:

> Put at its highest, our function is to determine, in the light of all facts which may enrich our knowledge and enlarge our understanding, whether the measure, enacted in the exercise of the police power and of a character inherently unobjectionable, transcends the bounds of reason. That is, whether the provision as applied is so clearly arbitrary or capricious that legislators acting reasonably could not have believed it to be necessary or appropriate for the public welfare.
>
> To decide, as a fact, that the prohibition of excess weights "is not necessary for the protection of the purchasers against imposition and fraud by short weights"; that it "is not calculated to effectuate that purpose"; and that it "subjects bakery and sellers of bread" to heavy burdens, is, in my opinion, an exercise of the power of a super-legislature—not the performance of the constitutional function of judicial review.

For Brandeis the Court's function was equally circumscribed when confronted with a legislative policy he [dis]approved. In 1925 the Oklahoma Legislature provided that no one could engage in the manufacture of ice for sale without obtaining a license. If on investigation the State Commission found that the community was adequately served, it might turn down the bid of a would-be competitor, and in this way, perhaps, advance monopoly. On its face, this legislation encouraged precisely the trend Brandeis had tried to prevent. "The control here asserted," the Court ruled in a 6-to-2 opinion setting aside the act, "does not protect against monopoly, but tends to foster it." Yet Brandeis, in dissent, voted to uphold the regulation. "Our function," he wrote, "is only to determine the reasonableness of the legislature's belief in the existence of evils and in the effectiveness of the remedy provided."

. . . .

Without exception the opinions Justice Brandeis embellished with social facts and statistics are in dissent. His factual dissenting opinion, like the factual brief, was an imposing apparatus to support his conviction that "the most important thing the justices do is not doing." In man's eternal pursuit of the more exact, Brandeis recognized that there are facts and facts. Facts have to be interpreted. For him "economic and social sciences are largely uncharted seas." Social science experiments rarely exhibit convincing proof comparable to that achieved in a laboratory of physics or chemistry. One can never be sure all the facts are assembled; and even if this were possible, exploration and study of them would rarely point to only one conclusion. Policy decisions are too complex to be left to statisticians. Their findings need to be informed by opinions based on less specialized knowledge. As to whether the shoe pinches and where, we want the verdict of the wearer, not that of the skilled craftsman who made it.

. . . Only in reviewing statutes affecting First Amendment freedoms and legislation directed against religious, national, or racial minorities need the Court subject legislation to "more exacting judicial scrutiny." Brandeis suggested that such encroachments run counter to "a fundamental principle of American government."

The primacy of facts, of informed action, is the hallmark of Brandeis' life and work. His brief in the Muller case is symbolic of his inflexible conviction that for wise action there must be "much and constant enquiry into facts." He relied on experts, utilized their findings, not their commands. Knowledge, along with promptings of the heart, alerted him to the perils of inaction, in the face of evils no one could deny. The solution of society's problems could not wait until every aspect was explored, every relevant fact presumably known. Overwhelming factual demonstrations alone do not account for the intensity of Brandeis' moral indignation and reformist zeal. . . .

Epilogue

Note. Books versus DEM

Law is further advanced than any other discipline in converting its information sources to machine-readable form. Databases in other disciplines generally contain indexes or bibliographies, whereas the two major databases of law, LEXIS and WESTLAW, contain full texts of judicial opinions, legislation, administrative regulations, and other legal sources—even scholarly articles.

Not only is the electronic storage of legal information in advance of other disciplines, so are the users of legal information. While databases in other disciplines are generally designed to be searched only by research specialists (usually librarians), LEXIS and WESTLAW are designed to be searched by end users. Since the advent of LEXIS in the mid-1970s, nearly all law students and lawyers have received training in database searching.

Full-text sources in specialized fields of law have also begun to appear on CD-ROM. West Publishing Company has developed "libraries" on CD-ROM in tax, bankruptcy, and other fields, and Mead Data Central has developed a CD-ROM "treatise" on Social Security law. Commercial versions of the most current technology—imaged discs—are not yet being marketed, but some law libraries are beginning to "image" parts of their book collections, "preserving the logic of a printed book and going beyond that with new forms of access."[1] Thus, between LEXIS, WEST-

LAW, and newer forms of technology, law, more than any other discipline, can contemplate replacing paper publications with electronic sources.

Law is not the only field in which some have predicted the death of the book. A sociologist has commented, "[E]ventually printform books will exist only as historical artifacts," as the "digital electronic medium" (DEM) will prevail.

> The adoption and ascendancy of the DEM is as immutable as was the Industrial Revolution. The difference is that the effect of DEM on our lives will be greater. It will pervade our daily endeavors in ways both obvious and subtle. ... [W]e will no longer use books in two senses: print books will become obsolete and electronic books will so differ from their print ancestors that they no longer will be books in the sense we use the term today.[2]

The immutability of the ascendancy of the electronic medium is ascribed to its advantages over paper books. Perhaps the greatest advantage is the fact that electronic media can be accessible from anywhere.

> Communication devices are improving as rapidly as computers particularly as they support the rapid transfer of digital information. The outcome will be that humans and machines are linked to a dense communications network that is spread across the globe.[3]

The existing Internet network and the emerging "Electronic Superhighway"[4] are bringing such predictions close to realization.

Among the advantages of "DEM" are its relative ease of production, transmission, storage, and preservation; access by any number at any time without waiting or interruption; the ability to handle large quantities of data; instantaneous revision or updating; and, above all, its interactive nature. The ability to interact gives researchers control not available in the "one-way process"[5] of a paper environment—including the ability to define and refine searches down to the level of individual words; to search texts at random; to "hypertext," or jump from one text to another, as from a citation to full text of the item cited; and to highlight and download or print portions of texts. Electronic media can also bring together diverse sources. For example, Mead Data's treatise on Social Security law unites the text of the treatise with full texts of the cases, statutes, and other materials on Social Security cited in the text. The author of the treatise has written:

> Today, we face a near-term future where, for many purposes, electronic media will supplant print altogether. Electronic resources, still viewe ˙ by many as case- or statute-finding tools, are positioning themselves so that they can not only point to but furnish the relied-on text of all relevant law documents.
>
> ·
>
> ... Both West and Mead Data Central are investing unprecedented amounts in the completeness, accuracy, and functional autonomy of their col-

lections. By functional autonomy, I mean the capacity of the collection to be used independent of print. Electronic publishers are acquiring print firms. Print publishers are consolidating and establishing new units to bring together the resources for new electronic legal information offerings. A few mavericks like me are devoting their careers to preparing new forms of law scholarship for this medium. The ambition underlying all these moves is unmistakable: to place in the end user's immediate work environment a comprehensive collection of relevant legal information with the full set of finding, browsing, and updating tools that print offers, but with the additional advantages of the electronic medium, including, but not limited to, full-text search. A related ambition is to wrap this information in a set of software tools that are as easy to use as books. "Point and click" is more streamlined and can be more precise than turning to a particular page indicated by a table of contents or following the citation to a particular page of a decision. "Block and copy" performed on text visible on the screen with use of a function key or mouse beats hand-copying or even photocopying for ease and accuracy in moving relevant passages of law text to notes or memoranda.[6]

The replacement of books by electronic media is also spreading to law school casebooks. Electronic versions of casebooks allow faculty to tailor and update readings and to use material dynamically in class; with proper software, they help students outline and synthesize materials; and students and faculty can communicate through E-mail.[7]

But even the most ardent proponents of electronic media allow that "[p]eople prefer to read paper rather than computer screens."[8] Books require no special equipment; they are not subject to downtime or hardware incompatibility; they are easily transported; and they may be easier to browse and clearer than databases in relating texts to footnotes or allowing back-and-forth flipping between parts to "zoom" in on specific provisions. Databases continue to have some handicap in dealing with charts, graphs, and images; the cost of electronic media remains relatively high, at least for nonacademic subscribers; and electronic media require not only initial training but constant maintenance of searching skills. Books also provide "rigor" in the selection of information to be published and "integrity" in the permanence of the information once published,[9] whereas the ease of manipulating and revising electronic media, advantages in some sense, can result in a lack of permanence and in problems of security and privacy as well as integrity.[10] Reliance on electronic media also denies access to those who cannot pay; books, on the other hand, are generally available without cost through the nation's libraries.

Many of the problems of electronic information can be overcome, and are being overcome, with improved software and design, and new developments, such as expert systems, artificial intelligence, and multimedia links of texts to sound and images, may create powerful new advantages over books. Nevertheless, the book has so far held its own. Law libraries at law schools, law firms, bar associations, and corporate law offices often

buy the same information on paper and on-line, and not one legal serial
title is known to have stopped publishing because of its alternate availability on-line.

Some who have tried to look into the future see a continuing division
of functions between books and electronic media:

> For much of our reading, and particularly for works requiring reconsultation
> and reference, the book remains more efficient, more convenient and less
> expensive than the most advanced electronic media we can imagine for the
> future. . . . While the storage and retrieval of all current primary sources of law
> on computer or laser disks is certainly within sight, similar access to retrospec-
> tive sources or the huge secondary literature seems unlikely. . . .
>
> After twenty years of remarkable growth in the use, capacity and effec-
> tiveness of a variety of electronic media, book production and sales continue
> to grow in the United States, in Canada, in Great Britain, and world-wide, in
> law and in all fields combined. Similarly, annual book acquisitions in law librar-
> ies and general research libraries have grown steadily despite their increasing
> use of and reliance on the new media.
>
> . . . I doubt that . . . you [would] be prepared to scrap the book collec-
> tions of your library, nor will the next generation of students, lawyers and
> researchers who may learn to read on computer terminals and tell time only
> from digital clocks. Even though they won't know what clockwise and coun-
> terclockwise mean, they will still rely on books for a significant part of their
> research. Books will continue to be the preferred medium for reading texts of
> more than a few pages, although electronic media may be the primary *access*
> tool in identifying, locating and perhaps ordering relevant sources.[11]

Thus, the future of books and electronic media may lie in coexistence
with a shifting mix of information migrating from one medium to
another—perhaps a long-term coexistence, much as there appears to be
between videotape, television, movie theaters, and the live stage. Some,
however, reject such a prospect: "[P]rint and the DEM will not coexist.
Events that advance DEM in any way have negative consequences for print.
It is too costly and complicated to run parallel systems."[12]

Both advocates for electronic media and those who see coexistence of
the two agree that what is at stake goes well beyond the mechanics of
research or the future of the publishing industry or of libraries. The implications are revolutionary. Like the revolutions sparked by Gutenberg's
press in the fifteenth century, new forms of communication can alter the
substance of the law, the fabric of society, and the very makeup of the
human mind.

Selection. The Substantive Impact of Technology

M. E. Katsh, *Communications Revolutions and Legal Revolutions: The New Media and the Future of Law,* 8 NOVA L. REV. 631, 631–69 (1984).

Introduction

Our age is noteworthy for the development of television and computers, media that transmit information over vast distances at electronic speed. In the mid-1400s, Gutenberg's invention of printing by moveable type was perceived to be equally miraculous and quickly became a powerful societal force. Francis Bacon wrote that "we should note the force, effect, and consequences of inventions which are nowhere more conspicuous than in those three which were unknown to the ancients, namely, printing, gunpowder and the compass. For these three have changed the appearance and state of the whole world." One rarely-noticed way in which printing changed the world was through its influence on law. The spread of printing led to fundamental changes in legal doctrines, legal institutions, legal values and attitudes about law. Printing technology helped create the modern legal order and has continued to be a major influence upon it.

We are living in an era in which the new electronic media are joining the traditional media of print, writing and speech and taking over some of their functions. . . . The new media can be expected to be used in ways that will cause a transformation in the legal order that has developed in the West in the last five hundred years.

. . . .

I. A Brief Overview of Law and Communications Research

. . . .

Analyses of law and the new media have focused almost exclusively on the new media's impact on either legal doctrines or legal institutions. The vast majority of such studies, unfortunately, are likely to reveal only short term surface changes in law. To identify changes that are likely to be more long lasting and affect fundamental aspects of the process of law, it is necessary to define law more broadly than is generally done by communications researchers. . . . The deepest change in law is likely to come about by the new media's impact on legal values, on individual habits of thought and on the social conditions that make law necessary for the resolution of conflict.

The initial impact of a new communications medium on law will be in the development of new rules to resolve problems caused by that medium. . . . Thus copyright law developed after the invention of printing, wiretapping laws followed shortly after the invention of the telephone, and laws of privacy were enacted as a result of the growth of newspapers. . . .

The second large body of literature concerning law and communications focuses on the employment of new media within legal institutions. Much of this literature describes experiments in which the new media are used in some novel way. Some research has attempted to assess whether these new uses will affect traditional legal policies. In general, however, very little is currently known about what it will mean in the future to begin employing the media in novel and widespread ways within our legal system.

. . . .

It is important, therefore, to determine how the values of the legal order and the habits of thought underlying the legal order, are influenced by processes of communication. Change which occurs in this facet of the legal process may occur slowly, but it will also be long lasting and will affect the subsequent development of both legal rules and institutions.

. . . .

II. The Nature of Media

. . . Just as law is falsely perceived by the public to be a set of rules, communications media are mistakenly looked at in terms of their content and not in terms of the influential qualities of the particular medium. How people communicate is usually thought to be much less significant than what is communicated. . . .

McLuhan tried to popularize a contrary point of view. In asserting that "the medium is the message," McLuhan argued that if one wants to understand the impact of a communication medium on a society, one should focus on the means of communication and not on the content of what is communicated by the medium. For example, McLuhan claimed, one could have learned much more about post-Gutenberg society from looking at the form of the printed page and the impact of printing on the spread of information, than from knowing that the first book printed was the Bible. . . .

The two most ardent proponents of the long term influence of communications media on society have been the late Marshall McLuhan and his colleague and mentor Harold Innis. The first theme of Innis' writings is that the use of a new medium of communication alters the distribution of information in a society and, as a consequence, its social structure. The development of writing, for example, led to societies being more hierarchical, since writing was a skill that only persons in power were apt to possess. Anthropologist Claude Levi-Strauss has noted that writing's first uses were "connected first and foremost with power. It was used for inventories, catalogues, censuses, laws and instruction. In all instances, whether the aim was to keep a check on material possessions or on human beings, it is evidence of the power exercised by some men over other men." Information in such societies, therefore, tended to flow down from the top rather than from citizens and groups to other citizens and groups. The invention of printing and the subsequent spread of literacy caused information to be disseminated to broader sectors of the population. The change which resulted from information flowing across classes as well as from the upper class downward, led to challenges to the traditional social order. It encouraged the development of liberal political theories and . . . increased demands for the protection of rights and for limits on state power.

The second main theme in Innis' writings is the influence of media on the concepts of time and space. Innis categorizes both media and societies as being either time-oriented or space-oriented. Speech, for example, is a time-oriented medium since it can be used to carry on a tradition, but is a poor medium for traversing large distances. He argues, therefore, that oral societies were highly concerned with the local community and its history, traditions, religion, and culture. Space-oriented media, such as print, by contrast are light and easily transportable, and, therefore, they encourage expansion over large areas, leading to the growth of secular states and a concern for the present and the future. . . .

McLuhan, unlike Innis, sees media more as devices which alter perceptual habits than as conveyors of information. He speculates that different media require the use of different senses and that, depending on which senses are used, individual and, ultimately, societal habits of thought are affected. The transformation of an oral culture into a literate one involves more, for McLuhan, than an increase in the amount of available information. When one talks to someone face to face, all of a person's senses may be used. Reading, however, uses only the eye. The effect of this, according to McLuhan, is profound. One who obtains information from a printed page rather than from another human being acquires new personality traits. He learns to think abstractly, to "act without reacting," and to confront social issues and problems in a detached, uninvolved and impersonal way. Typography, McLuhan asserts, separates the senses and, therefore, thought from feeling. These traits contribute to society which values rationality, uniformity, individuality, and systematic and abstract thought.

. . . .

There is one more explanation of the influence of media which is relevant to a discussion of the new media's cultural influence. This view holds that different media have different abilities to transmit some kinds of information and, therefore, affect the kind of information available to society. Abstract ideas and concepts, for example, are much more easily communicated in print than in televised form, whereas for portraying violent conflict or farcical humor, the opposite is true. . . . Each medium acts as a filter, letting some kinds of information through easily, some with difficulty, and some not at all. . . .

III. *The Influence of Printing on Law*

. . . .

A. THE DEVELOPMENT OF THE LEGAL DOCTRINES OF CENSORSHIP AND COPYRIGHT

The two most obvious legal doctrines related to the development of printing were censorship and copyright. The vast increase in the number of books which were printed and circulated in the last half of the fifteenth century was quickly perceived to be a threat to those in power. Professor Ithiel de Sola Pool has noted:

> Before printing, there had been no elaborate system of censorship and control over scribes. There did not have to be. The scribes were scattered, working on single manuscripts in monasteries. Moreover, single manuscripts rarely caused a general scandal or major controversy. There was little motive for central control, and control would have been impractical. But after printing, Pope Alexander VI issued a bull in 1501 against the unlicensed printing of books.

In 1529, Henry VIII issued a proclamation banning certain books which were odious to him or to the clergy who advised him.

Copyright came into being after the invention of printing because the nature of authorship changed. . . . Printing grew rapidly because it was possible to make money doing so. Authorship became important and protection of the author's work was made possible through copyright.

The legal rules which developed as a response to the new medium of printing are interesting but they do not provide great insights into the subsequent development of law. . . .

. . . .

B. PRINTING AND CHANGES IN LEGAL INSTITUTIONS

Less noticeable but more important were changes that occurred in legal institutions. The almost immediate affinity between law and print and the willingness of the law to employ the technology of print, is striking. William Caxton printed the first book in England in 1476. Five years later the first law books were printed and in 1485 the printing of parliamentary session laws began. The first printing of law books began a process that was to make the printed law book a central feature in the modern paradigm of law. The printing of law books gradually turned the law library into as central a legal institution as the courthouse. The printed book gradually became the repository of law and, in this country at least, the library became the heart of the modern law school. Christopher Columbus Langdell, the founder of modern legal education, was very sensitive to this point when he noted that "law is a science, and that all the available materials of that science are contained in printed books . . . law can only be learned and taught in a university by means of printed books . . . printed books are the ultimate sources of all legal knowledge."

Printing technology, through the creation of case reporters, has dominated legal education in this country for the past one hundred years. It has prompted analysis of and reliance upon precedent in ways not previously possible. One could simply not have had a system of precedent in a society that relied solely on writing. In a study of one of the earliest printed digests, Howard Jay Graham and John Heckel stated:

> The earliest digesters, with their printers, are the prophets and unsung heroes of the Common Law. It is strange more has not been made of their role and achievements. We can see very clearly today that it was in part because Nicholas Statham, Sir Anthony Fitzherbert, and later, Sir Robert Brooke, abstracted the "cases of the yeres," roughly ordered them by subjects, reduced practitioners' colloquies to procedural guides and principles, that English lawyers got to searching their books for *rules,* thinking more and more in terms of judicial *precedent* rather than in the old terms of judicial consistency, writs, cases and forms of actions. Fortuitously, printing made these first crude digests widely available at the very time English law was undergoing its heaviest challenge from the Continent. It doubtless would be an exaggeration to say that the Common Law was "saved" by printing. But certainly the Common Law as device, symbol, and system was in considerable part a product of its own compilation, ordering and improved distribution. During the crucial early Tudor period, in particular, printing and simpler indexing gave reader access, coherence and form; they accelerated future growth no less than did practice and utility.

C. THE INFLUENCE OF PRINTING ON VALUES, HABITS OF THOUGHT AND SOCIAL CHANGE

In her recent work, *Printing As an Agent of Social Change,* Elizabeth Eisenstein asserts that printing made possible the Protestant Reformation of the sixteenth century, the Scientific Revolution of the seventeenth century and preserved the contributions of the earlier Renaissance in a way that scribes would not have been able to do. Her analysis, along with the theories of Innis and McLuhan, explain many of the underlying changes in values which printing caused and which led to important changes in law.

1. Flow of Information: Challenges to Authority

Printing caused a radical change in the number of books produced and in the distribution of books. . . . Equally important, it made possible the spread of information in previously unforeseen ways. Legal information, too, began to circulate in new ways. In England, in the mid-1500s, "[t]he crucial acts of the reformation parliament were not only printed, published and proclaimed, but posted in every parish. . . ."

> Literate Englishmen now had what learned judges and serjeants even had lacked in . . . Littleton's time: ready access and reference to the texts of statutes on which their cases and problems turned. To encounter . . . what the scarcity of manuscript copies of the statute law had meant in the fourteenth and fifteenth centuries is to grasp something of the Tudors' excitement, relief, and sense of wonder. . . . [Printed statutes] thus were powerful factors in creating the Tudor image and tradition of constitutionalism. . . .

. . . .

2. Time and Space: Preserving and Distributing Information

. . . [P]rint was more successful than writing in overcoming problems of distributing information over wide areas. "Printing made it possible for the first time to publish hundreds of copies that were alike and yet might be scattered everywhere." Print also had considerable advantages in preserving texts over time. This was very different from scribal culture "where every copy was unique, with its own variations." In such a culture, it was impossible to be certain what the original author had written. The more a book was copied, the less authentic it became.

    . . . Thus, printing preserved the past and created continuity by making valuable data public, rather than secret. This "ran counter to tradition, led to clashes with new censors, and was central both to early modern science and to Enlightenment thought." The more permanent quality of print fostered notions of stability, consistency and predictability. These values, in turn, can be related to belief in the concept of rights. . . .

    Most importantly, by creating identical standardized copies that could be available everywhere, printing fostered notions of equality. . . . Particularly as court decisions began to be printed and distributed, pressures arose for national uniformity and equal treatment regardless of place. . . .

3. Changes in Perceptual Habits

Printing not only affected the flow of information but changed the image one perceived while reading. The first printed books looked very much like manuscripts. The typeface used was similar to a written script. After a period of years, however, printed pages began to look very different from a page of manuscript. . . .

    . . . Changes occurred not only in the appearance of the page, but in the organization of books. Printers were much more involved in indexing, cataloging and cross-referencing works than were scribes:

> The systematic arrangement of titles; the tables which followed strict alphabetical order; the indexes and cross-references to accurately numbered paragraphs all show how new tools available to printers helped to bring more order

and method into a significant body of public law. Until the end of the fifteenth century, it was not always easy to decide just 'what a statute really was' and confusion had long been compounded concerning diverse 'great' charters. . . .

4. The Communication of Abstract Ideals

Print is an ideal medium for fostering both the habits of thought and the values of a liberal legal order. . . . Theoretically, the legal model requires that "if a decision is to be rational it must be based upon some rule, principle, or standard. If this rule, principle, or standard is to make any appeal to the parties it must be something that pre-existed the decision." Alternative systems might rely on custom, compromise, discussion, force, or any technique other than reliance upon pre-existing rules. . . .

Respect for this idea of law is so traditional in our society that it is often forgotten what habits of thought and beliefs are required before a legal order can develop. One of these is belief in the power of abstract rules. For a society to have a legal system, one scholar has written, there must be a "belief in the power of certain words, put certain ways, to bring about certain effects denominated as legal. This kind of magic is necessary if law is to work." This "kind of magic" can only occur if the words have been put in tangible form, either in writing, or, more effectively, in print. . . .

IV. The Influence of New Media on Law

The foregoing analysis suggests that both law and society underwent a broad transformation following the invention of printing. Changes in rules, institutions and values led to a transformation that might be labeled revolutionary. Are comparable large scale changes likely to occur in our society due to the introduction of electronic media? . . .

A. CHANGES IN LEGAL DOCTRINE

Changes in traditional legal doctrines are the least important indicator of future change. They are usually responses to the first uses of the new medium. They often occur with little understanding of the qualities of the new media or of likely future uses that will be different from the initial use. Copyright law is the clearest example of an area of law that is fighting for its continued existence and is destined to lose. Copyright is a technique of regulation that is ideally suited to a medium such as printing where the location of making the copies can be identified. Copying machines and videotape recorders have presented the most publicized threats to copyright law but the computer, which will essentially provide each household with a copying machine, will provide the final blow to the copyright system of regulation. Yet, the demise of copyright, or, for example, the recent rise in privacy legislation in response to the new media, do not really help us in our search for what the role of law will be in the future. . . .

B. THE EFFECT OF NEW MEDIA ON LEGAL INSTITUTIONS

The effect of the new media on legal institutions will be visible less quickly than the impact on legal doctrine. In addition, the most quickly visible changes may not be the most important ones. For example, the struggle over whether television cameras should be allowed into the courtroom has received much attention but may be less important than other uses of video technology, such as the use of videotaped testimony. . . .

More basic, perhaps, is the effect of computerization of library resources on precedent and the notion of the common law. Computerization of case reporters has occurred at a point in time when the growth of reporters threatens to become unmanageable. A system of precedent will not function effectively when there are too few cases being decided and it also will not work when there are too many cases. In the past, the nature of printing technology imposed some limitation on how many cases could be printed and how quickly they would be published. The digest sytem made the whole process manageable. Where there are too many prior cases in an area and where cases are added to the data base much more quickly than in the past, unpredictability and instability will be the result. This will pose a challenge to the idea of precedent and to the foundation of the common law. Whereas print fostered the development of the idea of precedent, the use of computers may signal the erosion of this model of law.

. . . First, opinions are being added to the data base in greater and greater quantity. In future litigation, there will be more and more decisions on both sides of an issue, providing even more opportunity than there currently is for every party to a case to construct a legal argument supported by a host of cases. Second, cases are being added more quickly. Pressure will be exerted to use new cases, to continuously modify and to add to arguments in pending cases. At some point in this process the "myth of certainty" will become more obviously a myth and the system's allegiance to precedent, a fragile house of cards, may disintegrate. Can the computer provide an antidote or solution to prevent this from occurring? Can programs be developed to evaluate and reduce the amount of data that is retrieved from the data base? On one level, programs can assist the user to narrow the search for cases. . . . But, since computers are capable of more impressive feats, programs will be designed to do more, to apply some rule to cases the program identifies as relevant. In other words, if the model of storing decisions in a central data base continues, attempts will be made to employ the data manipulation function of the computer. At that point, when the process moves away from the current print model, some change in the law's attitude toward precedent will begin to change as well.

Third, computerization of law materials will probably broaden the range of materials users will come in contact with. Print made cases the center of the law collection and the digest system made the cases useable. Print has not dealt as efficiently with statutory or regulatory material. They are more difficult both to locate and retrieve. These areas are increasingly important areas of law and the computer data bases can be expected to include them and make them as accessible as judicial decisions. This broadening of the reach of the legal researcher involves much more than a change in research techniques. It has the potential for creating competition for the case as the building block of the legal system.

Although the image of cases as the heart of the library may remain for some time, the fact is that the computerized law library is already quite different from the print library, and the differences will grow more noticeable as time passes. Although LEXIS and WESTLAW began by storing cases, they have greatly broadened the information accessible from their terminals. In addition to cases, for example, the [WESTLAW] library includes access to DIALOG, a collection of 150 databases covering science, medicine, social science, current affairs and humanities . . . , and [LEXIS includes] NEXIS, a full-text library of general and business publications. It is as if a variety of non-law libraries have been moved into the law library. As these sources of information are discovered, they will begin to be used more than they are today and, along with the regulatory and statutory material that will become accessible, will change the image and authority of the judicial decision.

Ithiel de Sola Pool notes a fourth aspect of computerizing information that is worth considering.

> One change that computers seem likely to cause is a decline of canonical texts produced in uniform copies. In some ways this change will signal a return in print to the style of the manuscript, or even to the ways of oral conversation. . . . A small subculture of computer scientists who write and edit on data networks . . . foreshadow what is to come. One person types out comments at a terminal and gives colleagues on the network access to the comments. As each person copies, modifies, edits and expands the text, it changes from day to day. With each change, the text is stored somewhere in a different version.

The kind of future Pool envisions may portend a new attitude toward the authority or finality of decisions and toward the process of making decisions. The appearance of decisions in printed form, particularly Supreme Court decisions, emphasizes the idea that decisions are end points. Actually the decision is only an end point for the parties involved in the case. For the rest of us, every decision is a stopping point in a travel that includes the present case and future cases. It is a journey that never really ends. We perceive decisions as end points because it is convenient to do so and gives them authority they might not otherwise have. We should not assume that how we perceive decisions is inevitable. Rather, it is a culturally-based phenomenon that is partly related to print. If the method of recording cases, storing them and retrieving them changes, then the way they are perceived may change as well.

C. THE NEW MEDIA AND ITS INFLUENCE ON VALUES, HABITS OF THOUGHT AND SOCIAL CHANGE

1. Flow of Information

Assuming the existence of fairly unrestrictive governmental policies toward the new media, new patterns of communication between citizens and groups of citizens will begin to occur. The telephone and the postal service allow communication between two individuals. Computers allow for the sharing of information among much larger numbers of individuals in ways that are not now possible. New networks of communication will be created with information obtained by citizens being communicated to other citizens. Unlike broadcasting, which is a mostly hierarchical form of communication, microcomputers allow communication horizontally to other individuals or groups with similar interests. Until now, "[t]here has been no means for a group of people to adequately exchange information among themselves and reach decisions, other than to meet frequently face to face and talk it out." . . .

The analysis presented here leads to several conclusions that are different from most popular perceptions about the computer. Orwell's 1984 portrayed the technological era as one in which the state could control information and restrict the flow of information among citizens. The earliest use of computers, which could be afforded only by governments, corporations, or other large groups and institutions, reasonably led to this conclusion. Fairly soon, however, this model will probably be outmoded. Computers allow each individual to make his or her ideas available to others, to "publish" ideas in ways that were not previously possible. . . . Orwell's fear was reasonable for the first stages of the computer revolution, perhaps, but not necessarily for later stages.

What impact will this have on traditional values? . . . The spatial bias of the electronic media, the emphasis on the present, and the quickening of the process of change pose a threat to the model of law which is slow, methodical and relies on precedent. Print fostered the model of procedural justice, and of equal rights, but not of substantive equality. The pressures of the new media will be to demand actual equality. Law was often used to defuse conflict. Grievances were channeled into an institution that applied rules and appeared to be neutral. This model may be less satisfactory or workable in the future as "rights," "rules," and "neutrality" become less acceptable concepts.

Another effect of the speed with which information can now travel concerns privacy and its alter ego, secrecy. Privacy, as a concept, does seem endangered. But privacy is also a fairly recent concept. It was not a concept that was familiar in oral cultures where everybody knew everyone else.

Attempts to protect privacy, like attempts to maintain copyright, seem ultimately doomed to failure. . . . The lack of privacy has a governmental counterpart in the lack of secrecy. Government officials have complained that it is almost impossible to keep a secret. It is, therefore, both individual and governmental information that is accessible and not easily controlled. This analysis suggests that it is not necessarily true that governmental power will increase as a result of the new media. What does seem likely is that demands for justice and social change will increase and, as a result, the level of social conflict will increase as well. The legal mode of dealing with such a state of affairs seems dated and outmoded, not very well suited to social conditions of change and instability that are not even contained within the boundaries of the nation-state. As a result, new modes of conflict resolution can be expected to be developed to take their place alongside law.

2. Time and Space

The new media would, in Harold Innis' terms, have a very strong space bias. Their strength is in communicating information over vast distances. Conversely, they are also relatively impermanent. These qualities too, will ultimately have important legal and social consequences. For example, the electronic media are able to tell us what is happening in some distant place and it does this very quickly. Our frames of references have become expanded beyond national boundaries. As information flows across national boundaries in such quantity, some kinds of new institutions will be necessary to mediate demands and problems. While printing assisted in the creation of the modern nation state, the electronic media will likely lead to new institutions that are international in nature. . . . While traditional international law and legal tribunals have not been overwhelming successes, it may be that the necessary communications infrastructure for an effective international legal institution simply has not yet ever existed.

The impressive ability of the electronic media to conquer distance diverts attention from its main weakness, a quality of impermanence and tendency to focus on the present. Law is, of course, a process that insists on maintaining links with the past, with fostering continuity, consistency and predictability. Print played a pivotal role in developing a system with such values. The spatial bias of the new media will emphasize uniformity over space and should foster demands for equality over large areas. Print encouraged this, too, but could never do it as effectively as the electronic media are able to do. The effect of this change in focus will be to create additional pressures to change the traditions and goals of law.

[D.] THE VISUAL IMAGE

Video and computer technology . . . differ in one major way. Video relies on pictures and the spoken word while computers still rely on reading. . . .

. . . Print has acted as a catalyst and contributor toward the development of conceptual knowledge and allowed the seemingly unarbitrary categorization of knowledge, people, and actions by the legal system. The "myth of certainty," and the belief that law can be consistent, stable and predictable, are to some extent functions of the fact that these ideas are generally learned from books. . . .

. . . Professor Robert Ornstein has written that "one of the most basic differences between individuals is between those who tend to employ the linear, verbal mode and, those who are less verbal and more involved in spatial imagery." Law emphasizes linear, verbal abilities. The need to develop these abilities explains the absence of photographs in legal casebooks and may also explain some of the resistance to clinical legal education. Television, on the other hand, provides one possible explanation for Dean Walter Probert's statement that "something about these times makes legalistic conditioning more difficult in law schools."

V. Conclusion

. . . [I]n various ways, the message of the new media is anti-law. This may be one reason why "the law is becoming more fragmented, more subjective, geared more to expediency and less to morality; concerned more with immediate consequences and less with consistency or continuity." Yet, the effect of the new media is not necessarily authoritarian. It is just as possible that the new institutions which develop to resolve conflict will be more egalitarian, more participatory and, in the end, more just.

It should also be emphasized that the new media will not make printing or books disappear. The new ways of communicating will not cause the printed word to be obsolete, just as the invention of printing did not make writing disappear and the development of writing did not stop people from speaking to each other. The creation of new media for communicating will, however, affect the frequency with which printing is used. Some information which is now communicated through print will be transmitted much more quickly through different media in the future. It is impossible to predict what the nature or the mix of media will be, but it will inevitably be quite different from what it is now. . . .

Notes

Note 1(A)

1. *See* P. R. Hyams, *Trial by Ordeal: The Key to Proof in the Early Common Law, in* ON THE LAWS AND CUSTOMS OF ENGLAND 90, 93 (M. S. Arnold et al., eds., 1981).

2. R. C. VAN CAENEGEM, THE BIRTH OF THE ENGLISH COMMON LAW 67 (2d ed., 1988). The author, however, cites a "remarkable document" from the cathedral of Nagyvarad, Hungary, listing 389 trials by ordeal in thirteenth-century Hungary. *Id.* at 68.

3. M. T. CLANCHY, FROM MEMORY TO WRITTEN RECORD 123 (1979).

4. VAN CAENEGEM, *supra* note 2, at 69.

5. *Id.* at 70–84.

6. *See infra* Note 7(A).

7. CLANCHY, *supra* note 3, at 123.

Note 1(B)

1. J. H. Baker, *Records, Reports, and the Origins of Case-Law in England, in* JUDICIAL RECORDS, LAW REPORTS, AND THE GROWTH OF CASE LAW 15, 25 (J. H. Baker, ed., 1989).

2. *Id.* at 33.

3. *Id.* at 21.

4. *Id.* at 34.

5. L. W. ABBOTT, LAW REPORTING IN ENGLAND, 1485–1585, at 18–20 (1973).

Note 1(C)

1. P. H. WINFIELD, THE CHIEF SOURCES OF ENGLISH LEGAL HISTORY 217 (1925).

2. *Id.* at 228.

3. *See infra* Selection 7(A).

4. [J. Story, Book Review,] 23 N. AM. REV. 1, 9 (1826).

5. *Id.* at 8.

6. *Id.* at 10–11.

7. *Id.* at 11–12.

8. *See infra* Notes 1(F), 2(C), and 2(F).

9. W. W. S. Breem, *Historical Sources, in* MANUAL OF LAW LIBRARIANSHIP 249, 283 (E. M. Moys, ed., 2d ed., 1987).

10. *Id.* at 284.

11. L. W. ABBOTT, LAW REPORTING IN ENGLAND, 1485–1585, at 12 (1973), referring to William Stubbs.

12. *Id.* at 9.

Note 1(D)

1. J. W. WALLACE, THE REPORTERS ARRANGED AND CHARACTERIZED WITH INCIDENTAL REMARKS 1–2 (4th ed., 1882).

2. *Id.* at 40–44.

Note 1(E)

1. N. Lindley, *The History of the Law Reports,* 1 LAW Q. REV. 137, 141 (1885).

2. *Id.* at 142.

3. *Id.* at 147–48.

4. A. L. Goodhart, *Reporting the Law,* 55 LAW Q. REV. 29, 30 (1939). Reprinted with permission of Sweet and Maxwell, Limited.

5. *Id.* at 33.

6. Great Britain, Lord Chancellor's Dept., *Report of the Law Reporting Committee* 22 (1940).

7. *Id.* at 20.

8. *Id.* at 21.

Note 2(A)

1. *See* W. J. RITZ, AMERICAN JUDICIAL PROCEEDINGS FIRST PRINTED BEFORE 1801: AN ANALYTICAL BIBLIOGRAPHY (1984).

2. E. C. SURRENCY, A HISTORY OF AMERICAN LAW PUBLISHING 21–22 (1990).

3. *Id.* at 37–38.

4. C. M. COOK, THE AMERICAN CODIFICATION MOVEMENT 8–9 (1981).

5. A. V. Briceland, *Ephraim Kirby: Pioneer of American Law Reporting, 1789,* 16 AM. J. LEGAL HIST. 297, 306 (1972).

6. *Id.* at 307.

Note 2(B)

1. 33 U.S. (8 Pet.) 591 (1834).
2. *Id.* at 668.
3. *Id.* at 619–20.
4. T. J. Young, Jr., *A Look at American Law Reporting in the Nineteenth Century,* 68 LAW LIBR. J. 294, 295 (1975).

Note 2(C)

1. J. G. MARVIN, LEGAL BIBLIOGRAPHY 252 (1847).
2. E. C. SURRENCY, A HISTORY OF AMERICAN LAW PUBLISHING 175 (1990).
3. UNITED STATES DIGEST (1st ser., 1874).
4. *See infra* Note 2(F).
5. *See infra* Selection 7(B).
6. *See infra* Note 2(F).
7. *See supra* Selection 1(D).
8. SURRENCY, *supra* note 2, at 123.

Note 2(D)

1. SECOND REPORT OF THE COMMITTEE ON LAW REPORTING TO THE ASSOCIATION OF THE BAR OF THE CITY OF NEW YORK (December 3, 1873).
2. SPECIAL MEETING OF THE ASSOCIATION OF THE BAR OF THE CITY OF NEW YORK (December 17, 1873).
3. For an early example of "marginalia," see illustration at p. 9, *supra.*
4. P. Ogden, *"Mastering the Lawless Science of Our Law": A Story of Legal Citation Indexes,* 85 LAW LIBR. J. 1, 34 (1993).
5. J. L. High, *What Shall Be Done with the Law Reports?* 16 AM. L. REV. 435, 439 (1882).
6. T. J. Young, Jr., *A Look at American Law Reporting in the Nineteenth Century,* 68 LAW LIBR. J. 294, 301 (1975).

Note 2(E)

1. *ALR* began its fifth series in 1992.
2.

	ALR Fed (1969–)	ALR 5th (1992–) ALR 4th (1980–92) ALR 3d (1965–80)	ALR 2d (1948–65)	ALR (1919–48)
Index	*Index to Annotations: ALR 2d, 3d, 4th, 5th, ALR Federal* (6 v.)*			*ALR Word Index* (4 v.)
Digest	*ALR Digest to 3d, 4th, Federal* (9 v.)*		*ALR 2d Digest* (7 v.)	*Permanent ALR Digest* (12 v.)
Updating	Pocket part in each ALR volume		*ALR 2d Later Case Service* (28 v.)*	*ALR Blue Book of Supplemental Decisions* (7 v.)**

*Updated with pocket parts
**Updated with pamphlet

Note 2(F)

1. R. C. Berring, *Legal Research and Legal Concepts: Where Form Molds Substance*, 75 CAL. L. REV. 15, 23 (1987).

2. 33 U.S. (8 Pet.) 591 (1834). *See supra* Note 2(B). *See also* T. A. Woxland, *"Forever Associated with the Practice of Law": The Early Years of the West Publishing Company*, 5 LEGAL REFERENCE SERVICES Q. 115, 121–22 (1985).

3. Banks v. Manchester, 128 U.S. 244 (1888).

4. G. GILMORE, THE AGES OF AMERICAN LAW 58–59 (1977).

5. The numbers in the *Century Digest* are not the same as the key numbers used subsequently. A table in volume 21 of the *First Decennial* connects the pre- and post-1896 numbers.

6. A *U.S. Supreme Court Digest* is also published by the Lawyers Cooperative Publishing Company.

7. *See supra* Note 2(C).

8. Berring, *supra* note 1, at 25.

9. From 1951 to 1975, the opinions of the military courts were published in the *Courts-Martial Reports* of the Lawyers Cooperative Company.

10. The previously named United States Court of Claims opinions were reported in the *Federal Reporter* (to 1932) and the *Federal Supplement* (since 1932), as well as in a report published by the Government Printing Office, which ceased publication in 1981.

11. *See supra* Note 2(E).

12. The opinions of the United States Supreme Court are published not only twice but at least four times: in addition to West's *Supreme Court Reporter* (cited, S. Ct.), Supreme Court opinions are published by the Lawyers Cooperative Company in the *Lawyers Edition* (L.Ed.), by the Government Printing Office in the *U.S. Reports* (U.S.—which is the "official" report and is required to be cited, if available, but is always so tardy that other reports must be cited for current cases), and by the Bureau of National Affairs in the looseleaf *United States Law Week* (which is the most prompt source published on paper).

13. *See supra* Note 2(D).

14. *See supra* Selection 2(E).

15. E. C. SURRENCY, A HISTORY OF AMERICAN LAW PUBLISHING 127 (1990). *See also infra* Note 2(G).

Note 2(G)

1. West based an advertising campaign on the claim that its Insta-Cite was more current than LEXIS's Auto-Cite. LEXIS countered with the fact that Auto-Cite covers more cases. WESTLAW, more recently, has made updating of Shepard's itself more timely through its "Shepard's Preview" service.

2. Briefs of federal circuit and district courts or of state appellate courts are usually available only at the courts and at one or two large law libraries in the courts' localities. A proposal to have all federal circuit court briefs microfilmed by a non-profit consortium has been abandoned as too costly.

3. *See infra* Note 4(F).

4. *See infra* Note 6(F).

5. *See infra* Chapters 7 and 8.

6. J. K. Stephens, *LEXIS vs WESTLAW: The Contest Heats Up*, 6 LEGAL ADMIN. 42 (Sept./Oct. 1987).

7. *See* M. S. Klein, *Point: Comparing LEXIS and WESTLAW for Legal Research, in* WINNING WITH COMPUTERS 95 (J. C. Tredennick, Jr., ed., 1991).

8. *See supra* Note 2(F).

9. *See* D. P. Dabney, *The Curse of Thamus: An Analysis of Full-Text Legal Document Retrieval*, 78 LAW LIBR. J. 5, 32–34 (1986).

10. R. C. Berring, *Full-Text Databases and Legal Research: Backing into the Future*, 1 HIGH TECH. L. J. 27, 58 (1986).

11. *See supra* Note 2(E).

12. M. E. Maron and D. Blair, *An Evaluation of Retrieval Effectiveness for a Full-Text Document-Retrieval System*, 28 COMM. ASS'N FOR COMPUTING MACHINERY 289 (1985), cited in Dabney, *supra* note 9, at 6.

13. S. A. Childress, *The Hazards of Computer-assisted Research to the Legal Profession*, 55 OKLA. B. J. 1531, 1533–34 (1984).

14. Dabney, *supra* note 9, at 6.

15. W. G. Harrington, *A Brief History of Computer-assisted Legal Research*, 77 LAW. LIBR. J. 543, 544 (1984–85).

16. Berring, *supra* note 10, at 28.

17. *Id.* at 36.

18. R. Delgado and J. Stefancic, *Why Do We Tell the Same Stories?: Law Reform, Critical Librarianship, and the Triple Helix Dilemma*, 42 STAN. L. REV. 207, 218 (1989).

19. *Id.* at 222.

Note 3(A)

1. H. MAINE, ANCIENT LAW 5 (J. H. Morgan, ed., 1917).

2. *Id.* at 7.

3. *Id.* at 8–9.

4. *Id.* at 8. The Twelve Tables may have been influenced by the also famous code of Solon, adopted in Athens in 594–593 B.C. *See* H. F. JOLOWICZ and B. NICHOLAS, HISTORICAL INTRODUCTION TO THE STUDY OF ROMAN LAW 13 (3d ed., 1972).

5. JOLOWICZ and NICHOLAS, *supra* note 4, at 88.

6. *Id.* at 89. ("By their different kinds of advice, the pontiffs were able to influence the development of the law very considerably. They might even, under the cover of 'interpretation', create an entirely new institution.")

7. W. W. BUCKLAND, A TEXT-BOOK OF ROMAN LAW FROM AUGUSTUS TO JUSTINIAN 2 (2d ed, 1932).

8. JOLOWICZ and NICHOLAS, *supra* note 4, at 97.

9. *Id.* at 356, 451.

10. BUCKLAND, *supra* note 7, at 20–35. ("[T]he jurists of the classical age are the real builders of the great fabric of Roman law." *Id.* at 20.)

11. JOLOWICZ and NICHOLAS, *supra* note 4, at 479.

12. *Id.* (A second edition of the Code was prepared a few years later, and copies of the first edition were apparently destroyed.)

13. *Id.* at 481. (The prohibition on commentaries was hardly observed. "[I]n later ages the Digest has given rise to a greater literature than any other book except the Bible." *Id.* at 482.)

14. *Id.* at 492.

15. *Id.* at 496.

16. A. WATSON, THE MAKING OF THE CIVIL LAW 168 (1981).

17. *Id.*

18. H. G. RICHARDSON and G. SAYLES, LAW AND LEGISLATION FROM AETHELBERHT TO MAGNA CARTA 1 (1966), date the laws of King AEthelberht "before the end of the sixth century."

19. *Id.* at 15, 16.

20. *Id.* at 28–29.

Note 3(B)

1. 2 W. S. HOLDSWORTH, A HISTORY OF ENGLISH LAW 125 (4th ed., 1936).

2. H. G. Richardson and G. Sayles, *The Parliaments of Edward III, Part II,* 9 BULL. INST. OF HIST. RES. 1, 1–2 (1931).

3. HOLDSWORTH, *supra* note 1, at 437.

4. H. G. Richardson, *The Origins of Parliament,* 9 TRANSACTIONS ROYAL HIST. SOC'Y 146, 162 (4th series, 1928).

5. H. G. Richardson and G. Sayles, *The Early Statutes,* 50 LAW Q. REV. 201, 203–5 (1934). Reprinted with permission of Sweet and Maxwell, Limited.

6. *Id.* at 545, 548.

7. *Id.* at 216.

8. H. G. Richardson and G. Sayles, *The Early Records of the English Parliaments,* 6 BULL. INST. OF HIST. RES. 129, 140 (1929).

9. Richardson and Sayles, *supra* note 2, at 12–13.

10. H. G. Richardson and G. Sayles, *The King's Ministers in Parliament, 1272–1307,* 46 ENG. HIST. REV. 529, 540 (1931).

11. Richardson and Sayles, *supra* note 5, at 208, 209, 213, 216.

12. *Id.* at 548.

13. *Id.* at 544.

14. B. LYON, A CONSTITUTIONAL AND LEGAL HISTORY OF MEDIEVAL ENGLAND 553 (2d ed., 1980).

15. *Id.* at 554.

16. H. L. GRAY, THE INFLUENCE OF THE COMMONS ON EARLY LEGISLATION 405–16 (1932).

17. LYON, *supra* note 14, at 560.

18. H. G. Richardson and G. Sayles, *The Custody and Publication of the Parliamentary Rolls,* 51 ROTULI PARLIAMENTORUM ANGLIE HACTENUS INEDITI xviii (Camden Third Series, 1935).

19. G. R. ELTON, THE PARLIAMENT OF ENGLAND, 1559–1581, at 4 (1986).

20. HOLDSWORTH, *supra* note 1, at 440.

21. Richardson and Sayles, *supra* note 2, at 5, 9. Some paper bills also survive, most from the sixteenth century. *See* ELTON, *supra* note 19, at 10.

22. ELTON, *supra* note 19, at 6.
23. LYON, *supra* note 14, at 597.
24. *See infra* Note 5(B).
25. F. G. MARCHAM, A CONSTITUTIONAL HISTORY OF MODERN ENGLAND, 1485 TO THE PRESENT 66–67 (1960).
26. ELTON, *supra* note 19, at 7.
27. *See Introduction*, 1 STATUTES OF THE REALM xxx (1810).
28. LYON, *supra* note 14, at 612.
29. *See* Colt & Glover v. Bishop of Coventry, 80 Eng. Rep. 290 (1616).
30. Bonham's Case, 77 Eng. Rep. 638 (1610).
31. *See supra* Selection 1(C).
32. M. M. KNAPPEN, CONSTITUTIONAL AND LEGAL HISTORY OF ENGLAND 374 (1942).
33. *Id.* at 451–52.

Note 3(C)

1. M. M. KNAPPEN, CONSTITUTIONAL AND LEGAL HISTORY OF ENGLAND 505 (1942).
2. D. Alfange, *Jeremy Bentham and the Codification of Law*, 55 CORNELL L. REV. 58 (1969).
3. C. ILBERT, LEGISLATIVE METHODS AND FORMS 124 (1901).
4. *Introduction*, 1 STATUTES OF THE REALM xxx–xxxvii (1810).
5. T. F. T. PLUCKNETT, A CONCISE HISTORY OF THE COMMON LAW 74 (5th ed., 1956).
6. T. F. T. PLUCKNETT, LEGISLATION OF EDWARD I 19 (1949). For a more detailed critique, *see* T. F. T. PLUCKNETT, STATUTES AND THEIR INTERPRETATION IN THE FIRST HALF OF THE FOURTEENTH CENTURY 13–19 (1922).

Note 3(D)

1. C. ILBERT, LEGISLATIVE METHODS AND FORMS 57–62 (1901). Which statutes should be considered sleepers was often a matter of judgment, since new statutes often contained clauses simply repealing other statutes "inconsistent" with the new statute.
2. D. R. MIERS and A. C. PAGE, LEGISLATION 140–41 (2d ed., 1990).
3. *Id.* at 141.
4. *Id.* at 142–43.
5. *Id.* at 145.
6. *Id.* at 146.
7. ILBERT, *supra* note 1, at 162.
8. C. HUGHES, THE BRITISH STATUTE BOOK 121 (1957).
9. *Id.* at 122.
10. M. ZANDER, THE LAW-MAKING PROCESS 390–96 (2d ed., 1985).
11. *See infra* Chapter 7.
12. ILBERT, *supra* note 1, at 25.
13. MIERS and PAGE, *supra* note 2, at 150.
14. *See infra* Chapter 5.

Note 3(E)

1. V. Sacks, *Towards Discovering Parliamentary Intent,* 1982 STATUTE L. REV. 143, 143.

2. Millar v. Taylor, 4 Burr. 2303, 2332 (1769), quoted in T. F. T. PLUCKNETT, A CONCISE HISTORY OF THE COMMON LAW 335 (5th ed., 1956).

3. Beswick v. Beswick, [1968] A.C. 58, 74, quoted in R. CROSS, STATUTORY INTERPRETATION 155 (2d ed., 1987).

4. PLUCKNETT, *supra* note 2, at 336.

5. CROSS, *supra* note 3, at 161.

6. Sacks, *supra* note 1, at 157–58.

7. *Id.* at 158.

8. D. R. MIERS and A. C. PAGE, LEGISLATION 171 (2d ed., 1990).

9. *Id.* at 175.

10. *Id.* at 174.

11. *Id.* at 177, n. 54.

12. *Id.* at 176.

13. CROSS, *supra* note 3, at 165.

14. D. G. Kilgour, *The Rule Against the Use of Legislative History: "Canon of Construction or Counsel of Caution"?* 30 CANADIAN B. REV. 769, 784 (1952).

15. PLUCKNETT, *supra* note 2, at 335.

16. Kilgour, *supra* note 14, at 785.

17. Quoted in *Id.*

Note 4(A)

1. E. C. SURRENCY, A HISTORY OF AMERICAN LAW PUBLISHING 10 (1990).

2. M. L. Cohen, *Legal Literature in Colonial Massachusetts, in* LAW IN COLONIAL MASSACHUSETTS 243, 250–51 (1984).

3. *See supra* Note 3(B).

4. SURRENCY, *supra* note 1, at 10.

5. *Id.* at 14.

6. *Id.* at 13.

7. *Id.* at 79.

8. *Id.* at 19.

Note 4(B)

1. E. C. SURRENCY, A HISTORY OF AMERICAN LAW PUBLISHING 19 (1990).

2. *See supra* Selection 3(B).

3. C. M. COOK, THE AMERICAN CODIFICATION MOVEMENT 5 (1981).

4. *Id.* at 9.

5. *Id.* at 8.

6. *Id.* at 6–7.

7. *Id.* at 27.

8. *See supra* Note 3(C).

Note 4(C)

1. C. M. COOK, THE AMERICAN CODIFICATION MOVEMENT 89 (1981).
2. C. M. HAAR, THE GOLDEN AGE OF AMERICAN LAW 254–55 (1965).
3. COOK, *supra* note 1, at 172.
4. *Id.* at 187.
5. L. M. FRIEDMAN, A HISTORY OF AMERICAN LAW 403 (2d ed., 1985).
6. *Id.* at 403–4.
7. *Id.* at 406. Text at notes 6 and 7 © 1973, 1985 by Lawrence M. Friedman. Reprinted by permission of Simon & Schuster, Inc.

Note 4(D)

1. E. C. SURRENCY, A HISTORY OF AMERICAN LAW PUBLISHING 19 (1990).
2. R. H. Dwan and E. R. Feidler, *The Federal Statutes—Their History and Use*, 22 MINN. L. REV. 1008, 1009 (1938).

Note 4(E)

1. E. C. SURRENCY, A HISTORY OF AMERICAN LAW PUBLISHING 108 (1990).
2. *See supra* Note 2(A).
3. *See supra* Selection 2(A).
4. SURRENCY, *supra* note 1, at 108.
5. *See infra* Chapter 6.
6. *See infra* Note 4(G).

Note 4(F)

1. T. S. Dabagh, *The National Statutes System: A Plea for a New Publication*, 19 CAL. L. REV. 40 (1930).
2. *Id.*
3. W. B. Eldridge, *Legal Research Methods and Materials: A Proposal for the Establishment of a Current Legislation Index* (American Bar Foundation, 1962).

Note 4(G)

1. *See supra* Selection 3(D).
2. *CIS Congressional Bills, Resolutions, and Laws.* This set reaches back prior to World War II and is being extended further back. Congressional bills, 1789 to 1956, have also been microfilmed by the Library of Congress.
3. *CIS U.S. Committee Hearings on Microfiche,* 1833 to 1969; *CIS/Microfiche Library,* 1970 to date. Bills and resolutions introduced in Congress are initially considered by subcommittees that report to full committees that report to the Congress. When versions of bills passed by the House and Senate differ, conference committees are appointed to work out a uniform version.

4. *CIS U.S. Serial Set on Microfiche,* 1789 to 1969; *CIS/Microfiche Library,* 1970 to date.

5. *CIS U.S. Congressional Committee Prints on Microfiche,* 1830 to 1969; *CIS/Microfiche Library,* 1970 to date.

6. Unlike reports and House and Senate documents, hearings and committee prints are not numbered.

7. E. G. McPherson, *Reporting the Debates of Congress,* 28 Q. J. OF SPEECH 141, 141 (1942).

8. Pine Hill Coal Co. v. United States, 259 U.S. 191, 196 (1922).

9. R. DICKERSON, THE INTERPRETATION AND APPLICATION OF STATUTES 196 (1975).

Note 5(A)

1. U. A. Lavery, *"The Federal Register"—Official Publication for Administrative Regulations, Etc.,* 7 F.R.D. 625, 629 (1948).

2. B. LYON, A CONSTITUTIONAL AND LEGAL HISTORY OF MEDIEVAL ENGLAND 4 (2d ed., 1980).

3. *Id.* at 5.

4. *Id.* at 109.

5. F. W. MAITLAND, THE CONSTITUTIONAL HISTORY OF ENGLAND 9–10 (1950).

6. LYON, *supra* note 2, at 217–18.

7. *See supra* Note 3(B).

Note 5(B)

1. J. LOACH, PARLIAMENT UNDER THE TUDORS 8 (1991).

2. *Id.* at 11–12. Reprinted by permission of Oxford University Press.

3. R. STEELE, A BIBLIOGRAPHY OF ROYAL PROCLAMATIONS OF THE TUDOR AND STUART SOVEREIGNS AND OF OTHERS PUBLISHED UNDER AUTHORITY, 1485–1714, WITH AN HISTORICAL ESSAY ON THEIR ORIGIN AND USE, 3 vols. (1910).

Note 5(C)

1. C. T. CARR, DELEGATED LEGISLATION 55 (1921).

2. C. ILBERT, LEGISLATIVE METHODS AND FORMS 38–40 (1901).

3. G. HEWART, THE NEW DESPOTISM 91 (1929).

4. C. HUGHES, THE BRITISH STATUTE BOOK 41–42 (1957).

5. HEWART, *supra* note 3, at 80.

6. ILBERT, *supra* note 2, at 41.

7. *See supra* Note 3(D).

Note 5(D)

1. 2 MEMORANDA SUBMITTED BY GOVERNMENT DEPARTMENTS IN REPLY TO QUESTIONNAIRE OF NOVEMBER 1929 AND MINUTES OF EVIDENCE TAKEN BEFORE THE COMMITTEE ON MINISTERS' POWERS 206 (1932).

2. C. HUGHES, THE BRITISH STATUTE BOOK 43–44 (1957).

3. E. C. S. WADE and G. G. PHILLIPS, CONSTITUTIONAL AND ADMINIS-TRATIVE LAW 576 (9th ed., 1977).

4. *Id.*

5. *Id.*

6. *Id.* at 571.

7. D. L. KEIR, THE CONSTITUTIONAL HISTORY OF MODERN BRITAIN SINCE 1485, at 526 (9th ed., 1969).

8. J. F. GARNER, ADMINISTRATIVE LAW 71 (5th ed., 1979).

9. *Id.* at 73.

10. C. K. ALLEN, LAW AND ORDERS 108 (3d ed., 1965).

Note 5(E)

1. D. J. Way, *Primary Sources: Legislation, in* MANUAL OF LAW LIBRARI-ANSHIP 75, 107 (E. M. Moys, ed.; 2d ed., 1987).

2. *Id.* at 109.

3. W. W. S. Breem, *Primary Sources: Law Reports,* in *Id.* at 125, 149.

Note 6(A)

1. Proclamations are "of general interest and application within the United States." Executive orders "deal more exclusively with matters of an administrative and executive nature" such as civil service rules. J. HART, THE ORDINANCE MAK-ING POWERS OF THE PRESIDENT OF THE UNITED STATES 316 (1925).

2. *Decisions of the Department of the Interior Relating to Public Lands* (1881–1929).

3. L. C. DODD and R. L. SCHOTT, CONGRESS AND THE ADMINISTRATIVE STATE 26 (1979). See pp. 16–42 for much of the history recounted here.

4. R. D. STONE, THE INTERSTATE COMMERCE COMMISSION AND THE RAILROAD INDUSTRY 4–5 (1991).

5. Munn v. Illinois, 94 U.S. 113 (1876).

6. Wabash, St. L. & P. Ry. v. Illinois, 118 U.S. 557 (1886).

7. E. N. Griswold, *Government in Ignorance of the Law—A Plea for Better Publication of Executive Legislation,* 48 HARV. L. REV. 198, 212 (1934).

8. T. A. LAPP, FEDERAL RULES AND REGULATIONS (1918).

Note 6(B)

1. Schechter Poultry Corp. v. United States, 295 U.S. 495 (1935).

2. NLRB v. Jones & Laughlin Steel Corp., 301 U.S. 1 (1937).

3. PRESIDENT'S COMMITTEE ON ADMINISTRATIVE MANAGEMENT, REPORT 32 (1937).

4. *Id.* at 41.

Note 6(C)

1. Note, *The Federal Register and the Code of Federal Regulations—A Reap-praisal,* 80 HARV. L. REV. 439, 441 (1966).

2. 293 U.S. 388 (1935).

3. United States v. Public Utilities Commission of California, 345 U.S. 295, 320 (1953) (Jackson, J., concurring).

4. 59 A.B.A. REP. 148, 540 (1934).

5. *See supra* Selection 6(B).

6. 44 U.S.C. § 1507 (1988).

7. 44 U.S.C. § 1505(a) (1988).

8. 44 U.S.C. § 1505(b) (1988).

9. Ch. 417, sec. 11, 49 Stat. 500, 503 (1935).

10. N. J. Futor, *Searching the Federal Regulations: Forty-seven Steps Are Too Many,* 45 A.B.A. J. 43, 45 (1959).

11. U. A. Lavery, *"The Federal Register"—Official Publication for Administrative Regulations, Etc.* 7 F.R.D. 625, 638 n. 19 (1948).

12. J. C. Ruddy and B. S. Simmons, *The Federal Register—Forum of the Government and the People,* 32 GEO. L. J. 248, 255 (1944). *See also* N. J. Futor, *The Publication of Presidential Orders: A State of Chaos and Confusion,* 49 A.B.A. J. 69, 73 (1963) (estimates of "undiscovered presidential documents . . . have run as high as 50,000.")

13. J. H. Wigmore, *The Federal Register and Code of Federal Regulations,* 29 A.B.A. J. 10, 11 (1943).

14. *Id.*

15. Futor, *supra* note 12, at 72, 75. For the correction of the uncodified status of proclamations and executive orders, *see* Note 6(F), n. 5 *infra.*

16. L. A. Jaffe, *Publication of Administrative Rules and Orders,* 24 A.B.A. J. 393, 395 (1938).

17. *Id.*

Note 6(D)

1. Sec. 3, 60 Stat. 238, 5 U.S.C. § 1002 (1946).

2. *Id.*

3. 5 U.S.C. § 553(d) (1988).

4. F. C. Newman, *Government in Ignorance—A Progress Report on Publication of Federal Regulations,* 63 HARV. L. REV. 929, 933–34 (1950).

5. *Id.* at 945–46.

6. *Id.* at 944–45. (About 60 percent of the material published in the *Federal Register* had consisted of notices and other materials not later codified in the *C.F.R.* 105 CONG. REC. A7969 [1959].)

7. *Id.* at 951.

8. *Id.* at 949–50.

9. *Id.* at 951, n. 98.

10. Inexplicably, the director of the *Federal Register* division recommended this practice to librarians. [Remarks of B. R. Kennedy,] 51 LAW LIBR. J. 379 (1958).

11. [Remarks of J. Marke,] *Id.* at 378–79.

12. [Remarks of M. O. Price,] *Id.* at 379.

Note 6(E)

1. 105 CONG. REC. A7969 (1959).

2. Note, *The Federal Register and the Code of Federal Regulations—A Reappraisal,* 80 HARV. L. REV. 439, 450 (1966).

3. *Id.* at 450–51.

4. *Id.* at 445–49.

5. H. L. Cross, The People's Right to Know: Legal Access to Public Records and Proceedings (1953).

6. L. C. Dodd and R. L. Schott, Congress and the Administrative State 36–37 (1979).

Note 6(F)

1. Cervase v. Office of the Federal Register, 580 F.2d 1166 (3d. Cir. 1978).

2. *Id.* at 1167.

3. H. A. Hood, *Indexing and the Law,*, 8 Int'l J. L. Libr. 61 (1980).

4. *Id.* at 61–62.

5. CIS has also published the *CIS Index to Presidential Executive Orders and Proclamations* for the period prior to the *CIS Federal Register Index.* Twenty volumes cover 1787 to 1983. Proclamations and executive orders have also received their own official codification in *Codification of Presidential Proclamations and Executive Orders,* the first volume of which covers 1961 to 1989.

6. A private publisher, the Bureau of National Affairs, has published an "Administrative Interpretations" volume as part of its *United States Law Week* service. The separate volume has been discontinued, but some agency opinions are included with federal court opinions in the "General Law" volume of the service. In 1938, it was proposed that summaries of agency opinions be published in the *Federal Register,* with full texts of the most important opinions. J. H. Ronald, *Publication of Federal Administrative Legislation,* 7 Geo. Wash. L. Rev. 52, 88–89 (1938).

7. *See supra* Note 6(D).

8. P. R. Neal, *Loose-leaf Reporting Services,* 62 Law Libr. J. 153, 156 (1969).

9. Note, *The Federal Register and the Code of Federal Regulations—A Reappraisal,* 80 Harv. L. Rev. 439, 451 (1966).

10. M. L. Cohen, *Publication of State Administrative Regulations—Reform in Slow Motion,* 14 Buff. L. Rev. 410 (1965).

11. K. C. Davis, Administrative Law Treatise, sec. 6.11 at 400–401 (1958), quoted in Cohen, *id.* at 410.

12. States with administrative codes but no registers were Georgia, Maine, Nebraska, Nevada, North Dakota, and Vermont. M. L. Cohen, R. C. Berring, and K. C. Olson, How to Find the Law, app. B, at 614–62 (1989, 9th ed.).

13. Arkansas, Mississippi, Oklahoma, and Virginia. *Id.*

14. Delaware, Hawaii, Idaho, New Mexico, and Rhode Island. *Id.*

Note 7(A)

1. W. S. Holdsworth, Some Makers of English Law 8 (1938).

2. *Id.* at 15.

3. *Id.* at 13.

4. *Id.* at 18.

5. T. F. T. Plucknett, Early English Legal Literature 58 (1958).

6. HOLDSWORTH, *supra* note 1 at 17.

7. *See* E. C. SURRENCY, A HISTORY OF AMERICAN LAW PUBLISHING 22, 130 (1990).

Note 7(B)

1. J. H. Merryman, *The Authority of Authority,* 6 STAN. L. REV. 613, 648–49 (1954).

2. Contents notes in cataloging records are usually added for collections of essays. The individual essays, therefore, are retrievable by author and title in computerized cataloging systems that allow searches by keywords. The individual essays, however, are not assigned their own subject headings.

3. *Law Books Recommended for Libraries* (1967–1976). Entries in the bibliographies are marked A, B, or C according to the degree of the editors' recommendations.

4. J. A. McDERMOTT, RECOMMENDED LAW BOOKS (2d ed., 1986). The previous edition was published in 1969.

5. The *CLI/LegalTrac* index to book reviews grades the books reviewed—"A" if the review is favorable, "C" if unfavorable, and "B" if in between. *See infra* Note 8(B).

6. *See supra* Note 2(C).

7. Merryman, *supra* note 1, at 646, n. 116.

8. *See* H. Wechsler, *The Course of the Restatements,* 55 A.B.A. J. 147 (1969).

9. W. D. Lewis, *History of the American Law Institute and the First Restatement of the Law,* in 1 RESTATEMENT IN THE COURTS 1, 3 (1945).

10. *Id.* at 1.

11. *See supra* Note 4(G).

12. L. M. FRIEDMAN, A HISTORY OF AMERICAN LAW 676 (2d ed., 1985).

13. G. GILMORE, THE DEATH OF CONTRACT 59 (1974).

Note 8(A)

1. F. C. HICKS, MATERIALS AND METHODS OF LEGAL RESEARCH 200 (3d. ed., 1942).

2. *Id.* at 209.

3. M. I. Swygert and J. W. Bruce, *The Historical Origins, Founding, and Early Development of Student-Edited Law Reviews,* 36 HASTINGS L. J. 739, 763, n. 205 (1985).

Note 8(B)

1. F. Rodell, *Goodbye to Law Reviews,* 23 VA. L. REV. 38, 38 (1936).

2. *See, e.g.,* K. Lasson, *Scholarship Amok: Excesses in the Pursuit of Truth and Tenure,* 103 HARV. L. REV. 926 (1990).

3. In addition to a general law review, most law schools have added specialized periodicals. Especially popular topics are international law and environmental law.

4. Two notable examples of law school periodicals subject to faculty, rather than student, control are *Law and Contemporary Problems* published at Duke University and *Journal of Law Studies* published at the University of Chicago. Both are published in addition to, rather than in place of, student-edited law reviews. A proposal to have the Association of American Law Schools sponsor a national scholarly journal subject to peer review has been tabled.

5. Examples are the *Food, Drug, and Cosmetic Law Journal,* published by Commerce Clearing House, the *Intellectual Property Law Review,* published by Clark Boardman Company, and the *Journal of Agricultural Taxation and Law,* published by Warren, Gorham, and Lamont.

6. The availability of newsletters on any topic can be ascertained in an annual list—*Legal Newsletters in Print*—published by Info Sources.

7. A. S. Miller, *The Law Journals,* 5 CHANGE 64 (Winter 1973–74).

8. Examples are the *Administrative Law Review,* the *Antitrust Law Journal,* the *Family Law Quarterly,* and the *Tort and Insurance Law Journal.*

9. L. A. JONES, AN INDEX TO LEGAL PERIODICAL LITERATURE vi (1888).

10. Subsequent to the start of the *ILP,* the Jones-Chipman index was revived. The profession then had the overlap of two indexes until 1933, when the Jones-Chipman index ceased for good.

11. Association of American Law Schools, Committee on Libraries, *Report of the Subcommittee on the Index to Legal Periodicals,* 1976 A.A.L.S. PROCEEDINGS, pt. I, sec. I, 30.

12. *Id.* at 31.

13. *Id.* at 33–34.

14. *See supra* Note 7(B).

15. *See* V. Wise, *Of* Lizards, *Intersubjective Zap, and Trashing: Critical Legal Studies and the Librarian* 8 LEGAL REFERENCE SERVICES Q. 7, 14–15 (1988); R. Delgado and J. Stefancic, *Why Do We Tell the Same Stories?: Law Reform, Critical Librarianship, and the Triple Helix Dilemma,* 42 STAN. L. REV. 207, 210–13 (1989).

16. *See, e.g., Social Sciences Citation Index* (1973–   ).

17. California, Columbia, Cornell, Georgetown, Harvard, Law and Contemporary Problems, Michigan, Minnesota, Northwestern, NYU, Stanford, Texas, University of Chicago, University of Illinois, University of Pennsylvania, UCLA, Virginia, Wisconsin, Yale.

Epilogue—Note

1. J. L. Hoover, *Legal Scholarship and the Electronic Revolution,* 83 LAW LIBR. J. 643, 646 (1991).

2. L. H. Seiler, *The Concept of Book in the Age of the Digital Electronic Medium,* LIBR. SOFTWARE REV., Jan.–Feb. 1992, at 19, 28.

3. *Id.* at 20.

4. *See* TIME, Apr. 12, 1993, at 50 *et seq.*

5. Seiler, *supra* note 2, at 26.

6. P. W. Martin, *The Future of Law Librarians in Changing Institutions, or the Hazards and Opportunities of New Information Technology,* 83 LAW LIBR. J. 419, 421–22 (1991).

7. R. W. Staudt, *An Essay on Electronic Casebooks: My Pursuit of the Paperless Chase,* 68 CHI.-KENT L. REV. 291 (1993).

8. *Id.* at 305.

9. L. H. Seiler, *The Future of the Scholarly Journal,* ACAD. COMPUTING, Sept. 1989, at 13, 67–68.

10. *See, e.g., New York Times,* Mar. 14, 1993, at 25. (White House computer tapes destroyed by "sloppy handling" at end of Bush presidency, despite judge's order to preserve the tapes for use in pending litigation.)

11. M. L. Cohen, *Research in a Changing World of Law and Technology,* 13 DALHOUSIE L. J. 5, 10–11 (1990).

12. Seiler, *supra* note 2, at 27.

Index